THE

COMMONWEALTH AND PROTECTORATE

VOL. I.

HISTORY

OF

THE COMMONWEALTH

AND

PROTECTORATE

1649—1656

BY

SAMUEL RAWSON GARDINER

HON. D.C.L. OXFORD ; LITT.D. CAMBRIDGE ; LL.D. EDINBURGH ; PH.D. GÖTTINGEN;
FELLOW OF MERTON COLLEGE ; HONORARY STUDENT OF CHRISTCHURCH ;
FELLOW OF KING'S COLLEGE, LONDON

IN FOUR VOLUMES

VOLUME I.—1649–1650

AMS PRESS, INC.
NEW YORK
1965

AMS Press, Inc.
New York, N.Y. 10003
1965

PREFACE

THE publication of a new edition of *The History of the Commonwealth and Protectorate* renders a few words of preface necessary. The three volumes forming the first edition of Mr. Gardiner's book were published in 1894, 1897, and 1901 respectively. Only the first of these, which reached a third edition in 1901, had the advantage of revision and correction by the author himself. However, Mr. Gardiner appended to the third volume two pages of 'Corrigenda' for Volume II, and also inserted in his preface to Volume II some additional information which had come to hand too late to be employed in the text of his narrative. These corrections and additions are now incorporated in their proper place, either in the text or the notes. Besides this a certain number of verbal errors and small mistakes have been corrected, some of which were noted by Mr. Gardiner himself in his own copy of the book, while others were pointed out by reviewers.

It also seemed desirable, for the benefit of students of the period, to add occasional references in the notes to some recently published works on the history of the time and to some of the documents printed since the first edition of this book appeared. Mr. Gardiner himself edited for the Navy Records Society two volumes of *Papers relating to the first Dutch War*, issued by that Society in 1899 and 1900. He had previously utilised the evidence which these documents contained in his own account of the war, but as in his footnotes the references are to the manuscripts it was thought well to add references to the subsequently printed collection. In all cases in which something has been added to Mr. Gardiner's notes, or fresh notes have been inserted, the new matter is distinguished by square brackets.

Mr. Gardiner fell ill very soon after he began to work at the fourth volume of his History. For that reason he left but one chapter of the projected volume in a sufficiently advanced state for publication. The chapter in question treated principally of the reasons which led the Protector to summon his second Parliament and of the elections which preceded it, and it will form Chapter XLIX of this History. It will also be printed separately and in a larger form as a supplement to the Library Edition.

C. H. FIRTH.

CONTENTS

OF

THE FIRST VOLUME

CHAPTER I

THE COMMONWEALTH AND ITS ENEMIES

CHAPTER II

CROMWELL AND THE LEVELLERS

CHAPTER III

THE COMMONWEALTH ON ITS DEFENCE

CHAPTER IV

DUNDALK AND RATHMINES

CHAPTER V

DROGHEDA AND WEXFORD

CHAPTER VI

CORK, KILKENNY, AND CLONMEL

CHAPTER VII

THE TRIAL OF JOHN LILBURNE

CHAPTER VIII

THE CONFERENCE AT BREDA

CHAPTER IX

THE LAST CAMPAIGN OF MONTROSE

CHAPTER X

THE TREATY OF HELIGOLAND

CHAPTER XII

DUNBAR

CHAPTER XIV

SCOTLAND AFTER DUNBAR

MAPS

THE COMMONWEALTH

AND

PROTECTORATE

CHAPTER I

THE COMMONWEALTH AND ITS ENEMIES

THE execution of Charles I.—the work of military violence cloaked in the merest tatters of legality—had displayed to the eyes of the world the forgotten truth that kings, as well as subjects, must bear the consequences of their errors and misdeeds. More than this the actors in the great tragedy failed to accomplish, and, it may fairly be added, must necessarily have failed to accomplish. It is never possible for men of the sword to rear the temple of recovered freedom, and the small minority in Parliament which had given the semblance of constitutional procedure to the trial in Westminster Hall were no more than instruments in the hands of the men of the sword. Honestly as both military and political leaders desired to establish popular government, they found themselves in a vicious circle from which there was no escape. No government they could set up would be strong enough to remain erect unless the army were kept on foot, and if the army were kept on foot popular support would be alienated by its intervention in political affairs, and by the heavy taxation

*1649.
Jan. 30.
First results
of the King's
execution.*

*The power
of the sword.*

*A vicious
circle.*

required for its maintenance. Every serious attempt to rest the government on the voice of the nation itself would inure to the benefit of the young prince who had not offended as his father had offended, and who appealed to those whom he claimed as subjects on other grounds than the disposal of an armed force.

Though the efforts of the little group which now found it-self in possession of authority were predestined to failure, their The business strivings to loose the fetters of dynastic interest were of posterity. not without profitable result. In their own genera-tion their work struck but few roots. They were doing the business of a more distant posterity than that to which Eliot had devoted his life. Yet, though it is true that the proposals which they made were often such as to commend themselves to the men of the nineteenth, perhaps even to the men of the twentieth century, rather than to those of the seventeenth, it is not only by the immediate accomplishment of its aims that the value of honest endeavour is to be tested. Even when it fails to clothe itself in external fact, it contributes somewhat to the energy, and thereby to the ultimate vigour, of the race.

Anxious to liberate a people which still clung to its fetters, the leaders of the mutilated House of Commons could but Necessity of wait for better times, contenting themselves with a temporary the establishment of some makeshift constitutional settlement. arrangement, which might serve their turn till the day —not far distant, as they fondly hoped—when the misguided Feb. 1 people should come to a better mind. On February 1 Qualifica-tion of sit-ting mem-bers. the remnant of the House of Commons, now claiming for itself the name and authority of the Parliament of England,[1] attempted to make its own position regu-lar by resolving that no member who had voted on Decem-ber 5 that the King's offers afforded a ground of settlement,[2] or had been absent when that vote was given, should be allowed to sit until he had recorded his dissent from that resolution.[3]

At this stage the proceedings were interrupted by an invi-

---

[1] *Great Civil War*, iv. 290.   [2] *Ib.* iv. 266.   [3] *S.P. Dom.* i. 1.

tation from the Lords to discuss the future government of the

The Lords ask for a joint committee. country in a joint committee. Not only was permission to appear at the bar refused to messengers who brought it,[1] but on the following day the Com-

Feb. 2. The position of the Lords to be considered. mons resolved to take into consideration the position of the other House.[2] On the 6th some members—Cromwell being probably amongst them [3]—expressed

Feb. 6. The House of Lords abolished. a wish to retain the House of Lords as a purely consultative body, but the proposal was rejected by 44 votes to 29, and a resolution 'that the House of Peers in Parliament is useless and dangerous and ought to be abolished' was carried without a division. On

Feb. 7. The kingship abolished. the 7th a further resolution 'that it had been found by experience . . . that the office of a king in this nation, and to have the power thereof in any single person, is unnecessary, burdensome, and dangerous to the liberty, safety and public interests of the people of this nation, and therefore ought to be abolished,' [4] was carried, also without a division. Effect was given to these resolutions by the introduction of Acts—the name of Bills being now dropped—which were not finally passed till March 17 and 19,[5] but under the circumstances the delay was of no importance.

The reaction against monarchy naturally led to the introduction of government by a numerous body, and it was at once

A Council of State to be erected. agreed that a Council of State should be erected, and that a committee should be appointed to pro-

A committee discusses its composition pose to the House the names of its members and a draft of instructions for its guidance.[6] The discussions in this committee ranged far. Some of its members proposed that there should be no less than a hundred councillors, and that none of these should be peers.[7] In the end it was resolved that the number of councillors should be forty-one, and that peers should be capable of acting amongst them. The new Council of State was to have full executive

[1] *Perf. Weekly Account*, E, 541, 24. [2] *C.J.* vi. 129.
[3] *Ludlow*, i. 220. [4] *C.J.* vi. 132, 133. [5] *Ib.* 166, 168.
[6] *C.J.* vi. 133. [7] Grignon to Brienne, Feb. $\frac{12}{22}$, *R. O. Transcripts*.

authority in the management of home and foreign affairs, and
was authorised to administer oaths and to imprison or hold to
bail those who resisted its orders.   Its own existence was ter-
minable at the end of a year, 'unless it were otherwise ordered
by Parliament.'[1]   Parliament, in short, intended to retain
complete control over the Council, which would have no independent constitutional position, such as is secured to
the modern Cabinet by virtual possession of the power
of dissolution.   Far less would it attain the commanding position assigned to it in the latest edition of the *Agreement
of the People*, in accordance with which it would have sat con-
tinuously for two years, whilst a biennial Parliament, except on
special summons issued by the Council itself, would only have
remained in session during six months out of the twenty-four.[2]
The new Council, in short, was to be formed on the lines of the
Committee of Both Kingdoms and the Derby House Committee.[3]

and its con-stitutional powers.

The form of an engagement to be required from the
councillors was next discussed.   At Ireton's suggestion it was
resolved that they should declare their approval of
the establishment of the High Court of Justice, of
the trial and execution of the King, of the abolition
of the monarchy and of the House of Lords.[4]

An engage-ment pro-posed by Ireton.

[1] *C.J.* vi. 138.

[2] *Const. Doc.* 270.   According to the *Heads of the Proposals*, Parliament was to sit in the two years not less than 120 and not more than
240 days, ' or some other limited number of days now to be agreed on.'
Ib. 233.

[3] *Great Civil War*, iv. 52.

[4] " Plusieurs croyent," wrote the French agent nearly two years later,
" qu'il arrivera quelque brouillerie au Parlement sur la proposition qui y
fut faite un peu après la mort du deffunt Roy de la G. B. par Ireton . . .
que tous les membres du Parlement, du Conseil d'Estat, et les officiers
estant en emplois considerables eussent à souscrire à la condamnation
de mort donnée contre le deffunt Roy de l'Angleterre et au changement du
gouvernement qui ayant été opposé par quelques-uns fut eludé par Cromwell luy-mesme qui y trouva le temperament de l'engagement." Croullé
to Mazarin, Dec. $\frac{9}{19}$, 1650.   *Arch. des Aff. Étrangères*, lix. fol. 495.
The form of this proposed engagement has only been preserved in a

On February 13 the whole of these proposals were adopted by Parliament.[1] Algernon Sidney, indeed, objected to the imposition of the engagement, on the ground 'that such a test would prove a snare to many an honest man, but every knave would slip through it.' So sensitive were the regicides that Lord Grey of Groby cried out that Sidney had applied the epithet of knave to all who signed the engagement. Great was the uproar till Marten appeared as a peace-maker, pointing out, truly enough, that Sidney had merely said 'that every knave might slip through, and not that every one who did slip through was a knave.'[2] The influence of the regicides, however, prevailed, and an Act was passed enjoining on every councillor the signature of the engagement as it stood.

Algernon Sidney's objection to the engagement.

On the following day a vote was taken on the names of forty-one persons suggested by the committee as fit to sit in the new Council. Amongst those recommended were five peers—Denbigh, Mulgrave, Pembroke, Salisbury, and Grey of Warke. The lawyers were represented by three judges—Rolle, Chief Justice of the King's Bench, St. John, now Chief Justice of the Common Pleas, and Wilde, Chief Baron of the Exchequer, as well as by Bradshaw and Whitelocke. Amongst the officers were Fairfax, Cromwell, Ireton, Skippon, and Harrison. Of the forty-one names, those of Ireton and Harrison were alone rejected.[3] It is not unlikely that the rejection of these two officers was due to the support which had been given by them to the military demand for an immediate dissolution in the discussions preceding Pride's Purge.[4] Ireton's

Feb. 14. The Council of State nominated.

Ireton and Harrison rejected.

summary by Whitelocke (383), which should be compared with an entry in the Order Book of the Council of State, *Interr.* I, 62, p. 4. In Mrs. Everett Green's Calendar, the words 'court of justice' are misprinted 'board of justice.'

[1] Act of Parliament, Feb. 13 ; Order in Parliament, Feb. 13 ; *Interr. Papers*, 87, pp. 9–14.

[2] Sidney to the Earl of Leicester, Oct. 12, 1660 ; Blencowe's *Sydney Papers*, 238.

[3] *C.J.* vi. 140.   [4] *Great Civil War*, iv. 269.

known views in favour of strengthening the authority of the
Council of State may also have militated against him.   On the

Feb. 15.
The Council
completed.

15th the Council was completed by the substitution
of two other members, and at the same time the
resolution of Parliament not to allow the growth of
anything like personal authority was emphasised by its refusal
to allow the appointment of a Lord President of the Council.[1]

The consequences of Ireton's attempt to narrow the basis
of the new republic developed themselves with surprising

Feb. 17.
Its first
meeting.

rapidity.   When the Council met for the first time
on the 17th, it was found that only fourteen members
were in attendance, and of these all but one were
regicides.   The thirteen regicides took the engagement; the

Feb. 19.
The engage-
ment
resisted.

one, Sir William Masham, refused it.   On the 19th
it was taken by five more members, but twenty-two
dissentients still remained.   Of these, Grey of Warke
raised the insuperable objection that he would sign nothing
emanating from a single House.   The other four peers,
together with Fairfax, were ready to serve the new Government,
but refused to express approval of past actions which they had
opposed.   Various objections of a special character were
raised by others.[2]

Grey of Warke having been excluded by his own act, the
case of the remaining councillors was clearly one for com-

A case for
compromise.

promise; and Cromwell, who had been temporarily
placed in the chair,[3] set himself to correct the error
of his less practical son-in-law.   After an amicable conference
between the two parties in the Council, held at his instance on

Feb. 22.
A revised
engagement.

the 22nd, the House agreed to a new form of engagement, binding those who took it to concur in
'the settling of the government of this nation for
the future in the way of a republic without King or House of
Lords,' and to fulfil punctually the duty imposed on them by
Parliament.   Even this, however, appears not to have been

[1] *C.J.* vi. 143.
[2] C. of St. Order Book, *Interr.* I, 62, p. 4.
[3] *The Kingdom's Weekly Intelligencer*, E, 545, 13.

palatable to every one of the members of the Council, as the order by which the signature of the revised engagement was enforced was withdrawn by Parliament on the 23rd,[1] no directions being given for the substitution of a third form. It is only incidentally that we learn that Fairfax finally took the engagement in an unauthorised recension, binding himself to defend the proceedings of Parliament in settling the government ' in the way of a republic without King and House of Peers,' but not binding himself to concur in what was done.[2] It is by no means improbable that when the second form of the engagement was withdrawn it had been taken by all the other members of the Council, and that Fairfax alone was, though without official authority, permitted to accept it in an altered shape.

Feb. 23. Withdrawal of the revised engagement.

A final revision.

Of the forty members remaining in the Council after the exclusion of Lord Grey of Warke, the Earl of Mulgrave never took his seat. Three of the remaining members were judges,

---

[1] *C.J.* vi. 149. The Order Book of the Council of State has no reference to any subscription of the second engagement, whilst it has indirect evidence that it was not taken by all the members. An order of Feb. 23 directs the councillors to take an oath of secrecy, which would have been unnecessary if all of them had taken the engagement, which contains such an oath.

[2] We should have had no knowledge of the third engagement if it had not been mentioned in a resolution of the House on Feb. 20, 1650, that Fairfax had taken it. It is as follows : " I, A.B., being nominated member of the Council of State by this present Parliament, do testify that I do adhere to this present Parliament in the maintenance and defence of the public liberty and freedom of this nation as it is now declared by this Parliament, by whose authority I am constituted a member of the said Council, and in the maintenance and defence of their resolutions concerning the settling of the Government of this nation for [the] future in the way of a republic, without King or House of Peers ; and I do promise in the sight of God that, through His Grace, I will be faithful in performance of the trust committed to me, as aforesaid, and therein faithfully pursue the instructions given to the said Council by this present Parliament. In confirmation of the premises I have hereunto subscribed my name." *C.J.* vi. 369. The first engagement had been opposed by Vane. *State Trials,* vi. 164 ; *A Vindication of Sir H. Vane,* p. 7, E, 985, 21.

and three—Pembroke, Salisbury, and Denbigh—were peers. As two others, Bradshaw and Alderman Wilson, were not members of the House, there were thirty-one who sat both in Parliament and in the Council.[1]

As the average attendance on divisions in Parliament during the three months subsequent to the final institution of the Council of State did not exceed fifty-six,[2] the councillors, if they had been in constant attendance, and had always voted on the same side, would have been able to bear down all opposition. In fact, the average attendance in the Council was, during the same period, no more than fifteen, and the votes of fifteen councillors, even if they had been unanimous, could not overweigh the judgment of all the private members, though undoubtedly sufficient to turn the scale where opinion was anything like equally divided. An analysis of the division lists, indeed, shows that the Council had no such masterful weight in Parliament as has been sometimes ascribed to it.[3] The administrative recommendations of the Council, indeed, were almost always accepted by the House without hesitation or division, but when any controversial

Did the Council out-vote the House?

[1] Mrs. Everett Green, in the Preface to the *Calendar* for 1649–50, p. xv, note 1, says that the only members of the Council 'not identified as members of Parliament are Alderman Wilson, Lord Chief Baron Wylde and Major-General Skippon.' Skippon, however, was a member, whilst Bradshaw and Rolle were not, and St. John had, for the present, ceased to act on his appointment to the Bench. Mrs. Everett Green compares the Council of the whole of its first year with the Parliament of the first three months after Pride's Purge. I have preferred making the comparison for the three months after the institution of the Council of State.

[2] Including tellers.

[3] This is the view taken by Mrs. Everett Green in her Preface to the *Calendar of State Papers*, 1649–50. "It will at once be seen," she writes (p. xv), " that when they were unanimous and attending in force they would command a working majority in the House. Therefore their perpetual references to Parliament really mean, not an appeal to an independent governing power, but an appeal from themselves as a newly constituted power to themselves, with some additions, but bearing the august name of Parliament."

question was raised, it was almost invariably found that the division in Parliament was a mere echo of a previous division in the Council, as is shown by the fact that scarcely a division was taken during the first three months of the existence of the Council in which its members did not appear as tellers on opposite sides.

Important as it was to place the executive government in trustworthy hands, it was hardly of less importance to secure *Judicial institutions of the country.* the continuity of the judicial institutions of the country. Lawyers were more likely than politicians to refuse to take part in the administration of law under a Government which had set constitutional law at *Feb. 1. Hilary Term adjourned.* defiance, and on February 1, the House found it necessary to gain time for a negotiation with the judges by adjourning Hilary Term to the 9th.[1]

Feb. 8. Half of the judges continue in office. On the 8th the judges announced their decision. Of the two commissioners of the Great Seal, Sir Thomas Widdrington retired on the transparent plea of ill-health, whilst Whitelocke, in a laboured oration, announced his unwillingness to continue in office but for the pressure to which he had been subjected. Of the Common Law judges six agreed and six declined to accept new commissions, the acceptance of the former being conditional on the issue by Parliament of a declaration that it intended to maintain 'the fundamental laws,' and that it would repeal the Acts enforcing the oaths of allegiance and supremacy.

These conditions were at once accepted. To Whitelocke were given two colleagues, John Lisle and Sergeant Keble.[2] *Feb. 9. Judicial appointments.* It was not thought prudent for the present to fill the other vacancies. The customary reference to the King was omitted from the oaths of the judges, and the name of the Upper Bench was substituted for that of the King's Bench. In all other respects the administration of justice pursued its accustomed course.

---

[1] This is the date of the resolution, the Act was passed a few days later. *C.J.*, vi. 128, 130.

[2] *Ib.* vi. 134–136 ; *Whitelocke*, 378.

Anxious as Parliament was to lead the stream of ordinary justice through the ordinary channels, it was well aware that unless it was prepared to abandon the hope of meting out what, in the eyes of its members, was justice on political offenders, it must find some other way of securing its ends than a trial in the King's Bench by judge and jury.   On February 3 the House erected a new High Court of Justice, to try Hamilton, Holland, Norwich, Capel, and Owen.   Of this Court Bradshaw was President,[1] whilst the other members, men less notable than those who had sentenced the King, being nominated by Parliament, could be depended on to comply with its wishes.   It would have been more straightforward to put the prisoners to death by an Act of Attainder, but, as in the King's case, the House shrank from acknowledging even to itself that a mere semblance of judicial forms was all that it could employ.

How are political trials to be carried on ?

Feb. 3. A new High Court of Justice erected.

The proceedings opened on February 10.   All five prisoners pleaded that their captors had granted them quarter for their lives, and that they were therefore not liable to be tried on a capital charge.   This plea having been overruled on the ground that no promise of the military authorities could bar the action of a civil court, the result of the trials was a foregone conclusion.   Hamilton, indeed, pleaded that he was a foreigner by birth, and was therefore not amenable to English law, especially as his entrance in arms into England had been commanded by the Parliament of his own country.   He failed, however, to show that he had been born before the accession of James to the throne of England, and the court therefore held that he was, in accordance with the judgment in the case of the *post nati*,[2] a natural-born Englishman, as well as Earl of Cambridge in the English peerage.   No other points of legal importance were

Feb. 10. Trials of the Royalist prisoners.

March 6. The five Royalists sentenced.

---

[1] *C.J.* vi. 131.   Hamilton is throughout named by his English title, Earl of Cambridge, and Norwich is called Lord Goring, Parliament not recognising his earldom, which had been conferred since the outbreak of the Civil War.   [2] *Hist. of Eng.* 1603–1642, i. 356.

raised in the course of the trials, and on March 6 all five prisoners were sentenced to death.[1]

On March 8, petitions for mercy having been presented to Parliament by the relatives of the condemned men, their cases were taken into consideration. In spite of the influential advocacy of his brother Warwick, Holland was left to execution by a single vote. He was heavily weighted by his frequent tergiversations and his position in the very centre of the Royalist movement in the preceding year. The petitions in favour of Hamilton and Capel were rejected without a division. Owen, on the other hand, obtained a respite, which was equivalent to a pardon, by a majority of five, and Norwich owed his life to the casting vote of the Speaker. In all five cases Cromwell and Ireton had been systematically opposed to leniency.[2]

March 8. Two reprieved and the others left for execution.

On the 9th the three condemned Royalists were beheaded on a scaffold erected before the gate of Westminster Hall. Neither Hamilton nor Holland was much pitied by the spectators. With Capel it was otherwise. His frank and open nature, which had kept him unstained by the mire of political intrigue, had to the last attracted the admiration even of his enemies. Rejecting the services of a minister of a creed he detested, he stepped jauntily on to the scaffold with his hat cocked and his cloak under his arm. His religion, he said, was that of the Thirty-nine Articles, 'the best he knew of.' He was to die for his fidelity to the King and his obedience to the fifth commandment. His late master was 'the most religious of all princes of the world,' and his son was now the lawful king. Capel died nobly defiant, and in him English royalism could count one martyr more.[3]

March 9. Execution of Hamilton, Holland, and Capel.

The conclusion of these trials enabled the Council to complete its internal organisation. Hitherto it had been content

[1] *Clarke Trials*, in Worcester College Library.

[2] *C.J.* vi. 159. Whitelocke's statement that the Speaker gave his vote against Holland is disproved by the journals.

[3] *The Kingdom's Weekly Intelligencer*, E, 546, 19.

with temporary chairmen, but on March 10, the day after the
executions, it named Bradshaw its President,[1] avoiding the
title of Lord President, which had been condemned
by a vote of Parliament.[2] Before long, however,
Bradshaw was, by tacit consent, styled Lord President of the Council of State, Parliament itself finally
complying with established usage.

March 10.
Bradshaw
President
of the
Council
of State.

For the time no serious opposition was made in England
to the new Government. At Exeter, indeed, some Cavaliers
had torn down the Act prohibiting the proclamation
of another king,[3] and in London, as well as in
Devonshire, many of the clergy raised their voices against a
regicide commonwealth;[4] but the lesson taught by the last
campaign could not be ignored, and even the most enthusias-
tic Royalists acknowledged that without external assistance it
would be impossible to throw off the yoke of the victorious
army. It was on Ireland that for some time their hopes had
been mainly fixed.

England
quiet.

Since the autumn of 1648, Ormond had been doing his
utmost to bring the Supreme Council to terms.[5] The news
of Pride's Purge, and of Charles's imprisonment,
paved the way to an understanding, and on January
17, 1649, a treaty between the King's Lord Lieutenant and the confederate Catholics was signed at Kilkenny.
By this treaty the Roman Catholics were secured in
the free exercise of their religion, and to Irishmen
in general was offered the complete independence of
their Parliament, together with various salutary reforms. In
return for these concessions, the Confederates were to supply
Ormond with 15,000 foot and 500 horse, a force which, in
combination with that under Inchiquin, was expected to be
sufficient to reduce Dublin and to compel the submission of
O'Neill. To provide support for this army, twelve eminent

1648.
Ormond's
activity in
Ireland.

1649.
Jan. 17.
The Irish
peace.

---

[1] C. of St. Order Book, *Interr.* I, 62, p. 71.

[2] See p. 6.   [3] *Great Civil War*, iv. 321.

[4] *The Moderate*, E, 542, 11; *The Kingdom's Weekly Intelligencer*, E, 542, 14.   [5] *Great Civil War*, iv. 224.

members of the Supreme Council were appointed commissioners—Commissioners of Trust was the name by which they were generally known—for assessing taxes and appointing magistrates with the concurrence of the Lord Lieutenant. All consideration of the two burning questions of the possession of the churches and the jurisdiction of the Roman Catholic clergy was postponed till after the meeting of the promised Parliament.[1]

So well was Ormond satisfied with the outlook, that on January 22 he invited the Prince of Wales to hasten to Ireland,

Jan. 22.
The Prince
invited to
Ireland.

holding out hopes that he would soon be able to transport the Irish army into England. Lord Byron, who carried the invitation, was instructed to give a full report on the condition of the country.

The Royalist exiles in Holland had long been familiar with the idea of assailing England through Ireland. Their favourite

Rupert's
fleet in
Holland.

plan had been to send to Ormond's assistance that portion of the fleet which had rallied to the King, and Rupert's appointment as Admiral had done much to quicken the dilatory movements of those whose task it was to prepare the ships for sea. The Queen of Bohemia pawned her jewels, and with the money thus acquired, and by the sale of the guns of one of the ships, two small vessels were fitted out and sent forth to seize all shipping, the property of English rebels, which might fall in their way. Before long they brought back two prizes, the sale of one of which produced enough to equip the remainder of the fleet. On January 11

Jan. 11.
Rupert puts
to sea.

Rupert put to sea with eight vessels. He was accompanied by three Dutch East Indiamen, and though the commanders of these latter had no intention of giving him actual support, the combined fleet presented so imposing an appearance that the Parliamentary commander in the Downs made no attempt to interrupt his passage through the Straits.

Rupert struck the Irish coast at Crookhaven, whence, after

[1] Cox, *Hib. Angl.* App. xliii.

a short delay, he transferred his fleet to Kinsale. It was
miserably undermanned, and its commander's only
hope of being able again to put to sea with effect lay
in the attraction which the prospect of prize money
might have for Irish sailors.[1]

Jan. 29.
Rupert at
Kinsale.

In Scotland the effect of the resolution taken at Westminster to bring the King to a trial was to the full as great as
that produced in Ireland. When the Scottish Parliament met on January 4, the predominance of Argyle
appeared to be secured. The shires and boroughs
were represented by his partisans, and the nobles who had
recently opposed him did not venture to take their seats. In
1648 no fewer than fifty-six noblemen sat in the Parliament
House. In 1649 there were but sixteen, Argyle's supporters
to a man. The prevailing party seized the opportunity to
make a reaction impossible so far as legislation could effect
their object. On January 23, all who had supported, or had
even forborne to oppose, the Hamiltonian engagement were divided into three classes according to
their social or political importance, and excluded
respectively for life, for ten, or for five years from office and
Parliament. Those in the second and third class remained
under disability even after the expiration of the term till they
had given satisfactory evidence of repentance. A fourth class
was made up of those 'given to uncleanness, bribery, swearing,
drunkenness, or deceiving, or . . . otherwise scandalous in
their conversation, or who neglect the worship of God in their
families.' These were formerly excluded from office and
Parliament for a single year, but, when that year was at an end,
their exclusion was to continue till they gave evidence of re
pentance.[2] Pride's Purge was less drastic than this.

Jan. 4.
Effect of the
King's trial
on Scotland.

Jan. 23.
The Act of
Classes.

Argyle's party triumph only served to expose the weakness
of his position. He had attempted to maintain a friendly

[1] *Prince Rupert's Voyage*, Warburton, iii. 279 ; Rupert to Ormond,
Jan. 27 : Ormond to the Commissioners of Westmeath, Jan. 31 ; *Carte
MSS.* xxiii. foll. 347, 383.

[2] *Acts of the Parl. of Sc.* vi. part ii. 143.

attitude towards the dominant powers in England, and the clergy, who were his main supporters, were now thundering from the pulpit against his alliance with a sectarian English army. As the drama of the King's trial unfolded itself the hostile feeling increased, and Charles's execution rendered it uncontrollable. Not only was it unendurable that a King of Scotland should be done to death by a purely English tribunal, but it was taken for granted that the causes which had hindered a popular declaration in his favour were buried in his grave. It was thought impossible that a second Charles should share in that inexplicable repugnance to the Covenant which had stood in the way of the first. Scant justice would be done to the mental powers of Argyle in supposing that he had no forebodings of danger. For some time past one of his emissaries, Major Strachan, had been going backwards and forwards between him and the Independent leaders with the object of preventing a rupture between the two nations.[1] The tide was, however, running too strongly in the opposite direction, and Argyle, true to his nature, resolved to follow the multitude in order that he might appear to lead it.

Weakness of Argyle's policy.

Even before the King's trial Argyle had been preparing for a change of policy by an attempt to come to an understanding with the leading Engagers. Much as he disliked the Hamiltons, he disliked and feared Montrose more, and he knew that in the autumn of 1648 Montrose had arrived at Brussels, bringing with him from the Emperor the title of Field Marshal ; and, what was of far greater value, permission to levy troops in the Empire for his master's service.[2] Montrose was soon in friendly communication with Rupert, of whose expedition to Ireland he thoroughly approved, and it was understood that he intended to land in the North of Scotland in the hope of repeating, if fortune favoured, the exploits of Inverlochy and

1648. Nov. Argyle and the Engagers.

Montrose at Brussels.

---

[1] Graymond to Brienne, Feb. $\frac{6}{16}$, *Harl. MSS.* 4,551, fol. 310.

[2] Napier's *Memoirs of Montrose*, ii. 671.

Kilsyth.[1]   Before the end of November Hyde received from

An offer
from
Lanark. Lanark a communication that he was ready to serve even as a sergeant under Montrose, but Montrose would have no dealings with the Hamiltons, and Lanark humbled himself in vain.[2]

It is not unlikely that some hint of Lanark's overture to Montrose reached Argyle, and that he resolved to make use of

Dec.
Lanark in
Edinburgh. the repulse which his former opponent had received to bring him into his own service.   At all events, soon after the middle of December Lanark appeared in Edinburgh, where he disavowed the engagement and promised to desist from all opposition to the new Parliament. He was then confined to his own house and plied with inter-

1649.
Jan.
Lauderdale
summoned. rogatories, whilst Lauderdale was summoned from Holland on the pretext that he was required to give an account of his conduct in the service of the State. In the second week in January Lauderdale arrived at Leith. He would hardly have obeyed so meekly without secret assurances that he could come and go in safety.[3]   After his landing he promised never again to disturb the peace in

Jan. 27.
Escape of
Lanark and
Lauderdale. Scotland.   On January 27, both he and Lanark embarked clandestinely and sailed for Holland. On the day before that on which the Earls took ship, the guards in Edinburgh were doubled, and on the morning on which they went on board orders were given to secure them wherever they might be found.   Yet shrewd observers were of opinion that the two noblemen were acting in collusion with

The Earls in
collusion
with
Argyle. Argyle,[4] and there is every reason to believe that this explanation was true, especially as, though an outward show of hostility was maintained, Lanark and Lauderdale from that moment acted in complete harmony

---

[1] Graymond to Brienne, $\frac{\text{Jan. 23}}{\text{Feb. 2}}$, *Harl. MSS.* 4,551, fol. 292.

[2] Napier's *Memoirs of Montrose*, ii. 676–683.   The dates of the letters as given by Napier must be put back ten days to suit the old style.

[3] Graymond to Brienne, $\frac{\text{Dec. 26}}{\text{Jan. 5}}$, $\frac{\text{Jan. 30}}{\text{Feb. 9}}$, *Harl. MSS.* 4,551, foll. 282, 296.

[4] " Cependant, Monseigneur, ce depart si soudain, et beaucoup de petites particularités . . . m'ont fait apprehender qu'il n'y eut quelque

with their former rival. If the whole truth were known, it would probably be found that Argyle, aware that the King's execution was not to be averted, and believing that the younger Charles would make no difficulty about taking the Covenant, perceived that there would no longer be any practical barrier between himself and the Hamiltonians, if he abandoned, as he was now prepared to do, all thought of coming to an understanding with the English regicides. Once more Argyle was practising the art of swimming with the tide.

The news of the King's execution reached Edinburgh on February 4. On the 5th Prince Charles was proclaimed his father's undoubted heir as 'King of Great Britain, France,

mauvaise entreprise contre le Prince de Galles et que ce ne fust un effect de la bonne intelligence qu'on a tousjours reconnu estre entre les Hamiltons et les Argiles en ce qui concerne la ruine de la monarchie qui pourroit tendre ou à empescher que le Marquis de Montrose ne vint icy au cas qu'on veuille l'y envoier par la confiance que les Hamiltons donneroient d'eux mesmes, et par la crainte qu'auroit le Prince de Galles de leur imprimer de la jalousie, envoyant en Escosse le dit Marquis qui ne leur a jamais esté amy, ou pour decouvrir ses desseins à ce party et luy faire suivre leurs mauvais conseils dans ces entreprises ; car je ne voy pas pourquoy sciter le Comte de Laderdaill pour rendre raison des commissions qu'il a eues, et non pas ceux de Dumfermelin, Traquaire, et autres, qui en ont eu de pareilles ; outre je ne trouve pas que ce soit une ruse de dire à present qu'à la mesme heure qu'ils s'embarquerent on avoit mis des troupes en campagne pour les prendre, ce qui est en effet, et s'emprisonner dans le chasteau d'Edinburgh et d'en envoier de mesme à quelques autres pour voir s'ils estoient au pais et les y aians trouvez ne les prendre point, s'enforcer le vendredy et ce samedy le guet, et establir de nouvelles gardes à plusieurs avenues hors de la ville, comme aussy que le Baron de Balm-[erino] très attaché aux interestz du Marquis d'Argiles, ait revelé à ces deux comtes qu'on le vouloit saisir de leurs personnes, ce qui m'a esté asseuré qu'il avoit fait et qui ne se publieroit pas par ses meilleurs amis si cela luy pouvoit nuire envers son parti. Outre ce je ne comprends pas pourquoy ces deux Comtes passants en Hollande dans un bon vaisseau estant demeurez un jour en cette rade n'ont emmené avec eux tant de bons serviteurs du Roy d'Angleterre . . . qui sont en peine pour le dernier engagement." Graymond to Brienne, $\frac{\text{Jan. 30}}{\text{Feb. 9}}$, *Harl. MSS.* 4,551, fol. 296. Writing again on Feb. $\frac{6}{16}$, Graymond says that the Countess of Lanark had confirmed his suspicions. *Ib.* fol. 310.

and Ireland.' The young King, however, before he could be

Feb. 5
Charles II.
condition-
ally pro-
claimed at
Edinburgh. admitted to the exercise of his royal dignity, was to give satisfaction concerning religion, the union of the kingdoms, and the good and peace of Scotland, 'according to the National Covenant and the solemn League and Covenant.' [1]

The young heir thus conditionally acknowledged at Edinburgh, was at this time at the Hague, the guest of his brother-in-law, the Prince of Orange. On the 4th the fatal

Feb. 4.
Charles II.
assumes
the Royal
title. news of his father's death was conveyed to him by Dr. Stephen Goffe, who, after conversing for some time on other matters, addressed him as 'Your Majesty.'

Charles, seizing the meaning of the words, withdrew himself to his chamber and buried himself in a passionate outburst of grief. When he came forth he assumed the royal title as his

Feeling in
Holland. unquestionable right. At the Hague itself, where the influence of the Prince of Orange was predominant, popular opinion ran strongly against the murderers of the late King. The States General and the Dutch clergy presented the new claimant of the throne with addresses of condolence. Even the States of Holland gave public expression to their sorrow, though it was well known that the merchants and lawyers, of whom that assembly was mainly composed, had no wish to expose their commerce to the risk of a war with England. [2]

Charles, indeed, plainly understood that no foreign power would give him armed assistance until he could help himself,

Was Charles
to seek sup-
port in
Scotland or
Ireland? and that he could only become formidable by placing himself at the head of the enemies of England either in Scotland or in Ireland. For some time before any invitation reached him from either of those countries, the question whether he should throw himself on the Scots or the Irish was eagerly discussed in his council. Culpepper, Percy, and Secretary Long were eager for an alliance with Scotland and Presbyterianism, whilst Hyde, to whom all concessions to the Presbyterians were

---

[1] *Acts of Parl. of Sc.* vi. part ii. 157.

[2] Aitzema, *Saken van Staet en Oorlog*, iii. 323 ; *Clarendon*, xii. 1–3.

odious, warmly advocated a voyage to Ireland, where Ormond might be expected to ward off any unseemly yielding to the demands of the Catholic hierarchy.[1]

The choice of Ireland, indeed, as the scene of action, carried with it the choice of a Scottish policy very different *Hyde and Montrose.* from that which was about to be suggested by the Government at Edinburgh. Hyde's view of the case had the warm support of Montrose, who was eager to place himself at the head of a purely Royalist movement in *Montrose's reception of the news of the King's execution.* Scotland. The reception of the news of the execution of the late King had thrown Montrose into a frenzy of indignation. When he heard the bitter tidings he swooned away. As soon as he recovered he vowed to dedicate the remainder of his life to the task of avenging 'the death of the royal martyr, and of re-establishing his son upon the throne which was his due.' Then, returning to his chamber, he refused for two days to admit even his nearest friends. The fruit of this seclusion was the characteristic outburst—

> ' Great, Good, and Just, could I but rate
> My grief with thy too rigid fate,
> I'd weep the world in such a strain
> As it should deluge once again.
> But since thy loud-tongued blood demands supplies
> More from Briareus' hands than Argus' eyes,
> I'll sing thine obsequies with trumpet sounds,
> And write thine epitaph with blood and wounds.'[2]

If the verses were those rather of a soldier than of a poet, they were illuminated by the strong resolution of the writer. *Feb. 22. Montrose to be the King's Lieutenant-Governor of Scotland.* On February 22 Charles, carried away by the energetic insistence of his most heroic supporter, nominated Montrose as Lieutenant-Governor of Scotland and Captain-General of all forces raised in Scotland and of all others which might be brought thither out of England or Ireland.[3] Charles thus gave his

---

[1] Nicholas to Ormond, undated, Carte's *Orig. Letters*, i. 213.

[2] Napier's *Memoirs of Montrose*, ii. 692.

[3] Commission to Montrose, $\frac{\text{Feb. 22}}{\text{March 4}}$, *Hist. MSS. Com.* Rep. ii. 173.

sanction to the raising of a purely Royalist standard in the three kingdoms.

Charles's resolution to abide by any settled policy was soon put to the test. On February 20, two days before the issue of

Feb. 20.
Sir Joseph
Douglas in
Holland. Montrose's commission, Sir Joseph Douglas landed at Rotterdam with instructions from Argyle and his colleagues to feel his way, and, if he found Charles's inclination favourable to the acceptance of the Scottish terms, to promise that commissioners should be sent to treat with the new King.[1]

Argyle's messenger found his task heavier than he had anticipated. Young as Charles was—he had not yet completed

Difficulties
in his way. his nineteenth year—he was too shrewd to be willing to alienate his best supporters by accepting the Covenant; and though Lanark and Lauderdale, in pursuance of their tacit understanding with their former rivals, begged him to give way, they found him strongly inclined to

Charles
inclines to
Ireland. make Ireland rather than Scotland the basis of his operations. Even the Prince of Orange, who objected to any close relations between Charles and

Opinion of
the Prince
of Orange. the Irish Catholics, professed himself unable to understand the policy of the Act of Classes. To a Scotchman who alleged that there were in England three Presbyterians to one Independent, he replied with a warning against divisions. "How many Presbyterians soever ye be," he said, "if ye live at a distance, as I hear you do, ye will be

Charles's
answer
reserved. able to do nothing at all." Charles, who wished to gain time till the arrival of the expected message which Byron was bringing from Ormond, informed Douglas that he would reserve his answer till the promised commissioners arrived from Scotland.[2]

The Scottish Parliament, instead of appointing new commissioners to treat with Charles, sent orders to the three already at Westminster [3] to cross the sea to Holland as soon as

[1] *Acts of the Parl. of Sc.* vi. part ii. 124.

[2] Spang to Baillie, March $\frac{9}{19}$, *Baillie*, iii. 71.

[3] *Great Civil War*, iv. 305.

they had expressed their detestation of the execution of the
late King.[1] On February 24 they presented this last

Feb. 24.
Protest of
the Scottish
Commis-
sioners.

protest to the English Parliament, charging, with
undiplomatic directness, the Commons now sitting
at Westminster with the breach of the Solemn
League and Covenant, the suppression of monarchy and the
House of Lords, and with countenancing the Agreement of the
People, the aim of which was 'a licentious liberty and ungodly
toleration in matters of religion.' They therefore asked that
there should be no toleration and no 'change of the fundamental constitution and government of this kingdom by King,
Lords, and Commons,' and that nothing should be done which
could 'wrong King Charles II.' On the other hand, religion
was to be reformed by the establishment of the Presbyterian
discipline, and the King, 'upon just satisfaction given to both
kingdoms, to be admitted to the exercise of his government.' [2]

The 'Commons now sitting at Westminster' were naturally
irritated by the attempt of the Scottish Parliament to dictate a

Resentment
at West-
minster.

constitutional settlement for England. They at once
denounced it as laying 'the grounds of a new and
bloody war.' They directed that an appeal should
be made to Edinburgh which it was hoped might lead to a
disavowal of the protest, and they despatched Sexby to
Gravesend to arrest the Commissioners,[3] who were already on
their way to take shipping for Holland with the object of in
viting the young King to Scotland. Sexby arrested them on

Feb. 26.
The Scot-
tish Com-
missioners
sent home.

board and brought them back to London, whence
they were, on the 26th, despatched by land under a
guard to Scotland, so that their negotiation at the
Hague might at least suffer delay.[4]

On March 10, before the Scottish Commissioners could
reach Holland by this circuitous route, Byron reached the

[1] *Balfour*, iii. 388.

[2] *The Desires of the Commissioners*, E, 545, 28.

[3] *C.J.* vi. 151.

[4] *Ib.* vi. 152; Grignon to Brienne, $\frac{\text{Feb. 26}}{\text{March 8}}$, *R.O. Transcripts; Portland MSS. Hist. MSS. Com.* 13th Rep. App. i. vol. i. 511.

Hague with Ormond's invitation to Charles to put himself at the head of the Irish Royalists.[1] As Byron had visited Henrietta Maria on his way through France, and had secured her approbation to her son's projected journey on condition that he would do his best to allay the jealousy of the Scots, the opposition of her party in Charles's council fell to the ground, and by March 18 it was known at the Hague that Charles had given the preference to Ormond, and that he would go to Ireland if only he could find money enough for his journey.[2] For the moment, at least, Ireland was less exacting in her terms than Scotland was likely to prove.

March 10.
Byron in
Holland.

March 18.
Charles to
go to
Ireland.

At Westminster, either the possession of secret information or an intelligent perception of the dominant facts of the situation had for some time convinced the new Government that immediate danger was to be apprehended from Ireland rather than from Scotland. Long before Charles's resolution was made known, Rupert's occupation of Kinsale had brought home to Parliament the fact that unwonted efforts must be made to strengthen the navy, if the mercantile marine was to be protected. As early as on February 2 it resolved to add thirty merchant ships to the armed force of the Commonwealth.[3] At a time when Holland's trial was impending, it was impossible to allow his brother Warwick to retain control over the navy. The ordinance by which Warwick had been constituted Lord High Admiral was therefore repealed, and the powers of the office were formally transferred to the Council of State.[4] As that body was too numerous to exercise a proper supervision over the fleet, it

Feeling at
West-
minster.

Feb. 2.
The navy
to be
strength-
ened.

Feb. 23.
The
Admiralty
vested in
the Council
of State.

[1] See p. 13.

[2] Byron to Ormond, March $\frac{20}{30}$, Carte's *Orig. Letters*, i. 237.

[3] *C.J.* vi. 129.

[4] *Ib.* vi. 138, 149. Warwick had, in the preceding summer, been suspected of Royalist proclivities. Grignon to Brienne, $\frac{\text{Feb. 22}}{\text{March 4}}$, *French Transcripts, R.O.*

appointed from its own members a navy committee, of which Vane, who had long been officially familiar with maritime affairs, was the leading spirit, the direction of the fleet having been already entrusted to Colonels Popham, Blake, and Deane, with the title of Commissioners.

The increase of the number of ships would avail little unless they could be provided with crews. Unlike the late

Feb. 12.
Popham,
Blake, and
Deane.

King, the Government of the Commonwealth was fully alive to the importance of winning the sailors' hearts by assurances of good treatment. On the

Feb. 22-24.
Sailors to be
pressed and
rewarded.

22nd an Act was passed which, whilst authorising the impressment of men, promised a liberal distribution of prize money, and on the 24th a second Act assured the sailors a reward of 10l. for every captured gun.[1] On the 27th the three Commissioners, or—to give them the name by which they were generally known—the three Generals at Sea, received their commissions and instructions from the Council of State. On March 2, in view of the imminent danger from Rupert's fleet, Sir George Ayscue was specially appointed to command as Admiral on the Irish coast.[2]

If Ireland was to be made by the Royalists a basis of operations against England, an invasion of Ireland by the

An invasion
of Ireland
necessary.

soldiers of the Commonwealth was but a defensive measure. Parliament accordingly set itself to do everything in its power on the one hand to content the soldiers with their lot, and on the other hand to reconcile

March 1.
Parliament
asked to
grant settled
pay.

civilians to the maintenance of the army. On March 1 Fairfax and the Council of Officers asked Parliament to make free quarter unnecessary by granting settled pay.[3] On the 6th the Council of State reported that the army in England should consist of 32,000 men, besides 12,000 for Ireland.

March 6.
Men and
pay re-
quired.

---

[1] *Scobell*, ii. 4, 7.

[2] C. of St. Order Book, *Interr.* I, 62, pp. 33, 35 ; *C.J.* vi. 154.

[3] *The Moderate*, E, 546, 8.

The pay of both armies would be 120,000*l.* a month, that is to say, 1,440,000*l.* a year. On the 8th Parliament resolved that three-fourths of this sum, amounting to 90,000*l.* a month, should be assessed on the counties, and the remainder raised in some manner not yet specified.[1] On the 9th Fairfax was directed to ask the opinion of his officers on the best means of selecting the force needed for Ireland, and on the names of those most fitted to take the command.[2]

March 8.
Vote of
Parliament.

March 9.
The officers
to be con-
sulted.

Fairfax replied that the appointment of a commander-in-chief must precede the selection of the regiments to serve under him ;[3] and on the 15th the Council of State, acting with the authority of Parliament, named Cromwell.[4] Cromwell, however, hesitated to accept the nomination, and on the 23rd he explained his reasons to his brother officers. If Parliament, he said, commanded him to go, he was ready to obey, but he wished to have time to consider how far God would incline his heart to go voluntarily. Then, giving a practical turn to his words, he explained the reasons which made him for the present at least hang back. He did not wish, he said, to allow his name to be used to induce soldiers to volunteer for Ireland, unless he were first assured that there would be sufficient provision for the supply of their wants.[5] Warming as he went on, he protested that he had no thought of his own aggrandisement. " God," he said, " hath not blessed the army for the sake of any one man." " It matters not," he continued, " who is our commander-in-chief if God be so. . . . Truly I do believe that God hath so principled this army that there is none amongst us that, if God should set us out any man, we

March 13.
Reply of
Fairfax.

March 15.
Cromwell
named to
the com-
mand.

March 23.
Cromwell
hesitates to
accept the
offer,

and explains
his reasons.

---

[1] *C.J.* vi. 157, 159.

[2] Council of State to Fairfax, March 9, *Interr.* I, 94, p. 27.

[3] C. of St. Order Book, March 13, *Interr.* I, 62, p. 86.

[4] Ib. *Interr.* I, 62, p. 91.

[5] Compare the somewhat similar language of Gustavus Adolphus in 1625. *Hist. of England,* 1603–1642, v. 297.

should come to this to refuse to [1] submit to one another for the work's sake."

Then, taking a wider view of the situation, Cromwell reminded his audience that God had given them the first-

Cromwell's view of the situation. fruits of victory in 'the execution of exemplary justice upon the prime leader of all this quarrel in the three kingdoms, and upon divers persons of very great quality who did co-operate with him in the destruction of this kingdom '—inveterate habit would not allow him to give it any other name. They had now, he continued, to deal with their old enemies in Scotland and Ireland. After a few contemptuous phrases directed at the combination between the Scots and the English Presbyterians, Cromwell warned the army against internal distractions. "I must needs say," he continued, "I do more fear—not that I do think there is a ground to fear it will be, but as a poor man that desires to see the work of God to prosper in our hands—I think there is more cause of danger from disunion amongst ourselves than by anything from our enemies. . . . Now, if we do not depart from God and disunite by that departure, and fall into disunion amongst ourselves, I am confident, we doing our duty and waiting upon the Lord, we shall find He will be as a wall of brass round about us till He hath finished that work that He has for us to do."

God's work was, in the first place, to be found in Ireland. Recent intelligence from that country had been threatening.

His fear of danger from Ireland. "Truly," said Cromwell, "this is really believed : if we do not endeavour to make good our interest there, and that timely, we shall not only have . . . our interest rooted out there, but they will in a very short time be able to land forces in England and to put us to trouble here ; and I confess I have had these thoughts with myself that perhaps may be carnal and foolish; I had rather be overrun with a cavalierish interest than a Scotch interest ; I had rather be overrun by a Scotch interest

---

[1] The words ' refuse to ' are not in the MS.

than an Irish interest, and I think of all this is most dangerous ; and, if they shall be able to carry on their work, they will make this the most miserable people in the earth ; for all the world knows their barbarism, not of any religion almost any of them, but, in a manner, as bad as Papists, and truly it is thus far that the quarrel is brought to this State that we can hardly return into that tyranny that formerly we were under the yoke of, . . . but we must at the same time be subject to the kingdom of Scotland and the kingdom of Ireland for the bringing in of the King. Now it should awaken all Englishmen who perhaps are willing enough he should have come in upon an accommodation ; but now he must come from Ireland or Scotland." [1]

Cromwell's words did but echo the sentiments of the army. With Ormond planning an invasion, and with the Royalist

Royalist
hopes to be
crushed. gentry ready from Lancashire to Cornwall to welcome him and his Irish followers,[2] the army—or at least its commanders—could have no other thought than to tear up the mischief by the roots in its own soil. It is easy to say that England could never have been conquered by an Irish army, or that the party which endeavoured to profit by such aid would have been condemned to lasting obloquy. It was Cromwell's duty to take care that the danger should never arise. Ormond had without difficulty thrown English regiments from Ireland on the Western coast of England in 1643 ; and if he now succeeded in mastering Dublin it would be hard to prevent a repetition of the same operation with Irish regiments in 1649.

Even in the midst of this fierce denunciation of Irishmen, there was a limit beyond which neither Cromwell nor his

March 24.
Whalley's
recommen-
dations. followers were as yet prepared to go. On March 24 Whalley proposed with general acceptance that the officers should ask the Council of State to secure to those who went to Ireland their pay and arrears, that the com-

---

[1] Debate in the Council of Officers. March 23. *Clarke Papers*, ii. 200.

[2] Grignon to Brienne, $\frac{\text{March } 26}{\text{April } 5}$, *R.O. Transcripts.*

mander should be empowered to conclude peace, and that no
'ill terms be imposed upon him, as either to eradicate the
natives, or to divest them of their estates.' [1]　During the next
few days the negotiations with the Council of State proceeded
satisfactorily, and on the 30th, Cromwell having
been convinced that the army after landing in Ireland would not perish for lack of support, it was
notified that he would undertake the command under the
nominal superintendence of Fairfax, the commander-in-chief
of all the forces of the Commonwealth. [2]

March 30.
Cromwell
accepts the
command.

　Cromwell's acceptance of the command in Ireland was but
one step more in the evolution of the original quarrel.　For
some time it had been becoming clear that the
conflict between King and Parliament for supremacy at Westminster was widening out into a conflict for the
supremacy of England in the British Isles.　That it was so
was owing to the eagerness of Royalists to enlist the forces of
Scotland and Ireland in their own behoof, and it is no wonder
that Cromwell and his officers had made up their minds that
rather than Scotland or Ireland should interfere in the political
development of England, an English army should interfere in
the political development of Scotland and Ireland.

Cromwell's
intentions.

　There was strong probability that in Ireland at least the
English army, being what it was, would succeed in accomplish-
ing the task before it.　In Ireland, as in England, a negative
result was in the grasp of superior force.　The army had been
strong enough on one side of the Irish Sea to make
sure that it would no longer be mocked by the
illusory promises of Charles I.　It would be strong
enough on the other side to make sure that Irishmen should
no longer be used to threaten England for the benefit of an
English political party.　Yet unlikely as it was that the army
should secure in England the permanent triumph of Puritanism,
it was far less likely that it should found peace and order in Ireland by strengthening the 'English interest,' and by sacrificing

What
Cromwell
could do.

---

[1] *Clarke Papers*, ii. 2c8.　　[2] *C.J.* vi. 176.

the needs and the hopes of the ancient inhabitants to the greed and self-assertion of the English settlers. Yet to this hopeless task Cromwell had committed himself. It was the tragedy of the situation that he had the support of all but a very few of his countrymen. For evil as well as for good he stood forth, so far as Ireland was concerned, as the typical Englishman of his time.

CHAPTER II

CROMWELL AND THE LEVELLERS

IT was not without reason that Cromwell had warned the army against internal divisions. Men's minds had so far drifted from the anchorage of use and wont, that to some of them every counsel of perfection seemed capable of immediate realisation. Two of the leading ideas of the seventeenth century were that good and religious men had a right to rule the evil and irreligious, and that the nation ought to be governed according to the wishes of its representatives in Parliament. Incompatible as these two ideas were in themselves, they became still more incompatible in the exaggerated shapes which they were daily taking.

Risk of divisions in the army.

Two leading ideas.

The doctrine of the divine right of the religious to govern reached its furthest development in a petition prepared for presentation to the Council of Officers 'by many Christian people dispersed abroad throughout the county of Norfolk, and City of Norwich.' It asked for the establishment of the Fifth Monarchy, that is to say, of the reign of Christ and His saints, which, according to prophecy, was to supersede the four monarchies of the ancient world. What the petitioners meant was that, as only the godly were fit to govern, the Church should be the sole depository of civil authority. Independents and Presbyterians were to combine to choose delegates, who were in turn to elect 'general assemblies or Church Parliaments, as Christ's officers and the Church's representatives, and to determine all things by the

Feb. The Fifth Monarchy.

Word, as that law which God will exalt alone and make honourable.' [1]

Such a proposal might attract fanatics ; it could not attract the multitude. The Levellers who stood up for an exaggeration of the doctrine of Parliamentary supremacy were likely to be far more numerous. Advocating direct government by a democratic Parliament and the fullest development of individual liberty, the Levellers looked with suspicion on the Council of State as a body which might possibly be converted into an executive authority independent of Parliament, and thoroughly distrusted Cromwell as aiming at military despotism. Well-intentioned and patriotic as they were, they were absolutely destitute of political tact, and had no sense of the real difficulties of the situation, and, above all, of the impossibility of rousing the popular sympathy on behalf of abstract reasonings.

Principles of the Levellers.

It is unlikely that the officers would have interfered to hinder a purely civilian propaganda. About the middle of February, however, they discovered that the Levellers designed to tamper with the army by urging the soldiers to demand the reappointment of Agitators,[2] and the revival of the disused General Council of the Army, in order that these Agitators might again have an equal voice with the officers in determining the political action of the army.[3] As might have been expected, the officers took offence at the suggestion, and at a Council held on February 22, where there was a discussion on a petition from Fairfax's regi-

The Levellers and the army.

The reappointment of Agitators asked for.

Feb. 22.
The officers take offence.

---

[1] *Certain Queries*, E, 454, 5.

[2] In *A Plea for Common Right and Freedom* presented to Fairfax and his officers on December 28, 1648, by Lilburne and other Levellers (E, 536, 22), it was only asked that the Council of the Army should not sit except when the major part of the commission officers at the head-quarters and adjacent thereunto, not excluding of others, were present.

[3] The intention to urge the choice of Agitators is mentioned in Grignon's despatch of $\frac{\text{Feb. 22}}{\text{March 4}}$, (*R.O. Transcripts*), and is implied in the petition for the renewal of the General Council discussed on March 1. *Clarke Papers*, ii. 193.

ment, in which the views of the Levellers were embodied, much strong language was used. Hewson recommended that those who drew up such petitions should be tried by a court-martial on the ground that such a court 'could hang twenty ere the magistrate one.' [1] In the end the Council resolved that no soldiers should present petitions except through their officers, or through the General if the officers refused to do their part. Moreover, Cromwell and Ireton were instructed to ask Parliament to pass an Act for the punishment of civilians stirring up discontent in the army, by inflicting on them the same penalty which would be awarded to soldiers guilty of the same offence. [2]

An appeal to Parliament.

Of this agitation Lilburne was the heart and soul. On the 26th he laid before Parliament a remonstrance partly drawn up by himself, and afterwards published under the title of *England's New Chains.* In this he asked that the Council of State might be superseded by 'committees of short continuance, frequently and exactly accountable for the discharge of their trusts,' and that, in order to keep these committees in check, Parliament should remain in permanent session till the very day before a newly elected House was ready to take its place. Parliament was also asked to 'put in practice the Self-denying Ordinance,' and to consider how dangerous it was ' for one and the same persons to be continued long in the highest commands of a military Power.' In other words, not only Cromwell and Ireton, but also Fairfax, who had recently been elected a member of the House, were to be summarily cashiered. [3]

Feb. 26.
England's New Chains.

Three days later, on March 1, a petition was laid before the Council of Officers by eight troopers, one of whom was that Richard Rumbold who was afterwards an accomplice of the Rye House plotters, and who, as a follower of a later Argyle, was executed at Edinburgh, declaring

March 1.
A petition from eight troopers.

---

[1] *England's New Chains,* Sig. B., E, 545, 27 ; *The Hunting of the Foxes,* E, 548, 7 ; *The Legal Fundamental Liberties,* 2nd ed. p. 74, E, 561.   [2] *Clarke Papers,* ii. 192.

[3] *England's New Chains,* Sig. B. 2, F, 515, 27.

that 'he did not believe that God had made the greater part of
mankind with saddles on their backs and bridles in their mouths,
and some few booted and spurred to ride the rest.'[1]   The eight
petitioners now avowed their part in drawing up *England's New
Chains*, and argued that they were still bound by the engagement taken by the army on Kentford Heath [2] to maintain the
liberties of the people, and that those who resisted the right of
their comrades to petition Parliament were doing exactly what
they had themselves condemned in the case of Stapleton and
Holles.[3]   They indeed acknowledged that the officers did not
directly deny the right of soldiers to petition, but they argued
that, by the requirement that every petition should first receive
the approval of the officers, the concession was rendered
nugatory.   What, asked the troopers, could officers effect without the private soldiers who bore the burden and heat of the
day?   This home-thrust was followed by a sharp criticism of
the erection of the Council of State, of the substitution of a
High Court of Justice for trial by jury, and of the establishment
of the power of the sword in the self-same hand under one
military head.[4]

It would be difficult for Cromwell and Ireton with any
regard for consistency to meet the argument of the petitioners
Part of the
petition
unanswer-
able. that, to some extent at least, they were treading in
the steps of Stapleton and Holles.   Yet to give way
was to open the door, first to military anarchy, and
then at no long interval to a Stuart restoration.   Cromwell
cared little for consistency, and much for the maintenance of
March 3.
Five of the
petitioners
cashiered. order.   On March 3 the eight troopers were brought
before a court-martial, when five of them who re-
mained obstinate [5] were found guilty of writing a
letter 'scandalous to the Parliament, Council of State, High

---

[1] Burnet's *Hist. of his Own Time*, ed. 1823, iii. 30.   Compare
Macaulay, i. 555, 556.

[2] *Great Civil War*, iii. 279.   [3] *Ib*. iii. 229, 279.

[4] Petition, March 1, *Clarke Papers*, ii. 193, note *b*.   It is printed
with only five signatures in *The Hunting of the Foxes*, E, 548, 7.

[5] Ward, Watson, Graunt, Jellis, and Sawyer.

Court of Justice, and tending to breed mutiny in the army.'
They were accordingly sentenced to mount their horses in front
of their respective regiments with their faces towards the tails,
and to be cashiered after their swords had been broken over
their heads.[1]

On the 6th the sentence was carried into execution. As
soon as the five troopers were released, they called for a coach

March 6.
The sen-
tence exe-
cuted. and drove off triumphantly to their friends in London.
About a fortnight later they published an account of
their wrongs, under the title of *The Hunting of the*

March 21.
The
Hunting of
the Foxes. *Foxes from Newmarket and Triploe Heaths to White-*
hall by five small beagles late of the army. The key-
note of the whole lay in the assertion that Cromwell,
Ireton, and Harrison ruled the Council of Officers, and that the
Council of Officers ruled the State. " The old King's person,"
said the five beagles, " and the old lords are but removed, and
a new king and new lords with the Commons are in one House,
and so [we are] under a more absolute arbitrary monarchy than
before."

Cromwell's only reply was the before-mentioned appeal to
avoid divisions in the army, made to the Council of Officers on

March 23.
Cromwell's
appeal
against
divisions. the 23rd,[2] only two days after the appearance of the
book. On the 24th Lilburne returned to the charge
with the *Second Part of England's New Chains.*[3]
The first part had been mainly an attack on the

March 24.
The Second
Part of
England's
New
Chains. Council of State and the officers. In the second
Lilburne appealed to a new Parliament, on the
ground that the present one was coerced by the
officers. Yet at the same time he appealed to the
very members of Parliament of whose weakness he complained
to rise against the domination of the army, to reconstruct the
General Council of the Army by furthering the election of
Agitators, and to proceed heartily with the *Agreement of the
People.*

---

[1] The newspapers speak of only four being cashiered, but this is
evidently a mistake.

[2] See p. 25.　　　　　　　　　　　[3] E, 548, 16.

So imperiously to demand a settlement of the constitution with the enemy at the door was conduct too dangerous to be tolerated. On March 27 Parliament declared Lilburne's book to be seditious and destructive of the present government, to tend to mutiny in the army, and to hinder the present relief of Ireland by raising of a new war in the Commonwealth. Its authors were therefore to be proceeded against as traitors.[1]

March 27. Lilburne's book declared treasonable.

Accordingly, in the early morning of the 28th, Lilburne, together with three of his supporters, Walwyn, Prince, and Richard Overton, all of whom had had a hand in the composition of the incriminated pamphlet, were arrested by soldiers,[2] and carried before the Council of State. Lilburne was the first to be brought into the chamber in which its sittings were held. With his hat on his head he strode into the room, only removing it when he perceived that some of the councillors were also members of Parliament. Taking it for granted that he was about to be condemned by some new High Court of

March 28. Arrest of Lilburne and three of his supporters.

Lilburne before the Council.

---

[1] *C.J.* vi. 174.

[2] The circumstances of Overton's arrest indicate some of the causes of the unpopularity of the soldiers in London. Overton's landlord, a Mr. Devenish, whose wife was nursing a young child, slept according to the habit of those times, with his lodger, probably to escape the cries of the baby. The soldier who appeared to seize Overton found him sitting half dressed on the bed, and seeing that it had been occupied by two persons, charged him with having slept in it with Mrs. Devenish, naturally infuriating both the woman and her husband. *The Picture of the Council of State*, p. 25, E, 550, 14. It is to be noticed that the name of Wildman is not now to be found amongst Lilburne's associates. His defection seems to have occurred before the end of 1648. His name is not found amongst those who joined Lilburne on Dec. 28 in presenting *A Plea for Common Right and Freedom*, E, 536, 22. In *Defiance of the Act of Pardon*, published on July 4 (E, 562, 26), the author, Richard Overton, asks :—"And where's . . . my old fellow rebel, Johnee Wildman ? Mount Atlas, stand on tiptoes, where art thee ? And behold a mighty stone fell from the skies into the bottom of the sea, and gave a mighty plump, and great was the fall of that stone, and so farewell Johnee Wildman."

Justice, or even by the Council itself, he denied in the first place that there was any evidence that the Council had been appointed by Parliament; and, in the second place, that, if it were so, any such body had a right to proceed judicially against him. This time, however, there was no intention to resort to extraordinary measures, and Bradshaw was able to assure the prisoner that the Council of State claimed no jurisdiction over him. After this Lilburne was sent out of the room for a time. When he was readmitted, he was asked whether he was the author of the pamphlet to which objection had been taken. As might have been expected, he replied by a long tirade against the men who were reviving the exploded practice of the Star Chamber by asking him to incriminate himself.

Having thus relieved his mind, Lilburne threatened the Council with the consequences of committing him again to the custody of soldiers. "If you send me back to Whitehall," he said, "or any other such-like garrisoned place in England, I do solemnly protest before the Eternal God of heaven and earth, I will fire it and burn it to the ground if possibly I can, although I be burned to ashes with the flames thereof." "I must be plain with you," he added, looking fixedly at Cromwell as he spoke; "I have not found so much honour, honesty, justice, or conscience in any of the principal officers of the army as to trust my life under their protection, or to think it can be safe under their immediate fingers."

Lilburne threatens the Council.

The other three prisoners having also refused to incriminate themselves, all four were removed into an outer room. Lilburne listened through the door and recognised the voices of the speakers within. "I tell you, sir," said Cromwell, thumping the table as he spoke, "you have no other way to deal with these men but to break them, or they will break you; yea, and bring all the guilt of the blood and treasure shed and spent in this kingdom upon your heads and shoulders, and frustrate and make void all that work that, with so many years' industry, toil, and pains, you have done, and so render you to all rational men in the world as the most

Cromwell's strong language.

contemptiblest generation of silly, low-spirited men in the earth to be broken and routed by such a despicable, contemptible generation of men as they are, and therefore, sir, I tell you again, you are necessitated to break them." Ludlow then urged that bail should be allowed, but his motion was lost by a single vote, and all four were committed to the Tower to await their trial in the Upper Bench.[1]

A party which rules by the sword is seldom able to command the pen, and the Commonwealth was singularly weak in literary support. The newspapers which took its side were little more than mere chroniclers of passing events, and whenever they ventured on argument were too dull and unintelligent to be convincing. The Royalist press, on the other hand, though as devoid of true wit as its antagonists, was scurrilous and incisive, and was also entirely regardless of truth when anything might be gained by a falsehood. The one writer of genius to whom the new Government could look for help was Milton. Shortly after the King's execution, Milton had published *The Tenure of Kings and Magistrates* in defence of the proceedings against Charles. It was a work, indeed, of that kind which never convinces anyone, because it took for granted all that opponents denied, and because the author had too little knowledge of the human mind to adapt his reasoning skilfully, as the author of *Eikon Basilikè* had done, to the receptive powers of those whom he desired to persuade. Still, the book was a striking performance, and those in whose defence it was written would naturally assign to it higher merits than it possesses in the eyes of a later generation. They might well think that their champion was worth enrolling in the service of the Commonwealth.

Weakness of the literary supporters of the Commonwealth.

*Feb. 13.
Milton's Tenure of Kings and Magistrates.*

Accordingly, on March 15, an order of the Council of State appointed Milton its Secretary for Foreign Tongues. It was a post for a scholar, not for a statesman. Milton had to draw up, from instructions given to him, letters addressed to

[1] *The Picture of the Council of State*, E, 550, 14 ; C. of St. Order Book, March 28 ; *Interr.* I, 62, p. 126.

foreign States. Hitherto those letters had been couched in
two languages—in French to the French Government and to
other Governments such as that of the Dutch Republic to which the French language was familiar,
and in Latin to Governments like those of Spain or
the Empire, whose own diplomatic correspondence
was carried on in that tongue. The Council of State—very
likely at Milton's suggestion—resolved that all their communications with foreign powers should henceforth be carried
on in Latin, and Milton was, therefore, familiarly known as the
Latin Secretary.[1]

*March 15.
Milton
Secretary
for Foreign
Tongues.*

The Council now attempted to utilise Milton's services in
another fashion. Knowing his addiction to the writing of
pamphlets, they ordered him, on March 26, to make
some observations on the *Second Part of England's
New Chains*.[2] Milton, however, had a rooted objection to write excepting on themes chosen by himself,
and he may possibly have felt too much sympathy with
Lilburne's vindication of personal liberty to care to enter the
lists against him. Nothing could induce him to do
as he was bidden in this matter, and the attempt of
the Council of State to harness their Pegasus ended in failure.[3]

*March 26.
Milton
asked to
answer
Lilburne.*

*His dis-
obedience.*

The danger from the Levellers was the greater because the
City authorities maintained an attitude of opposition to the
Government. Measures indeed, as yet incomplete, had been
taken to coerce the City. In October, 1648, when
the mayoralty of the intrusive Warner came to an
end, Abraham Reynoldson, a sturdy Royalist, had
been chosen to succeed him. Parliament accordingly took

*1648.
Oct. 29.
The City
elections.*

---

[1] The whole subject of Milton's engagement is exhaustively treated in
Masson's *Life of Milton*, iv. 72-86. Professor Masson, however, was
not familiar with the diplomatic correspondence of the time, and his
suggestion that Milton might have difficulty in answering letters in French,
Italian, Spanish, Portuguese, German, or Dutch is founded on a mis-
apprehension. French was the only one of these languages in which
letters were received.

[2] C. of St. Order Book, *Interr.* I, 62, p. 177.

[3] See Masson's *Life of Milton*, iv. 96.

alarm lest a Royalist Common Council should be chosen as well as a Royalist Lord Mayor, and, having been itself purged by the army, it proceeded, on December 18, to purge the City by an ordinance directing that no one who had abetted the King's cause or the Scottish invasion, or had given his approbation to the apprentices' attack on the House of Commons, should thenceforward be chosen to hold any place of trust in the City, or should give a vote in the election of officers. At the same time orders were given that the posts and chains which had been set up as obstacles to charges of cavalry should again be removed from the streets.[1]

Dec. 18.
The purge
of the City.

As the result of this ordinance, the new Common Council, elected as usual on December 21, was as completely packed in the interests of the minority as the House of Commons itself. It was only to be expected that there would be fierce opposition between such a body and the Royalist Lord Mayor. At the first meeting of the Common Council, which took place on January 13, the Lord Mayor refused to put to the vote or even to listen to a petition to the House of Commons in support of the proceedings against the King, and for some hours maintained his position amidst a storm of outcries and abuse. At last he and the two aldermen who alone were present left the room, and thus, according to precedent, condemned the Council to impotence for want of a qualified chairman. The councillors, however, placed one of their own number in the chair, and carried the petition with unanimity.[2] On February 28 the Commons passed an Act for the removal of obstructions in the Common Council, authorising it to elect a chairman in the absence of the Lord Mayor or his representative.[3] They had already, on February 10, imposed an oath of fidelity to the Commonwealth on freemen hereafter admitted to citizenship, and this oath was now extended to all other municipalities.[4]

Dec. 21.
A packed
Common
Council.

1649
Jan. 13.
Its first
meeting.

Feb. 28.
Act for the
removal of
obstructions.

Feb. 10.
A freeman's
oath.

---

[1] *L.J.* x. 633.   [2] Corporation Records, *C.C. Journal Book*, xl. 313.
[3] The Act, which is not in *Scobell*, is in the *C.C. Journal Book*, xl. 312.   [4] *Scobell*, ii. 4.

It was not long before an opportunity presented itself of getting rid of the Lord Mayor, who was unaffected by this legislation. On March 17, the Act abolishing kingship was passed, and its proclamation ordered.[1] In London alone this order was stubbornly resisted. On April 2 the Lord Mayor was summoned to the bar of the House, and on his acknowledgment that his conscience would not allow him to break the oaths which he had taken, was deprived of his office, fined 2,000*l.*, and sent to the Tower for a month.[2] On the following day Alderman Andrews, who did not share the scruples of Reynoldson, was chosen Lord Mayor by the packed constituency of the City.[3] Even Andrews, however, did not venture to make the proclamation for some time to come; although, on the 7th, the five aldermen, who had been impeached in the preceding year, were not only discharged from their places by order of Parliament, but were declared incapable of holding office in future.[4]

March 17. Act abolishing kingship.

April 2. The Lord Mayor discharged and fined.

April 7. Five aldermen discharged.

Resolved to secure obedience, the Government was at least anxious to secure that popularity which seemed so hard to win. The persistent rains of the last summer had been ruinous to the crops, and food of all kinds was almost at famine prices. It is hardly to be wondered at that the men now in power had recourse to the measures which had commended themselves to the Privy Council of Charles I. during the scarcity which prevailed in 1630.[5] They held the same economical doctrines, and had the same desire to appeal to the masses for support against the country gentlemen and the upper middle class in the towns. On March 19 Parliament ordered the Justices of the Peace to enforce the laws against engrossing corn, and on April 6 it directed them to rate wages in accordance with statutes of Elizabeth and James, with a view to raising them in proportion to the rise of

Economical action of the Government.

March 19. Enforcement of the laws against engrossing.

April 6. Wages to be rated.

<hr/>

[1] *C.J.* vi. 166.   [2] *Ib.* vi. 177.   [3] *Ib.* vi. 179.
[4] *Ib.* vi. 181.   [5] *Hist. of Engl.* 1603–1642, vii. 162.

prices.[1] Somewhat later, on April 14, Parliament swept away the whole fabric of personal privilege which of late years had called forth loud and frequent protests. Actions brought against members of Parliament were in future to receive no hindrance, on the sole condition that notice should be given by the judge to the defendant if he happened to be a member.[2]

April 14.
Actions
to be
brought
against
members.

Apart from its other difficulties the Commonwealth, with its enormous army to keep up, was in grievous financial straits. The 30,000*l.* a month, left uncovered by the assessments,[3] must be found before Cromwell could sail for Ireland, and though there were many sources of supply ultimately available, such as the composition of delinquents, the property of the Royal family, and the lands of the suppressed Deans and Chapters, none of these would yield an immediate revenue sufficient for the purpose. It was therefore proposed that the City should be asked to lend 120,000*l.* on the security of fee-farm rents and the assessments. On April 12 a deputation from Parliament appeared at Guildhall to urge the citizens to lend. The war in Ireland, said Chief Baron Wilde, was between ' Papist and Protestant,' after which he quoted with approbation a saying attributed to James I., " Plant Ireland with Puritans and root out Papists, and then secure it." Cromwell contented himself with giving assurances that there was no truth in the rumours abroad that the army, when once supplied with money, would refuse to go to Ireland. In its discipline he professed perfect confidence. " As for divisions and distractions in the army, there was none, though it had been attempted." [4] In spite of these arguments the City professed doubts of the security offered, and Parliament had to fall back in hastening the sale of the Deans and Chapters' estates, in order to raise the money required. The official government of the City had no hold on the purses of its wealthy merchants.

Financial
straits.

April 12.
The City
asked for a
loan.

Eventually, too, a source of revenue would no doubt be

---

[1] *C.J.* vi. 167, 180.   [2] *Acts*, E, 1,060, No. 26.   [3] See p. 24.
[4] *The Moderate Intelligencer*, E, 551, 1.

opened in the compositions of delinquents engaged in the last
war, but the House, in passing resolutions concerning them on March 14 and 17, had left them ample
time to give in their accounts.   The question
whether the Commonwealth was to inflict further
penalties on those who had taken a prominent part in either
war was at the same time decided.   In addition to the two
sons of the late King, Charles and James, fifteen persons were
to be banished with entire confiscation of their estates, and
were forbidden to return under pain of death.   Two others,
the Marquis of Winchester and Bishop Wren, were
to be imprisoned and to lose all their property.
Two, one of whom was Judge Jenkins, were to be
tried for life in the Upper Bench, and five, Poyer,
Powell, Laugharne, Lingen, and Brown Bushell, were to be
tried for life by a court-martial.[1]   Of these latter five, the first
three were selected for an immediate trial, and after
a long and patient inquiry, all three were sentenced
to death as officers unfaithful to their trust.[2]   They
were, however, permitted to draw lots for their lives.
The lot fell on Poyer, who on April 25 was shot to
death in Covent Garden.[3]   Not long afterwards, on May 7,
Laugharne and Powell were pardoned and set at liberty.

There was little danger of any immediate movement of the
Royalists in England.   On March 21 their last stronghold,
Pontefract Castle, surrendered after a long blockade.
The officers of the garrison were particularly obnoxious, as it was amongst them that Rainsborough's
murderers were to be found, and six of their number were
excepted by name from the mercy shown to the remainder of
the defenders.   The Governor, Morris, with two of the excepted persons, however, forced their way through the lines of
the besiegers and made their escape.[4]   These two, having

March
14-17.
Delin-
quents'
composi-
tions.

March 17.
Persons
excepted
from
pardon.

April
10-12.
Poyer,
Powell, and
Laugh-
arne sen-
tenced
to death.

March 21.
Surrender
of Ponte-
fract.

[1] *C.J.* vi. 164–167.   [2] *A Perf. Diurnal*, E, 529, 13.
[3] *A Declaration of Col. Poyer*, E, 552, 3.
[4] *The Moderate*, E, 548, 21 ; *A True Copy of Articles of Surrender*,
E, 548, 25.

been ultimately captured, were tried at York assizes, and executed.

Far more pressing was the danger from the Levellers. On April 2 a petition for the release of Lilburne and his associates

April 2.
A petition
for Lil-
burne's
release.

was presented to Parliament, bearing, it is said, no less than 80,000 signatures. The petitioners urged that no one should be condemned except for some definite breach of the law.[1] Apparently in consequence of this petition Parliament, on April 11, ordered that the four prisoners should be prosecuted before the Upper

April 11.
Lilburne
to be pro-
secuted.

Bench with as little delay as possible.[2] It was, however, easier to prosecute Lilburne than to silence him. On April 16 appeared a new manifesto, in which he and his comrades protested against the application of

April 16.
A Lil-
burnian
protest.

the term Levellers to themselves, especially if it was understood to include a desire for the ' equalling of men's estates, and taking away of the proper right and title that every man has to what is his own.' [3]

In his most unpractical moments Lilburne had confined his demands to political reform, and his latest protest was

Lilburne
no socialist.

doubtless called out by his knowledge that some men, styling themselves the True Levellers, were now

The diggers
on St.
George's
Hill.

striking at the rights of property. On April 16, the Council of State, hearing that about fifty of these new social reformers having assembled on St.

April 16.
Fairfax
ordered to
disperse
them.

George's Hill, near Oatlands, had proceeded to dig up and sow the waste land, ordered Fairfax to disperse them,[4] a task which was easily accomplished on the 19th by two troops of horse.

On the 20th Everard and Winstanley, two of the principal

April 20.
Their
leaders
before the
Council.

diggers, were brought before Fairfax at Whitehall. They refused to remove their hats in the General's presence, saying that ' he was but their fellow-creature.' Everard explained that he had been

---

[1] *C.J.* vi. 178 ; *The Moderate*, E, 549, 12.
[2] *C.J.* vi. 183.   [3] *A Manifestation*, E, 550, 25
[4] C. of St. to Fairfax, Ap. 16 ; *Interr.* I, 94, p. 93*a*.

directed in a vision to dig and plough the earth. For the present, however, he and his followers intended to confine their operations to waste lands. Before long all men would voluntarily surrender their estates and agree to live in community, contenting themselves with food and clothing, money being wholly unnecessary.[1] In a manifesto which he and his comrades published on April 26, Everard was less reticent. All landlords, he declared, were thieves and murderers It was now time for the English, the true Israel, to free themselves from the landlords, the descendants and representatives of the Norman conquerors. Labourers were exhorted to work for hire no longer, but to dig the waste places for their own benefit. To the rulers, the Pharaohs of the day, was added a word of warning. " Therefore, if thou wilt find mercy, let Israel go free. Break in pieces quickly the band of particular property, disown this oppressing murder, oppression and thievery of buying and selling of land, owning of landlords and paying of rents, and give thy free consent to make the earth a common treasury, without grumbling ; that the younger brethren may live comfortably upon earth, as well as the elder, that all men may enjoy the benefit of their creation." [2]

April 26.
Manifesto
of the
diggers.

Too many Englishmen were interested in the social institutions of the country to allow this visionary hope to attain the smallest chance of realisation. An angry crowd, perhaps partly composed of freeholders who had right of common on St. George's Hill, dug up the seeds which had been sown.[3] The diggers were ill-treated by passing soldiers, as well as by the neighbours, and though the enterprise struggled on for some time, it ultimately came to nothing.[4]

Their work
destroyed.

Communism had no root in the England of the seventeenth

---

[1] *The Declaration and Standard of the Levellers*, E. 551, 11.

[2] *The True Levellers' Standard Advanced*, E, 552, 5.

[3] *A Modest Narrative*, E, 552, **7** ; *A Moderate Intelligence*, E, 557, 6.

[4] *A Declaration*, E, 557, 9 ; *A Letter to Lord Fairfax*, E, 560, 1 ; *A Declaration*, E, 561, 6 ; *An Appeal*, E, 564, 5 ; *A Watchword to the City*

century.   The political Levellers had followers enough.   On

April 18.
Another
Lilburnian
petition.
April 18 another body of petitioners, asking for Lilburne's release, appeared at the bar of the House, but were dismissed with the sharp answer that the prisoners would have a legal trial, and that no one would be suffered to interfere with the course of justice.[1]   On the 23rd

April 23.
A women's
petition.
a crowd of women attempted to do what the men had failed to accomplish, but they were forbidden even to enter the House, and were told to go home and wash their dishes.[2]

As long as the army maintained its discipline, such manifestations were of little moment.   Hitherto Cromwell's assertion

The discipline of the army.
at Guildhall [3] that there was no disunion amongst the soldiers had been justified by the course of events. It was now, however, to be seen that it had been

April 17.
Regiments
for Ireland
chosen by
lot.
premature.   On April 17, according to arrangement, lots were cast for the selection of regiments to go to Ireland.   The lots fell on four regiments of horse, those of Ireton, Scrope, Horton, and Lambert ; on four of foot, those of Eure, Cook, Deane, and Hewson, and upon five troops of dragoons.   The soldiers were, however, informed that none who wished to remain behind would be compelled to go to Ireland, though, if they elected to stay in England, they would not be permitted to remain in the army.   On this, some who had resolved not to leave England till the demands of the

---

of London, E, 573, 1 ; A New Year's Gift, E, 587, 6.   Compare Clarke Papers, ii. 215–221, where there is a curious song beginning—

> You noble diggers all, stand up now, stand up now,
>   You noble diggers all, stand up now,
> The waste land to maintain, seeing Cavaliers by name,
> Your digging does disdaine, and persons all defame,
>   Stand up now, stand up now.

[1] C.J. vi. 189, 190.

[2] A Petition of Well-affected Women, E, 551, 14 ; Merc. Militaris, E, 551, 13.   In the latter is given a conversation in which Cromwell takes part, but it would be rash to guarantee its authenticity.

[3] See p. 40.

Levellers had been granted—300 in Hewson's regiment alone—threw down their arms. They were promptly cashiered and received each of them a small sum to carry them to their homes. That the disaffection was not general was shown by the alacrity with which volunteers from regiments not selected for Irish service came forward to fill their places.[1]

Some soldiers refuse to go and are cashiered.

Though the number of those who shared the political opinions of the Levellers was comparatively small, the discontent caused by the dismissal of those who refused to go to Ireland spread rapidly. To them, as to every other soldier in the army, large arrears were still due, and as nothing had been said to the cashiered men about the payment of these arrears, it was taken for granted that they would be forfeited. A feeling grew up akin to that which had bound together all classes of soldiers in opposition to Parliament in 1647. If the Independents followed the example of the Presbyterians in dealing with the rising danger, it would go hard with the new Commonwealth.

Question of arrears.

The prevailing discontent first came to a head in Whalley's regiment, which received orders on April 24 to march from its quarters in Bishopsgate Street to a rendezvous at Mile End Green. In one of the troops a dispute about pay ended in some thirty of the soldiers seizing their colours and refusing to leave their quarters. On the following morning the mutineers resisted all the arguments of their officers, and it was not till Fairfax and Cromwell appeared on the scene that they submitted. Fifteen of their number were carried to Whitehall, where a court-martial, sitting on the 26th, condemned six of them to death and five to be cashiered after riding the wooden horse. Cromwell, however, pleaded for mercy, and in the end all were pardoned with the exception of Robert Lockyer, who was believed to have been the ringleader.

April 24. Mutiny in Whalley's regiment.

April 25. The mutiny suppressed.

April 26. Sentence of a court-martial. Lockyer to die.

[1] *A Modest Narrative*, E, 547, 9; *The Perf. Weekly Account*, E, 552, 2; *A Paper Scattered about the Streets*, E, 551, 21.

Lockyer, though young in years, had fought gallantly through the whole of the war. He was a thoughtful, religious man, beloved by his comrades, who craved for the immediate establishment of liberty and democratic order. As such, he had stood up for the *Agreement of the People* on Corkbush Field, and he now entertained against his commanding officers a prejudice arising from other sources than the mere dispute about pay, which influenced natures less noble than his own. Unfortunately his friends, in petitioning for his release, rested their case on the ground that all sentences given by a court-martial were made illegal by the Petition of Right and the law of the land. Such a doctrine would have dissolved the army into chaos, and when Lilburne and Overton wrote to Fairfax, threatening him with the fate of Joab and Strafford, all chance of pardon was at an end. On the 27th, Lockyer, firmly believing himself to be a martyr to the cause of right and justice, was led up Ludgate Hill to the open space in front of St. Paul's, and there, after expostulating with the firing party for their obedience to their officers in a deed of murder, he was shot to death.[1]

April 27.
The execution.

Thousands of Londoners were found to sympathise with anyone who placed himself in opposition to the military authorities. On the 29th, Lockyer's funeral was made the occasion of a remarkable demonstration of civilian sentiment. Some thousands of men walked in procession, wearing, mixed with the customary black of mourning, the sea-green ribbons which had been first seen in London at Rainsborough's funeral,[2] and had since been adopted as the distinguishing mark of the Levellers, whose principles in the main coincided with those of the murdered Rainsborough. Lockyer's horse was led before his coffin, an honour usually reserved for officers of high rank. On the coffin itself were sprigs of rosemary dipped in blood, in the midst of which lay the dead man's sword. In the whole long

April 29.
Lockyer's funeral.

---

[1] Opposite views of this affair are to be found in *The Army's Martyr*, 2nd edit., E, 554, 6, and *A True Narrative*, E, 552, 18.

[2] Perhaps the colour was considered appropriate to a sailor.

procession there was nothing to provoke opposition. Orderly and silently, save for the sound of trumpets announcing a soldier's funeral, the long column tramped through the streets, a body of women closing up the rear. At last the Army's Martyr, as his admirers styled him, was laid in a grave at Westminster.[1]

The thousands of law-abiding citizens who took part in the procession were assuredly not moved by any sympathy with mutineers. Their protest was against military inter-

Motives of those who took part in it.

ference with political affairs. "England," Lilburne had said when he was brought before the Council of State, "is a nation governed, bounded, and limited by laws and liberties." Lockyer was held to be a martyr, because it was suspected that those who had condemned him to death were of a contrary opinion. The tragedy of the situation lay in this, that those who attempted the suppression of the Levellers were as desirous as Lilburne could possibly be that England should be 'governed, bounded, and limited by laws and liberties.' It was not, however, in human nature that the men who had the sword in their hands should throw away the results of their toil, in the hope that at some future day laws and liberties might again revive under softer influences than could proceed from the armed ranks of soldiers.

As long as possibility of speech or writing remained Lilburne would be a thorn in the sides of the men whom he regarded as the worst of usurpers. On May 1 he

May 1. Lilburne's new Agreement of the People.

issued yet another version of the *Agreement of the People*, in which he showed himself as distrustful of the existing Parliament as he had hitherto been of the executive government. The new representative body, he held, was to be annually elected by manhood suffrage; servants, persons in receipt of alms, and those who had fought on the King's side being alone excluded from voting. No one in receipt of public money nor any treasurer, receiver, or practising

[1] *Merc. Pragm.* E, 552, 15; *The Moderate*, E, 552, 20; *The Kingdom's Weekly Intelligencer*, E, 552, 21. *The Moderate* was the Levellers' organ.

lawyer might be elected. Members of any one Parliament were to be incapable of sitting in the next, which was to take the place of its predecessor with but one night's intermission. Each Parliament was to name a Committee of its members to carry on business in times of adjournment, and to bind it by suitable instructions. Not only was there to be complete religious liberty, but each parish was to choose its minister, on the understanding that he was to be maintained by voluntary offerings alone.[1]

On May 2 fresh bodies of petitioners urged Parliament to liberate the four prisoners and to provide for the speedy

May 2. Another Lilburnian petition.

election of its successor.[2] Far more serious was the news that Scrope's regiment, which had advanced as far as Salisbury on its way to Ireland, had refused to

May 1. Declaration of Scrope's regiment.

leave England till the liberties of the country were secured. With the exception of two troops, Ireton's regiment concurred with that of Scrope, and the greater part of Reynolds's regiment quartered round Bristol was of the same opinion. A similar declaration was apprehended from those of Harrison and Skippon.[3]

Another centre of resistance was formed at Banbury, where, on May 6, a body of local forces rallied to a manifesto issued

May 6. England's Standard Advanced.

under the title of *England's Standard Advanced.* Its author was a certain William Thompson, who had formerly been a corporal, but who had been cashiered for taking part in a tavern broil. Having insisted on following the regiment from which he had been dismissed, he was condemned to death by a court-martial for provoking to

---

[1] *The Agreement of the Free People of England*, E, 552, 23.

[2] *C.J.* vi. 199.

[3] *The Moderate Intelligencer*, E, 555, 3 ; *England's Standard Advanced*, E, 553, 2. There is a second and enlarged edition, published on May 12, E, 555, 7. The title-page is missing in the Museum copy, but Mr. Firth tells me that his copy has, in bold black type, ' For a New Parliament by the Agreement of the People,' and that if the tract were doubled up and stuck in the hat, as the Agreement was at the rendezvous on Corkbush Field (*Great Civil War*, iv. 25), these words would show out well.

mutiny, though he had finally been pardoned by Fairfax.[1]   A kind of military Lilburne, he inveighed loudly against the tyranny of courts-martial, and called for the execution of the new Lilburnian *Agreement of the People.*

The Banbury rising was not of long duration.   Before the day was over Colonel Reynolds, at the head of three troops which

Thompson's rising suppressed.

had remained faithful out of his mutinous regiment, fell upon the mutineers.   Thompson resisted to the uttermost, killing with his own hand a lieutenant who pressed him hard.   The bulk of his followers, however, had little mind to fight against their old comrades, and finding himself about to be deserted, he took to flight, whilst about twenty of his men rode off to join Scrope's regiment at Salisbury.[2]

For some days Parliament had been striving to find means to satisfy the material demands of the soldiers.   On April 30

April 30. Deans and Chapters abolished.

an Act was passed for the abolition of Deans and Chapters, as the first step towards the appropriation of their estates.[3]   Landed property, however, could not speedily be converted into money, and as the London citizens persisted in refusing a loan they were ordered, on

May 8. Demands on the City.

May 8, to pay immediately 27,400*l.* due for the arrears of former assessments.[4]   By this time the case was urgent, as news had arrived that the dis-

News from Salisbury.

content of the regiment at Salisbury was about to pass into actual mutiny.[5]   Prompt measures were

The Tower occupied.

taken to avert the danger.   Four hundred soldiers who could be trusted were sent to occupy the Tower,[6]

May 9-12. Restrictions on the liberty of Lilburne and his companions.

and on the 9th Parliament ordered that no one should have access to Lilburne and his three companions except their wives, children, and servants.   Three days later even this relaxation of their close imprison-

---

[1] *England's Freedom, Soldiers' Rights,* E, 419, 23 ; *A Vindication of L. G. Cromwell,* E, 431, 7 ; *A True and Impartial Relation,* E, 432, 23 ; *The Prisoners' Mournful Cry,* E, 441, 17.

[2] *The Impartial Intelligencer,* E, 530, 8.   [3] *C.J.* vi. 198.

[4] *Ib.* vi. 204.   [5] *The Moderate Intelligencer,* E, 555, 3.

[6] *Merc. Elencticus,* E, 556, 9.

ment was forbidden,[1] doubtless in order to make it impossible for them to send fresh manifestoes to the press. On the 9th, too, an Act was brought in for charging the soldiers' arrears on the estates of the late King and his family.[2] For the present at least nothing could be done to satisfy the more ideal aims of the soldiers. On May 4, indeed, the House had ordered that a debate on due elections and equal representation should be opened on the morrow ; but when the morrow came the debate was postponed to the 9th, on which day the House might fairly plead that it was justified in deferring the consideration of such far-reaching changes to a season of greater tranquillity.[3]

May 4. Order for a debate on elections.

May 9. Debate postponed.

It was for Fairfax and Cromwell to hasten the arrival of such a season. On the 9th they reviewed their own two regiments of horse in Hyde Park. Cromwell addressed the men, telling them that any who wished to leave the army were at liberty to do so with the assurance of ultimate payment of all that was due to them. He begged them not to be unmindful of the labours of the House or of its care for the provision of an adequate navy for the defence of the country. He further announced that it was resolved to find a way of paying the soldiers' arrears, and that Parliament intended to bring its sittings to a close, and to provide as soon as possible for the election of a more representative successor. Cromwell, in short asked the soldiers to trust Parliament to do all that could reasonably be required of it, and not to give the victory to the common enemy because a new constitution could not be brought into existence at a moment of imminent peril.[4] Language so eminently sensible could not fail of its effect with the men whom he had so often

May 9. A review in Hyde Park.

Cromwell's address.

---

[1] *C.J.* vi. 205, 208. *A Discourse between Lilburne and Hugh Peters* (E, 556, 26), in which Peters is made to give his opinion that there is no law in England but the sword, is manifestly, in the face of this order, a pure invention, and is declared to be such in *Merc. Pacificus*, E, 557, 7.

[2] *C.J.* vi. 205.   [3] *Ib.* vi. 201, 202.

[4] Heads of Cromwell's speech are given in *A Perfect Summary*, E, 530, 3.

FAIRFAX'S PURSUIT OF THE MUTINEERS.

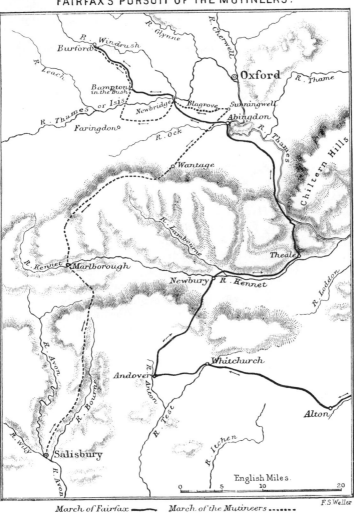

March of Fairfax ————   March of the Mutineers ·······

F.S.Weller

E 2

led to victory. By his orders the sea-green ribbons which a few of them had placed in their hats were plucked out by force, and the two regiments professed themselves ready to obey all orders given by their officers.

With these two regiments of horse and three others of foot, making together upwards of 4,000 men, Fairfax and Cromwell

March of
Fairfax and
Cromwell. set out for Salisbury, quartering at Alton on the night of the 11th. On the following morning Colonel Scrope, followed by about eighty other officers, made his appearance, bringing news that his own regiment

May 12.
They hear
of the open
mutiny of
Scrope's
regiment. had absolutely refused obedience, and had been joined by four of Ireton's troops, the whole of the mutineers being about 600 men. By the advice of a Council of War, Fairfax ordered the issue of an appeal to the mutineers, which embodied the arguments used by Cromwell in Hyde Park, and which, to judge by its style, was composed by Cromwell himself.[1]

On the 12th Fairfax reached Andover. On the morning of the 13th he learned that the mutineers had removed to Marl-

They reach
Andover.
May 13.
The muti-
neers at
Marl-
borough. borough, and inferred that their object was to make their way in the direction of Buckinghamshire, where Harrison's regiment was quartered. Policy as well as good feeling led him to desire to win back the soldiers without bloodshed, and he took the op-portunity of a letter addressed to him by their Agitators to send

Fairfax
opens com-
munications
with them. Major White and three other officers to open com-munications with them. " Let them know," cried Cromwell to White as he rode off, " that though we have sent messengers to them we will not follow with force at their heels." [2]

Before White could come up with the mutineers they had

They
march to
Sunning-
well. pushed on to Wantage, whence wheeling to the right they made their way to Sunningwell, between Oxford and Abingdon.[3] Here, as Fairfax had supposed,

---

[1] *A Declaration from his Excellency*, E, 555, 6.

[2] White's *True Relation*, E, 574, 26.

[3] Bridger's narrative in *A Perfect Summary*, E, 530, 12. Fairfax, in

they hoped to have been met by Harrison's whole regiment. Only two troops, however, reached the rendezvous, the rest having perhaps been deterred by Fairfax's rapid march to Theale, from which place an easy road led to the valley of the Thames. Before the morning of the 14th was far spent Fairfax knew that any further danger of the mutineers, who now numbered about 1,200 men, combining with Harrison's regiment was at an end, as they had drawn back through Berkshire with the intention of rallying to their cause other regiments further west. To effect this object they marched to Newbridge, in the hope of crossing the Thames, but, finding Reynolds posted too strongly on it to be attacked with any chance of success, they made their way westwards on the southern side of the river till, in despair of finding another bridge, they swam across not far from Faringdon. They then made their way to Burford, where they imagined themselves safe for the night.[1]

Fairfax at Theale.

May 14. Movements of the mutineers.

Fairfax had started early in pursuit, and, after a splendid march, in which some of his cavalry covered forty-five miles, he drew near to Burford at midnight. By his orders Cromwell at once attacked the mutineers. Roused from their sleep, and unprepared for a surprise, they made but short resistance. After a few shots nearly four hundred of them surrendered at discretion. The remainder were either quartered in the surrounding villages or escaped under cover of the night.[2]

Fairfax in pursuit.

The attack on Burford.

On the following morning a court-martial was held, and two cornets, Denn and Thompson, a brother of the more notorious William Thompson, were, together with two corporals, con-

his letter to the Speaker, in *A Full Narrative*, says they slept at Blagrove. There is a Blagrove Farm about a mile west of Sunningwell, which must be the place intended.

[1] [The map probably represents the crossing as taking place too far to the West. According to Fairfax's letter in *A Full Narrative* the mutineers crossed by a ford about a mile beyond Newbridge. See also a review in *The Guardian* for Jan. 2, 1895.]

[2] *A Full Narrative*, E, 555, 27 ; *A Declaration of the Proceedings of the Lord Gen. Fairfax*, E, 556, 1 ; White's *True Relation*, E, 574, 6.

demned to die, the remaining prisoners being posted on
the leads of the church to witness the execution. Denn's
penitence obtained his pardon at the last moment.
The other three were shot in the churchyard;
Thompson with some appearance of regret, the two
corporals, Church and Perkins, defiant to the last.
Then Cromwell went into the church and, summoning the prisoners before him, told them that though they had deserved deci-
mation, the general had mercifully pardoned them all. For the
time they were exiled to Devizes, but were ultimately
re-embodied in the ranks. Colonel Eyre, who had
given trouble at Corkbush Field,[1] being no longer a
member of the army, was sent to Oxford to receive a civil trial.

William Thompson, who was still at large, having gathered
round him two troops of horse, had broken into Northampton
and carried off money and arms. Reynolds, sent in
pursuit, came up with him in a wood near Welling-
borough. Thompson would take no quarter, and
after killing two of his adversaries was shot dead by a corporal.[2]

With Thompson's death, on the 17th, the rising of the
Levellers was brought to an end. On the same day Fairfax,
attended by his principal officers, visited the new
Oxford which was growing up upon the ruins of that
old one which had received its mould from Laud.
On the 19th the now Puritan University gave to the
successful soldiers the highest honours it could
bestow. Fairfax and Cromwell donned the scarlet
gowns of Doctors of Civil Law, whilst Harrison, Hewson,
Okey, and other martial figures were decked in the soberer
costume which designates a Master of Arts.[3] The new
authorities were in the right in what they did. The maintenance of that religion which they loved depended on the strong
arms and buoyant hearts of those who had shown themselves
capable of enforcing discipline.

May 15.
A court-
martial.

Three of the
mutineers
executed.

The re-
mainder sent
to Devizes.

May 17.
Fate of
William
Thompson.

Fairfax and
Cromwell at
Oxford.

May 19.
The Fair-
faxian
Creation.

---

[1] See *Great Civil War*, iv. 22.

[2] *Perf. Diurnal*, E, 530, 14 ; *The Moderate*, E, 556, 3.

[3] Wood's *Annals of the University*, 619.

CHAPTER III

THE COMMONWEALTH ON ITS DEFENCE

STEP by step the Government of the Commonwealth was compelled to accommodate itself to its true position, and to rule by *April-Sept.* means which every one of its members would have *Three peers in the House.* condemned if they had been employed by Charles or Strafford. No additional reputation was gained by the fact that three discredited peers, Pembroke, Howard of Escrick, and Salisbury, were elected to serve as members of what had once been the House of Commons.[1] The failure of Parliament to conciliate public opinion necessitated the pass-*May 14.* ing of a new Treason Act, which became law on *A new Treason Act.* May 14. It transferred to Parliament the safeguards with which the monarchy had been surrounded, but it also—for the first time since the reign of Henry VIII.—created a fresh treason outside the limitations of the great Statute of Edward III. The part played in political affairs by the army was indirectly acknowledged by a clause making it treasonable for civilians to stir up mutiny in the ranks.[2]

Still more significant was the imposition of fresh restrictions on the press. In the first days of the Commonwealth Parlia-*Feb. 9.* ment had contented itself with prohibiting all un-*Prohibition of unautho-rised re-ports.* authorised reports of the proceedings in the second High Court of Justice.[3] On March 16 an order,

---

[1] Pembroke took his seat in April, Howard in May, and Salisbury in September.

[2] *Acts*, E, 1,060, No. 62. Soldiers stirring up mutiny could be dealt with by martial law. [3] *Acts*, E, 1,060, No. 5.

which proved entirely futile, was given for the seizure of all

March 16.
*Eikon
Basiliké* to
be seized.

copies of the *Eikon Basiliké*.[1] On the 19th even strenuous assertors of liberty of conscience took alarm at the news that a translation of the Koran was

March 19.
Proceedings
against the
printers of
the Koran.

in the press ; but after further discussion the proceedings taken against the printers were dropped, and on May 7 the book appeared, without causing a change in the religious views of a single Englishman.[2]

On May 7 the armed resistance of the Levellers and the concentrated attack of a host of scurrilous calumniators drove

May 7.
Complaint
against
Mabbott.

a Council of State, in which Vane and Cromwell sat, to report to the House that Mabbott, the licenser, had allowed the publication of 'divers dangerous books,' and to recommend his dismissal, as well as the preparation of measures for the suppression of seditious writings, especially of *The Moderate*, the decided though cautious organ of the Levellers.[3] Mabbott's offence, it appears, was the licensing of Lilburne's new *Agreement of the People*.[4]

Mabbott on
the liberty
of the press.

Being called to account, Mabbott expressed his concurrence in the request for his own dismissal. It was lawful, he thought, 'to print any book, sheet, &c., without licensing, so as the authors and printers do subscribe their true name thereunto, that so they may be liable to answer the contents thereof, and, if they offend therein, then to be punished by such laws as are or shall be for those cases provided.'[5] Accordingly, on May 22, Mabbott having been dismissed, the House requested the Council of State to prepare

May 22.
Mabbott
dismissed.

'an Act for preventing the printing of scandalous books and pamphlets.'[6] Though the Council of State had already directed Bradshaw to prepare such an Act,[7] some time was allowed to pass till these orders were complied with, and it is just possible that the delay was caused by a

---

[1] *C.J.* vi. 166.   [2] *Ib.* vi. 168 ; *The Alcoran of Mahomet*, E, 553, 3.

[3] C. of St. Order Book, *Interr.* I, 62, p. 267.

[4] *Ib.* 62, p. 264.   [5] *Perf. Diurnal*, E, 530, 21.

[6] *C.J.* vi. 214.   [7] C. of St. Order Book, *Interr.* I, 62, p. 294.

lingering hope that, after the collapse of the Levellers, no legislation of the kind would be needed.

To do them justice, the men now in power took no pleasure in repressive legislation. They kept before their eyes at least the ideal of a popular legislature. On May 15 the House appointed a Committee to report, in the first place, on 'the succession of future Parliaments and the regulating of their elections'; and, in the second place, on the time for 'putting a period to the sitting of this Parliament'[1]—Vane being one of two members specially directed to keep the matter in view. Though it was hardly likely that the report of this Committee would be speedily forthcoming, it was at least possible to notify the good intentions of Parliament, and on the 19th an Act was passed declaring England to be a Free Commonwealth, and therefore to be governed by 'the representatives of the people in Parliament . . . without any King or House of Lords.'[2] A further outward sign of increasing self-confidence was the transference, on May 28, of the Council of State from Derby House to Whitehall.[3]

May 15.
A committee to
report on
elections.

May 19.
England to
be a Free
Common-
wealth.

May 28.
The
Council of
State at
Whitehall.

It was hard, however, to obtain more than the outward show of submission, and even this was with difficulty to be obtained in the City. Though Andrews, who had sat in the High Court of Justice and had consented to the sentence of the King, occupied the civic chair, he had not hitherto ventured to publish the proclamation of the abolition of the monarchy. At last, on May 30, the Lord Mayor, accompanied by fourteen aldermen, summoned up courage to read the proclamation in the Exchange. Some at least of the bystanders interrupted the proceedings with their exclamations, and one of them, a merchant, was led away in custody.[4]

May 30.
The aboli-
tion of
kingship
proclaimed
in the City.

On the following day a deputation of aldermen invited the

---

[1] *C.J.* vi. 210.   [2] *Scobell*, ii. 30.

[3] *Merc. Pacificus*, E, 557, 7.

[4] *A Moderate Intelligence*, E, 557, 6; *C.J.* vi. 221.

House to a banquet to be given in the City on June 7, the
date fixed for a thanksgiving for the suppression of
the Levellers. The invitation was cheerfully accepted,
and at the same time two aldermen, Soames and
Chambers, who had absented themselves at the time of the
proclamation, were ordered to account for their absence. On
June 1 both of them were deprived of their dignities
and disqualified from future office. Soames, being
a member of the House, was also disabled from sitting in the existing Parliament.[1] Chambers, who had been the
first citizen to resist the illegal taxation of Charles, was amongst
the first to refuse compliance with the orders of the Commonwealth. No less than seven aldermanships were
now vacant ; but there was considerable delay in
filling their places, as it was hard to find men
qualified for the post who would serve under the conditions
imposed. In other directions, however, the Commonwealth
gathered strength. The success of Fairfax and Cromwell had,
at least, impressed the lawyers with a sense of its stability, and
it was at last found possible to complete the Bench of
Judges by filling the six vacancies created by the
resignations of those who had refused to acknowledge the new
order of things four months before.[2]

May 31
The House
to dine in
the City.

June 1.
Two aldermen deprived.

Aldermanships left vacant.

Six judges appointed.

On the 6th preparations were made for the banquet which
was to celebrate the union of the purged Parliament and the
purged City. It was arranged that the Speaker,
as representing the House of Parliament, should be
received with royal honours, the Lord Mayor
temporarily surrendering to him his official sword.[3] Some one
even proposed that the Speaker should confer knighthood on
the Lord Mayor and two other aldermen ; but the suggestion
was not adopted by Parliament.[4]

June 6.
Preparations for the City banquet.

As the guests drove into the City on the 7th to attend the
sermons which were to precede the banquet, signs of their
unpopularity were not wanting. Though the streets were lined

---

[1] *C.J.* vi. 222. [2] *Ib.* vi. 222.
[3] C. of St. Order Book, *Interr.* I, 62. [4] *S.P. Dom.* xi. 3

with soldiers, uncomplimentary remarks were freely uttered, and some Royalist or Leveller contrived to take out the linch-

June 7. Arrival of the guests. pin of Cromwell's coach, thereby effecting a block in the line when the wheel came off. In few of the City churches was the Day of Thanksgiving observed at all, and where the churches were open prayers for King Charles were in many cases offered. At the banquet itself there was gaiety enough, and if political parties could be strengthened by mutual compliments amongst its members, the position of the Commonwealth would have been assured.

June 8. Presents to Fairfax and Cromwell, and to the poor. On the next day the official representatives of the City presented Fairfax with a basin and ewer of gold, and Cromwell with plate valued at 300*l.* as well as 200 pieces in gold. The food left from the feast was distributed amongst the poor, together with 400*l.*[1]

The dissatisfaction of Londoners, even if they were neither Royalists nor Levellers, with an ever-present soldiery is easily accounted for. Increasing numbers of citizens were in the habit of seeking recreation on Sundays on the river and frequenting the villages on its banks. To stop the practice,

June 4. A fatal shot. soldiers were posted by the side of the stream, and on June 4, one of them, firing at a waterman who refused to stop rowing at his summons, missed his aim, but wounded a child in a boat beyond it.[2]

Amidst general discontent there could be no thought of an immediate dissolution. According to a not unfriendly writer,

The dissolution of Parliament postponed. the opinion prevailed at Westminster, 'that this Parliament shall not suffer a dissolution till the people love them, and that not till the delivery from taxes, which may probably within a few months be effected, and then they shall be beloved, elected, and what not.'[3]

He must have been indeed sanguine who expected a speedy reduction of taxation in the face of internal discontent and

---

[1] *The Moderate*, E, 559, 12 ; *The Perf. Weekly Account*, E, 559, 13 ; *Whitelocke*, 406.

[2] *The Kingdom's Weekly Intelligencer*, E, 558, 12.

[3] *A Modest Narrative*, E, 537, 13.

external danger.   The information forwarded from Holland

March 21.
Arrest of
Lady Car-
lisle.

was not reassuring, and on March 21, in order to obtain fuller information of the designs of the English Royalists, the Government ordered the arrest of Lady Carlisle, who was known to have had in her hands the threads of the combination of the preceding year.[1]   In April

April.
Attempt to
frighten her.

an attempt, probably successful, was made to frighten her into a disclosure of her secrets.   " The Countess of Carlisle," wrote a Royalist intelligencer, " hath been again shown the rack, but she desires them not to hurt her, for she is a woman and cannot endure pain, but she will confess whatsoever they will have her." [2]

Whatever may have been the secrets thus disclosed, it is unlikely that the Government of the Commonwealth depended

March.
Plans of the
Court at the
Hague.

Hyde's
opinion.

solely upon the Countess for information of the plans of the exiled Court at the Hague.   At that Court the project of striking England through Ireland was gaining ground.   Even Hyde, in whose eyes to seek help from the Presbyterian Scots was the lowest degradation, had nothing to say against the proposed intervention of Ormond's army.   His feeling on this score was, at least for the time being, shared by Charles, and on March 19 a

March 19.
The States
General
asked to
assist
Charles.

paper presented to the States General in the name of the young King asked for an advance of money for the expenses of a voyage to Ireland.   In this paper the conditions imposed at Edinburgh on the King's admission to the crown of his fathers, as well as the exclusion of five-sixths of the Scottish nobility from Parliament by the Act of Classes, were strongly denounced.[3]   On the

March 27.
A specific
sum
demanded.

27th the sum of 20,000*l.* was specified as needed for the proposed expedition.[4]   The States General, however, showed so little inclination to comply with

---

[1] C. of St. Order Book, *Interr.* I, 62, 100.

[2] Letter of Intelligence, $\frac{\text{April 25}}{\text{May 5}}$, Carte's *Orig. Letters*, i. 286.

[3] Representation to the States General, March $\frac{19}{29}$, *ib.* i. 260.

[4] Advices from the Hague, $\frac{\text{March 27}}{\text{April 5}}$, *Carte MSS.* xxiv. fol. 378.

Charles's request that he thought it well to send begging-letters
Begging-
letters. to such of his adherents as still retained property in
England.[1]

Crying as was Charles's need of money, his need of a
settled policy was still more urgent. Though the choice between Ormond and the Scots was in reality a choice between
the Episcopal and the Presbyterian parties in England, it was
hard to persuade him of the impossibility of securing the
assistance of both. It is true that, early in March, Hyde had
Hyde's
proposed
Declaration. prepared a draft of a Royal Declaration which would
have left no doubt on the matter. As might have
been expected, this projected manifesto breathed
implacable enmity against the Commonwealth and the army,
exempting from pardon not only those who had consented to
the death of the King in the High Court of Justice, but those
by whose votes that Court had been erected. The special note
of the Declaration was, however, the offensive attitude of its
Its eccle-
siastical author to the English Presbyterian party in its ecclesiastical as well as in its political aspect. The Church
was to be settled in accordance with the demands of a National
Synod, that is to say, of the two Convocations in conjunction,
and though a few foreign divines were to be admitted, they were
not likely to effect anything in the presence of the serried ranks
of bishops and cathedral clergy, who took so large a part in the
Convocations.

Nor was Hyde's attack on the constitutional reforms of the
Presbyterian party less incisive. He boldly declared for going
and
political
proposals. back to the state of things which had existed before
the outbreak of the Civil War. The Constitution as it
stood at the beginning of the Long Parliament before
the formation of parties, when as yet no disputed question had
been thoroughly settled and no authority acknowledged to be
supreme, was Hyde's political ideal. Too much of a lawyer to
approve of absolute royal power, he was too little of a statesman
to recognise the necessity of subjecting the King's authority to

---

[1] Circular Letters, *Clarendon MSS.* ii. 29, 30.

parliamentary supremacy, and he could see nothing but the germ of rebellion in the constitutional scheme of the Presbyterians. He told them plainly, as Milton had told them in his *Tenure of Kings and Magistrates,* that the deeds of which they now complained were but the outcome of their own former misdeeds, and that 'by the same principles upon which an army was raised to rebel against the King, that army hath oppressed the power and authority that raised them, and have conquered those masters who raised and employed them to conquer others.' [1]

Hyde's declaration found little support in the shifty counsels of Charles's Court. It was assailed on many sides, but
especially on the ground that it was certain to give
The Declaration dropped.
offence to the Presbyterians. Lauderdale and Lanark, who, since his brother's execution, had become Duke of Hamilton, were the loudest in calling for its rejection ; and, in consequence of their outcries, the idea of issuing a declaration of any kind was silently dropped. It was probably in consequence of this rebuff that Hyde welcomed the opportunity
Hyde and Cottington to go to Spain.
of absenting himself from Court by accepting a mission, in conjunction with Cottington, to the Court of Spain, where he hoped to extract from Philip a loan to meet Charles's growing requirements.[2]

March 27.
The Scottish Commissioners apply to Charles.
Charles was now to listen to pleadings on the other side. The Scottish Commissioners arrived and had their first audience on March 27. They hoped, before their main negotiation commenced, to obtain from Charles an order dismissing Montrose from attendance on his person, and were much disappointed at his

[1] Draft of a Declaration, *Eng. Hist. Review,* for April, 1893.

[2] " I confess Sir E. H. is not troubled to be for some time absent from this company." Hyde was told of his appointment about March 24 ; Hyde to Hatton, $\frac{\text{March } 27}{\text{April } 6}$, *Nicholas Papers,* i. 124. We learn from a letter from Hyde to the Prince of Orange, dated Jan. $\frac{21}{31}$, 1650, that the Prince suggested this mission ; Wijnne, *Geschilling van de afdanking van 't Krijgsvolk,* 101. This can only have been in order to get rid of Hyde, as the Prince of Orange was no friend to Spain.

refusal to reply to a single request until their whole budget had been opened.[1]

Annoyed as they were, the Commissioners did not break off the negotiation. On April 5 they asked Charles, not merely to accept the two Covenants so far as Scotland was concerned, but to promise his assent to Acts of Parliament enjoining them on England and Ireland.

April 5.
The Scottish demands.

Charles could not fail to be aware that by so doing he would alienate his staunchest English supporters ; and though he did not at once break with the Scots, he took care to postpone his reply as long as possible, in the vain hope that the Commissioners might be inclined to modify their exorbitant demands.[2]

The pertinacity of the Commissioners was the more obnoxious to Charles as those who sent them had ostentatiously disregarded his personal feelings. On March 16 the Parliament at Edinburgh sentenced Huntly to death for the crime of taking up arms for his King ; and on the 22nd the sentence was carried into effect.[3]

March 16.
Sentence on Huntly.

March 22.
His execution.

Huntly's execution was no doubt intended as a warning to Charles that, if he wished to protect his supporters in Scotland, he must accede to the demands of the Commissioners. Such a warning must have appeared to be the more needed as, before the end of February, a party of Royalists seized Inverness, and, after no long delay, took the field under the command of Seaforth's brother, Thomas Mackenzie of Pluscardine. Middleton, who had escaped from England—it is said by a breach of parole—threw himself amongst them. The men were, however, undisciplined, and on May 8 a body of

Feb.
Inverness seized by Royalists.

May 8.
The rout of Balvenie.

---

[1] Committee of Estates to Charles ($\frac{\text{March 28}}{\text{April 7}}$, $\frac{\text{March 30}}{\text{April 9}}$), *Clar. St. P* ii. 474 ; iii. App. lxxxv ; Charles's answer, $\frac{\text{March 29, 31}}{\text{April 8, 10}}$, *Baillie*, iii. 513.

[2] Commissioners of the Kirk to Charles, April 5, *ib.* iii. 514 ; Commissioners of Parliament to Charles, April 10, *Clar. St. P.* ii. 475.

[3] *Acts of Parl. of Sc.* VI. part ii. 327 ; *Balfour*, iii. 393 ; Graymond to Brienne, March $\frac{20}{30}$, $\frac{\text{March 27}}{\text{April 6}}$, *Harl. MSS.* 4,551, fol. 322, 331.

1,200 was surprised and routed at Balvenie on the Spey by a small force of no more than 120 horse sent against them by Leslie.[1]

Whilst the Scottish Presbyterians were vainly urging Charles to constitute himself their champion in the three kingdoms, their English brethren were receiving overtures from Cromwell.   He was ready, he assured them, to consent to the establishment of the Presbyterian system—no doubt without coercive jurisdiction—and to the readmission to Parliament of the members excluded by Pride's Purge.[2]   The gulf between Cromwell and the Presbyterians was, however, too wide to be bridged over.

April.
Cromwell
makes
overtures
to the
English
Presby-
terians.

It was a more hopeful plan to aim at securing the neutrality of the States General.   Accordingly, on April 18, it was resolved to despatch a special envoy to the Hague, who should announce the intention of Parliament to send a brilliant embassy to cultivate a good understanding between the two republics.   The person selected for this mission was Dr. Dorislaus, a Dutchman by birth, though he had been for some years in the service of the English Parliament as a lawyer.   It seems not to have occurred to those who sent him that, as he had taken part in the prosecution of the King, his name was in bad odour with the English and Scottish refugees who swarmed in the streets of the Hague.[3]

Mission of Dorislaus.

On April 29 Dorislaus reached the Hague.   Among the Scottish followers of Montrose the feeling against the regicides was especially bitter, and it was amongst these that a scheme was laid to murder the new envoy, or, as they probably said, to execute justice upon him.[4]   The assassins, however, did not keep their own

April 29. He reaches the Hague.

A plot to murder him

---

[1] *Acts of Parl. of Sc.* VI. part ii. 216, 222 ; Graymond's despatches, April to May, *Harl. MSS.* 4,551, ff. 331–369.   *Balfour*, iii. 401, 407.

[2] Walker's *Hist. of Independency*, ii. 157.

[3] C. of St. Order Book, *Interr.* I, 62, p. 204.

[4] The connection of the murderers with Montrose's following was rumoured at the time, and that the rumour was correct is shown by the

counsel; and Strickland, the accredited English ambassador, having heard rumours of their designs, communicated his suspicions to Dorislaus. When, therefore, on the following day, a message was brought to the new envoy, ostensibly from Strickland, inviting a visit, he refused to leave his inn. The assassins, however, were not to be thus baffled. On the evening of May 2, just as Dorislaus was sitting down to supper, six men, leaving one of their companions to guard the street door, burst into his room, and whilst some of them secured his servants, one, whose name was Whitford,[1] after slashing him over the head, passed a sword through his body. The whole party, leaving their victim dead upon the ground, made their escape. The States General, indeed, professed innocence, and denounced the perpetrators of the deed; but Whitford succeeded in crossing the frontier into the Spanish Netherlands, where he was in perfect safety. In England a public funeral was accorded to the murdered servant of the Commonwealth, a pension granted to his son, and gifts of money to his daughters. All Royalists received the news of the murder with unbounded satisfaction. Even the staid and kindly Nicholas wrote of the assassination as 'the deserved execution of that bloody villain.'[2]

May 2. His assassination.

A public funeral voted.

To the exiles at the Hague the Scottish Commissioners were almost as hateful as Dorislaus himself. On May 1 they pressed Charles for a final answer to their demands presented more than a month before.[3]

May 1. The Scots ask for an answer.

fact that two of them, Whitford and Spottiswoode, and probably others, accompanied Montrose to Scotland in 1650. *A Perf. Diurnal*, E, 777, 12, 14.

[1] A son of Dr. Walter Whitford, the Bishop of Brechin. Wood's *Ath. Oxon.* iii. 667.

[2] Strickland to the C. of St. May $\frac{3}{13}$, Cary's *Mem. of the Civil War*, ii. 131; Nicholas to Ormond, $\frac{May\ 28}{June\ 7}$, *Carte MSS.* xxv. fol. 10; *C.J.* vi. 209; Andrée to Count William Frederick, May $\frac{2}{12}$, Groen van Prinsterer, *Archives de la Maison d'Orange Nassau*, Série 2, iv. 309.

[3] The Commissioners to Charles, May $\frac{1}{11}$, *Clar. St. P.* iii. App. lxxxvi. See *Clarendon MSS.* No. 60.

Charles applied for advice to the Scottish lords in attendance on the Court. Hamilton excused himself on the plea of ignorance of the existing state of affairs in Scotland. Montrose replied that, though Charles might, with considerable reservations, accept the Scottish National Covenant, he must imperatively reject the Solemn League and Covenant. To do otherwise would be to alienate all his faithful subjects in the three kingdoms. As to the proposed adoption of the Presbyterian worship in his own household, it did not become those who had rebelled against the father, because 'they but imagined he intended to meddle with them in that kind,' to interfere with the religion of the son. It was well, Montrose ironically added, for commissioners sent by the very men who had sold the late King to his enemies, and who were now engaged in murdering the best subjects of the present one, to offer 'to continue the same faithfulness unto his Majesty as they had formerly shown to his royal father.' Lauderdale with more worldly wisdom recommended Charles to grant all that was asked so far as Scotland alone was concerned, and to use the Scottish form of worship whenever he was in that country or with a Scottish army.[1]

Opinions of Hamilton, Montrose, and Lauderdale.

On May 11 these opinions were submitted to the Council. The result was that on the 19th Charles delivered to the Commissioners a reply in which he declared himself ready to accept the Scottish Acts relating to the National Covenant and the Presbyterian doctrine and discipline. He could do nothing regarding England or Ireland without the consent of the Parliaments of those kingdoms. As for the Solemn League and Covenant, he would adopt anything in it which was for the good of Scotland without prejudice to England or Ireland. Moreover, he would do nothing to disturb the peace lately concluded in Ireland.[2] Holding this answer to be equivalent to a rejection of their demands the Commissioners returned to Scotland.

May 11. The Council consulted.

May 19. Charles's answer.

---

[1] Napier's *Memoirs of Montrose*, ii. 700; *Clarendon MSS.* 68, i.

[2] The King's answer, May $\frac{19}{29}$, *Clar. St. P.* iii. xciii.; The King's final answer, *Clarendon MSS.* 62.

On May 27 they landed at Leith to give an account of their failure.[1]

Charles had thus adopted the policy of suiting the ecclesiastical institutions of the three kingdoms to the wishes of their respective populations. Scotland was not to coerce England, or England to coerce Ireland. It is unnecessary to discuss the merits of an idea which was only entertained as a weapon of political warfare. Charles not unnaturally thought more of recovering his throne than of laying the foundations of a constitutional settlement. For the present he was shrewd enough to discover that it was hopeless to regain England on Argyle's terms, and he was meanwhile doing his best to encourage the enterprise on which Montrose had set his heart.

Policy adopted by Charles.

He encourages Montrose.

Montrose with his usual idealism was planning a scheme for the invasion of Scotland by aid of the Continental sovereigns, who, as he fondly hoped, would, in mere defence of their own crowns, support him to the utmost against a regicide republic. Unfortunately for him, the dominant feature of European politics was the rivalry between France and Spain, and neither France nor Spain was likely to assist an exile who had nothing to offer in return, whilst other Powers, having recently freed themselves from a desolating war, would shrink from rekindling its flames for the benefit of a young prince in whose success they had little or no interest.

Montrose's hopes.

Montrose's first application was to some extent successful. On March 31 he obtained from the Danish Chancellor Ulfeldt, who was at the time in Holland, eleven diamond rings valued at 5,000 rixdollars, about 1,125$l.$ in English money. His further request for permission to sail from Stavanger in Norway with an expedition directed against Argyle's Government was referred to Copenhagen.[2] As the negotiation with Scotland showed itself to be more and

March 31. His negotiations with Ulfeldt.

---

[1] *The Moderate Intelligencer*, E, 558, 10.

[2] Acquittance by Montrose, $\frac{\text{March 31}}{\text{April 10}}$; Montrose to Ulfeldt, April $\frac{1}{11}$; *Clarendon MSS.* ii. Nos. 35, 89, i., where these papers are incorrectly dated in the Calendar.

more hopeless, Charles turned decisively to Montrose. On

April 13.
Montrose
to negotiate,

April 13 he empowered him to treat with European kings and states, and on May 19, the day on which Charles gave his final answer to the Scottish Com-

May 19.
and is named
Admiral of
Scotland.

missioners, Montrose was named Admiral of Scotland.[1]

Charles, however, was in need of money for his own projected expedition to Ireland, and whilst he relegated Montrose to the German and Scandinavian States, it was to the western Governments that he looked for personal assistance.

Charles
needs
money for
himself.

Disappointment tracked him at every turn. In vain the Prince of Orange urged the States General to assist him with a loan, and the exiled Prince had

A Dutch
loan refused.

to content himself with the profits, such as they were, of the prizes made by Rupert's fleet at Kinsale.[2] From France, distracted by internal commotions, nothing was

May 27.
Cottington
and Hyde
set out for
Madrid.

to be hoped, but, on May 27,[3] Cottington and Hyde were finally despatched to Madrid with instructions to promise, in consideration of pecuniary assistance, to relax the execution of the penal laws against the

English Catholics in the event of a restoration. If this offer— raised, if necessary, to a promise absolutely to repeal the laws— proved insufficient, the goods of English merchants trading in Spain were to be offered as security for a loan.[4] On their way through Brussels the ambassadors were to apply to the Archduke Leopold, the Spanish Governor of the Low Countries, and to urge the Duke of Lorraine, whose army had been thrown out of employment by the Peace of Westphalia, to give to Charles the assistance which he had at one time promised

June 22.
Charles at
Brussels.

to his father. Charles himself followed fast on the heels of his ambassadors. On June 22 he arrived at Brussels to press his claims.

Both in Spain and at Brussels these claims were scouted as

---

[1] Commissions, April $\frac{13}{23}$, May $\frac{19}{29}$, *Hist. MSS. Com. Rep.* ii. 173.

[2] Edgeman to Nicholas, May $\frac{15}{25}$, *Nicholas Papers*, i. 125.

[3] Edgeman's Diary, *Clarendon MSS.*

[4] Instructions to Cottington and Hyde, May 24 (?), *Clar. St. P.* ii. 481.

ridiculous. The Spanish Government, indeed, had hitherto

Charles and Spain. refused to recognise the Commonwealth, as its chances of survival appeared precarious, but it had no wish to give assistance which it could ill afford to a Prince whose chances of restoration were equally precarious. Philip had written hurriedly to the Archduke to stop the mission of the ambassadors, and the Archduke and his ministers let Charles plainly know that a Spanish king at war with France could do nothing for one who was about to transfer himself to French soil, and whose mother, to say nothing of Jermyn his mother's chief adviser, was notoriously under French influence.[1] After this rebuff Charles had no choice but to pursue his way across the frontier, to carry out his Irish adventure as best he might. The only encouragement which reached him was from the enthusiasm of Montrose. In word, at least, Charles showed his gratitude. On June 12, when he halted at Breda

June 12. Charles renews his commissions to Montrose. on his way to Brussels, he, somewhat superfluously, renewed all the commissions which he had already granted to him, and promised that he would never take a step in Scottish affairs without his advice.[2] On the 18th he pressed Ulfeldt to continue his assistance, a request to which Ulfeldt responded by an additional gift of 7,500 rix-dollars, equivalent to 1,687$l.$ 10$s.$, and of a considerable stock of arms and ammunition.[3] Montrose was thereby enabled to start on his mission, for which Charles, on June 26, after his own arrival at Brussels, gave him fresh authority. Meanwhile

Charles goes to St. Germains. Charles himself made his way to St. Germains, where he remained for some time awaiting news from Ireland.

As Charles's resolution to look for help from Montrose and Ireland rather than from Argyle and the Scots led him to seek aid at Brussels and Madrid, so also it led him to seek aid from

[1] Consulta of the Council of State, $\frac{\text{May 27}}{\text{June 8}}$; Cardenas to Peñaranda, June $\frac{10}{20}$; Peñaranda to Cardenas, $\frac{\text{June 23}}{\text{July 3}}$; Peñaranda to Navarro, $\frac{\text{June 25}}{\text{July 4}}$; Peñaranda to Philip IV. $\frac{\text{June 26}}{\text{July 6}}$; *Guizot*, App. 389, 393, 395–403.

[2] Charles to Montrose, June $\frac{12}{22}$, Napier's *Memoirs of Montrose*, ii. 706.

[3] *Clarendon MSS.* ii. No. 89, ii.–vi.

Pope Innocent X. On July 28 he sent Robert Meynell to Rome with general credentials addressed to all and singular to whom he had anything to communicate. This vague expression was interpreted in a letter from Cottington to Cardinal Capponi, in which it was plainly stated that if the Pope would give money to help Charles to recover his Crown, Charles would engage in return to show favour to his Catholic subjects.[1]

July 28.
Meynell to ask help from the Pope.

On turning his back on the Scots, Charles was at least angling for the support of a combination more homogeneous than that to which he had looked for aid a few weeks before, as Catholics and English churchmen had more in common than Catholics and Presbyterians. Yet even under these conditions the difficulties in the way of party co-operation were practicably insuperable, and nowhere were they more evidently insuperable than in Ireland. The differences which existed between Ormond and the Confederate Catholics were but thinly skinned over. Ormond was seeking to make use of his new allies in order to re-establish the monarchy in England, whilst the Confederate Catholics were seeking to make use of Ormond in order to establish the Roman Catholic religion and an independent Parliament in Ireland. Even if these hindrances to united action could be overcome, it was hard to see what strength of military comradeship could arise between the Catholic soldiers of the Confederation and the regiments—mainly composed of Protestants of English birth or descent—which followed Murrough of the Burnings,[2] and had, in his service, defiled the sanctuary of Cashel with the blood of slaughtered priests. Nor would it be easy to lure Owen O'Neill from his seclusion in the North to join hands even with his fellow Catholics who had been excommunicated by Rinuccini in consequence of their adhesion to the Supreme Council.

Want of cohesion amongst the Irish Royalists.

Ormond was, however, sanguine. Like Montrose, he

---

[1] Charles's letter of credence, $\frac{\text{July } 28}{\text{Aug. } 8}$; Cottington to Cardinal Capponi, $\frac{\text{July } 29}{\text{Aug. } 8}$, *Clar. St. P.* ii. 488.

[2] *Great Civil War*, iv. 106.

fancied that the horror of the late King's death would excite all men of good will in a desperate resistance to the regicides. So hopeful indeed was he that he attempted to win over the commander of the Parliamentary forces in Ireland.

Ormond sanguine.

A message received from Michael Jones's brother, the Protestant Bishop of Clogher, induced Ormond to believe that even the Parliamentary Governor of Dublin was ready to make common cause with him and the Confederate Catholics against his own employers.[1]   Accordingly, on March 9, he wrote to urge Jones to take the only course worthy of an honest man, 'now that the mask

March 9.
His overture
to Jones.

of hypocrisy by which the Independent army hath ensnared and enslaved all estates and degrees of men, is laid aside, now that . . . they have barbarously and inhumanly laid violent sacrilegious hands upon and murdered God's anointed and our King, not, as heretofore some parricides have done, to make room for some usurper, but in a way plainly manifesting their intentions to change the monarchy of England into anarchy ; unless their aim be first to constitute an elective kingdom, and Cromwell or some such John of Leyden being elected, then, by the same force by which they have thus far compassed their ends, to establish a perfect Turkish tyranny.' By forsaking the service of such as these, Jones would give his aid to the restoration of the ' Protestant religion to its purity . . . Parliaments to freedom, and our fellow subjects to their liberty.' [2]

[1] "I have been persuaded to write to Jones, and am now satisfied that the encouragement given me by some pretending your Majesty's service and of near relation to Jones, was only to give him opportunity to manifest his resolution to adhere to the bloody rebels and to gain the more reasonable and considerable supplies from them." Ormond to Charles, April 10, *Carte MSS.* xxiv. fol. 405. That the informant referred to was the Bishop of Clogher appears from Inchiquin's vindication of himself written on Dec. 6. *Carte MSS.* xxvi. fol. 330. The motive ascribed to Jones is improbable, as, if it had existed, he would not have cut off the negotiation so promptly.

[2] Ormond to Jones, March 9, *The Marquis of Ormond s Declaration*, E., 548, 28.

It is possible that Jones had in private expressed his disapprobation of regicide, and that some strong language of his on the subject had formed the basis of his brother's message to Ormond. However this may have been, it is noticeable that Jones in his reply made no attempt to justify the execution of the King. His whole argument moved in another plane. He attacked Ormond for his alliance with rebels and for talking of the restoration of the purity of religion with the help of an army of 'Papists.' "Most certain it is," he continued, "and former ages have approved it, that intermeddling of governors and parties in this kingdom with sidings and parties in England hath been the very betraying of this kingdom to the Irish whilst the British forces here had been thereupon called off and the place therein laid open,[1] and, as it were, given up to the common enemy." Finally, Jones reminded Ormond 'that the English interest in Ireland must be preserved by the English and not by the Irish.'[2]

March 4.
Jones's
reply.

Jones's words would find an echo in England even amongst those who disapproved of regicide as heartily as Ormond. Englishmen were, with rare exceptions, of one mind in thinking that the threats of invasion from Ireland must be brought definitely to an end, and that the only way to bring them to an end was by tightening the grip of England upon the Irish people and the Irish soil. They had too little knowledge of Irish feeling and Irish grievances to be aware that they were entering on a course of oppression from which their children's children would suffer, and, unfortunately for both sides in the quarrel, there was as yet no compact Irish nation to compel them to take its wrongs into account. The divisions of the Irish had originally invited the conquest of Ireland. They now rendered impossible the reconquest of Irish independence. "The Gael," wrote a bard

The
English
interest in
Ireland.

---

[1] The reference is to the recall of English troops by the King in 1643.

[2] Jones to Ormond, March 14, *A True Copy of Two Letters*, E, 529, 28, where the correspondence is continued by one other letter from either side.

who had imbibed the traditions of the most purely Celtic part
of the island,

> " are being wasted, deeply wounded,
> Subjugated, slain, extirpated
> By plague, by famine, by war, by persecution.
> It was God's justice not to free them,
> They went not together hand in hand." [1]

For the moment, however, resolute as Jones had shown
himself, his position seemed hopeless to those whose eyes were
fixed only on the immediate present. His soldiers
deserted in shoals, whilst Ormond felt himself able
to announce that as soon as the grass grew to provide
forage for his cavalry he would be able to take the field at the
head of 8,000 foot and 2,000 horse, and that unless
Jones were plentifully supplied from England, a siege
of a few days would be sufficient to reduce Dublin. [2]

Desertions from Jones's army.

Ormond hopes to reduce Dublin.

Difficult as Jones's position would be if he were opposed
by Ormond alone, it would easily become desperate were
Ormond to find allies in the North who could pour
down to support his attack on Dublin by way of
the coast-road leading through Drogheda. Drogheda,
indeed, was itself held by a Parliamentary garrison, and Monk,
whose troops occupied Dundalk, Carlingford, and
Carrickfergus on the coast, as well as Lisburn and
Newry further inland, was as staunch to ' the English interest '
as Jones himself, whilst Sir William Cole at Sligo and Sir
Charles Coote at Londonderry, though too isolated to bring
him active support, might at least serve to distract the forces of
the enemy. [3]

Feb. State of affairs in the North.

Monk's position.

What forces might be opposed to Monk depended on
the skill of Ormond's diplomacy, and on the strength of the

---

[1] The Irish vision at Rome, Gilbert's *Cont. Hist. of Aff. in Irel.* vol.
iii. 194.

[2] Ormond to Nicholas, March 5, *Carte MSS.* xxiv. fol. 52.

[3] D. O'Neill to Ormond, Feb. 14 ; Ward's advices, Feb. 16 ;
Carte MSS. xxiii. fol. 485. The place now called Lisburn was then
known as Lisnegarvy.

indignation aroused by regicide. No two parties could be
more widely separated by past hostility and by moral and intellectual antagonism than the Ulster Celts who followed
Owen O'Neill, and the Scottish Presbyterian colonists who had occupied their lands and proscribed
their religion. Yet Ormond was so far encouraged by his apparent success in the South that he fondly imagined it possible
to bring even these incompatible forces into line in the service
of the King. It was at least helpful to him that Rinuccini,
discouraged by the signature of the Peace, had sailed from
Galway on February 23,[1] leaving Ormond, if he
thought of winning over those Irish who had as yet
refused to bow their necks under the yoke of English
royalism, to negotiate with a soldier rather than with a priest.

Irish and Scots in Ulster.

Feb. 23. Rinuccini leaves Ireland.

It would be difficult for Ormond to win over Owen
O'Neill, but it would be more difficult for him to win over the
Scottish Presbyterians. Unpractical as their brethren
on the other side of the sea, they were hardly inclined to meet him even half-way. On February 15
the Presbytery of Belfast issued a long tirade against
sectaries on the one hand and the malignants of Hamilton's
engagement on the other,[2] and though some influential person-
ages, such as Lord Montgomery of Ards, wished to turn the
movement to the advantage of the Royal cause, the Presbytery
insisted that they could do nothing for an uncovenanted king,
though they were ready to defend themselves against an army
of sectaries. Their view of the situation was widely
supported by their countrymen, and their first step
was to call on Monk to renew the Covenant himself
and to order his troops to do the like, if he wished them to
continue to co-operate with him.[3]

Feb. 15. Declaration of the Presbytery of Belfast.

Monk asked to renew the Covenant.

When Monk took the Covenant in 1646, he could regard it
as a mere form of declaring his allegiance to the authority he
was about to serve in arms. His strong sense of military honour

---

[1] *Vind. Cath. Hib.* 174.

[2] *A Necessary Representation*, prefixed to Milton's *Observations on the
Articles of Peace.*   [3] Adair, *A True Narrative*, 154–156.

forbade him to renew it in 1649, when it would have been tantamount to a declaration of an intention to disobey the authority to which as a soldier he now owed obedience.

Military honour, however, did not prevent Monk from beguiling those who had announced themselves as his antagonists.

Monk makes delays.
If he gave a straightforward refusal, the Scottish troops would be at once withdrawn from him, and his position, perilous already, would become well-nigh desperate. He accordingly spun out time by giving answers which bound him to nothing.[1]

The Scots were no less determined to persist in their own narrow resolutions. On March 30 they denounced Ormond's combination with ' Papists ' as strongly as they denounced the sectaries, and called on Monk to submit the direction of the war to a council of officers elected by the soldiers. Monk was hardly the man to place himself under the dictation of a body of Presbyterian agitators, inspired by a Presbyterian clergy, especially as he knew that its first step would be to assail the Commonwealth of England, whose servant he was. " I desire to know," he sarcastically asked, " in regard of our dependence upon England, whom it is we shall serve for the present." [2] It was this resolution of men like Jones and Monk to obey the Government of England without regard to political party, which, to some extent, counterbalanced the weakness of the hold of the Commonwealth on English feeling.

March 30.
Declaration of the Scots.

April 9.
Monk's query.

Loyal as Monk was to ' the English interest,' he was in

[1] Adair, *A True Narrative*, 156, 157. " Monk," wrote Jones afterwards, " hath informed me that his letters and answers and offers to the Scots was intended only for breaking them, and giving thereby some seeming satisfaction to the common people, and well knowing that his offers would not be accepted by the others without taking the Covenant, which he was resolved not to do ; and if the Scots had taken him at his word, he would have fallen off." Jones to Cromwell, June 6, *Carte MSS.* cxviii. fol. 332.

[2] Montgomery of Ards and others to Monk, March 30, *Carte MSS.* xxiv. fol. 332 ; *The Declaration of the British*, E, 556, 15 ; Adair's *Narrative*, 159.

little sympathy with English prejudices, or even with English
feelings. It was enough for him if he could find
assistance in any quarter by which he could be aided
in the difficult task of maintaining his post till reinforcements could reach him from beyond the sea. Now that
the Scots were likely to assail him, he turned to Owen O'Neill.

*Monk re-
gardless of
English
prejudices.*

O'Neill was by this time in a mood to respond to his
advances. It is true that he detested the Confederate
Catholics and the regicide Commonwealth with
impartial energy, and in his confidential correspondence he declared that rather than permanently associate
himself with either, he would pass the remainder of his days
in exile from his beloved country.[1]   In the last winter, however,
his position had been deplorable. His followers, scattered
over the counties of Cavan, Leitrim, Longford, and Westmeath,[2] were on the verge of starvation, and gunpowder was as
hard to come by as food. The Nuncio, indeed, had promised
to send him supplies from the continent, but even if that
promise were fulfilled, O'Neill's army was in danger of perish-
ing before help could reach it, and his only chance of safety
lay in his procuring temporary aid from one or other of the
combatants who divided the field in Ireland. For some time
he had been in communication with Jones with little
or no result,[3] and in February he turned to Ormond,
,asking him, through his nephew Daniel O'Neill, to
despatch commissioners to treat on the conditions of alliance.
Ormond seized the opportunity, and on February 20
sent the commissioners.[4]   Little information of the

*O'Neill in
straits.*

*His over-
tures to
Jones and to
Ormond.*

*Feb. 20.
A negotia-
tion opened.*

[1] O'Neill to Massari, May 13; O'Neill to Rinuccini, May 18;
Gilbert's *Cont. Hist. of Aff. in Irel.* vol. ii. 435, 436.

[2] Westmeath to Ormond, Jan. 31 ; *Carte MSS.* xxiii. fol. 373.

[3] O'Neill to Monk, April 25, *Vind. Cath. Hib.* i. 188.   It is evident
from this letter that the negotiation, which had roused the suspicions
of the Supreme Council (Gilbert's *Cont. Hist. of Aff. in Irel.* vol. i.
747-9), had not gone far.   See Rinuccini to Panzirolo, Oct. 31, Nov. 9,
29, 1648, *Nunziatura*, 340, 342, 354.

[4] Ormond to Clanricarde, Feb. 27, *Carte MSS.* xxiii. fol. 405.

course of their negotiation has been preserved, but difficulties undoubtedly arose, and on April 10 Ormond wrote to Charles that though there had as yet been no formal breach, he did not think that it could be long averted.[1]

April 10.
Its failure.

It was, in fact, about this time that O'Neill, knowing of the straits to which Monk was reduced, turned to the Parliamentary commander in the North, hoping, no doubt, to obtain the powder which he needed on easier terms than those offered him by Ormond. O'Neill opened the game by taking up a threatening position in the immediate neighbourhood of Dundalk ; Monk, who was within its walls, and was utterly unable to cope with O'Neill and the Scots at the same time, wrote on April 21 to the Ulster chief inviting him to negotiate. O'Neill at once accepted the proposal, and on May 8 the negotiations resulted in a cessation of hostilities for three months ending on July 3, in order that time might be given for the presentation to Parliament of certain propositions in O'Neill's favour. In the meantime the two armies were to assist one another, and if, in consequence of an attack from Ormond or Inchiquin, O'Neill needed more powder than he had, his wants in that respect were to be supplied by Monk.[2]

O'Neill
turns to
Monk.

He moves
towards
Dundalk.

April 21.
Negotiation
between
Monk and
O'Neill.

May 8.
A cessation
of hos-
tilities.

As a mere temporary convention this agreement satisfied both parties. Monk and O'Neill were equally anxious to gain a shelter against impending ruin, until the supplies which they expected arrived, and both Monk and O'Neill had got precisely what they wanted. Neither of them had overreached the other. As to O'Neill's propositions for a permanent settlement, it is hardly likely that he expected them to be accepted at Westminster, and at all events Monk had bound himself to nothing except to transmit them to England, and to help him to defeat those who were the enemies of both. Monk had reason to know, from a conversation held some little time before with Jones, under whose orders

Character of
the conven-
tion.

[1] Ormond to Charles, April 10, *Carte MSS.* xxiv. fol. 405.

[2] *The True State of the Transactions,* F., 569, 11.

he was placed, that he would approve of any device for gaining time ; and that it was merely a temporary expedient which Monk had in view is shown by his long delay in forwarding to Westminster a copy of the articles of cessation. It is difficult to account for this delay except on the supposition that Monk, expecting that they would be rejected, wished to continue on good terms with O'Neill as long as possible.

If this was so, Monk's hand was forced by the danger of Londonderry. Sir George Monro had been sent by Ormond to besiege it, and the hostility of the Ulster Scots to all who resisted their predominance in the North was now open and avowed. Sir Charles Coote, the commander of the garrison, was even less likely than Monk to come voluntarily to terms with O'Neill. His father, who had been one of the English settlers in Ulster, had been stripped of his entire possessions by the insurgents in 1641 ; and, after avenging himself by a cruel and unrelenting warfare, had been slain by them in the following year. The younger Coote had inherited his father's hatred, yet he now, as the only means of saving the garrison entrusted to his charge, called upon O'Neill for help.

The danger of Londonderry.

Coote's hostility to the Irish.

On May 22 Coote and O'Neill signed an agreement very similar to that which Monk had accepted a fortnight before.[1] On the 25th, when O'Neill's co-operation in the defence of a Parliamentary garrison was actually impending, Monk at last despatched to England his own convention, accompanying it with a letter to Cromwell as Lord Lieutenant of Ireland, in which he explained his conduct as having been prompted by military necessity. He showed, however, that he had no personal objection to a permanent under-standing with the Ulster Celts. " O'Neill's propositions," he wrote, " are wonderful high, but I believe will descend much

May 22.
His convention with O'Neill.

May 25.
Monk sends his own agreement to England.
His letter to Cromwell.

---

[1] *A True Relation of the Transactions between Sir C. Coote and Owen Roe O'Neill*, E, 571, 33. There had been an earlier negotiation which had been broken off. See *Des. Cur. Hib.* ii. 518.

lower." [1]   It was hardly likely that Cromwell and his associates would speak so lightly of an alliance on any terms with men whose hands had, according to the prevalent belief, been imbrued, almost without exception, in the blood of murdered Protestants.

[1] *The True State of the Transactions*, E, 569, 11.

CHAPTER IV

DUNDALK AND RATHMINES

THE association of the Ulster Celts with the massacre of 1641 made it difficult for any English party to avail itself of their services. As far as the Independent leaders were concerned the mere religion of the Irish would hardly have stood in the way of the projected alliance. In the summer of 1647 a clause modifying the penal laws of which the English Catholics complained had been inserted in *The Heads of the Proposals*.[1] Later in the year it was only on the ground of expediency that the Independents had voted [2] against the reception of a petition in which a certain number of Catholics offered an abjuration of the Pope's claim to absolve from obedience to the civil government, to permit the breach of promises made to heretics, and to command the destruction of excommunicated persons.[3]

On the rejection of this petition at Westminster it was forwarded to Rome, strengthened by the signatures of fifty of the Catholic laity. Though it was condemned by a congregation at Rome it obtained the approval of an unnamed French divine, who asserted that decrees issued from Rome were constantly set at naught by the French courts whenever they were opposed to the rights of civil government. The articles were

Relations between Independents and Catholics. 1647.

A Catholic petition.

It is rejected at Westminster and at Rome.

1648. April 2. Opinion of a French divine.

---

[1] *Great Civil War*, iii. 330.   [2] *Ib.* iii. 377.

[3] The petition itself has not been preserved; but a memorandum on which it seems to have been founded is in *The Westminster Archives* at the Oratory in London. It bears nine signatures, all of them apparently those of priests.

printed at Paris with this opinion appended, and in the summer of 1648 copies found their way into England.[1]

It little matters to the oppressed from whose hand the boon of liberation comes, and in November, when the Presbyterian Parliament was tottering to its fall, an Independent agent reported from Paris that the English Catholics there were favourably disposed towards the army, and were prepared to welcome the approaching Commonwealth. Sir Kenelm Digby, by whom these views were advocated, had already received from Lord Say a pass to return to England.[2] In February Scout-master Watson was despatched to Paris to carry on the negotiation and to repeat to Digby the invitation to come back to his native country.[3] That the idea of extending toleration to Catholics who would accept the government of the Commonwealth and would renounce all doctrines subversive of civil authority did not extend to England alone, is shown by the project entertained soon after the King's execution, of sending Sir John Winter, a noted Royalist Catholic, to Ireland, with a mission to conciliate his co-religionists in that country.[4]

Nov. English Catholics at Paris.

Proposed negotiation with the Catholics.

1649 Feb. Sir K. Digby invited to England.

Proposed toleration of Catholics.

It is probable that Winter's mission related principally, if not exclusively, to the Confederate Catholics. The case of the Catholics of Ulster was in other hands. Father Crelly, the abbot of a Cistercian monastery at Newry,[5] had, in 1647, been sent to Rome by the Marquis of Antrim to urge the Pope to contribute money for the support

Abbot Crelly's mission.

[1] *Articles proposed to the Catholics of England*, E, 458, 9. These articles are the same as those in the memorandum, with slight modifications.

[2] Letter of an Independent Agent, Nov. 28, 1648, in *A True and Full Relation*, E, 476, 14.

[3] Digby, coming from Paris in Watson's company, arrived at Rouen on Feb. 13. Winstad to Nicholas, Feb. $\frac{17}{27}$, Carte's *Orig. Letters*, i. 220.

[4] Advertisement from London, Feb. $\frac{15}{25}$, *ib.* i. 224.

[5] *Lord Leicester's MS.* fol. 2,792b.

of a fresh expedition to Scotland, which that nobleman was planning in conjunction with Montrose. Failing in his immediate purpose, Crelly betook himself to England, where he was received by a small committee of five members of the

A Spanish alliance proposed.

Council of State. To them he propounded a plan for an alliance with Spain, in which Antrim and O'Neill should be included, and supported it by real or pretended revelations of the intention of the French Government to assist Ormond and the Confederate Catholics. He gathered from his interviews with the committee that its members were favourably disposed towards him. Cardenas, too, the Spanish ambassador, wrote hopefully to Madrid of the project, and demanded powers to negotiate with the Commonwealth for the assistance of an English fleet against France. Such a proposal was not likely to be adopted at Madrid.[1]

Philip had as yet no mind to enter into an alliance with a regicide republic, especially with one so ill-consolidated as the

Hesitation at Madrid.

English Commonwealth appeared to be, and he therefore rejected the proposal of his ambassador. Before, however, the King's reply arrived, Cardenas and Crelly learned that the Council of State had abandoned, if it had ever

The idea of tolerating Catholics abandoned.

seriously entertained, the idea of tolerating Catholics, partly, it would seem, in consequence of its discovery that the great majority of the English Catholics would remain faithful to the Royalist cause, partly, no doubt, because it could not but be aware that the step it had contemplated would be extremely unpopular amongst its

March 14. Winter excepted from pardon.

own supporters.[2] On March 14, finding that Sir John Winter was no longer useful, Parliament excepted him from pardon, though it allowed him time to leave the country in safety.[3] Crelly had already dis-

Crelly's disappointment.

covered the fruitlessness of his errand, and on March 6 he wrote to Antrim that he was only remaining in England till Cardenas had received an answer from

---

[1] Consulta of the Council of State, March $\frac{3}{13}$, *Guizot*, i. App. v. No. 3.

[2] Letter from an English Catholic, March 26, *Lord Leicester's MS.* fol. 2,795b.   [3] *C.J.* vi. 164.

Madrid.[1] By this time Antrim had made his submission to
Ormond, and the negotiation had therefore broken down on
both sides. When, towards the end of May, Sir Kenelm Digby
arrived in England from Paris he found little disposition to
listen to his proposals.[2]

Under these unfavourable circumstances, Monk's letter,
announcing his arrangement with O'Neill, was laid by Crom-

June.
Monk's
letter laid
before the
Council of
State.

well before the Council of State. It is highly probable that Cromwell had already authorised Jones to
take advantage of any negotiations which might be
offered by one or other of the hostile commanders,
but it is almost certain that, till Monk's letter reached him, he
knew nothing of the actual terms of the agreement with
O'Neill, and that he was absolutely opposed to any permanent

The cessa-
tion to be
kept secret.

alliance with the Ulster Celts. The three months'
cessation was, however, another matter, and the
Council of State, refusing to ratify it, nevertheless
resolved to keep it secret.[3] There is no ground for supposing
that Cromwell dissented from the course then taken; nor,
when all the circumstances of the case are taken into consideration, is there any reason why he should have done so.[4]

[1] Crelly to Antrim, March 6, *Carte MSS.* xxiv. 49, 54. This letter
is incompatible with the supposition that Crelly had received promises
from the Independents.

[2] Relation of an Irish gentleman, Gilbert's *Cont. Hist. of Aff. in
Irel.* vol. ii. 204; Salvetti's despatch, June $\frac{1}{11}$, *Add. MSS.* 27,962, M.
fol. 306.

[3] "It was not then thought fit, for divers reasons, to return any
answer thereupon to Col. Monk, but enjoined secrecy on the whole."
Order Book of the C. of St. *Interr.* I, 62, p. 601. This is passed over
in The Report of the Council to Parliament, *C.J.* vi. 277.

[4] That Cromwell directly authorised Monk's treaty was suggested by
Walker (*Hist. of Ind.* ii. 233), and has since been maintained by Mr.
Julian Corbett (*Monk*, ch. v.). Monk's letter to Cromwell is, however,
to my mind incompatible with the supposition that he was acting under
instructions more definite than the general ones which he states that he had
received from Jones. Mr. Corbett, as I learn from him, rests his case
upon two grounds. In the first place, there is a letter from the Council
of State of May 7, hurriedly countermanding the despatch from Chester

An explosion of popular sentiment against the three months'
cessation, which would prematurely have converted O'Neill
Cromwell's   into an enemy, would at this time have been
need of   disastrous to Cromwell's plans. Having made up
supplies.   his mind not to cross the sea without the means of

of money intended for Monk, whilst on May 11 a letter was written to
Monk thanking him for his services, and on the 15th orders were given
to despatch the money (C. of St. to Walley, May 7, *Interr.* I, 94, p.
147 ; Order Book of the C. of St. *Interr.* I, 62, p. 287 ; C. of St. to
Walley, May 15, *Interr.* I, 94, p. 169).   The simplest explanation is that
the Council heard on the 7th that Dundalk was in danger from the Scots,
and had learnt by the 15th that no immediate danger was impending,
and that therefore the money could be sent with safety.   This is pretty
much what they say themselves, and I see no reason to disbelieve them.
The theory that they were offended with Monk's negotiation, and that
Cromwell smoothed things down, presupposes that they already knew
something of the negotiation, and that Cromwell was at hand to combat
their objections.   The former supposition is in the highest degree
improbable, and though Cromwell was present in the Council on May 7,
he did not reappear till the 28th, being called away from London to
suppress the Levellers.
    In the second place, Mr. Corbett refers to an extract from a letter,
the contents of which were forwarded by Nicholas to Ormond on
$\frac{\text{July 28}}{\text{Aug. 7}}$, in which Nicholas's unknown correspondent says that he had been
told by ' a great Papist ' that the business between Cromwell and the
Catholics was asleep, and that, as to Owen O'Neill, 'for this he could
not speak with so much confidence to it as to the former, but he had it
from a good author (which afterwards he named, viz. the Lord Brudenel)
that that gentleman had about three weeks ago written a letter to
Cromwell to thank him for his care he had of him and his army in
paying this half-year ; but he desired him withal to consider that his
promise was but conditional, as presupposing the Pope's approbation,
which he could never obtain, but on the contrary had received a present
command to do nothing prejudicial to the Crown of England, and upon
that, it is probable, came that report a while since, that O'Neill was joined
with the Marquis of Ormond ' (Carte's *Orig. Letters*, i. 297).   The day
three weeks before this extract was enclosed was July 7, and presupposes
a letter written by O'Neill to Cromwell towards the end of June.   If at
that time he told Cromwell that in consequence of the Pope's intervention
he could do nothing for him, how came he subsequently to take part in
the relief of Londonderry, when it was besieged by the very Royalists whom

paying his men, he found himself hampered with innumerable delays. It is true that Parliament had done what it could in favour of the army. On May 12 an Act was passed to enable soldiers to pay for their quarters by borrowing money on the security of the assessments, and a second Act on May 28 ordered the issue of debentures bearing a 'visible security,' in order to save the owners of such debentures from being driven, as had often been the case before, to sell them for no more than three shillings in the pound.[1] The difficulty was to find 'visible security.' To entice men to purchase the lands of Deans and Chapters now put up for sale, persons who had formerly lent to the State money which had not been repaid were offered the opportunity of 'doubling.' If they now paid in ready money a sum equal to the amount of their original loan, they were to receive lands equal in value to both payments, and would thus obtain payment in land for what was coming to be held as a bad debt. Yet, even with this temptation, buyers came in but slowly.

May 12. Act for paying quarters.

May 28. 'Visible security' offered for debentures.

'Doubling' on the lands of Deans and Chapters.

It was not by financial difficulties alone that Cromwell's

---

he was ordered to support? How, too, came Cromwell, who, for some time to come, was notoriously unable to obtain money to transport his own army to Ireland, to find pay for that of O'Neill?

If the whole of Jones's correspondence with Cromwell had been preserved, it would perhaps be possible to ascertain Cromwell's part in the attempts at this time made by Jones to break up the coalition against him. One passage of the few of Jones's letters which have reached us may, however, be quoted. " I have hitherto," he wrote, " fomented — as still I do—the differences between Owen Roe and Ormond, and am now on the same design for taking Preston off also with his Irish party, which is now also taking. It will be of high consequence to the utter and speedy breaking of their whole powers." Jones to Cromwell, June 6, *Carte MSS.* cviii. fol. 44b. This looks as if Cromwell had given Jones to understand that he might intrigue as much as he pleased, but had left details to his subordinate.

[1] *Acts of Parl.* E, 1,060, pp. 223, 263 ; *The Levellers Vindicated*, E, 571, 11.

departure was stayed. On June 9 Parliament resolved that the seats of the members who had voted for the continuance of the Treaty of Newport, and who had not satisfied the committee appointed to receive retractations of that vote, should be declared vacant and be filled up by fresh elections.[1] At this proposal, which would have introduced into the House more than a hundred new members of uncertain politics at a time when he would himself be on the other side of the sea, Cromwell took alarm. He made an alternative proposal that Parliament should adjourn for two or three months, leaving the reins of government in the hands of the Council of State.[2] The House, which was at all times disinclined to share its authority with new comers, followed Cromwell's lead, and on June 11 requested the Council to draw up a list of Bills fit to be passed into law before the adjournment.[3]

June 9. Partial elections resolved on.

Cromwell proposes an adjournment.

June 11. His view adopted.

Definite preparations were now made for the Irish expedition. On June 15 Ireton was named Lieutenant-General, and on the 22nd Cromwell was formally appointed Commander-in-Chief and Governor of Ireland, a title which, even in official parlance, was speedily abandoned for the time-honoured designation of Lord Lieutenant, the civil and military authority being combined in his person for three years.[4] On June 27, to provide resources for his army, an Act was passed charging the excise with 400,000*l.*, and on the 29th another Act authorised the immediate borrowing of 150,000*l.* on that security.[5] A popular government, indeed, would have found no difficulty in raising the money on such good security ; but the Government was not popular, especially in London, and the city merchants, instead

June 15. Ireton Lieutenant-General.

June 22. Cromwell Commander-in-Chief.

June 27-29. Financial expedients.

The City will not lend.

---

[1] *Whitelocke,* 406.

[2] Walker's *Hist. of Ind.* ii. 202 ; Salvetti's despatch of July $\frac{6}{16}$, *Add. MSS.* 27,962, M. fol. 327b.

[3] *C.J.* vi. 229.   [4] *Ib.* vi. 232, 239.

[5] *Ib.* vi. 245.

of taking up the loan, offered to bet twenty to one that Cromwell would never leave England.[1]

The delay was the more annoying as news of the increased activity of the enemy had for some time been pouring in from News from Ireland. Ireland. On the other hand, it was satisfactory to know that the mastery of the sea had passed into the hands of the Commonwealth. On May 22 Blake arrived May 22. Kinsale blockaded. off Kinsale and blockaded the harbour. Rupert's ships were as yet too scantily manned to break out,[2] and if Dublin and Londonderry were to be besieged by the Royalists, they would be besieged, like Hull and Plymouth in the English Civil War, on the land side alone. Yet, even with the sea open behind them, Dublin and Londonderry were exposed to no slight danger. About the middle of May, Ormond sent Castlehaven in advance to clear the way for his own march to Dublin, and Castlehaven reduced Maryborough May. Castlehaven reduces Maryborough and Athy. on the 16th and Athy on the 21st. Yet even in the midst of these successes the inherent weakness of a military undertaking based on no sound financial organisation was plainly to be seen. Castlehaven had started with 5,000 foot and 1,000 horse. His half-starved men deserted in shoals, and he had to complain Desertions from his army. after the capture of Athy that only 1,500 of his infantry remained with him, and that they were only kept alive by stealing cows. " God Almighty," he wrote to Ormond, " bless all, but to my thinking our business for as much as concerns this army hath but a scurvy face." [3]

Ormond was more sanguine. He thought that so small a May 23. Ormond hopes for the best. sum as 5,000*l.* would make the King absolute master of Ireland, and that there would not be much difficulty in raising it.[4] Encouraged by this hope, he deter-

---

[1] *The Moderate*, E, 565, 11.

[2] Legge to Ormond, May 22 ; Castlehaven to Ormond, May 26 ; Sir E. Butler to Ormond, May 27 ; *Carte MSS.* xxiv. fol. 765, 782, 784 ; *A Perfect Summary*, E, 531, 20.

[3] Castlehaven's *Memoirs* (ed. 1680), 85 ; Castlehaven to Ormond, May 14, 16, 19, 21, 22 ; *Carte MSS.* xxiv. fol. 701, 719, 742, 755, 764.

[4] Ormond to Jermyn, May 23, *ib.* xxiv. fol. 772.

mined to set out for Dublin, the gate of Ireland, where the
girdling wall of mountains falls back for a space and leaves free
access to the central plain.   On May 29 he assured Nicholas

May 29.
His view
of the
military
situation.

that the King could dispose of at least 10,000 foot
and 3,000 horse.   On the other hand, he allowed
that if Irish soldiers were to be brought under
military discipline, they must be constantly paid,
which, added the unhappy Lord Lieutenant, 'they can never
be.'   Inchiquin's men, mainly recruited amongst the English
settlers in Munster, were no less clamorous 'for impossible
sums of money.'   Yet Ormond was full of hope to carry
Dublin 'and, in consequence, the whole kingdom.'   As yet
he knew nothing of the agreement between Monk and O'Neill,
and he hoped that the hostility of Royalists and Levellers
would be enough to hinder Cromwell from bringing or sending
any considerable assistance to Jones.[1]

On May 30 the combined forces of Ormond and Inchiquin,
numbering 6,000 foot and 2,000 horse, broke up from Kil-

May 30.
Ormond's
advance.

kenny.   It was not an army from which united
action could be expected.   Between Inchiquin's
Protestants and the Catholics who had been handed
over to Ormond by the Supreme Council no good understanding prevailed.   It was comparatively easy to smooth away
personal asperities.   Preston, for instance, who was annoyed by

Preston
to be a
viscount.

the appointment of Lord Taaffe to the post of Master
of the Ordnance, which he coveted for himself, and
who had even entered into a correspondence with
Jones, was consoled with the promise of a viscountcy.[2]

[1] Ormond to Nicholas, May 29, Carte's *Orig. Letters*, ii. 379.

[2] Ormond to Charles, June 1 ; Ormond to Long, June 1 ; *Carte MSS.*
xvi. foll. 1, 3.   For Preston's communication with Jones, see the extract
at p. 85, note.   According to a letter from Rochfort to Jones of June 4
(*ib.* cxviii. 45), Preston engaged in a plot to seize Ormond at a dinner
to which he was invited, as he passed through Carlow on the 31st.   The
plot, wrote Rochfort, failed, because Ormond came accompanied with an
armed guard.   It is possible that Preston listened to the scheme in order
to frustrate it, and the evidence is, at all events, insufficient to fix so deep
a stain on his character.

Such rivalries might be dangerous in the future, but for the present Ormond was, at least in appearance, in the full tide of success, whereas it was amongst his opponents that the disintegrating effect of differences of opinion and sentiment was most clearly to be seen.   It was not only by the Scots in the north that regicide was abhorred.   One fortified post after another was voluntarily surrendered to Ormond by officers in the employment of the English Parliament, Ballysonan being the only one to hold out.

*June.
Surrender of fortresses to Ormond.*

Sir Thomas Armstrong deserted to him with a strong body of horse, and his example was followed by other Parliamentary officers. On June 14, indeed, Jones, accompanied by Monk, who had come southwards to consult him on his own difficulties, sallied forth from Dublin to obstruct Ormond's march, but he was sadly out-numbered, and on the 17th he was out-manœuvred and forced to draw back into the city.[1]   On the 21st Ormond reached Castleknock, and occupied the grounds of Phœnix Lodge with his cavalry. Before long he established his headquarters at Finglas on the northern side of Dublin.[2]

Desertions from Jones.

*June 14.
Jones attempts to check Ormond's advance.*

*June 17.
Jones's retreat.*

*June 21.
Ormond before Dublin.*

In reality everything depended on Ormond's promptness in assailing Dublin before succour could arrive. Yet he determined to play a waiting game. He may have distrusted the quality of his troops, and he certainly underestimated the power of the English Government to hasten the succours which had been so long delayed. He appears to have thought that the difficulty of obtaining provisions from the neighbourhood of Dublin, together with the pressure exercised by a disaffected population, would compel Jones to surrender, although the sea was still open for the introduction of supplies. Jones, on the other hand, with none of the unconquerable optimism of his

Ormond resolves to play a waiting game.

---

[1] Ormond to the King, June 28, Carte's *Orig. Letters*, ii. 383 ; *The Moderate Intelligencer*, E, 562, 2 ; *The Moderate Mercury*, E, 562, 4 ; *The Present Condition of Dublin*, E, 562, 11.

[2] Blacknall's advices, *Carte MSS.* xxv. fol. 35.

opponent, busied himself in repairing the fortifications, and
drove out of the gates the Roman Catholic citizens
and all others, whether civilians or soldiers, whom
he suspected of treachery.[1]

Jones's prepara-tions.

Ormond at all events had no fear of the result. He despatched Inchiquin first to reduce Drogheda, and then to fall
upon Monk and rally the Ulster Scots to the Royal
cause. On the 28th he invited his young sovereign
to consider how the total reduction of Ireland might
' be best improved and made use of towards the regaining of '
his other dominions. How great were the difficulties
in the way of that final consummation was not unknown to him. Irishmen, he was well aware, thought
far more of seeing their own grievances redressed in their own way
than of restoring Charles to the throne. " It is easily foreseen,"
he wrote, " that, upon the full subduing of those that hold in this
kingdom for the rebels in England, and before those heretofore
of the Confederate party will consent to the sending away or
disbanding of any considerable number of their best men, they
will expect a confirmation by Act of Parliament of what they have
gained by the late peace ; and it is to be feared that their clergy
will not rest there, but will press for such enlargement in point
of ecclesiastical livings and jurisdiction—the true and original
ground of the Irish rebellion—as may not consist with your
Majesty's honour, safety, or conscience to allow them. Yet I
conceive it is not impossible but that your Majesty,
by securing to the generality by Parliament and by some particular instances of bounty and trust what is already granted,
which carries with it all reasonable advantages and security as
to temporal interests and very large freedoms for the exercise
of their religion, may so far gain upon them that it will not be
difficult to carry them to what new action your Majesty shall
please, and yet not entangle yourself in such further concessions to them as may lose the hearts of the Protestants without
whom your Majesty's work here, much less in England and
Scotland, is not to be done."

Inchiquin sent against Drogheda.

June 28.
Ormond's fore-bodings.

His advice.

[1] *The Present Condition of Dublin*, E, 563, 4.

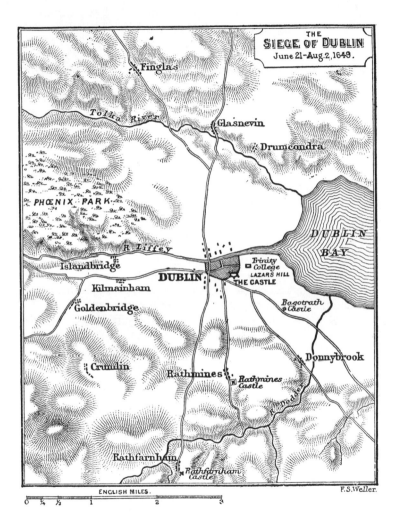

THE
SIEGE OF DUBLIN
June 21-Aug.2,1649.

Finglas

Tolka River

Glasnevin

Drumcondra

PHŒNIX PARK

R. Liffey

DUBLIN BAY

Islandbridge

DUBLIN

Trinity College
LAZARS HILL
THE CASTLE

Kilmainham

Goldenbridge

Bagotrath Castle

Crumlin

Donnybrook

Rathmines

Rathmines Castle

Dodder

Rathfarnham

Rathfarnham Castle

ENGLISH MILES.

F.S.Weller.

0   ¼   ½   1   2   3

The disruption of the alliance which he had so laboriously
concluded stared Ormond in the face. " How this Parliament,"
he continued, " can be without your Majesty's presence . . . I cannot see ; nor any assurance without a Parliament of sending any considerable body
of Irish hence with the consent of those entrusted by them [1] to
see the performance of the conditions with them ; and unless
the greater number be of them,[2] the Protestants interested
here will not hold it safe that any number of themselves be
sent." The expected conquest of Ireland, in short, must lead
to an outbreak of hostility between the two sections of Ormond's supporters, which could only be averted by Charles's
personal intervention.[3]

Evidently the danger of an Irish invasion of England was
greater in appearance than in reality ; but history is full of
examples of menaces which become formidable
if they are not met with vigour and decision.
Cromwell at least had no doubt as to the necessity
of putting an end for ever to threats which had been suspended
over England since the utterance of those hasty words which
more than anything else had cost Strafford his head. Another
Royal Lord Lieutenant appeared to be repeating Strafford's
words : "Your Majesty hath an army in Ireland which you
may employ to reduce this kingdom." Yet Cromwell, eager as
he was to set forth, was still tied to Westminster by his financial needs, perhaps, too, by the necessity of assuring himself
that there was no immediate risk of a Scottish invasion.

About the time that Ormond sat down before Dublin,
public attention was called to the events passing in
Ulster.[4] On June 20 a rumour was spread in
London, with no basis of fact, that Monk and O'Neill
had marched together to relieve Dublin   More accu-

---

[1] *I.e.* the Commissioners of Trust, see p. 13.   [2] *I.e.* of Protestants.

[3] Ormond to Charles, June 28, Carte's *Orig. Letters*, ii. 383.

[4] *The Moderate Mercury*, E, 561, 1 ; *The Moderate Intelligencer*,
E, 561, 2.   From the Royalist *Merc. Pragmaticus* (E, 561, 17) published on
June 26, it appears that no definite information had as yet been published.

rate information was on the way, and on June 28 a part of
the correspondence between Monk and O'Neill was
published in London; and soon afterwards arrived a
pamphlet containing, not only the correspondence,
but the treaty itself. This pamphlet had been
printed at Cork, and was sent to the press by an
officer serving under Monk, who was almost certainly
Colonel Mark Trevor, and who announced his intention of
deserting to Ormond, partly on the ground of his abhorrence
of the murderers of the king, but still more on account of the
treaty with O'Neill.[1]

Marginal notes: June 28. Correspondence between Monk and O'Neill published. The treaty published.

There is no doubt that the Council of State shared Trevor's
opinions on the last point, but the treaty had still more than a
month to run, and the Council was most unwilling
to drive O'Neill into active warfare sooner than was
necessary. Doubtless with this object, the Council,
which had hitherto shown little disposition to give
ear to the propositions of the Abbot Crelly on behalf of Antrim
and O'Neill,[2] now instructed its committee to hear
what he had to say. Crelly asked, as O'Neill had
asked before, for indemnity for the Irish in arms in
Ulster, and for 'the enjoyment of their religion and estates for
the time to come.' As far as can be gathered from his own
language, he also asked for a general toleration of all Catholics
within the jurisdiction of the Commonwealth.[3] Every one of

Marginal notes: The Council anxious to keep the cessation unbroken. July. Crelly before a committee.

---

[1] *General Owen O'Neill's Letter*, E, 562, 1 ; *The Propositions of Owen
Roe O'Neill*, E, 562, 15.   [2] See p. 82.

[3] *Ludlow*, i. 228 ; Ludlow, as usual, gives no date, but Crelly's own
account points to his having been before the committee early in July.
" Intra paucos dies," he writes, " confidenter præsume me intellecturum
realem eventum propositi de quo quantocyus Dominationem vestram
illustrissimam certiorem reddam. . . . Deum Maximum testor quantum
in iis laboravi et cum quibus periculis ac difficultatibus; licet nondum
absolverim censeo, et non absque fundamento, quod infra terminum
viginti dierum per me ipsum vel per alium expressum Dominationi suæ
illustrissimæ," *i.e.* Rinuccini, " omnia referre valuero. Res de quibus
ago sunt generales et graves, et cum grandibus consilio grandium
deliberate ductus in iis procedo, quandoquidem de re totius Religionis

his demands was ultimately rejected, but for the present he was put in hope of a satisfactory answer. Evidently the Council expected that O'Neill would thereby be induced to observe the cessation to the end. The maxim that it is as justifiable to defeat a public enemy by craft as by valour finds easy access to the breasts of even high-minded statesmen.

It can hardly be doubted that Cromwell gave his assent to this manœuvre of his fellow-councillors. His own plans were

Cromwell's plans. grounded on a policy very different from that of an alliance with any body of Irish Catholics. He was prepared to make his own the old policy of Strafford and to subordinate every other consideration in the government of Ireland to the work of upholding the 'English interest,' and of making Protestant English colonists supreme in that country. Thus alone, he imagined, could chaos be reduced to order.

With this object in view, Cromwell, whilst pushing forward towards Chester a sufficient force to relieve Jones from danger,

Jones to be relieved by way of Chester. was despatching the bulk of his army towards Bristol and Milford Haven, from which port was the nearest passage to Cork and the southern coast of Munster.

Cromwell intends to land in Munster, There was to be found the English colony which had sprung up mainly through the enterprise of the first Earl of Cork, which had kept its ground against the Confederate Catholics at the time of the cessation in 1643,[1] and which furnished the strength of Inchiquin's army now fighting, not without reluctance, by the side of the Confederates.

and communicates with Inchiquin's officers. Through one of his officers, Colonel Phayre, Cromwell had already been in communication with some of the officers in Inchiquin's army, and had asked them to continue their service in that army, in order that when the proper moment arrived they might turn against their own commander with more effect.[2]

Catholicæ agitur et aliquando demonstrabitur." Crelly to ——(?) July $\frac{9}{19}$, *Lord Leicester's MS.* fol. 2,800b.

[1] See the map in *Great Civil War*, i. 224.

[2] "Some of these," Phayre afterwards declared, "stayed, by his advice, in Inchiquin's army on purpose to serve said interest." Phayre's

By this time, too, Cromwell had on his side a man whose influence over the English in Munster was beyond dispute. Lord Broghill, the fifth son of the Earl of Cork, had taken part with Inchiquin in his early resistance to the Confederate Catholics, but had been for some time living in retirement, first in Ireland and then in Somerset. The execution of the King roused him from his life of ease, and in the spring of 1649 he came to London with the intention of crossing to the Continent to ask Charles for a commission in Ireland. Whilst waiting for a passport he was surprised by a visit from Cromwell, who told him that his design was discovered, and that he would soon be in the Tower unless he consented to abandon it. He had himself, said Cromwell, obtained leave from the Council to make the attempt to bring him to a better mind. If he would serve against the Irish, ' he should have a general officer's command, and should have no oaths nor engagements laid upon him, nor should be obliged to fight against any but the Irish.' He must, however, make up his mind at once, one way or other. On this, Broghill, in whom antipathy to the Irish was more deeply seated than devotion to the Royal cause, accepted the proposal, and from that time became one of Cromwell's most trusted supporters in Ireland.[1]

Lord Brog-hill intends to serve as a Royalist.

Cromwell wins him over.

deposition, Caulfield's *Council Book of the Corporation of Cork*, p. 1165. The passage is not quite free from ambiguity, as it might mean that they stayed after the defeat at Rathmines; but I feel very little doubt that the interpretation given to it in the text is right.

[1] Morrice's *Memoirs of Orrery*, prefixed to *The State Letters of Roger Boyle, Earl of Orrery*, 10. This is the same source from which the story of Cromwell and Ireton at the Blue Boar is taken (*Great Civil War*, iv. 27). It would be unwise to guarantee the story as accurate in every detail, but it fits in with Cromwell's designs at the time, though his intention to land in Munster must have been forgotten when it was written. Indirect confirmation of the part relating to Cromwell's promise that Broghill should fight with the Irish only is given by a letter from Inchiquin to Ormond of Dec. 9 (*Clarendon St. P.* ii. 500). " My Lord of Broghill," he writes, " sent me some messages; first, that he assures me he does not act for them, nor by their commission, that he will never

The beginning of July found Cromwell still in straits for money, and he adhered to his resolution that without money he would not lead his men across the sea. His presence in the West of England was, however, needed to restore discipline among his troops. A few weeks before a party of thirty soldiers burst into Prynne's house in Somerset, climbing over the walls and breaking down the doors. When entrance had been gained they beat his servants, drew their swords on himself, forced their way into his beer-cellar, and possessed themselves of the money and clothes of his household. Having done thus much they 'hollowed, roared, stamped, beat the tables with their swords and muskets like so many bedlams, swearing, cursing, and blaspheming at every word.' They smashed the crockery, threw a joint of beef at the head of the maid who was placing it on the table for their use, and insisted on having turkeys fetched out of the farmyard. At supper they drank so hard that 'most of them were mad-drunk, and some of them dead-drunk under the table.'[1] Prynne's experience was probably exceptional, but men guilty of such conduct, even in the house of so notorious an antagonist of the Commonwealth, were not likely to be well-behaved elsewhere.

Cromwell needed in the west of England.

Prynne ill-treated by soldiers.

It was time for Cromwell to intervene. On July 12 he set out for Bristol with unwonted state, in a coach drawn by six grey Flanders mares and protected by a life-guard every member of which was 'either an officer or an esquire.' Above him floated a milk-white standard,[2] symbolising, as it would seem, his hope to bring back white-robed Peace from amidst the horrors of war. Yet, long as the starting of his expedition had been delayed, it seemed likely to be kept back for some time longer. He arrived at Bristol on the 14th, but was then com

July 12. Cromwell sets out for Bristol.

July 14. His arrival at Bristol.

disserve the King, though he act in this national quarrel, and that, though perhaps I may not believe it, yet he would be glad to do me personal service."

[1] *A Legal Vindication*, E, 565, 3.   This took place on May 22.
[2] *A Perfect Diurnal*, E, 531, 21.

pelled to assure his troops that until money arrived for their support he would not order them to embark.[1] He did everything necessary to complete his preparations for sailing when the proper moment arrived, and whilst pushing on his regiments towards Milford Haven, he continued to keep up his communications with the English soldiers in Munster.   Unless

His offer to the Governor of Cork. Ormond was grossly misinformed, Cromwell offered 6,000*l.* to the Governor of Cork to open the gates of that city on his arrival, and there is reason to believe that similar overtures were made to persons in authority in Kinsale and Wexford, and possibly in other ports on the southern coast.[2]

Whilst Cromwell was thus preparing for a landing in Munster he did not neglect those who were holding out in

Reinforcements for Jones and Coote. other parts of Ireland.   Three regiments of foot under Venables, Moore, and Huncks, and one of horse under Reynolds, were forwarded to Chester, part of that under Huncks being destined for Londonderry, whilst the remaining forces were to make all speed to Dublin. Some of Reynolds's troopers mutinied on their way through Wrexham, and committed outrages in the neighbourhood;[3] but the greater part remained with their colours, and the four regiments reached Chester without much loss.

Whilst these reinforcements were still on the way, events were occurring in Ireland which seriously increased the difficul-

July 11. Surrender of Drogheda to Inchiquin. ties of the Parliamentary commanders.   On July 11 Drogheda surrendered to Inchiquin. Of the 700 foot and 255 horse of which the garrison was composed,

---

[1] *Merc. Pragmaticus*, E, 565, 21 ; *The Moderate Intelligencer*, E, 564, 6.

[2] Advices from Blacknall, June 21 ; Long to Ormond, $\frac{July\ 24}{Aug.\ 3}$, *Carte MSS.* xxv. fol. 35, 140 ; Ormond to Digby, July 19 ; Ormond to Byron, Sept. 29 ; Carte's *Orig. Letters*, ii. 391, 407 ; Intelligence of Cromwell's Embarkation, Gilbert's *Cont. Hist. of Aff. in Irel.* vol. ii. 223.

[3] C. of St. to Walley, June 26, *Interr.* I, 94, p. 264 ; Order Book of the C. of St. *Interr.* I, 62, p. 533 ; Wrexham is there miswritten Wexford. See C. of St. to Cromwell, July 17, *Interr.* I, 94, p. 313.

no fewer than 600 foot and 220 horse took service with the victorious party.[1]

Inspirited by this success, Inchiquin pursued his march. In Ulster, Sir George Monro, who was in arms for the King, after reducing Coleraine, had crossed the Bann, and had opened communications with Lord Montgomery of Ards, and other commanders, who were chafing under the unpractical refusal of the Presbyterian clergy to permit them to fight for an uncovenanted king. They now resolved to throw off the yoke, and Montgomery, having obtained admission into Belfast on the plea of defending it against Monro, had gained over the soldiers of the garrison,[2] and joining with Monro had made himself master of Carrickfergus as well. Montgomery then openly declared himself for Charles II., in the teeth of the protests of the clergy.

Monro and the Scots in the North.

Montgomery declares for the King.

The storm would soon fall on Dundalk, where Monk still held out. In his desperation he sent to O'Neill for assistance against Inchiquin in accordance with their agreement, offering to supply him with the gunpowder of which he stood in need. Accordingly on July 23 a party of O'Neill's men appeared in Dundalk to fetch away the store. Once within the walls, the Irishmen dispersed amongst the drink shops, and when at last they staggered through the gates with their loads, they were in no plight to resist an enemy. Unluckily for them Inchiquin was in the immediate neighbourhood. The Irishmen were cut down or put to flight, whilst the ammunition they carried passed into the hands of the victors.

Monk at Dundalk.

He applies to O'Neill.

July 23. O'Neill sends for ammunition.

His party defeated by Inchiquin.

On the morning of the 24th Inchiquin opened an attack on the fortress. Monk's own garrison, however, refused to fight

[1] Letter from an officer, July 16, in *Perf. Occurrences*, E, 532, 1 ; Ormond to Charles, July 18 ; Carte's *Orig. Letters*, ii. 388.

[2] Adair's *Irish Presb. Church*, 165–173 ; the complaint of the Boutefeu, E, 566, 18 ; Monro to Gemill, July 30 ; *Carte MSS.* xxv. fol. 105.

for the ally of O'Neill, and he had no course open but to
come to terms with Inchiquin. On a promise that he and all

July 24.
Surren-
der of
Dundalk.

who chose to follow him should be allowed to depart
unharmed, he threw open the gates. Inchiquin
received a hearty welcome, and almost the whole of
the garrison took service under him.[1]   Inchiquin had now
accomplished his work in the North, and leaving Monro and
Montgomery to overpower Coote in Londonderry, he returned

Surrender
of Trim
and Sligo.

to take his share in the siege of Dublin. The Castle
of Trim surrendered to him as he passed, and, as
Sligo had about the same time submitted to
Clanricarde, Dublin and Londonderry were at the end of July
the only fortified posts of any importance holding out against
the Royalists.

Whilst these operations were in progress, Ormond had
clung to his head-quarters at Finglas, probably in order to

Ormond at
Finglas.

hinder Jones from marching to the relief of Monk.
Though he knew that Cromwell was expected in
Ireland, he looked forward to his coming without anxiety.   " If

July 18.
He pro-
fesses not
to fear
Cromwell.
Wants of
his army.

Cromwell come over," he wrote on the 18th, " we
shall more dread his money than his face.[2] We
have none but what we force from this exhausted
kingdom." In spite of this avowal, he was strangely
confident.   " That," he continued, " which only
threatens any rub to our success is our own wants, which have
been and are such that soldiers have actually starved by their
arms, and many of less constancy have run home ; yet, upon a
view yesterday taken, we are about 5,000 foot and 2,000 horse
here, besides 1,200 horse and 2,000 foot about Dundalk and
Trim. Many of the foot are weak, but I despair not to be
able to keep them together and strong enough to reduce Dublin
if good supplies come not speedily to relieve it.   I am confident
I can persuade the one-half of this army to starve outright, and

---

[1] Gilbert's *Cont. Hist. of Aff. in Irel.* vol. ii. 37 ; *A Perfect Diurnal*,
E, 552, 10.

[2] So in the MS.   ' force ' as printed.

I shall venture far upon it rather than give off a game so fair on our side and so hard to be recovered if given over." [1]

A few days after this letter was written the four regiments destined to relieve Jones reached Dublin. On July 26 the last

July 22-26. Four regiments land at Dublin.

man of them stepped on shore.[2] Jones thus found himself at the head of a force at least equal in numbers to the enemy and far superior in cohesion as well as in all military qualities. This inauspicious moment was, however, seized by Ormond to assume the offensive. On the 25th, encouraged by the news of Inchiquin's success at Dundalk, he transferred the bulk of his forces to Rathmines on the southern side of Dublin, leaving Lord Dillon at Finglas

July 27. Inchiquin sent to Munster.

with 2,000 foot and 500 horse.[3] On the 27th, when Inchiquin had brought back his forces, another council of war was held to discuss the course to be taken in view of Cromwell's landing in Munster, a danger which was believed to be immediately impending. In the end Inchiquin was despatched with a regiment of horse to Munster, whilst Ormond was to push on the siege of Dublin, beginning with an attack on Rathfarnham, a fortified house owned by Sir Adam Loftus and situated in the rear of the quarters of the Royalists.[4]

On the 28th Rathfarnham was taken without much difficulty, and though, at another council of war, voices were raised

July 28. Rathfarn-ham taken.

against remaining so near a powerful garrison which had recently been reinforced, it was determined to fall back on a plan for reducing the city without exposing

A plan of action.

the besiegers to the hazard of an assault. The horses of Reynolds's newly arrived cavalry, it was thought, might be deprived of the necessary forage if the besiegers could

---

[1] Ormond to Charles, July 18, Carte's *Orig. Letters*, ii. 388. About this time there was a plot to betray Dublin Castle, but the negotiation was carried on directly with the King, and Ormond appears to have known nothing of it. Advices from Blacknall, July 11; Wilson to Blacknall, July 30; Ormond to Long, Sept. 28; *Carte MSS.* xxv. fol. 35, 203, 614.

[2] Jones to Lenthall, Aug. 6, Cary's *Mem. of the Civil War*, ii. 153.

[3] Carte's *Ormond*, v. 120.

[4] Minutes of a Council of War, July 27, *Carte MSS.* xxv. fol. 39.

gain possession of the meadows which stretched from Trinity College to Ringsend on the shore of Dublin Bay.

Accordingly, on the 29th, Ormond ordered Sir Thomas Armstrong to sweep these meadows with a party of horse, and to carry off the horses and cattle grazing on them.

July 29.
Sir T.
Armstrong
driven
back.

He was, however, driven back with some loss. Amongst the prisoners taken by the garrison was a young nephew of Jones named Eliot, who had recently gone over to the Royalists. Jones promptly hanged him as a deserter, thus reaping the admiration of the Parliamentary newspapers in London as a second Brutus.[1]

Armstrong's failure stirred Ormond to more decisive action. On the evening of August 1 he directed Major-General Purcell to lead 1,500 foot under cover of the night to the

Aug. 1.
Bagotrath
to be forti-
fied.

ground in dispute, and to fortify the old castle of Bagotrath, which not only commanded the meadows which fed Jones's horses, but was also near enough to the sea to throw shot across the entrance of the Liffey, and thereby to hinder Jones from receiving further supplies. Purcell, however, was led astray in the dark by incompetent or

Aug. 2.
Purcell at
Bagotrath.

treacherous guides, and did not reach Bagotrath till an hour before daybreak on the 2nd. When Ormond arrived on the scene, accompanied by Sir William Vaughan and a party of horse, he found that little progress had been made with the works, but that large parties of Jones's men were clustering in front of the city wall.

Ormond gave directions to Purcell and Vaughan to protect the working party, after which, having waited in vain for an

Purcell
routed.

attack, he retired to his tent at nine in the morning to sleep off the fatigues of the night. He was soon aroused by the sound of firing, and he then discovered that Jones had fallen on Purcell with superior force, and had recovered Bagotrath.[2] More than this Jones had not hoped to

---

[1] *Perf. Occurrences*, E, 532, 13.

[2] The statement that Purcell was dismissed by Ormond for his conduct on this day is an exaggeration, as he is frequently mentioned afterwards as Major General Purcell.

do, but his victory had been so easy that he resolved to follow
it up, and pushed on against Ormond's main station at Rath-
Ormond
routed at
Rath-
mines.   mines.   In vain Ormond, now roused from sleep,
drew out his troops and exhorted them to stand firm.
One regiment after another either threw down its arms
or fled, and though Ormond summoned to his aid the regiments
quartered at Finglas they refused to stir, in spite of the urgency
of their commanders.   In a very short time a grave disaster had
befallen the Royal cause.

The two commanders were even more at variance than is
usual in their accounts of the losses suffered by the defeated
Ormond's
losses.   army.   Jones declared that he had slain 4,000 and
had captured 2,517.   Ormond put the number of the
killed no higher than 600, and alleged that most of them had
been ' butchered in cold blood after they had laid down their
arms upon promise of quarter and had been for almost an hour
prisoners, and divers of them murdered after they were brought
within the works of Dublin.' [1]   So definite a statement is not
refuted by the silence maintained on the other side, but it must
be remembered that a considerable number of Ormond's
soldiers had gone over to him from the enemy, and that it is
not unreasonable to conjecture that Jones held, as he had held
in the case of his own nephew, that no promise of quarter could
be successfully pleaded by a deserter.[2]

However this may have been, Jones's victory turned the
tide of affairs in Ireland.   Till the news of it reached England
The tide
turned in
Ireland.   the Royalists had been confident of Ormond's
success.   On the very day when the two armies
were struggling at Rathmines a pamphlet, published
Expecta-
tions of the
English
Royalists.   in London, announced that an infant had been found
in a field near Leominster, which had prophesied in
articulate speech that Charles, after rallying Ireland
to his cause, would cross into England and would in three

[1] Narrative of Military Operations, *Carte MSS.* xxvi. fol. 440.

[2] Ormond to Charles, Aug. 8 ; Ormond to Byron, Sept. 29 ; Carte's
Orig. Letters, ii. 392, 407 ; Jones to Lenthall, Aug. 6, Cary's *Mem. of
the Civil War*, ii. 159.

years be restored to the throne of his ancestors.[1]   In the City wagers were freely offered that Dublin had already surrendered, at the enormous odds of 100*l.* to 5*s.*[2]

Against Jones's success was to some extent to be set Monk's expulsion from Dundalk.   On July 26 Monk himself

July 26.
Monk at
Chester.

landed at Chester, whence he hastened on to London, where he arrived on August 1.[3]   After a hurried interview with the Council of State he was despatched to give an account to Cromwell of the state of affairs in Ireland, and doubtless also to seek his advice on the

Aug. 1.
He passes
through
London
and goes
on to see
Cromwell.

best way of meeting the outcry which had been raised in London against the convention with O'Neill. He found Cromwell at Milford Haven with a pro- spect of embarking speedily.   At last the financial difficulties in his way had been overcome, and on July 31, 100,000*l.* had been forwarded to him from London, thus enabling him to start without violating the promise made to his soldiers that he would not lead them across the sea until he had enough money to secure their pay on the other side.[4]

The exact nature of Monk's communications with Cromwell on the subject of his agreement with O'Neill must remain

Probable
nature of
his com-
munica-
tions with
Cromwell.

uncertain, but it was probably arranged between them that Monk was to make public the truth, if not the whole truth.   He was to take upon himself the blame of accepting the agreement, saying nothing of

[1] *Vox Infantis*, E, 566, 27.   The field is there strangely said to have been near Leominster in Herefordshire, 'hard by a village called the Hove, not far from Corfe Castle.'

[2] *The Army's Painful Messenger*, E, 566, 25.

[3] A letter from Chester dated July 26 in *The Moderate* (E, 532, 4) says that Monk had gone to meet Cromwell ; but almost every other newspaper speaks of his arrival in London.   In *Perfect Occurrences* (E, 532, 7) we find, under the date of Aug. 1, 'Colonel Monk came over to Chester and to London, but went away the same night again towards the Lord Lieutenant in Pembrokeshire.'   Very likely he originally intended to go to Cromwell, but thought it best to see the Council of State first.

[4] *Merc. Pragmaticus*, E, 565, 21 ; *The Moderate Intelligencer*, E, 566, 23.

Cromwell's preliminary authorisation of some kind of negotiation, if such authorisation there was,[1] and keeping silence on the secrecy maintained by the Council of State with the view of postponing a rupture as long as possible.[2]

Accordingly, on August 10, Scot, in the name of the Council of State, laid a report before Parliament. As soon as it had been read Monk was called to the bar and asked by whose advice the convention had been made. "I did it," he replied, "in my own name only, having formerly had discourse with Colonel Jones ; Colonel Jones told me that if I could keep off Owen Roe [3] and Ormond from joining it would be a good service." To a further question he answered no less positively.

Aug. 10. Scot's report cn the convention with O'Neill.

"I deny expressly," he said, "that I had any advice or direction from the Lord Lieutenant of Ireland or from the Council of State or from Parliament or any member of either ; but I did it only on my own score, considering it was for the preservation of the English interest there, and that they have had some fruits thereof accordingly." On this, the House, after perfunctorily censuring the agreement,

Monk censured and excused.

----

[1] See p. 83, note 4.

[2] "What we have greatest reason to take notice of was a letter from Oliver to the Council of State, wherein he certifies in the behalf of Colonel Monk, the bearer, how well he did approve of the reasons he gave for endeavouring a conjunction with O'Neill, but, because the soldiery were much startled at the news thereof and many deserted him only on that ground, he therefore desired that the design might be wholly disowned by the House, and get the Colonel cleared, and something published to give satisfaction to the people." *Merc. Pragmaticus*, E, 569, 7. The evidence is not of a high order, but it is likely that the story was true in the main, and that Cromwell thought Monk justified in concluding a cessation for three months for practical reasons, though he disliked any actual combination with O'Neill, and agreed, on that score, with popular opinion. The dates favour the supposition that Cromwell was consulted. Monk left London on the night of Aug. 1, and was back on the 7th, so far as can be inferred from an Order of the Council of State relating to the affair being dated on that day. Milford Haven is 257 miles from London.

[3] *I.e.* Owen Roe O'Neill.

declared that as Monk's motives had been good, he should not 'at any time be called in question.'[1]

Monk's steadfast adherence to military duty would in itself have been enough to secure Cromwell's goodwill, and Cromwell certainly had no wish to blame him for the act by which he had sheltered 'the English interest' in the North from the storm by which it had been threatened. It can hardly be doubted that Monk seized the opportunity of his visit to Milford Haven to warn Cromwell against the danger of throwing his whole force into Munster. Jones's victory was not at that time known in England, and Cromwell's plans must have been affected by the tidings that Drogheda and Dundalk were in the hands of the Royalists, and that the way to Dublin lay open to the march of Montgomery and the Scots. In any case it appears to have been about this time that Cromwell resolved not to betake himself in person to Munster, but to send thither two-thirds of his army under Ireton, whilst the remaining third proceeded, under his own command, to Dublin. He was now ready to set out. The money he needed had arrived, and some signs of mutiny which had showed themselves amongst his troops died away. On August 12, as he was preparing to embark, he was gladdened by the news of Ormond's defeat. "This," he wrote, "is an astonishing mercy, so great and seasonable that we are like them that dreamed. . . . These things seem to strengthen our faith and love against more difficult times. Sir, pray for me that I may walk worthy of the Lord in all that He hath called me unto."[2]

On August 13 Cromwell sailed with his portion of the army. The sea was rough, and Hugh Peters, who had been on board before the sailing of the expedition, noted that 'the Lord Lieutenant was as sea-sick as ever I saw a man in my life.'[3] On the 15th

Marginal notes: Monk gains Cromwell's goodwill. / Cromwell's army to be divided. / Aug. 12. He hears of Jones's victory. / Aug. 13. Cromwell sails, / Aug. 15. and lands in Dublin.

[1] *C.J.* vi. 277.

[2] Cromwell to Mayor, Aug. 13, *Carlyle*, Letter C.

[3] Peters to the Council of State, Aug. 16, *A Perfect Diurnal*, E, 532, 32.

Cromwell landed in Dublin. Before many days he was re-joined by Ireton and the remainder of the army. Ireton's change of plan was publicly ascribed to the direction of the wind,[1] but there is some reason to think that he had expected to be admitted into Youghal by the treachery of its governor, Sir Pierce Smith, and that his hopes had been baffled by Inchiquin's arrest of those who had been entrusted with its defence.[2] Not long after Ireton reached Dublin Hugh Peters arrived with the stragglers left behind at Milford Haven for want of shipping to convey them.[3]

---

[1] Peters to the Council of State, Aug. •16, *Great Britain's Painful Messenger*, E, 571, 22; *The Moderate*, E, 571, 7; *The Moderate Intelligencer*, E, 572, 10; *Perf. Occurrences*, E, 532, 29.

[2] "We have also certain assurance . . . that the crossness of the winds was not the only cause that drave Ireton into Youghal Road, but the hopes he had of being admitted to land there—as formerly he thought to have done at Cork but failed of it—by the treachery of Pierce Smith, the Governor of Youghal, who had contracted with Cromwell to deliver the town to him for 2,000*l*." Inchiquin, continues the writer, had arrested Smith, and so baffled the design, *Merc. Elencticus*, E, 573, 2. *The Moderate Intelligencer* (E, 572, 26), after attributing Ireton's return to a calm of six days, prints a letter from Chester in which it is said that 'Major-General Ireton designed for Munster, hovering at Cabel Island' (*i.e.* Capel Island off Knockadoon Head) 'some days, did not see ground to put in there.' The same newspaper states that 'Inchiquin hath purged all Munster garrisons of such as he suspected might prove friends to the Lord Lieutenant.'

[3] Peters to ——, Sept. 1, *Perf. Occurrences*, E, 533, 1.

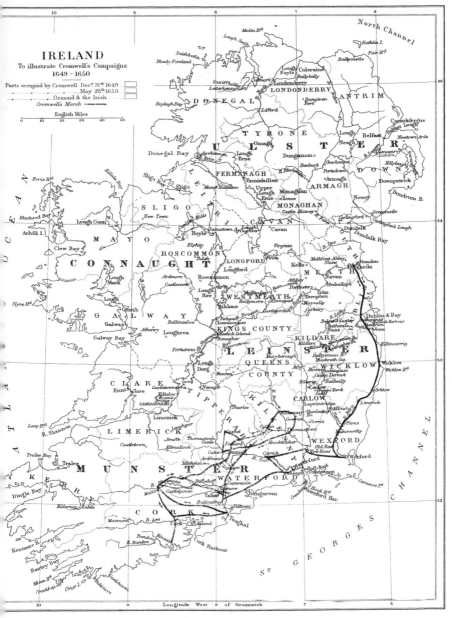

IRELAND
To illustrate Cromwell's Campaigns
1649 – 1650

Parts occupied by Cromwell Dec.r 31.st 1649
" " " May 26.th 1650
Ormond & the Irish
Cromwell's March

English Miles
0   10   20   30   40   50

Longmans, Green & Co. London, New York & Bombay.

CHAPTER V

DROGHEDA AND WEXFORD

THE first news which met Cromwell on his landing was that Ormond, whose constancy in adversity was as great as his helplessness in action, had reinforced the garrison of Drogheda, and that Jones had been repulsed in an attempt to surprise the town. Whatever might be Cromwell's ultimate design, it was imperative on him to begin by mastering Drogheda, and thus to gain command of the road along which the Ulster Scots would advance if they came to Ormond's relief.

Aug. Jones fails to take Drogheda.

Importance of the place.

By this time, indeed, Cromwell had to guard himself against a new foe in the North of Ireland. O'Neill had already discovered that his convention with Monk had gained him nothing. That convention expired on the last day of July, and early in August the Ulster chieftain proposed to Ormond through Sir Luke Fitzgerald to renew the dropped negotiations with the Royalist party,[1] and about the same time he dispatched a certain Fitzmorris to urge Rupert to support his request. O'Neill, therefore, did not wait to hear that his convention with Monk had been disavowed at Westminster. It was enough for him that it had not been renewed at the date of its expiry.[2]

Aug. O'Neill's overtures to Ormond.

[1] See p. 76.

[2] Ormond to Clanricarde, Aug. 8; Rupert to Ormond, Aug. 12; *Carte MSS.* xxv. 193, 240. The first of these letters, written from Kilkenny, mentions that O'Neill's overtures had reached Fitzgerald, which implies that they had been sent off by O'Neill at least four or five days before the 8th, whilst O'Neill's convention was not denounced at Westminster till the 10th. Letters purporting to be Ormond's were about

Whatever might be the course of this negotiation, O'Neill had no intention of neglecting any opportunity of possessing himself of ammunition, whether it was to be had from Ormond O'Neill's or from Ormond's enemies. Even before he sent dealings with messages to Ormond and Rupert he had come to Coote. an understanding with Coote, the Parliamentary governor of Londonderry, to break up the siege,[1] on condition of receiving three hundred oxen and thirty barrels of powder.[2] Little as O Neill cared for either of the parties contending for the soil of his country, he never forgot to perform punctually what he had promised on the word of a soldier. On August 7 Aug. 7-9. he appeared within sight of Londonderry, and on He relieves London- th 9th the Royalist army under Montgomery and derry. Monro marched away. For some days O'Neill loyally co-operated with Coote, capturing the fortresses which girdled Londonderry with Scottish garrisons.

Whatever may have been O'Neill's real feelings before, there can be little doubt that the reception of the news of Ormond's defeat at Rathmines settled his determina- He resolves to join tion to ally himself with Ormond rather than with Ormond. Coote. "Gentlemen," he is reported to have said to his officers, "to demonstrate to the world that I value the service of my King and the welfare of my nation, as I always did, I now forget and forgive the Supreme Council and my enemies their ill practices, and all the wrongs they did me from time to time, and will now embrace that peace which I formerly denied out of a good intent." [3] There was doubtless something of impetuous generosity in the words in which O'Neill announced

this time printed in London, but they were mere forgeries. Ormond had lost his cipher at Rathmines, and did not dare to write secrets when there was danger of their being disclosed.   [1] See p. 78.

[2] Col. Henry O'Neill's relation, Gilbert's *Cont. Hist. of Irish Affairs*, vol. iii. 211. This seems the most trustworthy statement. Sir R. Stewart, writing to Charles on $\frac{Oct. 25}{Nov. 4}$, says that O'Neill had 5,000*l.* and some oxen, *Carte MSS.* cxxx. fol. 94.

[3] Henry O'Neill (*Gilbert*, iii. 211) is mistaken in thinking that Daniel O'Neill was with Owen when these words were spoken, but this does not militate against the general truthfulness of his narrative.

his intention of restoring the fortunes of his King; but there was probably also the shrewd calculation that his country was more in danger from Cromwell than from Ormond, and that he would serve her best by throwing all his weight into the scale of the weaker party.

Ormond had gathered from O'Neill's overtures that he might look to him for aid in his dire necessity. On August 12

Aug. 12.
Ormond
asks help
from
O'Neill, he entreated him ' to bring those seasonable and, we hope, real inclinations which we hear you have lately expressed to his Majesty's service to a due and wished-for perfection.' On the same day he urged

as well as
from Mont-
gomery, Montgomery to bring up his Scots at once. In a letter to Clanricarde on the 13th his sanguine nature

Aug. 13.
and Clanri-
carde. once more asserted itself; when the troops he now expected had come up, he would, he said, be able ' to attempt the reduction of Dublin.' [1]

Such was the position of affairs when Cromwell landed. Until this cloud in the North had been dispersed, his Munster scheme must be postponed. He knew, however, that there was scarcely one of Inchiquin's officers who was not eager to change sides, and he therefore released some of them who had been taken at Rathmines, sending them to Munster, with as-

Cromwell's
message to
Munster. surances that his coming would be as little delayed as possible.[2] For the present he must strain every

He aims at
Drogheda. nerve to break up Ormond's new combination, and the first blow must be aimed at Drogheda that it might not serve as a screen behind which Ormond could collect the scattered forces on which he counted for the renewal of the campaign. He could not, however, move at

Jones's regi-
ments re-
organised. once. His men required rest after their voyage, and Jones's regiments had to be re-organised to fit them to take part in the coming campaign.[3]

---

[1] Ormond to O'Neill, Aug. 12; Ormond to Montgomery, Aug. 12; Gilbert's *Cont. Hist. of Aff. in Irel.* vol. ii. 227, 229; Ormond to Clanricarde, Aug. 13, *Carte MSS.* xxv. fol. 252.

[2] Phayre's Deposition, Caulfield's *Council Book of the Corporation of Cork*, 1164.

[3] *The Moderate* (E, 573, 7) says they were ' dissolute and debauched,'

Cromwell was determined that under his command the plundering habits of the soldiery in Ireland should be abandoned.

Aug. 24.
Cromwell's
Declaration.

On August 24 he issued a declaration ordering that no violence was to be offered to the life or property of persons not in arms. A market would be opened in his camp where ready money would be paid to all who brought provisions for sale. Those who wished to remain in their homes would, on payment of contributions fairly imposed, be protected in their persons and estates till January 1, when they would have to apply to the Attorney-General for what further protection they might require.[1]

Whilst Cromwell was, out of necessity, tarrying at Dublin, Ormond was doing everything in his power to strengthen Drogheda.

Aug. 17.
Ormond at
Drogheda.

On the 17th he appeared in person in the town, and superseded Lord Moore, who had been appointed Governor by Inchiquin, in favour of Sir Arthur Aston,[2] a Catholic officer who had been Governor of Reading in 1643 and of Oxford in 1644.

Aug. 24.
Sir Arthur
Aston appointed
Governor.

In the latter employment he had lost a leg through a fall from his horse,[3] and the wooden substitute had made him a well-known figure in Charles's army. He was no less notorious for his stern and unbending nature.

On August 30, by which time all the regiments detailed for service had marched in, the garrison was composed of 2,871 men including officers.[4]

Aug. 30.
Numbers of
the garrison.

They were in truth the flower of Ormond's army; his own regiment, under the command of Sir Edmund Verney, having lately arrived to support the three foot regiments which were already in the place when it was attacked by Jones. Of the other three regiments one under Colonel Byrne which had been left behind

but, according to *Perfect Occurrences*, it was a mere matter of the thinness of the ranks. Two regiments had to be combined into one, and the superfluous officers got rid of.

[1] *A Declaration*, Aug. 24, *Carlyle*, following Letter cii.

[2] Commission to Aston, Aug. 24, *Carte MSS.* clxii. fol. 46.

[3] Wood's *Fasti*, Ann. 1644.

[4] Garrison in . . . Drogheda, Aug. 30, Gilbert's *Cont. Hist. of Aff. in Irel.* vol. ii. 496. There were 2,552 foot and 319 horse.

by Inchiquin was composed of Englishmen and Protestants, whilst the other two under Wall and Warren were for the most part, if not altogether, composed of Irish Catholics. Of Ormond's own regiment we have no certain information, but if it was, as may reasonably be supposed, levied in the neighbourhood of Kilkenny, it is not likely that there were many Englishmen or Protestants to be found in its ranks. The seven troops of horse were mainly composed of Irish Catholics.[1]

It is mainly composed of Irish.

Whilst Ormond was thus, as he fondly hoped, securing Drogheda against danger, he was unremitting in his urgency with O'Neill to hasten to its aid. On August 23 he dispatched the Catholic Bishop of Raphoe and Colonel Audley Mervyn to press him to march at once.[2] Mervyn took the opportunity of deserting to Coote. On September 1 the bishop reported that he had received a friendly message from O'Neill excusing himself from receiving him, on the ground 'that he was in Sir Charles's quarters,' and 'that his honour was engaged, which to him was dearer than his life.' The bishop shrewdly suspected that O'Neill was waiting for payment of the money still due to him from Coote. O'Neill, added the bishop, had with him about 5,000 foot and 300 horse, but would have no difficulty in increasing his army to 10,000 foot and 2,000 horse.[3]

Aug. 23. Ormond sends to O'Neill.

Sept. 1. O'Neill hangs back.

No wonder Ormond was eager to obtain the assistance of

[1] When Jones appeared before Drogheda the two regiments which had just marched in ' had scarce time to quarter themselves conveniently, much less to contract such an acquaintance with the inhabitants, who were, for the most part, English ; or the regiment of English commanded there by one Colonel Byrne since the taking of it by the Lord Inchiquin, as was in truth necessary for the security of each other's fidelity and concurrence in the defence of so important a garrison.' *Narrative of Military Operations, Carte MSS.* xxvi. fol. 440. According to the *Moderate Intelligencer,* ' Sir A. Aston chose rather to have Irish than English for his garrison.' E, 573, 19.

[2] Ormond to O'Neill, Aug. 23, Gilbert's *Cont. Hist. of Aff. in Irel.* vol. ii. 230 ; Instructions to the Bishop of Raphoe and Col. Mervyn, Aug. 23, *Carte MSS.* xxv. fol. 351.

[3] The Bishop of Raphoe to Ormond, Sept. 1, *ib.* fol. 442.

such a force.   He had himself taken up a position at Tecro-

Ormond at
Tecroghan. ghan, the house of Sir Luke Fitzgerald in the south-
western corner of Meath, ready, if occasion served, to
carry aid to the defenders of Drogheda ; but he had with him
merely a small force of 1,000 horse, and though he hoped to
make up his numbers to 4,000 foot and to 2,400 horse, he based
his expectations only on the problematical arrival of a detachment
from the Ulster Scots, of Clanricarde's men from Connaught, and
of a detachment which he expected Inchiquin to send him from
Munster.[1]   Even before the bishop's despatch was written, Or-

Mission of
Daniel
O'Neill. mond, to add weight to his mission, had sent after him
Daniel O'Neill, who had negotiated with his uncle,
Owen O'Neill, in the spring.   On September 5, Or-

Sept. 5.
Finds Owen
O'Neill. mond's new emissary wrote that he had found Owen
at Ballykelly, twelve miles east of Londonderry, and

O'Neill's
sickness. therefore still in Coote's quarters, but unable to move
as quickly as he wished on account of a swelling in
his knee.   "This day," added Daniel, " he has a litter made for
him ; if to-morrow he has any manner of ease he intends to
march.   Whether it be his sickness or that he intends to oblige
your Excellency the more, he has not talked anything as yet

His eager-
ness to help
Ormond. of his conditions.   All his officers to a very few, and
those of least consideration, are as passionate for his
submission to his Majesty's service as Sir Luke Fitzgerald would have them.   The number of foot he hopes to bring
your Excellency will be near 6,000, and about 500 horse, truly
not so contemptible for their number as some persuaded me
they were ; they are well horsed and armed to a very few." [2]

Sept. 1.
Cromwell
leaves
Dublin. Ormond's forces, in short, were scattered whilst
his opponent's were well in hand.   On September 1
Cromwell, having sent Michael Jones in advance, set

Sept. 3.
Cromwell
before
Drogheda. out from Dublin.   On the 3rd his whole army,
numbering about 10,000 men, was before Drogheda.
On his way he was gladdened by the desertion of

---

[1] Ormond to Clanricarde, Aug. 21, *Carte MSS.* xxv. fol. 337.

[2] D. O'Neill to Ormond, Sept. 5, Gilbert's *Cont. Hist. of Aff. in
Irel.* vol. ii. 251.

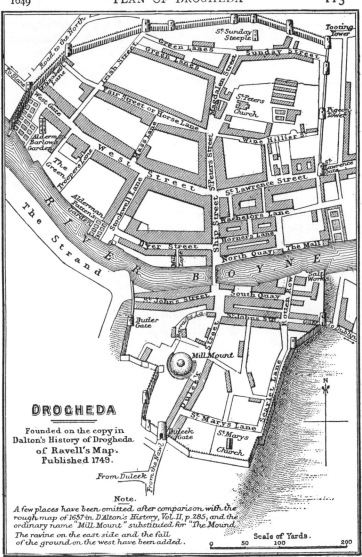

DROGHEDA

Founded on the copy in
Dalton's History of Drogheda
of Ravell's Map.
Published 1749.

From Duleek

Note.

A few places have been omitted after comparison with the
rough map of 1657 in D'Alton's History, Vol. II, p. 285, and the
ordinary name "Mill Mount" substituted for "The Mound".
The ravine on the east side and the fall
of the ground on the west have been added.

Scale of Yards.
0　　50　　100　　　　200

F.S.Weller.

Captain Wentworth from the enemy with 150 of Inchiquin's horse, forming part of the cavalry which was with Ormond at Tecroghan. The divisions between English and Irish in the hostile ranks were beginning to serve Cromwell well.[1] It would still, however, be some days before batteries could be opened. Trenches had to be dug and the siege cannon brought by sea from Dublin.

In one way Drogheda was admirably situated for resistance. It was divided into two parts, separated by the deep channel of the Boyne, and only joined by a single bridge. It was therefore impossible for a besieger, unless his numbers were far greater than those of which Cromwell could dispose, to assail it on both sides, or even to stop the entrance of supplies. On the other hand, these advantages would be of little value unless Ormond had a force outside strong enough to make use of them, and it soon became evident that he was in too destitute a condition to aid the garrison. On September 8 Aston informed Ormond that his ammunition was running short, his money spent, his stock of provisions low. On the 9th he begged Ormond to fall on the camp of the enemy.[2] Neither he nor his subordinates, however, allowed their courage to fail. " Warren and Wall," wrote Verney to Ormond, "are my most intimate comrades, and indeed I have not in my life known more of diligence and circumspection than in these two gentlemen. We ordinarily meet once a day to discourse of our condition and what is fit to be done. . . . We are informed that your Excellency hath a considerable army, and our humble opinions have been that you might advance and lodge at Slane Bridge with safety, and that the enemy could no way force you to fight unless to their

Margin notes:
Situation of Drogheda.

Sept. 8.
Wants of the garrison.

Sept. 9.
Verney's letter.

---

[1] *The Kingdom's Weekly Intelligencer*, E, 373, 10; · *A Moderate Narrative*, E, 574, 17 ; Narrative of Military Operations, *Carte MSS.* xxvi. fol. 440.   Sir Theophilus Jones, Michael's brother, was left behind as temporary Governor of Dublin.

[2] Aston to Ormond, Sept. 5, 8, 9, Gilbert's *Cont. Hist. of Aff. in Irel.* vol. ii. 250, 253, 258.

infinite disadvantage, and certainly they could much less maintain their siege ; their camp is much subject to wants, they bringing their supplies by sea."[1]

Unhappily for the besieged, Ormond had no 'considerable army' to dispose of, and the preparations of the enemy were

Sept. 10.
Cromwell
summons
Aston and
opens a
cannonade.

De'ences
of Drog-
heda.

being rapidly completed. On the 10th Cromwell summoned Aston to surrender, and on his rejection of the offer opened a steady cannonade. Both parts of the town rising steeply from the river were protected by a high wall of the mediæval type, and it was against the southern face of this wall that Cromwell's attack was necessarily directed. A deep ravine protected the eastern wall of the southern part against attack, whilst there was a less pronounced falling away of the ground on the western side. Here, however, the comparative weakness of the barrier was supplemented by a huge artificial mound known as the Mill Mount, on two sides of which the western wall ran, making a re-entering angle, the southern wall being therefore the only assailable part of the defences on the southern bank of the Boyne. Near the western end of this southern wall was the Duleek Gate, whilst just behind its eastern extremity was St. Mary's Church, offering a strong position to the defenders.

Against the wall at the south-eastern corner and the church behind it, Cromwell had erected two batteries. By the evening

Position of
Cromwell's
batteries.

of the 10th he had demolished the steeple of the church, had made a small breach apparently near the corner of the wall, and another more considerable in its southern face.[2]

---

[1] Verney to Ormond, Sept. 9, *Carte MSS.* xxv. fol. 501.

[2] Cromwell speaks of breaches ' on the east and south wall,' and of both being stormed. It seems impossible that he should have stormed across the ravine, and it is therefore probable that by the east wall he means the eastern end of the south wall. The story of the siege is given in Cromwell's despatch to Le' thall (*Carlyle*, Letter cv.), which should be compared with Hewson's letter in *Perfect Occurrences*, E, 533, 15, and two anonymous letters in *The Kingdom's Faithful and Impartial Scout*, E, 533, 16.

Though even the larger breach was not yet practicable, Aston had little doubt what would be the result of the next

Aston
resolves
to die at
his post.

day's cannonade. "The soldiers," he wrote to Ormond, "say well—I pray God, do well. I will assure your Excellency speedy help is much desired. I refer all things unto your Excellency's provident care. Living I am, and dying will end, my Lord, your Excellency's most faithful and most obliged humble servant, Arthur Aston." Then came a postscript referring to a letter just received, in which Ormond had announced that Colonel Trevor was approaching with supplies from Dundalk. "I hear nothing," wrote Aston, "nor have not done, of Colonel Trevor. My ammunition decays apace, and I cannot help it." [1]

These were the last written words of a brave and honourable soldier. On the day on which they were penned Ormond

Ormond
disap-
pointed of
succour.

heard of O'Neill's sickness, and of the uselessness of expecting immediate help from that quarter.[2] Neither Inchiquin nor Clanricarde had sent the reinforcements on which he had counted, and though Trevor was on the way, he advanced so slowly that it was hardly possible for him to arrive in time.

On the morning of the 11th, whilst Cromwell's batteries were enlarging the breach, the defenders of Drogheda were not

Sept. 11.
Prepara-
tions for
the de-
fence.

idle. They threw up a triple line of earthworks, starting from behind the church, and reaching to the wall on either side, so as to form a protection after the enemy had poured over the outer defences. It was not till five in the afternoon that Cromwell gave the word

The storm.

to storm. Three regiments—those of Ewer, Hewson, and Castle—rushed up the perilous slope, and endeavoured to surmount the fragments of the broken wall. They were met by hearts as stout as their own. Twice [3] they

---

[1] Aston to Ormond, Sept. 10, Gilbert's *Cont. Hist. of Aff. in Irel.* vol. ii. 259.

[2] Ormond to D. O'Neill, Sept. 11, *ib.* 261.

[3] Cromwell writes of only one repulse, but even his own narrative countenances the other witnesses who mention two.

were hurled back with loss, Colonel Castle being amongst the slain. Then Cromwell himself leapt forward to head the baffled column to one last attempt. Encouraged by their great captain's word and presence, the men whom he had so often led to victory showed themselves invincible. The breach so hotly contested was won at last, and the English veterans,

The position round St. Mary's carried.

when once they had poured over the broken rampart, carried the newly raised earthworks as well. Unless the accounts of those few Royalists who survived are to be altogether rejected, many of the defenders were at this time admitted to quarter.[1]

Whilst the mass of the defeated garrison fled hurriedly down the sloping streets to gain the bridge, Aston and his principal officers, followed by some three hundred of

Aston on the Mill Mount.

the soldiers of the garrison, climbed the lofty steep of the Mill Mount, either to seek a refuge or to sell their lives as dearly as they could. It is possible that Cromwell, heated by the passion of the fight, ascribed their action to the latter motive. Cromwell's rages were never premeditated, and it always required some touch of concrete fact to arouse the slumbering wrath which lay coiling about his heart. Was the struggle, he may well have thought, not to be

---

[1] Sir Lewis Dyves, writing some months after the event, expressed his belief that Aston would have made his defence good 'had not Colonel Wall's regiment, after the enemy had been twice bravely repulsed, upon the unfortunate loss of their colonel in the third assault, been so unhappily dismayed as to listen, before they had need, unto the enemy offering quarter, and admitted them in upon these terms, thereby betraying both themselves and all their fellow-soldiers to the slaughter.' *A Letter from Sir L. Dyves*, E, 616, 7. Ormond, writing to Byron nearer the time, says that Cromwell carried the breach on the third assault, ' all his officers and soldiers promising quarter to such as would lay down their arms, and performing it as long as any place held out, which encouraged others to yield ; but when they had once all in their power and feared no hurt that could be done them, the word " No quarter !" went round.' Ormond to Byron, Sept. 29, Gilbert's *Cont. Hist. of Aff. in Irel.* vol. ii. 271. This account is doubtless too highly coloured, but it is unlikely that the statement that quarter was offered is without foundation.

ended after he had burst over wall and entrenchment? [1]   At
all events, it was not till he reached the foot of that mighty
mound that a command to put to the sword all who were upon
the height above rose to Cromwell's lips.   The law
of war as it stood then, and long afterwards, [2]
authorised him to give the order to slay the
defenders of an indefensible post, and what better
evidence would there be that the post was indefensible than
that its appointed guardians had failed to make good their
ground?

Cromwell
orders the
slaughter
of the de-
fenders.

The deed of horror was all Cromwell's own.   Till he spoke
the words of fate, the soldiers above were breaking down the
defences of the Mount, and some of them were
offering quarter to its defenders. [3]   Cromwell's order
put an end to these proffers of mercy, and with few

Massacre
on the Mill
Mount.

[1] To appreciate the probability that this thought must have come into
Cromwell's mind, it is necessary to have stood at the foot of the Mill
Mount.

[2] Mr. Firth has drawn my attention to the following extract from one
of Wellington's letters : " I believe it has always been understood that
the defenders of a fortress stormed have no claim to quarter ; and the
practice which prevailed during the last century of surrendering a fortress
when a breach was opened in the body of the place, and the counterscarp
had been blown in, was founded on this understanding.   Of late years the
French have availed themselves of the humanity of modern warfare, and
have made a new regulation that a breach should stand one assault at
least.   The consequence of this regulation was to me the loss of the flower
of the army in the assaults of Ciudad Rodrigo and of Badajoz.   I certainly
should have thought myself justified in putting both garrisons to the
sword ; and if I had done so to the first, it is probable I should have
saved 5,000 men in the assault of the second.   I mention this in order to
show you that the practice of refusing quarter to a garrison which stands
an assault is not a useless effusion of blood."   Wellington to Canning,
Feb. 3, 1820.   *Despatches, Correspondence, and Memoranda of Arthur,
Duke of Wellington*, I, 93.

[3] This is shown in the only full account of the taking of the Mill
Mount from the Parliamentary side.   "The mount was very strong of
itself, and manned with 250 of their principal men, Sir Arthur Aston being
in it, who was Governor of the town, which, when they saw their men
retreat, were so cast down and disheartened that they thought it in vain to

exceptions the Royalists on the Mill Mount were butchered as they stood. Aston's head, it is said, was beaten in with his own wooden leg, which the soldiers had torn away in the belief that he had concealed treasure in it.[1] Still Cromwell's wrath was not satiated. In the heat of action there stood out in his mind, through the blood-red haze of war, thoughts of vengeance to be taken for the Ulster massacre confusedly mingled with visions of peace more easily secured by instant severity. Save at the storming of Basing House, he had never yet exercised the rights which the stern law of war placed in his hands ; but

None in arms to be spared.

he had one measure for Protestants and another for ' Papists,' and especially for Irish ' Papists.' The stern command to put all to the sword who ' were in arms in the town,' leapt lightly from his lips.

Then ensued a scene, the like of which had seldom been witnessed in the English war. Amidst shrieks and groans and

A general massacre of the garrison.

shouts of triumph, pike and sword plied their fiendish work down the sloping streets. The flying wretches were in no case to block the narrow passage of the bridge, and the slaughter continued as pursuers and pursued breasted the steep hill on the northern side of the Boyne. A thousand were slain in or around St. Peter's Church at the top of the hill.

When Cromwell came up he found that about eighty had

The refugees in St. Peter's steeple.

taken refuge in the steeple. These he summoned to surrender to mercy, but such a summons did not necessarily imply that their lives would be spared,

make any further resistance, which, if they had, would have killed some hundreds of our men before we could have taken it. Lieutenant-Colonel Axtell, of Colonel Hewson's regiment, with some twelve of his men, went up to the top of the mount and demanded of the Governor the surrender of it ; who was very stubborn, speaking very big words, but at length was persuaded to go into the windmill on the top of the mount, and as many more of the chiefest of them as it would contain, where they were disarmed, and afterwards all slain." Letter from Drogheda, *Perf. Diurnal*, E, 553, 17.

[1] After his death, however, 200 gold pieces were found in his girdle. Wood's *Fasti*, ii. 72 ; Ludlow's *Memoirs* (ed. 1751), i. 261.

and hopeless as their position was they refused the offer. After a fruitless attempt to blow up the tower with gunpowder, Cromwell gave orders to drag the seats in the church beneath it and to set them on fire. As the flames gained the structure above, the unhappy victims attempted to escape to the roof. Some fifty of them were there killed by the soldiers, whilst the remaining thirty perished in the burning steeple. The authors of this cruel deed comforted themselves by recording the imprecations of the tortured wretches, as if no fate could be too horrible for men who died with profane oaths upon their lips.[1]

The steeple burnt.

On the following morning it having been discovered that a few survivors who had taken refuge in two towers in the wall refused to yield, Cromwell set a guard to watch them till hunger drove them down. From one of the towers shots were fired, and some of the watch were killed and wounded. When the inevitable surrender came, Cromwell, instead of directing a promiscuous slaughter, ordered that the officers should be ' knocked on the head, and every tenth man of the soldiers shipped for the Barbados,' whilst the whole garrison of the other tower was spared, though they too were sent to Barbados.[2]

Sept. 12.
Two towers captured.

---

[1] In *Perfect Occurrences* (E, 533, 15) we are told that ' they refusing to come down, the steeple was fired, and then fifty of them got out at the top of the church, but the enraged soldiers put them all to the sword, and thirty of them were burnt in the fire, some of them cursing and crying out " God damn them ! " and cursed their souls as they were burning.' I have added some particulars from a tract by Dr. Bernard lent me by Mr. Firth. Its title-page is lost, so that I am unable to quote it more precisely.

[2] Cromwell to Lenthall, Sept. 17, *Carlyle*, Letter cv. It will be seen that I have made no use of the story told by Thomas Wood, a soldier in Cromwell's army, to his mother and his brother the antiquary, Anthony Wood, in 1650, and related by the latter in his own life, prefixed to *Ath. Oxonienses.* " He told them," writes the latter, " that 3,000 at least, besides women and children, were, after the assailants had taken part and afterwards all the town, put to the sword on Sept. 11 and 12, 1649 ; . . . that when they were to make their way up the lofts and galleries in the church and up to the tower where the enemy had fled, each of the assailants would take up a child and use [it] as a buckler of defence when

With these exceptions Cromwell showed no pity. What
was worse, even the few who by the connivance of the soldiers
had escaped death on the Mill Mount were sought out and
killed in cold blood. Amongst these was Verney,
Death of
Verney and the noble son of a noble father, who was enticed even
Boyle, from the presence of Cromwell by a certain Roper,
who then ' ran him through with a tuck.' Lieutenant-Colonel

they ascended the steps, to keep themselves from being shot or brained.
After they had killed all in the church, they went into the vaults under-
neath, where all the flower and choicest of the women and ladies had hid
themselves. One of these, a most handsome virgin, arrayed in costly and
gorgeous apparel, kneeled down to Thomas Wood with tears and prayers
to save her life ; and, being strucken with a profound pity, took her under
his arm, went with her out of the church with intentions to put her over
the works to shift for herself ; but a soldier, perceiving his intentions,
he ran his sword up her belly, . . . whereupon Mr. Wood, seeing her
gasping, took away her money, jewels, &c., and flung her down over the
works, &c."

Anthony further tells us that his brother had served as a Royalist, and,
having engaged in the Cavalier plot in 1648, had fled to Ireland, where,
to escape the gallows, he became an officer in the regiment of Colonel
Henry Ingoldsby. Ingoldsby said of him that he was 'a good soldier,
stout and venturous, and, having an art of merriment called buffooning,
his company was desired and loved by the officers of his regiment.' Just
the sort of man, in short, to invent a story to shock his mother and his
steady, antiquarian brother.

This suspicion is confirmed by Dr. Bernard, to whose tract I have
referred in the last note. He was the preacher at St. Peter's, and lived
hard by. He narrates at some length the dangers which he had himself
escaped, and then proceeds to tell what happened in the church. "Not
long afterwards," he says, " came Colonel Hewson, and told the Doctor
he had orders to blow up the steeple (which stood between the choir and
the body of the church), where about threescore men were run up for
refuge, but the three barrels of powder which he had caused to be put
under it for that end, blew up only the body of the church, and the next
night "—this should have been ' the same night '—" Hewson caused the
seats of the church to be broken up, and made a great pile of them under
the steeple, which, firing it, took the lofts wherein five great bells hung,
and from thence it flamed up to the top, and so at once men and bells and
roof came all down together, the most hideous sight and terrible that ever
he was witness of at once." Not only does Bernard say nothing of Wood's

Boyle was summoned from dinner by a soldier, and shot as soon as he had left the room.[1]   Though we have no particulars of the deaths of Colonel Warren and Captain Finglas, it can hardly be doubted that they shared the fate of Verney and Boyle.[2]

and of
Warren
and Finglas.

It was not only upon the soldiers of the garrison that destruction fell.   Every friar in the town was knocked on the head, and a few civilians perished, either being mistaken for soldiers or through the mere frenzy of the conquerors.[3]

horrors, but he implicitly denies their existence when he writes that ' when that town was stormed and all that bare arms in it put to the sword.' Bernard was a strong Royalist, having taken a prominent part in proclaiming Charles II. at Drogheda.   He had been threatened with death by Cromwell and had no reason to spare him, especially as his tract was published after the Restoration.

In examining the story itself we come upon inherent improbabilities. It makes children to be found in the church, where they are said to have been caught up by the soldiers, and the women in the vaults beneath. Surely the children would have been with their mothers, either below, or, far more probably, in their own houses.   Moreover, when handsome virgins want to hide themselves on such an occasion, they are not accustomed to array themselves in jewels and gorgeous apparel.   After this it is hardly worth while to ask what Wood meant by saying he dropped the girl's corpse over the works.   The works were high walls—at least twenty feet high.   Did he really take the trouble to climb up for the purpose ?

[1]   Lady Verney's *Verney Family*, ii. 344.

[2]   " Many men and some officers have made their escapes out of Drogheda. . . .   All conclude that no man [had] quarter with Cromwell's leave ; that yet many were privately saved by officers and soldiers ; that the Governor was killed in the Mill Mount after quarter given by the officer that came first there ; that some of the towers were defended until yesterday, quarter being denied them ; and that yesterday morning the towers wherein they were were blown up ; that Verney, Finglas, Warren, and some other officers were alive in the hands of some of Cromwell's officers twenty-four hours after the business was done, but whether their lives were obtained at Cromwell's hands, or that they are yet living, they cannot tell."   Inchiquin to Ormond, Sept. 15, Gilbert's *Cont. Hist. of Aff. in Irel.* vol. ii. Pref. xxviii.

[3]   Carlyle was exceedingly indignant with the editor of the Old Parliamentary History for printing a postscript to one of Cromwell's letters, in which a list of the slain soldiers is given with the addition ' and many

When all was over Cromwell appears to have felt the
necessity of justifying himself.   On the 12th he despatched

Sept. 12.
Cromwell
excuses
himself.
Venables with a compact force to recover Dundalk,
and gave him a letter to the Royalist governor of
that town.   " I offered mercy," he wrote, " to the

inhabitants,' which he says has no authority in contemporary copies.   It,
however, appears in the official contemporary copy in *Letters from Ireland*,
E, 575, 7.   Dr. Bernard's experience, as told in the pamphlet referred to
in the note to p. 120, throws some light on the question.   After telling
how the mayor and other principal Protestants took refuge in his house,
and how it was the first to be attacked after the town was fully taken, he
proceeds as follows :   " There came five or six who were sent from a
principal officer—the Doctor's former acquaintance – under a pretence of a
guard for his house, but had a command from him, as soon as they were
entered, to kill him, which an ear-witness hath since assured him of.   The
Doctor denying to open the door to them, one of them discharged a musket
bullet at him ; it passed through the door, and only fired the skin of one
of his fingers, leaving a spot upon it, which burned four or five days
after, and did him no more hurt.

" Then a cornet of a troop of horse came to his relief, and pretending
he had order from the General to take care of that house, the soldiers
withdrew, and so at a back door he brought in his quartermaster, whom
he left to secure him.   About a quarter of an hour after another troop of
horse came to the window, and demanded the opening of the door.   The
quartermaster and himself, with an old servant, left him . . . stood close
together, and told them it was the minister's house, and all therein were
Protestants.   As soon as they heard the Doctor named and his voice, one
of them discharged his pistol at him, wherein being a brace of bullets, with
the one the quartermaster was shot quite through the body, and died in
the place, and the other shot his servant through the throat, but recovered ;
the Doctor only was untouched."   Ultimately the soldiers betook themselves to plunder the house till the arrival of Ewer, who turned them
out.

This was written after the Restoration, but in a sermon preached in
Feb. 1649, appended to the third edition of *The Penitent Death of a
Woful Sinner*, p. 310 (1121, b. 19), Bernard speaks of the storming of the
town " when not only your goods —according to the custom of war—were
made a spoil of, but your lives were in the like danger, and were in an
equal hazard, but by a special providence of God was preserved."   This
is hardly language which would have been used if more than a very few of
the inhabitants had been killed, and it is therefore possible that ' the many

garrison of Drogheda [1] in sending the Governor a summons before I attempted the taking of it, which being refused brought this evil upon them.   If you being warned thereby, shall surrender your garrison to the use of the Parliament of England . . . you may thereby prevent effusion of blood. If upon refusing this offer, that which you like not befalls you, you will know whom to blame." [2]

Cromwell was probably the only man in the victorious army who imagined that what had taken place needed any excuse at all.[3]   The persistency with which he defended his conduct is sufficient evidence that his conscience was not altogether at ease.   " Truly," he wrote to Bradshaw on the 16th, " I believe this bitterness will save much effusion of blood through the goodness of God.   I wish that all honest hearts may give the glory of this to God alone, to whom indeed the praise of this mercy belongs."   On the following day, writing more fully to Lenthall, he brought forward yet another argument.   " I am persuaded," he wrote, " that this is a righteous judgment of God upon these barbarous wretches who have imbrued their hands in so much innocent blood, and that it will tend to prevent the effusion of blood for the future, which are the satisfactory grounds to such actions, which otherwise cannot but work remorse and regret." [4]

Cromwell further excuses himself.

Sept. 16.

Sept. 17.

inhabitants' was an exaggeration.   That any civilians were killed in Ireland without an attempt to punish their murderers, was afterwards explicitly denied by Cromwell.   "Give us," he wrote, "an instance of one man since my coming into Ireland, not in arms, massacred, destroyed, or banished, concerning the massacre or destruction of whom justice hath not been done, or attempted to be done." *Declaration* printed by Carlyle after Letter cxviii.

[1] ' Tredah ' in the original.

[2] Cromwell to the chief officer at Dundalk, Sept. 12, *Carlyle*, Letter ciii.

[3] When Monk's storm of Dundee in 1651 was followed by a massacre, he said nothing in his own justification.

[4] Cromwell to Bradshaw, Sept. 16 ; Cromwell to Lenthall, Sept. 17 ; *Carlyle*, Letters civ. cv.   It is necessary to keep in mind the prevalence

It is in the highest degree unlikely that any single man amongst the defenders of Drogheda had had a hand in the Ulster massacre ; but to Cromwell, as to the majority of Englishmen of his time, every Irishman, and still more every English defender of the Irish cause, had made himself an accomplice in the misdeeds of certain Irishmen. For that which appears now to have been the blackest part of his conduct, the killing of Verney and his companions in cold blood, twenty-four hours after the general massacre was ended, Cromwell made no excuse. If conjecture as to his motives be allowed, he may be credited with a determination that where the private soldiers had suffered, the English officers, whose guilt was, in his eyes, far greater, should not be permitted to escape.[1] Having once convinced himself that he was but executing justice on criminals, it was easy for Cromwell to bolster up his case with the further argument that the slaughter of well-nigh three thousand men would tend to prevent the effusion of blood. For a time, indeed, this horrible slaughter might procure for him an easy entrance into strongholds to which he would not otherwise have been readily admitted ; but, in the long run, the indignation caused by the butchery which he had ordered would steel the hearts of brave men to defy the worst rather than yield to the perpetrator of the massacre of Drogheda.

Of the thoughts and feelings of Irishmen, Cromwell took no heed.[2] " We are marching our army to Dublin," wrote Crom-

Examination of his arguments.

of a belief in the most exaggerated accounts of the Ulster massacre. Sir J. Temple's *Irish Rebellion*, in which they were contained, had been published in 1646, and they were again given in May's *Hist. of the Parliament* published in 1647.

[1] Elucidation of Cromwell's views on the criminality of the Irish will be found in his reply to the Declaration of the Prelates at Clonmacnoise ; see p. 147.

[2] Those modern critics who argue that Cromwell merely put in force the law of war, as exercised by Tilly and others, forget that the question is whether he did more than he had himself done in England. There, except at Basing House, he had been uniformly merciful. He now treated Irishmen worse than he treated Englishmen. This is the only thing of

well to Bradshaw on September 16, "and then shall, God
willing, advance towards the southern design—you know what

—only we think Wexford will be our first undertaking
in order to the other."[1] Wexford, in short, the home
of the privateers from which English commerce had
grievously suffered, was first to be taken and converted into a
basis of operations before Cromwell made his way into the
friendly districts on the Munster coast.

Before marching, Cromwell appointed Hewson Governor of
Dublin. As had been arranged before the army left England,

Hewson
Governor
of Dublin.

Michael
Jones to
be Lieu-
tenant-
General.

Success of
Venables
in the
North.

Michael Jones, who had previously held that post, was
now to serve as Lieutenant-General,[2] whilst the lower
office of Major-General was given to Ireton. Theophilus
Jones was sent to support Venables in the North.
Venables had very soon accomplished the greater part
of his task. Trim and Dundalk were abandoned by the
enemy without fighting, and Carlingford and Newry
submitted without difficulty.[3] Cromwell need have
no fear lest the Ulster Scots should advance to
Dublin in his absence.

importance. The question of his allowing prisoners, who had been
admitted to quarter, to be put to death stands apart. It was contrary to
the military practice of his own day. At the siege of Limerick Ireton
cashiered an officer who had killed prisoners received to quarter by a subordinate, and made ample apologies to the commander of the place.
Several Proceedings, E, 786, 29. It has, however, to be proved that
Cromwell knew at the time that he gave the command that some of the
enemy had been admitted to quarter.

[1] Cromwell to Bradshaw, Sept. 16, *The Kingdom's Weekly Intelligencer*,
E, 575, 5. This passage is omitted in most of the copies printed in the
newspapers, and is not to be found in *Carlyle*.

[2] Jones is first styled Lieutenant-General in a letter of the Council of
State (*Interr.* I, 94, p. 376). It was written just after the reception
of the news from Rathmines, but a formal appointment by the Council or
Parliament would have been officially recorded, and it is, therefore,
probable that the appointment proceeded directly from Cromwell.

[3] Cromwell to Lenthall, Sept. 27, *Carlyle*, Letter cvi. ; Sir E Butler
to Ormond, Sept. 29 ; Castlehaven to Ormond, Oct. 1 ; *Carte MSS.*
xxv. foll. 624, 644 ; Hewson to ——? Oct. 29, *Collections of Letters,*

Cromwell therefore set out with high hope for Wexford. Paying his way and maintaining the strictest discipline, he met

Oct. 1.
Cromwell's
advanced
posts before
Wexford. with no resistance on the march. On October 1 his advanced posts were before the town, and the remainder of his army arrived on the following day.

Oct. 2.
His whole
army
arrives. He had already been obliged to dissipate some of his troops in garrisons, and he now counted about 7,000 foot and 2,000 horse under his orders. Wexford is a town of no great breadth, but it runs to a considerable length

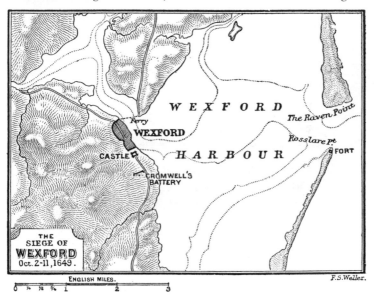

THE SIEGE OF WEXFORD Oct. 2-11, 1649.

ENGLISH MILES.

F.S.Weller.

along the shores of its harbour. At its south-western extremity

He prepares
to attack
the castle. was a castle, and it was opposite this that Cromwell prepared to plant his batteries on a rocky eminence.

E, 579, 10. In addition to Cromwell's letters, the best authorities for the siege of Wexford from the besiegers' point of view are two letters printed in *A very Full and Particular Relation*, E, 576, 6. As both are anonymous, I shall quote them as *First Letter* and *Second Letter* respectively.

For some days the inhabitants had been fluctuating between fear and hope. A lawyer named Rochford had been active in persuading them to surrender. On September 28 Castlehaven, who had been entrusted by Ormond with a special command over forces destined for the relief of the southern towns, now acting at the request of the Corporation, appointed Colonel Synott Governor of the town. Synott, however, had served under Preston, the General of the Confederation, whereas the most vigorous of the inhabitants of Wexford had attached themselves to the party of the Nuncio. Before the day was over the Corporation urged Castlehaven to cancel his nomination. Castlehaven refused, and, but for the appearance of Sir Edmund Butler, who had been specially despatched by Ormond to provide for the defence of the town, the population would have settled the question in dispute by a resolution to open the gates to Cromwell. Though this danger was averted, Synott wrote to Ormond that he would soon be driven to throw up his command.[1]

Divisions within the town.

Sept. 28. Synott appointed Governor.

Arrival of Sir E. Butler.

Sept. 29. Synott in despair.

Cromwell on his side had to suffer from heavy rain. The ground on which he bivouacked was converted into a quagmire and his army was thinned by dysentery. Ormond's flying parties hovered about and cut off supplies. It was therefore indispensable to open a communication with the sea. On October 2 Jones was sent against Fort Rosslare, which commanded the entrance to the harbour. The garrison fled at his approach, and the Parliamentary fleet at once entered the harbour with provisions and the siege-train from Dublin.[2] On the following day Cromwell summoned the town. Synott,

Cromwell's difficulties

Oct. 2. Fort Rosslare taken.

Oct. 3. Cromwell summons Wexford.

---

[1] Castlehaven to Ormond, Sept. 28 ; Sir E. Butler to Ormond, Sept. 29 ; *Carte MSS.* xxv. fol. 608, 624 ; Synott to Ormond, Sept. 30, Gilbert's *Cont. Hist. of Aff. in Irel.* vol. ii. 282 ; Castlehaven's *Memoirs*, 78.

[2] Cromwell to Lenthall, Oct. 14, *Carlyle*, Letter cvii. ; *First Letter*, E, 576, 6 ; Hugh Peters to ——? Oct. 3, *Several Proceedings*, E, 533, 20.

having reconsidered his resolution to throw up his command, opened a dilatory correspondence with the object of gaining time till reinforcements should arrive from Ormond.[1]

Synott obtained what he wanted. On the 6th, when 1,500 Ulster foot had been thrown into the town by Castlehaven,[2]

Oct. 6. Synott broke off his correspondence with Cromwell.
The garrison reinforced. By this time Ormond had advanced to Ross, where he learnt that Sir Pierce Smith, who had formerly
Treason of Sir Pierce Smith. been prepared to surrender Youghal to Ireton, had declared for Cromwell in concert with three of Inchiquin's cólonels. The treason was premature, and Youghal was speedily reduced, but Inchiquin's army was honeycombed with disaffection, and it was thought advisable to make no serious attempt to punish the offenders.[3]

Ormond hoped better things from the Governor of Wexford. On the 8th he appeared in person on the northern side of the

Oct. 8. Ormond at the Ferry. ferry which connected the town with the country to the north of the harbour. He there conferred with Synott, and on the following morning with the prin-
Oct. 9. cipal townsmen. To them he gave promises of further support and of the appointment of Sir Edmund Butler
Oct. 11. Sir E. Butler in Wexford. to supersede the unpopular governor. On the 11th Butler, who had gone off to fetch help, reappeared, and gave orders to ferry over 500 men whom he had brought with him. Before his orders could be carried out Wexford was in the enemy's hands.[4]

Cromwell batters the castle. On that very morning Cromwell's batteries had opened fire upon the castle. So destructive was the result, that Synott renewed his correspondence with

---

[1] Correspondence, Oct. 3-6, appended to *Carlyle*, Letter cvii.

[2] Castlehaven's *Memoirs*, 6-8; Synott to Ormond, Oct. 6, Gilbert's *Cont. Hist. of Aff. in Irel.* vol. ii. 286; Cromwell to Lenthall, Oct. 14, *Carlyle*, Letter cvii.

[3] Ormond to Clanricarde, Oct. 6, *Carte MSS.* xxv. fol. 674.

[4] Ormond to the Mayor of Wexford, Oct. 10; Ormond to the Commissioners of Trust, Oct. 11; Narrative of Military Operations, *Carte MSS.* xxv. fol. 717, xxvi. 440.

Cromwell, this time offering to surrender if complete religious
liberty and municipal independence were granted to the town.

A futile negotiation.
Cromwell scouted the proposal, offering in turn to
protect the lives and property of the inhabitants and
give quarter to the officers, and to allow the privates
to return to their homes on engaging never again to take arms
against Parliament. Before Synott's commissioners returned

Stafford betrays the castle.
with this answer, one of their number, Captain
Stafford, the governor of the castle, agreed to betray
his trust and to admit the besiegers into his fortress.

Stafford's treason had an immediate effect upon the
defenders of the wall opposite. Seeing the guns of the castle

Effect of his treason on the town.
turned on them, some leapt over the works and
called for quarter, but the greater number deserting
their posts hurried to the shore, hoping to escape
across the water. Cromwell's soldiers were not slow to take
advantage of their flight. Planting their pikes in the crannies

The wall scaled.
of the wall, a few clambered up to the undefended
top. Then ladders were brought, and masses of
soldiers poured over into the town. It was in and round the
market-place that they first met with resistance. The streets

Resistance in the town.
approaching it were guarded by cables stretched
from wall to wall.[1] Behind these improvised barri-
cades stood at bay a party of soldiers supported by
a larger body of townsmen, whom a long course of privateering
had made bitterly hostile to the English.[2] Before long, however, their resistance was overpowered and the horrors of

---

[1] The author of the *First Letter* (E, 576, 6) says that 'they had
gabled all their streets.' Dr. Murray and Mr. Henry Bradley are both
of opinion that 'gabled' is a form of 'cabled,' unless, indeed, it is a mis-
print, and that ropes were fastened across the streets. At all events, some
form of obstruction is implied.

[2] "Occupato insperatè . . . castro . . . in civitatem irruit; oppo-
suêre se viriliter aggressori Præsidiarii, simul cum civibus; pugnatumque
est ardentissimè per unius horæ spatium inter partes in foro." Bruodinus,
Propugnaculum Catholicæ veritatis, 681. The testimony of this hostile
witness disposes of the usual supposition that the soldiers originally fell
upon harmless townsmen.

Drogheda were repeated at Wexford. Here, too, priests and friars were butchered without mercy. It is said that some of Another massacre. these unfortunate men, hoping to move the infuriated soldiery to mercy, approached them with crucifixes in their hands, and were at once put to death as idolators.[1] Cromwell and his officers refused to interfere on behalf of those who had stood to arms in the market,[2] and these in their rush to the water's edge found themselves in the midst of a struggling multitude of men and women. All who could threw themselves into boats, but boats pressed down by an agonised crowd could not long float, and it was reckoned that about 300 persons were drowned. The wrath of the soldiers was indeed mainly directed against those who had resisted, but it was impossible to distinguish between one townsman and another, and all were involved, at least in the belief of the soldiers, in the common guilt of piracy.[3] It is possible that some women

[1] The *Second Letter*, E, 576, 6.

[2] "Seeing thus the righteous hand of God upon such a town and people, we thought it not good nor just to restrain off our soldiers from their right of pillage nor from doing of execution upon the enemy, where the entrance was by force, and a resistance endeavoured, though too late." The *Second Letter*, E, 576, 6.

[3] There can be no doubt that many of the townsmen were killed. Cromwell writes that 'most of them are run away, and many of them killed in this service.' The evidence of the writer of the *Second Letter*, E, 576, 6, is to the same effect. "There was more sparing of lives, of the soldiery part of the enemy here than at Drogheda ; yet of their soldiers and townsmen here were about 1,500 slain and drowned in boats sunk by the multitude and weight of people pressing into them." This number exactly agrees with that given in a petition from the inhabitants of Wexford to Charles II. after the Restoration, printed in Gale's *Inquiry into the Ancient Corporate System of Ireland*, App. cxxiv. After asserting that Cromwell put ' man, woman, and child to a very few to the sword,' the petitioners estimate the loss of life of ' the soldiers and inhabitants ' at 1,500. It is obvious that if this figure is correct the whole population, ' man, woman, and child,' cannot have been killed. No doubt we have sweeping statements, especially from ecclesiastics. Dr. French, Bishop of Ferns, for instance, writing as late as in 1673, and not having himself been present at the siege, tells us that priests were massacred and a young gardener and a sacristan (*Spicilegium Ossoriense*, i. 510), both of whom

fell victims to the madness of the slaughterers, though on this head it is impossible to speak with certainty, and it is probable that most of those women who actually perished were either crushed in the throng or drowned in attempting the passage across the water.[1]

it may be remarked were connected with the clergy. In another letter printed in the introduction to Moran's *Memoirs of O.iver Plunket*, xxiii., the same writer speaks generally of 'the inhabitants weltering in blood and gore,' and of 'the few survivors of' his 'flock.' Writing in 1650, and, therefore, not long after the occurrence, Dr. Lynch, Archbishop of Dublin, says that there were killed 'multi sacerdotes, nonnulli religiosi, plurimi cives, et duo millia militum' (*Spic. Oss.* i. 341), the latter being an evident exaggeration. We have no direct evidence from the side of the besieged as to the townsmen bearing arms, but Synott, in one of his early letters, complains that he cannot get the townsmen to muster (Synott to Ormond, Sept. 30, Gilbert's *Cont. Hist. of Aff. in Irel.* ii. 282), and they may have come forward on Sir E. Butler's appointment. The evidence of Bruodinus has already been quoted. From the other side we have the statement of the author of the *First Letter* (E, 576, 6) that 'the town within had 2,000 able men, mostly mariners,' besides the soldiers of the garrison. This seems to regard them as joining in the defence. It may be added that according to the law of war at a much later period, men defending a fortified town after the defences had been captured were liable to be put to death. "Je m'empressai," wrote Marbot of the siege of Ratisbon in 1809, "de dire au chef de bataillon que, la ville étant prise d'assaut et occupée par nos troupes, il ne lui restait plus qu'à mettre bas les armes sous peine d'être passé au fil de l'épée." Marbot, *Mémoires*, ii. 138.

[1] The legend of the two or three hundred women killed round the cross need not be taken seriously. It first appears in a volume published in 1763, where it is said that Cromwell 'fit égorger au pied de la Croix de cette ville au nombre de deux cens qui imploroient en vain miséricorde à genous, les yeux baignés de larmes.' MacGeoghegan's *Histoire de l'Irlande*, iii. 691. It is to no purpose to say that the story is confirmed by local tradition, unless it can be shown that the tradition existed before the story was in print. Against it is the silence of all contemporary writers. The cross, too, appears to have stood in the market-place, and if so it was the least likely place in the whole town to be chosen as a place of refuge, it being in the centre of the preparations for resistance. With respect to the slaughter of women generally, we have nothing but generalities. The author of the Aphorismical Discovery (Gilbert's *Cont.*

As at Drogheda, Cromwell sought to thrust the responsibility for the slaughter upon God. "Indeed," he wrote to Cromwell's comment. Lenthall, "it hath not without cause been deeply set upon our hearts that we, intending better to this place than so great a ruin, hoping the town might be of more use to you and your army, yet God would not have it so ; but by an unexpected providence in His righteous justice brought a just judgment upon them, causing them to become a prey to the soldiers who in their piracies have made preys of so many families, and now with their bloods to answer the cruelties which they exercised upon the lives of divers poor Protestants." [1] Such language seems strange enough now, though there was nothing in it which sounded strange to Puritan Englishmen of that day. Those who regard war from a more mundane point of view, can only say that the slaughter of Wexford was at least Comparison between the two massacres. less unjustifiable than the slaughter at Drogheda. At Drogheda soldiers had fought hard to drive back the enemy from a breach so far defensible that two assaults were repulsed from it. At Wexford soldiers and townsmen resisted after the defences of the place had been captured, and, striving to inflict a purposeless loss of life on the victorious enemy, paid the penalty in their own persons.

Hist. of Aff. in Irel. vol. ii. 54), for instance, says Cromwell slaughtered 'all that came in his way without exception of sex or person, age or condition, only such as were of the conspiracy ; many of the soldiers . . . saved themselves by boats or swimming, but great mortality did accompany that fury of both soldiers and natives, all sex and age indifferently then perished.' Bruodinus continues his account of the fight in the market-place (see p. 130, note 2) with the words ' sed impari congressu, nam cives ferè omnes unà cum militibus sine statûs sexûs aut ætatis discrimine Cromweli gladius absumpsit.' All this looks like mere rhetorical exaggeration, and is easily accounted for by the writers mixing up the losses by drowning with those by massacre. If any large number of women had been deliberately killed, I feel sure that it would have been mentioned somewhere in Ormond's voluminous correspondence.

[1] Cromwell to Lenthall, Oct. 14, *Carlyle*, Letter cvii.

CHAPTER VI

CORK, KILKENNY, AND CLONMEL

" The town," wrote Cromwell to the Speaker, after the capture of Wexford, " is now so in your power that of the former Cromwell recommends the introduction of English settlers. inhabitants I believe scarce one in twenty can challenge any property in their houses. Most of them are run way, and many of them killed in this service ; and it were to be wished that an honest people would come and plant here." [1] Once more the keynote of Cromwell's policy, the subordination of Ireland to the English, was clearly sounded. What Elizabeth, and James, and Strafford had attempted in vain, was to be carried out thoroughly at last. For the moment, at least, Cromwell gained strength by his avowal of a resolution to protect ' the English He sets out for Munster. interest.' He was now ready to march where his policy, fraught with future evil, would stand him in good stead. As soon as the plunder of Wexford had been shipped for Dublin,[2] he took the road leading to the port towns of Munster, with which he had long been in communication.

The first obstacle on his way was New Ross, a fortified town commanding a ferry over the Barrow. On October 17 Oct. 17. Ross summoned. Cromwell summoned its governor, Sir Lucas Taaffe. " I have this witness for myself," he wrote, " that I have endeavoured to avoid effusion of blood—this

---

[1] Cromwell to Lenthall, Oct. 14, *Carlyle*, Letter cvii.
[2] Roche to Taaffe, Oct. 14, *Carte MSS.* xxv. fol. 759.

being my principle that the people and places where I come may not suffer except through their own wilfulness." The terror of Drogheda and Wexford was upon the garrison, and

Oct. 19. *A negotiation opened.*
Taaffe began to waver. On the 19th he asked for leave for his soldiers and such of the townsmen who wished it to depart in safety, and for liberty of conscience to such as remained. " I meddle not with any man's conscience," was Cromwell's prompt reply ; " but if by liberty of conscience you mean liberty to exercise the mass, I judge it best to use plain dealing, and to let you know where the Parliament of England have power that will not be allowed of." Before

Capitulation of Ross.
the end of the day terms of capitulation were agreed to. The soldiers were to march away, leaving behind their cannon and ammunition. Those of the townsmen who within three months elected to depart were to be allowed to do so. Those who remained behind were to be protected in person and goods.[1]

When Taaffe marched out, five hundred of his soldiers took service under Cromwell. They were of English birth,

Deserters from Taaffe.
and their example was likely to prove contagious. Cromwell, indeed, sadly stood in need of help. His

Cromwell's army diminished.
army was thinned by dysentery and fever, as well as by the necessity of garrisoning the fortresses that he had taken, and it is doubtful whether he could now place more than 5,000 men in the field. For the moment, too,

He constructs a bridge over the Barrow.
his movements were hampered by the necessity of constructing a bridge over the Barrow, without which he did not venture to continue his forward march. Yet he could not endure to be idle, and a spell of fine weather having set in he despatched Jones with 2,000 men to assail

The siege of Duncannon.
Duncannon fort, which, being situated on the eastern side of the united estuaries of the Barrow and the Suir, guarded the access to Waterford from the sea. A few days later Cromwell followed in person.[2]

[1] Correspondence between Cromwell and Taaffe, Oct. 17, 19, *Carlyle*, Letters cviii.–cxi.

[2] Cliffe's Narrative, *Borlace* (ed. 1743), App. 5.

At first the fort seemed unlikely to give much trouble to the besiegers. The Irish soldiers within it deserted in such numbers that Roche, the governor, assured Ormond that it was impossible to hold out. Ormond, in reply, superseded Roche, appointing in his place Wogan, who, in 1648, had deserted Fairfax and carried his troop over to the Scots. With Wogan, Ormond sent his own life-guard [1] to stiffen the resistance. Wogan soon made it evident that Taaffe's example was not to be followed at Duncannon.

Oct. 23.
Wogan
supersedes
Roche.

The siege had not proceeded long before Cromwell was gladdened with the news for which he had been long thirsting. On October 16 the English officers and soldiers of the garrison of Cork backed by the English in-habitants declared for Parliament, expelled their governor, and drove out the Irish, wounding many of them in the fray. The example of Cork told upon Inchiquin's English soldiers. Before the 24th he had been deserted by all but two hundred of his foot, and Ormond, when he heard of the disaster, was of opinion that even these would join their comrades on the following day.[2]

Oct. 16.
Rising at
Cork.

Desertions
from
Inchiquin.

The direct accession of strength which accrued to Cromwell from the revolt of Cork was but a part of his advantage. It widened the breach, wide enough already, in the ranks of his opponents. Ormond was assailed with Irish complaints of his folly in trusting English Protestants. "It is noted by many," wrote Muskerry in the part of a candid friend, "that Protestants and English do share your favours amongst them in that measure as there is no room left for the Catholic natives to pretend unto them." Ormond's soldiers, continued the writer, were charged with oppressing the country, and it was said that every article of the treaty was explained to the disadvantage of

Irish dis-
trust of
English
Protestants.

Oct. 27.
Muskerry's
remon-
strance.

---

[1] These are the 'kurisees' who puzzled Carlyle. See his observations on Letter cxvii.

[2] Depositions in Caulfield's *Council Book of the Corporation of Cork*, App. B; Lady Fanshawe's *Memoirs*, **77**; Ormond to Castlehaven, Oct. 24, *Carte MSS.* xxvi. fol. **23**.

the clergy. Ormond's reply was dignified and pathetic,[1] but he could not harmonise the discordant elements of his party.

Oct. 30.
Ormond's
reply.

So loud was the outcry against his alleged favour to Protestants that he was obliged to send the incompetent Roche back to Duncannon, though he insisted that he should serve under Wogan till the siege was at an end.[2]

Within the fort this conciliatory measure had its full effect. The Catholic priest and the Protestant minister were on the

The defence
of Dun-
cannon.

best of terms, and shared in the use of the garrison chapel. The constancy of the defenders was crowned with success, and in the night of November 5

Nov. 5.
The siege
raised.

the besiegers, unwilling to continue their operations at so advanced a season, marched away. It seemed as if the effect of the massacres at Drogheda and Wexford was already spent.[3]

In the meanwhile the revolt of the English settlers in Munster was assuming larger proportions. On the first news

Progress
of the
revolt of
Munster.

of the rising of Cork, Cromwell despatched Broghill to spread and organise the insurrection. With him went Colonel Phayre, who held the threads of the secret negotiation which had preceded it.[4] Broghill was also accompanied by another companion, in after days more illustrious than any other Englishman then living save Cromwell himself. Blake, whose squadron had been driven by a storm from before Kinsale, had had the mortification of knowing that

Rupert's
escape.

Rupert had effected his escape in the interval. Cromwell knew his worth too well to chide him for his misfortune, and after vainly urging him to return to the

Blake
sent to
Cork.

land service as major-general under himself,[5] sent him to Cork in the frigate in which Broghill and Phayre

[1] Muskerry to Ormond, Oct. 27 ; Ormond to Muskerry, Oct. 30, *ib.* fol. 45, 55.

[2] Ormond to Castlehaven, Oct. 30, *ib.* fol. 54.

[3] Castlehaven to the Commissioners of Trust, Oct. 27 ; Castlehaven to Ormond, Nov. 4, 6, *Carte MSS.* xxvi. fol. 78, 97, 106.

[4] Cromwell to Scot, Nov. 14 ; Cromwell to Lenthall, Nov. 14, *Carlyle*, Letters cxiv. cxv. See pp. 95, 97.   [5] *C.J.* vi. 30.

were conveyed as passengers.   On the way Cromwell's com-
Nov. 3.
An enthu-
siastic re-
ception. missioners learnt that Youghal had declared for
Parliament.   On their arrival at Cork, on November 3,
they were received with boundless enthusiasm.[1]

So strongly pronounced was the manifestation of English
feeling in Munster, that even Inchiquin fell under suspicion.
Inchiquin
charged
with offering
to join
Cromwell. Antrim accused him of having agreed to come to
terms with Cromwell.   Ormond accepted Inchiquin's
disclaimer, but it is certain that a letter was in
circulation, dated October 16, the day before
Cromwell summoned Ross, which, if it were, as many believed
it to be, in Inchiquin's handwriting, would place his treason
beyond doubt.[2]   Whatever the truth may have been, the mere
fact that the charge was made weakened the authority of
Inchiquin, weak enough already.

Every blow struck at the alliance between Inchiquin's
English Protestants and the Irish Confederate Catholics made
The Celtic
element
in Ireland. Ormond more anxious to rally the purely Celtic
element in the Irish population to the Royal cause,
He had already made some progress in this direction.
In the latter part of September Daniel O'Neill was able to
report well of his uncle's disposition to bring real assistance to

---

[1] Blake to Cromwell, Nov. 5, *Tanner MSS.* lvi. fol. 137.

[2] In a letter to Ormond of Nov. 17 (*Carte MSS.* xxvi. fol. 223) it is
said that Father John Farral declared publicly in Waterford that he had
Inchiquin's contract with the Parliament under his own hand.   On the 18th
(*ib.* fol. 227) he said that Father Patrick stated that he had seen a copy of
Inchiquin's contract with Cromwell, dated Oct. 16, and that after the
delivery of Youghal Inchiquin was to have the command of 6,000 men.
Further, a colonel in Ormond's army wrote in the following year, that
' the original of Inchiquin's propositions to Cromwell when he was before
Ross,' was taken from Bishop Egan when he was captured and hanged
(*Clarendon MSS.* ii. 355).   On the other hand, we have Inchiquin's
own vindication of Dec. 6 (*Carte MSS.* xxvi. fol. 330), which is vague
and inconclusive, and a letter of the same date to Michael Jones (*ib.* fol. 33),
in which he begs him to state that the part assigned to him was not in
accordance with fact.   The story seems to have been that Jones got the
letter and gave it to Antrim to take to the Bishop of Clogher.

Ormond. On the 25th Owen, who was then at Omagh, talked of reaching Westmeath in six days, and he was en-

Sept. 25. Report of Daniel O'Neill. couraged in his purpose by a special offer of favours to be conferred on himself sent from Charles by the hands of Father Talbot.[1] In the meanwhile commissioners appointed by Ormond and Owen O'Neill met at Finnea

Oct. 20. Agreement between Ormond and O'Neill. in the county of Longford, and there, on October 20, an agreement was signed. Ormond bound himself to accept O'Neill as commander of 6,000 foot and 800 horse, to allow the nobility and gentry of Ulster to name his successor in the event of his death, to annul all grants of lands formerly belonging to him and his partisans, which had been confiscated since the rising in 1641, and even to admit O'Neill and his followers as tenants of lands which they and their predecessors had lost at the time of the Ulster plantation. Moreover the Roman Catholic clergy were to retain all churches and livings held by them in Ulster at the date of the signature of the treaty, and to be reasonably contented—whatever that might mean—in respect of churches and livings still in possession of the enemy.[2]

The acceptance of a dominant Roman Catholic Church with a virtually independent Celtic Ulster was the policy to *Ormond's policy.* which Ormond had now perforce committed himself. His old allies, the Confederate Catholics of the South, had also been compelled to humiliate themselves before O'Neill by engaging to sue at Rome for absolution from the excommunication which Rinuccini had pronounced against them.[3] The common enemy had become too strong to allow *Sept.-Oct. Parliamentary successes in the North.* the continuance of intestine quarrels. In the North of Ireland the Parliamentary commanders had overpowered their enemies. After narrowly escaping a defeat, Venables had secured Lisburn and Belfast,

---

[1] Commission from Charles, $\frac{\text{Aug. 30}}{\text{Sept. 9}}$, Ormond to O'Neill, Sept. 28, Gilbert's *Cont. Hist. of Aff. in Irel.* vol. ii. 255, 279.

[2] Articles between Ormond and O'Neill, Oct. 20, Gilbert's *Cont. Hist. of Aff. in Irel.* vol. ii. 300.

[3] *Aphorismical Discovery, ib.* 52.

whilst Coote, now strengthened by the whole of Huncks's regiment, had recaptured Coleraine and had almost completely subdued Down and Antrim. By the end of October the only important places holding out for the King in those counties were Charlemont and Carrickfergus.

All this would doubtless have served as a spur to O'Neill if his condition had been such as to allow him to move forwards.

O'Neill's illness Ill as he had been when he left Coote's quarters, he was now rapidly growing worse, and on November 6 Nov. 6. and death. the one commander who had succeeded in inspiring Celtic Ireland with enthusiasm breathed his last.[1] Contemporary admirers without a shadow of foundation attributed his death to poison. Later writers have fondly imagined that if he had lived to cross swords with Cromwell, the event of the war would have been other than it was. He was in fact a trained soldier, who had gained the hearts of the Irish peasants, and had thereby succeeded in keeping them together under the most adverse circumstances. The forces which he commanded were badly supplied and badly paid, and were driven of necessity to subsist by plunder. It is highly to O'Neill's credit that under such circumstances he succeeded in maintaining discipline at all, and still more that his career was not stained, like that of Cromwell, by any acts of deliberate cruelty. It was totally impossible for him with the materials at his disposal to display the qualities of a great commander.

O'Neill's last wish[2] was that Ormond would procure for his son, Colonel Henry O'Neill, those Royal favours which had His last message to Ormond been offered to himself. The appointment of his successor in the command of the Ulster army lay, according to agreement, with the nobility and gentry of the province.[3] Before his death he had pushed on a considerable detachment under Lieutenant-General Ferrall to Ormond's assistance in the South.

[1] Aphorismical Discovery in Gilbert's *Cont. Hist. of Aff. in Irel.* vol. ii. 62.

[2] O'Neill to Ormond, Nov. 1, *ib.* 315.   [3] See p. 139.

Before Ferrall appeared on the scene Cromwell had completed his bridge at Ross, and had been joined by reinforcements which enabled him to place 7,000 men in the field.[1] On November 15, being himself confined to bed by illness, he sent Jones and Ireton across the Barrow to bring Ormond if possible to a decisive action. Ormond, however, took refuge in an unassailable position at Thomastown, and the Parliamentary commanders, having but a short supply of provisions, were compelled to return to Ross, though they were able to despatch Reynolds to seize Carrick, an operation which he performed without difficulty. The possession of Carrick gave Cromwell, who was now recovered, a bridge over the Suir, thus enabling him to approach Waterford on the land-side. He at once took advantage of the opportunity thus offered to him. On November 24 he arrived before Waterford, finding the country untouched by the ravages of war and well stocked with provisions.

The bridge at Ross.

Nov. 15. Jones and Ireton cross the Barrow.

Carrick seized.

Nov. 21. Cromwell leaves Ross

Nov. 24. and appears before Waterford.

The weather had suddenly improved, but Cromwell would hardly have undertaken so hazardous an operation as a siege merely on the chance of the continuance of fair weather in the last week of November. In reality he counted on the divisions which existed amongst the townsmen. So strong was the party of the late Nuncio within the walls of the palace, and so bitterly were Ormond and his supporters detested, that when Castlehaven appeared on the 21st to strengthen the garrison he was refused admission. On the 23rd, indeed, when Cromwell's approach was known, the municipal authorities appealed to Ormond for assistance, but they imposed on him the condition that no troops were to be sent unless they belonged to Ferrall's contingent from Ulster. In order to gain time they applied to Cromwell for a cessation for fifteen days, and, though Cromwell

Nov. 21. Castlehaven rejected.

Nov. 23. Ormond to send Ferrall's men.

---

[1] Cromwell to Lenthall, Nov. 14, *Carlyle*, Letter cxv. ; Cliffe's Narrative, *Borlace* (ed. 1743), App. 5.

refused their request as exorbitant, he granted a cessation for five. As his siege-guns would certainly not arrive before the time had expired he lost nothing, and he made use of his leisure to seize the fort at Passage, on the western side of the estuary, nearly opposite Duncannon.[1]

Nov. 24.
Cromwell grants a cessation.

The difficulty thrown in the way of the relief of Waterford cut Ormond to the heart. " The Roman Catholics," he complained, " that stood so rigidly with the King upon religion—and that, as they called it, in the splendour of it—are with much ado withheld from sending commissioners to entreat Cromwell to make stables of their churches. An army we have superior in numbers to the enemy, but no industry of mine is able to provide so for it as to keep it one week at once together."[2] Depressed as he was, Ormond started for Waterford, taking with him Ferrall and two thousand Ulster Celts, who could easily find admittance, as the town was not blocked up on the river-side.

Nov. 30.
Ormond's complaint.

He sets out for Waterford.

Even before Ormond's arrival Cromwell had found his undertaking desperate. The short spell of fine weather came to an end, and the soaking rain made the roads impassable for the heavy guns on which the besiegers counted. Even if the guns had arrived it was doubtful whether they could be placed in position on the sodden ground. Provisions, too, ceased to find their way into the camp, and diseases again spread rapidly amongst the besiegers.[3] On December 2, ' being,' as he wrote, ' as terrible a day as ever I marched in all my life,' Cromwell raised the siege. As he took his course by the southern bank of the river he witnessed the approach of Ferrall's troops on the opposite side.

Cromwell in straits.

Dec. 2.
He raises the siege.

[1] The Mayor of Waterford to Ormond, Nov. 21, 23 ; Castlehaven to Ormond, Nov. 22, *Carte MSS.* xxvi. fol. 247, 263, 252 ; Cliffe's Narrative, *Borlace* (ed. 1743), App. 6 ; Cromwell's Correspondence with the Mayor of Waterford, Nov. 21-24, *Carlyle*, App. No. 15.

[2] Ormond to Jermyn, Nov. 30, Carte's *Orig. Letters*, ii. 415.

[3] Rushworth to Lenthall, Dec. 20, *A Perf. Diurnal*, E, 533, 35.

On the following day Cromwell received a better welcome. Broghill met him at the head of 1,200 horse and foot which he had raised in Munster, bringing news that the garrison of Dungarvan had come over that very morning.[1]

Dec. 3.
A meeting
with Brog-
hill.

Bandon and Kinsale had submitted not long before, and the outlying garrisons of Baltimore and Castlehaven soon followed their example. In the North, Carrickfergus surrendered to Coote on December 13,[2] and at the end of the year Cromwell's hold upon the coast line from Londonderry to Cape Clear was broken at Waterford alone.

Surrender of
Dungarvan,
Bandon, and
Kinsale.

The line held by Cromwell was indeed a thin one, exposed to attack from a vigilant and well-prepared enemy. The enemy, however, was neither vigilant nor well prepared, and the only loss suffered by Cromwell was that of Enniscorthy, which was betrayed by some soldiers of the garrison. Everywhere else his soldiers showed themselves capable of holding their own. At Arklow, at Carrick, and at Passage they repulsed attacks made by enemies considerably superior in number.

Loss of
Ennis-
corthy.

Cromwell's army, in fact, suffered far more from disease than from the sword of the enemy, and amongst the many victims to the dampness of the Irish climate was one who could ill be spared. Jones was stricken down with fever on the march from the camp before Waterford, and was left behind at Dungarvan, where he died on December 10. "What England lost thereby," wrote Cromwell, "is above me to speak. I am sure I lost a noble friend and companion in labours. You see how God mingles out the cup unto us. Indeed we are at this time a crazy company :—yet we live in His sight, and shall work the time that is appointed to us, and shall rest after that in peace." [3]

Illness of
Jones.

[1] Broghill to ——? Dec. 19, *Several Proceedings*, E, 533, 36 ; Cromwell to Lenthall, Dec. 19, *Carlyle*, Letter cxvii.

[2] Basil to Bradshaw, Dec. 12 ; Coote to Lenthall, Dec. 13, *Several Proceedings*, E, 433, 32, 34 ; *The Irish Mercury*, E, 592, 5.

[3] *Carlyle*, Letter cxvii. The story told in Morrice's *Memoirs* of Orrery (p. 16) that Jones in his illness urged Broghill to declare against

Cromwell was now compelled to go into winter quarters till the weather improved sufficiently to allow the resumption of active enterprise. If he had actually subdued but a small portion of the country, he had potentially subdued it all. It was hardly likely that any place would be more bravely defended than Drogheda had been, and it was still more unlikely that any Irish army would be sufficiently well supplied to hold the field against Cromwell's regiments with the whole of England at their backs. Ormond was now as depressed as nine months before he had been exuberant.

Cromwell in winter quarters.

On September 17 Charles had landed in Jersey [1] on his way to Ireland, but he did not venture to move further till he received from Ormond information which the Lord Lieutenant, whose cipher had been lost at Rathmines, was unable to give him. At last Charles, impatient of delay, sent Henry Seymour with orders, after conveying to Ormond the garter which was the token of his sovereign's gratitude, to bring back a full report of the condition of the country.

Sept. 17. Charles in Jersey.

Mission of Henry Seymour.

Ormond's report, which was drawn up on November 30, was indeed gloomy. He could still dispose, he said, of 5,000 foot and 1,300 horse, as his own immediate following, but he knew not how to maintain such a force in the field ; 'our wants,' he complained, 'having occasioned disorder, and that disorder the spoil of the country, and that spoil the flight of the country from us as from an enemy.' In Connaught the only county which might be looked to for assistance was that of Galway, and Galway was

Nov. 30. Ormond's report on the state of Ireland.

Cromwell is inadmissible, but it may possibly have a foundation in some words uttered in delirium. We have reason to think (see p. 72) that Jones disapproved of Cromwell's part in the King's execution, and this thought may have come up in his mind when he was under the fever. It is noteworthy that none of the letters telling of his death speak of him as making a pious end, though we hear much of this in other cases. See especially one from Jones's brother, the Bishop of Clogher, in *A Perf. Diurnal* (E, 533), in which the contrast is marked.

[1] Hoskins' *Charles II. in the Channel Islands*, ii. 310.

so devastated by the plague as to be altogether helpless. Elsewhere the Irish were too jealous of the English, and the English too diffident of their own ability to resist, to make it easy to keep them together. The Ulster army was indeed considerable in numbers, but now that O'Neill was dead it would fall into disputes about the succession to the command. Possibly an army of 20,000 foot and 5,000 horse might be brought together out of the whole of Ireland, but for this it was absolutely necessary that his Majesty should send money enough not only to raise troops, but subsequently to maintain them. Without such supplies—and Ormond must have known perfectly well that it was entirely out of Charles's power to provide them—he did not dare to advise him to come to Ireland.[1]

Ormond thus virtually acknowledged that his policy of effecting a Royalist restoration in England by a combination of Irish parties with English and Scottish settlers had failed disastrously. If resistance to a fresh English conquest of Ireland was to be prolonged, the burden of the war must fall on the Irish population alone, and especially on that purely Celtic population by which the English agrarian system was still regarded with loathing. In proportion as this Celtic resistance predominated power would naturally fall into the hands of the Catholic priesthood, the only bond of union between otherwise discordant parties.

Failure of Ormond's policy.

Increasing predominance of the Celtic element.

To take upon themselves the authority thus thrust upon them, the Irish prelates met on December 4 at Clonmacnoise. Their first act was the issue of a Declaration warning their flocks that Cromwell intended to extirpate the Catholic religion, which could not ' be effected without the massacring or banishment of the Catholic inhabitants.' Those whose lives were spared, they argued, could not hope to retain their property. By English Acts of Parliament ' the estates of the inhabitants of this kingdom are

Dec. 4. Manifesto of the prelates at Clonmacnoise.

[1] Ormond's statement, Nov. 30, Gilbert's *Cont. Hist. of Aff. in Irel.* vol. ii. 329.

sold, so there remaineth now no more but to put the purchasers
in possession by the power of forces drawn out of England,
and for the common sort of people, towards whom they show any
more moderate usage at the present,[1] it is to no other end but
for their private advantage and for the better support of their
army, intending at the close of their conquest—if they can
effect the same, as God forbid—to root out the commons also,
and plant this land with colonies, to be brought hither out of
England—as witness the number they have already sent hence
for the Tobacco Islands—and put enemies in their place.'

On the 13th the prelates sent forth a second Declaration, in
which they announced that, as far as they were themselves con-

Dec. 13.
A second
manifesto.

cerned, they had brought to an end the feud which
had divided the partisans of Rinuccini from the
partisans of the Supreme Council.   From henceforth
they would be united in contending ' for the interest and im-
munities of the Church and every prelate and bishop thereof,
and for the honour and dignity, estate, right, and possession of
all and every said archbishop, bishop, and other prelates ; and
we will, as one entire and united body, forward by our counsel,
action, and device the advancement of his Majesty's rights and
the good of this nation in general.'[2]

1650.
January.
Cromwell
hears of
the mani-
festoes.

His
counter-
declara-
tion.

News did not circulate freely in Ireland, and it
was not till the middle of January that these declarations fell into the hands of Cromwell on his return
to Youghal after completing a tour of inspection
amongst the Munster garrisons.[3]   He at once dashed
off a reply ' for the undeceiving of deluded and
seduced people.'   He flew at once at the assumption

---

[1] Carlyle imagined that these words showed that the prelates did not
believe in the massacre of civilians at Drogheda and Wexford.   The
sentence, however, clearly refers to property only.

[2] Declarations of the prelates at Clonmacnoise, *Spicilegium Ossoriense*,
ser. ii. 38, 39.

[3] Kinsale is the farthest point indicated as reached by Cromwell in
contemporary newspapers.   His alleged visit to Glengariff and the legend
of the bridge may be safely left to the guide-books.   The reception of the

by the clergy of a right to guide the laity, and asserted that
the very words 'clergy' and 'laity' were 'unknown to any

He attacks the claims of the clergy ; save the anti-christian Church and such as derive
themselves from her.' At the call to Irishmen to
combine against 'the common enemy' Cromwell
blazed up into indignation. "Who is it," he asked the clergy,
"that created this common enemy? I suppose you

and pro- tests that English- men are not 'the common enemy.' mean Englishmen. The English! Remember, ye
hypocrites, Ireland was once united to England;
Englishmen had good inheritances which many of
them purchased with their money; they or their
ancestors from many of you and your ancestors. They had

Cromwell's view of the relation- ship be- tween English and Irish. good leases from Irishmen for long time to come,
great stocks thereupon; houses and plantations
erected at their cost and charge. They lived peaceably and honestly amongst you; you had generally
equal benefit of the protection of England with them,
and equal justice from the laws—saving what was necessary for
the State, upon reasons of State, to put upon some few people
apt to rebel upon the instigation of such as you. You broke
the union, you unprovoked put the English to the most unheard-of and most barbarous massacre, without respect of sex
or age, that ever the sun beheld, and at a time when Ireland
was in perfect peace, and when through the example of English
industry, through commerce and traffic, that which was in the
natives' hands was better to them than if all Ireland had been
in their possession and not an Englishman in it; and yet then,
I say, was this unheard-of villainy perpetrated by your instigation
who boast of peace-making and union against the common
enemy. What think you by this time? Is not my assertion
true? Is God—will God be with you? I am confident He
will not."

As a contribution to Irish history, nothing could be more
ludicrously beside the mark than these burning words. The

Declarations at Youghal is shown by the tone in which Cromwell writes in
a letter written to Lenthall on Jan. 16, not printed by Carlyle. It is in
Several Proceedings, F., 534, 4.

idyllic picture drawn of Irishmen and Englishmen living
together in peace till wicked priests stirred up the sleeping
Cromwell's interpretation of the past. passions of the Irish has no foundation in the domain
of fact. Cromwell knows nothing of the mingled
chicanery and violence which made the Ulster Plantation hateful in the eyes of every Irishman. He knows nothing of
lands filched away, of the injustice of legal tribunals by which
judgments were delivered in an alien speech in accordance
with an alien law, of the bitterness caused by the proscription
of a religion clung to all the more fondly because it was not the
religion of the English oppressor.

Nevertheless, as an explanation of Cromwell's own conduct
in Ireland, this Declaration is of supreme importance. Granted
His own conduct explained by it. his honest belief in the view of Irish history which he
here puts forth, it becomes impossible to convict
him of anyth'ng worse than ignorance in ordering the
slaughter of Drogheda. If the collective priesthood of Ireland
had hounded on a peaceful people to outrage and massacre,
every priest taken deserved to be knocked on the head. If
Irish, or, still worse, English soldiers, stood to arms to defend
a system based on outrage and massacre, they deserved all that
the cruel law of war of that age allowed to the captors of a
besieged fortress. Poisonous as in this case was the fruit which
grew upon the tree of error, the error was not Cromwell's only.
He said no more than was said by every writer in England who
touched on Irish affairs.[1]   His belief in English innocence and

---

[1] Mr. Firth had drawn my attention to a passage in May's *Hist. of the
Parl.* lib. ii. 4, published in 1647. "The innocent Protestants were
upon a sudden deprived of their estates, and the persons of above two
hundred thousand men, women, and children murdered, many of them
with exquisite tortures, within the space of one month. That which increased the amazement of most men was the consideration that the ancient
hatred which the Irish—a thing incident to conquered nations—had borne
to the English did now seem to be quite buried and forgotten; forty years
of peace had compacted those two nations into one body and cemented
them together by all conjunctures of alliance, intermarriages, and con-
sanguinity, which was in outward appearance strengthened by frequent
entertainments and all kinds of friendly neighbourhood. . . . The present

his exaggeration of Irish crime were common to all who thought or spoke on the subject. He had the mind of England as well as its sword at his disposal.

For the rest Cromwell's intentions were as benevolent to the mass of the Irish people as Strafford's had formerly been.

Cromwell's intentions. " We are come," he says, " to take an account of the innocent blood that hath been shed, and to endeavour to bring them to account—by the blessing and presence of Almighty God, in Whom alone is our hope and strength—who by appearing in arms seek to justify the same. We come to break the power of a company of lawless rebels who, having cast off the authority of England, live as enemies to human society, whose principles—the world hath experience of—are to destroy and subjugate all men not complying with them. We come—by the assistance of God—to hold forth and maintain the lustre and glory of English liberty, in a nation where we have an undoubted right to do it, whereas the people of Ireland—if they listen not to such seducers as you are—may equally participate in all benefits to use liberty and fortune equally with Englishmen, if they keep out of arms." [1]

Not to meddle with any man's conscience, but to prescribe

Substance of Cromwell's policy. the worship which confirmed and strengthened it ; to put to death all who resisted him in this enterprise, but to treat non-combatants with moderation in the hope that they would become like Englishmen, was the substance of Cromwell's policy in Ireland.

To carry out this policy, Cromwell set forth from Youghal on January 29, having heard rumours that his recall had been

Jan. 29.
Cromwell
leaves
Youghal. determined on in England, and being therefore anxious to accomplish as much as possible before positive orders reached him. By this time he had received considerable reinforcements, new uniforms for his

government was full of lenity and moderation, and some redress of former grievances had been newly granted by the King to his Irish subjects." Surely Cromwell had found time to read this.

[1] *A Declaration of the Lord Lieutenant of Ireland*, E, 596, 6. Printed with some alterations by Carlyle.

infantry, and money wherewith to pay his men.[1] His object
was to master the counties of Kilkenny and Tipperary, where
the head-quarters of the Catholic Confederation had
formerly been. For seven weeks he and his subordinates reduced one stronghold after another, for
the most part receiving the submission of the
garrisons, but slaughtering without mercy those who ventured
to reject a summons, even when it had been tendered before a
breach had been effected. By the end of the third week in
March, Hewson from Dublin had overrun a great part of the
county of Kildare, Cook from Wexford had recovered Enniscorthy, Broghill had gained ground in the county of Limerick,
whilst in the region in which Cromwell himself was operating,
two fortresses alone, those of Kilkenny and Clonmel, still held
out. The enemy had no army in the field strong enough to
resist him, and Cromwell already regarded the two places as
his own.[2]

*Jan. 29-
March 12.
Cromwell
in Kil-
kenny and
Tipperary.*

The two sieges cost him more than he had anticipated. On
March 23 he summoned Kilkenny in vain. Though the plague,
imported from Galway, was raging within the walls,
Sir Walter Butler, the governor of the town, held
out bravely, and though Cromwell's troops gained
ground in the suburbs, they were repulsed in every attempt to
storm the main defences. The civilian population with the
mayor at its head was, however, anxious to treat, and the
soldiers of the garrison were too few to enable the governor to
resist the importunity of the citizens. Cromwell being probably
impatient to finish his work before he was summoned from
Ireland, abandoned his claim to devote to death soldiers who
had resisted him so stubbornly, and granted favourable terms.
The soldiers were merely to evacuate the place. The
townsmen were to be freed from plunder on
payment of 2,000*l.*[3] After Kilkenny was occupied

*March 23.
Cromwell
summons
Kilkenny.*

*March 28.
Surrender
of Kil-
kenny.*

---

[1] *The Irish Mercury*, E, 594, 5.

[2] Cromwell to Lenthall, Feb. 15, April 2, *Carlyle*, Letters cxix. cxxx.

[3] *Carlyle*, Letters cxxii.–cxxx. ; Butler to Ormond, Nov. 3, *Carte
MSS.* xxvii. fol. 240.

there was much smashing of crosses and fonts, of altars and coloured glass, but no injury was offered to any laymen, and the statement that priests were slain rests merely on rumour or tradition.[1]

Cromwell, whilst conducting the siege of Kilkenny, had been protected by the activity of Lord Broghill. On April 10 Broghill fell on a large body of the enemy, which had advanced out of Kerry as far as Macroom. Their rout was complete. Prisoners were few, as Broghill had given orders to knock on the head all who were taken. Amongst the captives was Egan, the Catholic Bishop of Ross. Broghill sent him before the walls of the castle of Carrigadrohid, bidding the officer who conducted him to spare his life if the governor would surrender, but to hang him if the governor refused. The answer was a

Bishop
Egan
hanged. refusal, and the bishop was promptly hanged.[2] In his pocket was found a letter, alleged to be in Inchiquin's handwriting, in which that nobleman offered to submit to Cromwell.[3]

Whatever may have been the truth about Inchiquin, there could be no doubt that the English who still served under him were anxious to obtain honourable terms. Scouted by the

Inchiquin's
English
officers
and men Irish, they knew their very lives to be in danger from their own allies,[4] and they despatched two emissaries, Captain Daniel and Dean Boyle, to make an arrange-

April 26.
make
terms with
Cromwell. ment with Cromwell. Cromwell received the messengers gladly, and, on April 26, signed articles allowing all Protestant Englishmen and Scotchmen, whether soldiers or not, to betake themselves to the Continent,

---

[1] Against the tradition mentioned by Mr. Prim (*Transactions of the Kilkenny Arch. Soc.* 1851, p. 460) and the vague rumour recorded by Dr. Lynch (*Spicilegium Ossoriense*, i. 335) must be set the Jesuit relations (*ib.* ii. 58), in which nothing is said of the murder of priests.

[2] Broghill to —— ? April 16, *Several Proceedings*, E, **777**, **6**.

[3] Letter from Ja. Barn. (?) *Clarendon MSS.* ii. 355. Broghill in the letter quoted above says : 'I found some papers of singular consequence in the bishop's pocket, which I hope shall not want improving.'

[4] Inchiquin to the Commissioners of Trust, April 17, *Carte MSS.* xxvii. fol. 311.

or to retire into such parts of Ireland as were under the authority
of Parliament.   As to their estates, if they had any, they were
to retain them till the pleasure of Parliament was known; or
till they had paid compositions in the same proportion as had
been paid by other English Protestants who had recently submitted.[1]

Cromwell, indeed, did his best to urge the deputies to
include both Ormond and Inchiquin in the agreement, and he
Cromwell wishes to include Ormond and Inchiquin. actually sent passes to enable these two noblemen to
leave Ireland without molestation.[2]   By Ormond the
passport was contemptuously returned.[3]   Inchiquin,
deserted by his followers and distrusted by the Irish,
remained for a time in Ireland, though Ormond thought it
expedient to deprive him of a command which had by this
time become merely nominal.[4]

Ormond was now driven to rely almost entirely on Celtic
Ireland.   In Waterford, indeed, Ferrall and his Ulstermen,
having been discredited by their defeat at Passage and being
Feb. 8. Preston succeeds Ferrall at Waterford. ill-supported by the townsmen, had returned to their
own country.   Ferrall's place was taken by Preston,
who had early in February been appointed by Ormond to the command.[5]   In the north and west of
Ireland, the only organising force lay in the prelates of the
The pre- lates and the war. Roman Catholic Church, and there the appointment
of Preston, who had sided with the Supreme Coun-
cil against Rinuccini, to any office whatever would
have been out of the question.   Making a virtue of necessity

---

[1] Cromwell's articles, April 26, Gilbert's *Cont. Hist. of Aff. in Irel.*
vol. ii. 393.

[2] Boyle to Ormond, April 30; Passport for Ormond, May 7, *ib.*
vol. ii. 400, 405 ; Passport for Inchiquin, May 7, *Carte MSS.* xxvii.
fol. 463.

[3] Ormond to Cromwell, May 17, Gilbert's *Cont. Hist. of Aff. in Irel.*
vol. ii. 411.

[4] Inchiquin to Ormond, May 24, *Carte MSS.* xxvii. 553.

[5] Ormond to the Commissioners of Trust, Feb. 7 ; Commission to
Preston, Feb. 8, *ib.* xxvi. fol. 28, clxii. fol. 131, Aph. Disc. in Gilbert's
Cont. Hist. of Aff. in Irel. vol. ii. 67.

Ormond summoned the prelates, together with the Commissioners of Trust, to meet at Limerick on March 8. When they came together, instead of taking measures for the steady prosecution of the war, they proposed to tie Ormond's hands by the appointment of a Privy Council, and to give to themselves—though the demand was expressed with some circumlocution—a veto on all military appointments. On March 21 Ormond replied with dignity, pointing out that in time of war control over the army must be in a single hand, and asking for further explanation on points in which the intention of the authors of the proposals was only too clear.[1]

March 8.
Meeting at Limerick.

March 21.
Ormond's reply.

Ormond would hardly be benefited by the retention of authority over his diminishing regiments in the south unless the Ulster army was at his disposal to create a diversion in the north. According to agreement the gentry and nobility of Ulster met at Belturbet on March 18, to choose a successor to Owen O'Neill. The rival candidates were many; some of the principal officers of the army were naturally mentioned, and Antrim, in spite of his recent tergiversations, was suggested as being likely to reconcile the Scottish Royalist Presbyterians under Monro with the Catholic Celts who abounded around them. In the midst of distracted counsels the clergy steadily pushed their way, and in the end, on the pretext of avoiding a ruinous competition, they obtained the election of one of themselves, Emer Macmahon, Bishop of Clogher. The bishop was a man of energy and capacity, but he was singularly unfitted by his profession from exercising military command, and it was hardly likely that the old warriors, the Ferralls and O'Neills who had supported Owen's authority without a thought of rivalry, would willingly submit on the field of battle to even the most energetic priest.

March 18.
Ulster meeting at Belturbet.

The Bishop of Clogher chosen general.

Nothing could have served Cromwell's interest better than

----

[1] Remedies proposed, March 13; Ormond's reply, March 21, Cox, *Hib. Angl.* ii. App. xlv. The date of Ormond's reply is taken from the copy in the *Carte MSS.* xxvii fol. 104.

this election.   In it the Celtic element in the Irish resistance asserted itself without contradiction.   In Ulster the children

The Celtic element predominant.

or grandchildren of the men who had been expelled by the great Plantation threw themselves on the lands still remaining in the possession of the settlers, and appropriated them without scruple.   Monro, who had charge of the garrison of Inniskillen, and had long been discontented with the turn of events, now admitted a Parliamentary force into the castle.   Ormond, as a Protestant, was an object of special detestation to the party now in the ascendant, and proposals were openly made to replace him by Antrim, or by some other Catholic.[1]

Ormond was despondent, and talked of leaving Ireland to its fate.   Castlehaven urged him to reconsider his determina-

March 28. Castlehaven urges Ormond to remain.

tion.   "Leave not this kingdom," he wrote ; "you and your family will perish abroad . . . Recover the kingdom or perish.   Make friendship with the bishops and nation."   Ormond bowed his head to necessity,

April 1. Ormond's commission to Bishop Macmahon.

as he had often done before, and on April 1 signed a commission appointing Bishop Macmahon to the command of the Ulster army.   Yet he felt the blow severely.   In Limerick, he complained, the clergy had 'absolute dominion.'   He found it hard to say whether it was better for the King's interest 'to prevail by such hands or to be destroyed by Cromwell.'[2]

Bishop Macmahon and Ormond.

It is probable that Bishop Macmahon did everything in his power to soothe the wounded feelings of the Lord Lieutenant.   His own language was con-

---

[1] Galbraith to Ormond, March 26, Monro to Ormond, March 26, April 18, *Carte MSS.* xxvii. foll. 200, 333 ; Bishop Macmahon to Ormond, May 4, Gilbert's *Cont. Hist. of Aff. in Irel.* vol. ii. 404, Aph. Discovery, *ib.* vol. ii. 70.   The author of the *Hist. of the War in Irel.* tells the story (p. 113), but he cannot be trusted in details.   He ascribes the bishop's election to the showing of a commission from Ormond, which, however, was not signed till April 1.

[2] Castlehaven to Ormond, March 28, Ormond to Bramhall, April 10, *Carte MSS.* xxvi. foll. 217, 285 ; Commission to Bishop Macmahon, April 1.   Gilbert's *Cont. Hist. of Aff. in Irel.* vol. ii. 390.

ciliatory [1] and he showed by his actions his determination to prosecute the war vigorously. It is possible that it was through his influence that the language of the Catholic prelates and nobility assumed a milder tone. They met again at Loughrea, on April 25, and on the 30th they offered to do their utmost to incline the people to obedience to his Majesty's authority, though, as they truly remarked, they could 'not undertake to remove at present the distrusts and jealousies the people entertain through the want of success in services, the sense of their sufferings and apprehensions for want of redress of their grievances.' [2]

April 25.
Meeting at Loughrea.

April 30.
Offer of the prelates and nobility.

Since the taking of Kilkenny, Cromwell's activity had been for some little time intermitted. He was occupied in making arrangements with the English of Inchiquin's army, [3] and it was not till these had been completed that he moved forward to assail Clonmel. The town, which lies along the north bank of the Suir, [4] had in February been entrusted by Ormond to Hugh O'Neill, [5] Owen's nephew, an officer of undoubted vigour and capacity, who like his uncle had served in the Spanish army in the Low Countries. O'Neill had under his command a force of Ulster Celts numbering some 1,200 men, of whom all but fifty-two were infantry. [6] The place had been more or less blocked up ever since his appointment, but it was only on April 27 that Cromwell appeared before it to open a formal attack. O'Neill called on Ormond for succour ' to prevent any bloody tragedy to be acted here as in other places for want of timely relief.' [7] Ormond

Cromwell moves towards Clonmel.

February.
Hugh O'Neill in Clonmel.

O'Neill asks for succour.

---

[1] Bishop Macmahon to Monro, April 20; Bishop Macmahon to Ormond, April 27, *ib.* vol. ii. 390, 398.

[2] The address of the clergy and nobility, April 30, Cox, *Hib. Angl.* ii. App. xlvi.   [3] See p. 151.

[4] In the map of Ireland the town is wrongly placed to the south of the river.

[5] Ormond to Hugh O'Neill, Feb. 16, Gilbert's *Cont. Hist. of Aff. in Irel.* vol. ii. 361.   [6] Muster Roll, *ib.* vol. ii. App. 3.

[7] Hugh O'Neill to Ormond, April 27, *ib.* vol. ii. 398; *Perf. Diurnal,* E, 777, 1.

would gladly have responded to the appeal, but it was hopeless to expect that the Ulster army would march so far away whilst their own province remained in danger, and all that he could do was to direct Lord Castle Connell to reinforce the garrison with 400 men.[1]

May 2.
A small
relief
ordered.

Before this petty relief had time to arrive the crisis of the siege had come. Cromwell's batteries had effected a breach, and on the 9th he gave the order to storm it. Never had the Parliamentary army met with such stout resistance. It was hard enough to surmount the breach in the teeth of the dogged resistance of the defenders ; but when once the breach was surmounted those who entered found the prize slipping from their grasp. A new wall drawn in a semicircle and approachable only by crossing a deep ditch confronted them, and the wall, as well as the houses behind, was manned by men who did not flinch in their death struggle with their hereditary foe. Caught in a trap the Cromwellian soldiers bore themselves bravely as was ever their wont, but the plunging shots tore their ranks, and strewed the ground with slain. To break through that semicircle of fire was beyond their power, and when night fell the survivors staggered back, to acknowledge that for once they had been foiled. Their loss had been enormous ; according to one account it was reckoned at no less than 2,500 men.

May 9.
A storm
repulsed.

Successful as they had been, the victorious garrison could prolong the struggle no longer. Neither Ormond nor Castlehaven was strong enough to take the field against the besiegers, and their own ammunition had run out in the fierce wrestle. In the dead of night Hugh O'Neill with his brave followers slipped away, marching in the direction of Waterford. He left instructions with the mayor to make his peace with the enemy, and accordingly, on the morning of the 10th, Cromwell received a deputation, to which he readily granted the lives and estates of the inhabitants, on condition of the surrender of the

The retreat
of the
garrison.

May 10.
Surrender
of Clonmel.

---

[1] Ormond to Byrne, May 2, *Carte MSS.* cxlii. 227.

'town and garrison.' Only after the articles had been agreed on did he discover that he had been deceived. Angry as he was, he stood by his word, and when his soldiers entered the town, they offered no damage to life or property.[1]

The abortive storm of Clonmel was Cromwell's last feat of arms in Ireland. Pressing letters of recall compelled him to abandon all thought of continuing the campaign in person, and on May 26,[2] leaving Ireton behind him as Lord Deputy, he sailed for Bristol. If he had not conquered Ireland he had done enough to make its conquest a mere matter of time, though it was likely to take a longer time than he himself anticipated. So far from sparing effusion of blood, his cruelty at Drogheda and Wexford, successful at Ross and at a few lesser strongholds, had only served to exasperate the garrisons of Duncannon, of Kilkenny, and of Clonmel, and in his later movements Cromwell, always prepared to accept the teaching of events, had discovered that the way of clemency was the shortest road to conquest. Neither he nor any of his fellow-countrymen were prepared to concede to the conquered Irish even such reasonable consideration of their demands as was compatible with the military and political predominance of England.

That the predominance of England would be secured when once an armed struggle began was a foregone conclusion. In the first place, Ireland was divided, whilst at least for military purposes England was united as it had never been before. In the second place, Ireland, especially that part of Ireland which maintained its independ-

Marginal notes:
May 26. Cromwell leaves Ireland.

The conquest a matter of time.

Causes of the predominance of England.

---

[1] Letter from Clonmel, May 10, *Several Proceedings*, E, 777, 6, Aph. Disc. in Gilbert's *Cont. Hist. of Aff. in Irel.* vol. ii. 611. I am doubtful about this story of Fennell's treachery. The alleged attempt to storm the gate is only mentioned by this last authority, and seems to be merely a misplaced account of what really happened in the final storm. Other authorities are collected by Mr. Gilbert, *ib.* vol. ii. 412.

[2] Bishop Jones's Diary, in the *Journal of the Soc. of Antiquaries of Ireland*, for March 1893, p. 52.

ence when Cromwell left it, was miserably poor, whilst England was exceedingly rich.   Whilst Hugh O'Neill was compelled to abandon the blood-stained walls of Clonmel because neither Ormond nor anyone else could either keep an army in the field to relieve him or supply him with enough ammunition to enable him to hold out longer, Cromwell had no such difficulties to face.   Reinforcements, siege-guns, clothing, ammunition, and provisions were at his disposal, if not at every moment in the campaign, at all events in sufficiency.   The financial difficulties which had prevented Parliament from supplying him with money whilst he lingered in London and in Wales had at last been got over, and between March 1, 1649,

Large pay-   and February 16, 1650, no less than 715,166*l*. had
ments to the   been disbursed in money or in money's worth for
Cromwellian
army.   the use of the Cromwellian army in Ireland.[1]

In the weakness of Ireland lies in some sort the justification of the Cromwellian conquest.   A nation politically ripe and strong with the consciousness of its unity can be treated with respect as a friend or as a foe.   A people divided internally, and without the elements of political organisation, invites the sword of the conqueror.   To do the Irish justice, not one of the parties which disputed for the pre-eminence had seriously aimed at sending forth an army to invade England ; but they had allowed themselves to be dragged in the wake of an English political party, and to threaten even more than they were themselves inclined to perform.   From the days of Strafford to the days of Ormond the apprehension of an irruption of an Irish army had weighed like a nightmare on the breasts of Englishmen, and what wonder was it that Englishmen roused themselves at last to bring the danger to an end?   Historians may remember that but for former wrongs Irishmen would never have thought of assisting one English party or another.

---

[1] *Interr*. I, p. 118. Mrs. Everett Green gives a total of only 535,590*l*., but she omits a statement of additional payments, which is at the end of the MS. she was calendaring. Of the sum paid, 100,028*l*. was on account of arrears previously due.

Large bodies of men do not even note such considerations. They see the present danger, and they strike home.

That his policy served to inflame, and not to extinguish, the distractions of Ireland was the true 'curse of Cromwell.'

The 'curse of Cromwell.' Yet it is hard to see how he could have done other than he did. In dealing with Ireland, as in dealing with the King, he imposed an emphatic negative on a situation which had become intolerable. In England there was to be no kingship without good faith. In Ireland there was to be no meddling with English political life, no attempt to constitute an independent government in the hands of the enemies of the religion and institutions of England.

CHAPTER VII

THE TRIAL OF JOHN LILBURNE

THE victories of Cromwell had no doubt strengthened the position of the Government of the Commonwealth; but, on the other hand, nothing had been done to dispel the belief that it was the creature of the army. That belief was the chief source of its weakness, and as long as Lilburne was able to wield the pen it was not likely to be forgotten.

There had been long delay in bringing Lilburne to trial, probably through fear of provoking so redoubtable an antagonist. Early in May 1649 an attempt was made to provoke him to treasonable action. Tom Verney, the ignoble member of an honourable family, was employed to write to Lilburne offering to bring men from Buckinghamshire [1] and the neighbouring counties to assist the

1649.
Position of the Government.

Delay in bringing Lilburne to trial.

---

[1] Levellers, in the extreme form of Diggers, had some hold on Bucks. See *Light Shining in Buckinghamshire*, E, 548, 9 ; *A Declaration of the Well-affected in the County of Buckinghamshire*, E, 555, 1. Verney's letters are in *A Preparative to a Hue and Cry after Sir Arthur Hazlerigg*, E, 573, 16. Tom Verney was the second son of Sir Edmund Verney, slain at Edgehill. Lilburne adds that Tom Verney had recently been employed to kidnap Charles. As a confirmation of Lilburne's view that Verney was in the pay of the Council of State, it can be shown that on June 18 the Council ordered his apprehension, and called on him to answer certain charges (Warrant, *Interr.* I, 62, p. 448). On the 27th, however, an order was made to give him satisfaction for his services (C. of St. Order Book, *Interr.* I, 62, 482). It looks as if he were imprisoned that he might act as a spy.

mutineers, who had not yet, at that time, been chased into Burford. Lilburne knew Verney too well to trust him, told him that he was a villain, and refused to hold any further communication with him.

It was impossible to keep Lilburne from writing, and on June 18 he published *The Legal Fundamental Liberties of the People of England,* a long, rambling production, in which, after vindicating his own conduct, he denounced Cromwell and his principal officers as having established a despotism by means of Pride's Purge.[1]

June 18.
The Legal
Fundamental
Liberties.

A still more violent attack on Cromwell and Ireton was completed on July 17, though it was not immediately published. On the 18th, however, an order of Parliament, procured by Henry Marten, gave permission to the Lieutenant of the Tower to set him at liberty on bail, thus enabling him to visit his wife and children, who were seriously ill.[2] In the end two of his children died. Severe as the blow was it did not distract his attention from matters of public concernment, and it was at this time that he listened to certain members of Parliament who were anxious to induce him to desist from his extreme pretensions.

July 18.
Lilburne
liberated on
bail.

Whatever may have been the precise nature of these overtures, they led to nothing. On August 10 Lilburne published the pamphlet which he had written in the Tower, giving it the title of *An Impeachment of High Treason against Oliver Cromwell and his Son-in-law Henry Ireton.*[3] Stripped of the violent personalities in which his argument was clothed, Lilburne's position was that in exceptional cases it was lawful to take arms against a tyrant, but only on condition that the armed force should at once give way to the sovereign people organised in accordance with the democratic principles of the latest edition[4] of the *Agreement of the People.* So bitterly was Lilburne opposed to the rule of the sword that he preferred a restoration of the monarchy on

Aug. 10.
An Im-
peachment
of High
Treason.

---

[1] *The Legal Fundamental Liberties,* E, 560, 14.   [2] *C.J.* vi. 264.
[3] *Impeachment of High Treason,* E, 568, 20.   [4] See p. 47.

fair conditions to a continuance of the present usurpation of the people's authority.   " If we must have a king," he declared, " I for my part would rather have the Prince than any man in the world because of his large pretence of right, which if he come not in by conquest, by the hands of foreigners—the bare attempting of which may apparently hazard him the loss of all at once by gluing together the now divided people to join as one man against him—but by the hands of Englishmen by contract upon the principles aforesaid," that is to say, the principles of the *Agreement of the People,* "which is easy to be done, the people will easily see that presently thereupon they will enjoy this transcendent benefit, he being at peace with foreign nations, and having no regal pretended competitor, viz. the immediate disbanding of all armies, garrisons, and fleets, saving the old cinque-ports, and so those three grand plagues of the people will cease, viz. free-quarter, taxations, and excise ; by means of which the people may once again really say they enjoy something they can in good earnest call their own, whereas for the present army to set up the pretended Saint Oliver or any other as their elected king, there will be nothing thereby from the beginning of the chapter to the end thereof but wars and the cutting of throats year after year ; yea and the absolute keeping up of a perpetual and everlasting army under which the people are absolute and perfect slaves."

It is impossible to treat the man who could write these words as a mere vulgar broiler.   Unfortunately he had no sense
Merit of Lilburne's view.   of the line which divides the practicable from the impracticable, and he was at the mercy of impostors who persuaded him, often on very little ground, that his political opponents were villains of the deepest dye.[1]

Up to this time the Council of State had treated Lilburne with considerable leniency.   He had been allowed to

---

[1] See, for instance, the wild story in *A Preparative to a Hue and Cry after Sir A. Hazlerigg* (E, 573, 16), which is given on the authority of William Blank.   Blank's story was not only inherently improbable, but is shown to have been a fabrication in *An Anatomy of L. C. Lilburne's Spirit,* by T. M[ay], E, 575, 21.

pass his time in or out of the Tower at his pleasure.[1]   On
August 20 they issued a warrant for his apprehension and the
seizure of his books and papers.[2]   Though the execution of the warrant was entrusted to forty musketeers,
Lilburne so terrified the soldiers by the strength of
his language that they came away without making any
serious attempt to carry out their orders.[3]   For some
time the Council made no attempt to recover the ground
they had lost, and, on September 1, Lilburne published a small
tract even more audacious than those which had preceded it.

Aug. 20.
An order to
seize Lil-
burne and
his books.

Aug. 21.
Lilburne
resists.

It bore the title of *An Outcry of the Young Men and
Apprentices of London*, and was printed with the
signatures of ten apprentices, Lilburne's own name
not appearing on the title-page or anywhere else.   It was a
mere incitement to the soldiers to rise in vindication of the
Agreement of the People, and to show by their actions their
sympathy with the martyrs of Burford.[4]   That after this outburst Lilburne should have been allowed to remain at liberty
can only be accounted for by the timidity of the Council of State.

Sept. 1.
*An Outcry
of the
Young Men.*

The time soon arrived when it ceased to be possible to
treat Lilburne with consideration.   A copy of the *Outcry of the
Young Men* having been transmitted to a soldier at
Oxford fell upon well-prepared soil.   On September 8
the garrison called on its officers to join in demanding
a free Parliament according to the *Agreement of the People*, the
restitution of the General Council of the Army, the immediate
abolition of tithes, and the payment of arrears without deduc-
tion for food consumed.   Failing to elicit a satisfactory re-
sponse, they seized on New College where the magazine was
stored, and placed their officers under arrest.   The Council of
State took alarm, the more readily as it had reason to suspect
a combination between Royalists and Levellers, and as the

Sept. 8.
A mutiny at
Oxford.

---

[1] On Aug. 18 he writes from the Tower, *A Preparative*, E, 575, 16.
On the 21st he is at liberty.

[2] Warrant, Aug. 20, *Interr.* I, 63, 7.

[3] *Great Britain's Manifest Messenger*, E, 571, 22.

[4] *An Outcry*, E, 572, 13.

M 2

mutineers had boasted that half the army in England was prepared to join them. At the request of the Council, Fairfax at
once despatched Ingoldsby, the Governor of Oxford, to his post,
and gave orders for a considerable force to follow under the
command of no less a personage than Lambert. Fortunately
no movement of troops on a large scale was needed. Ingoldsby's
presence was sufficient to win back the soldiers to their duty,
and on the morning of the 10th the ringleaders were in custody,
and discipline restored.[1]

The next step was taken on the 11th, when Parliament
ordered the contrivers of the *Outcry of the Young Men* to be pro-

Sept. 11.
The con-
trivers of the
Outcry to be
prosecuted.
secuted under the clause of the new Act of treason
directed against those who stirred up mutiny in the
army.[2] On the 13th, in a new pamphlet,[3] Lilburne
assailed Hazlerigg with extraordinary virulence, and

Sept. 13.
A Prepara-
tive to a
Hue and
Cry.
published the letters in which Tom Verney had
attempted to lure him into treason. On the 14th he
was brought before the Attorney-General, but, as he
refused in any way to acknowledge his offence, a warrant for his
recommittal to the Tower was at last issued on the 19th, though

Sept. 27.
Lilburne
sent back
to the
Tower.
it was not till the 27th that he was actually lodged
within its walls.[4] On October 13 the Council of
State after long consultations with Prideaux, the
Attorney-General, announced to Parliament that
sufficient evidence had been discovered to convict Lilburne,
and directed a special commission to be issued for his trial at
Guildhall, the date ultimately fixed being October 24.[5]

Accordingly on that day thirty-nine of the forty-one com-

---

[1] The fullest account is in Wagstaff's report, in *The Kingdom's Weekly
Intelligencer*, E, 573, 27. See also *The Moderate*, E, 573, 7 ; *The Impartial Intelligencer*, E, 573, 13 ; *The Moderate Intelligencer*, E, 573, 19.

[2] See p. 55.

[3] *A Preparative to a Hue and Cry after Sir A. Hazlerigg*, E,
573, 16.

[4] *Strength out of Weakness*, E, 575, 18.

[5] C. of St. Order Book, Oct. 13, *Interr.* I, 63, p. 38 ; C. of St. to the
Sheriffs of London, Oct. 22, *Interr.* I, 94, p. 502.

missioners nominated appeared at Guildhall, the approaches to
which were strongly guarded by a large force of the City trained

Oct. 24.
The com-
missioners
at Guildhall. bands.[1]   Keble, as one of the commissioners of
the Great Seal, presided over the Court, and was
assisted by no fewer than seven of the common
law judges, amongst whom Jermyn took the leading part.
The first day's proceedings took place before the grand jury,

A true bill
found. and in the end a true bill was found, though if the
report made by Lilburne's friends is to be trusted,
some of the jurors only intended to avow that part of the
charge against him was true.

On the morning of the 25th John Lilburne took his place
at the bar.   Voluble and pugnacious, he had a memory well

Oct. 25.
Lilburne
in court. stored with legal lore, and an absolute contempt for
the time-honoured commonplaces which passed as
legal wisdom.   He soon discovered that the court
which was to try him was as much upon its defence as he was
himself, and would be loth to interrupt him lest any appearance

He refuses
to plead to
the indict-
ment. of harshness should alienate the jury.   When called on
to plead to his indictment he entered on a long argu-
ment against his case being heard with closed doors,
which only came to an end when the presiding judge attracted
his attention to a door that stood open, perhaps in consequence
of an order given after his argument had begun.   Then came an
almost interminable wrangle as to the legality of the commis-

He consents
to plead, sion under which he was tried.   In the end he consented to plead Not guilty, though not in the usual form.

[1] The account of the trial printed in *State Trials*, iv. p. 1269, is a
reprint of the *Trial of L. C. Lilburne* (E, 584, 9), published by Theodorus
Verax, *i.e.* Clement Walker.   This report was taken in the shorthand of
the day, according to *Truth's Victory* (E, 579, 12), by Mr. Reade—perhaps John Reade, one of the grand jury—and others.   Subsequently
appeared *The Second Part of the Trial of Lieutenant-Colonel John
Lilburne* (E, 598, 12), adding an account of the proceedings which took
place before the grand jury on the 24th, and containing errata, as well as
additions to the former report of the proceedings on the 25th and 26th.
These additions are not to be found in the reproduction in the *State Trials*,
where, moreover, the date is wrongly given.

So far Lilburne had presented himself in the character of the litigious disputant. He now stepped on firmer ground. In defending his own person he stood forward as the legal reformer. He asked that counsel might be assigned to him as legal points were certain to arise upon the evidence produced against him, and that some days might intervene between his first sight of the indictment and his trial, in order that he might have time to consider how to meet the charges against him, and to summon witnesses in his favour. The Court would hear nothing of his objections. Counsel should be assigned to him when any point of law arose, but not before, and the only delay granted should be to the following morning. Subsequent legislation on trials for treason in the reign of William and Mary did justice to Lilburne's reasoning. Even in his own day his condemnation of the irrational conclusions of the lawyers was shared by many, and would probably have been shared by more if he had not been himself too ready to take refuge in those very technical niceties which he condemned in others.

and asks for counsel and delay.

The next day's proceedings opened in an unexpected way. Lilburne produced in support of his demand for counsel the case of Major Rolph, who in the preceding year had been accused of treason.[1] Counsel had then been assigned to the prisoner, whose life had been saved by the ingenuity of that counsel. The Court refused to be bound by the precedent, silenced Lilburne for the time, and ordered the jury to be impanelled. When this had been done the indictment was read. There was no mention of the publication on account of which Lilburne had been committed to the Tower in March,[2] the charge of treason being made to rest on his more recent pamphlets.

Oct. 26. Rolph's case quoted.

A jury impanelled.

Evidence was then brought that the incriminated books had either been written or circulated by Lilburne, and passages were read which showed that Lilburne regarded the power of Parliament since Pride's Purge as an illegal

Evidence brought.

---

[1] *Great Civil War*, iv. 131, note 2.   [2] See p. 36.

and tyrannical usurpation resting on the sword alone, and that he had proposed the calling of what in modern language would be styled a Convention to prepare for a new representative body chosen in accordance with the rules laid down in the Levellers' *Agreement of the People*.[1] When the Attorney-General had completed his task, Lilburne once more pleaded for counsel and for further time to consider the indictment. He was weary, he said, with standing for many hours. Yet weary as he was he was bidden to proceed with his defence.

Lilburne's defence is to those who look for an argument going to the root of the questions in dispute in the highest degree disappointing. There is much urging of legal technicalities, much questioning whether the books which everyone knew had issued from his pen had legally been proved to be his own, and a flattering call to the jury to remember that they were judges of law as well as of fact, and that the judges on the bench were no more than Norman intruders and in truth, as soon as the jury pleased to pronounce their verdict, no more than ciphers.[2]

Lilburne's defence.

Impossible as it is to pry into the hearts of the jury, it is hardly likely that when, at five in the afternoon, after having sat for ten hours, they began to consider their verdict, they were much moved by any of these things. The broad issue had been revealed, if not in Lilburne's speech in defence, in the copious extracts from his writings which had been read aloud by the clerk at the instigation of the Attorney-General. Was England to be governed in accordance with the will of its freely elected representatives, or by a little knot of men who owed what authority they possessed to the swords of a victorious army? The decision was the easier because the jury had not to come to a resolution on a question of abstract politics. They had simply to determine whether they would hang the prisoner for expressing his disapproval of acts which had so dubious an origin.

Real point before the jury.

[1] See p. 47.

[2] In the text it is ' are no more but ciphers to pronounce their verdict,' which is evidently corrupt.

The substance of Lilburne's best defence lay in a passage
in the *Outcry of the Young Men*, a portion of which had been
read in Court : " It is not imaginable—except

among bears, wolves, and lions—that brethren of
one cause, one nation and family, can without
remorse and secret check of conscience, impose such iron yoke
of cruelty and oppression upon their fellows as by the awe and
force of your sword rampant is imposed upon the people of
this nation ; we are at the best but your hewers of wood and
drawers of water ; our very persons, our lives and properties,
are all over-awed to the supportation only of the raging lawless
sword, drenched in the precious blood of the people. The
ancient and famous magistracy of this nation, the Petition of
Right, the Great Charter of England, above thirty times confirmed in open and free Parliament, with all other the fundamental laws, safeties, and securities of the people, which our
ancestors at an extraordinary dear rate purchased for the
inheritance of us and the generations after us, and for which
you pretendedly took up arms against the late King and his
party, are now all subverted, broken down and laid waste, the
military power being thrust into the very office and seat of
civil authority :—the King not only most illegally put to death
by a strange, monstrous, illegal, arbitrary court such as England
never knew, monarchy extirpated not rectified, without and
beside the consent of the people, though the actors of that
bloody scene have owned and declared them to be the original
of all just human authority, but [1] even our Parliaments—the
very marrow and soul of all the native rights of the people—
put down, and the name and power thereof transmitted to a
picked party of your forcible selecting, and such as your
officers—our lords and riders—have often and frequently
styled no better than a mock Parliament, a shadow of a
Parliament, a seeming authority, or the like, pretending the
continuance thereof but till a new and equal Representative,

---

[1] The extract read in court begins, for obvious reasons, with this word,
The Trial of L. C. John Lilburne (E, 584, 9), p. 94.

by mutual agreement of the free people of England, could be elected, although now, for subserviency to their exaltation and kingship, they prorogue and perpetuate the same, in the name and under colour thereof introducing a Privy Council, or, as they call it, a Council of State, of superintendency and suppression to all future successive Parliaments for ever, erecting a martial government by blood and violence impulsed upon us." [1]

Rhetorically exaggerated as the words were, Lilburne's diagnosis of the situation was sufficiently near the mark to win sympathy from the tradesmen who composed the jury, and who detested nothing so much as the military compulsion which bore them down. When after an adjournment of an hour, the Court called on the foreman of the jury for the verdict, he was able to reply in a loud voice, 'Not guilty,' in the name of all the twelve.

The verdict.

Then ensued a scene, the like of which had in all probability never been witnessed in an English court of justice, and was never again to be witnessed till the seven bishops were freed by the verdict of a jury from the rage of James II. From every part of the crowded hall 'a loud and unanimous shout' arose in triumph. For a full half hour the cries of joy continued to be raised. The only man unmoved was the prisoner himself, who had just escaped from the jaws of death. The judges grew pale with alarm lest the excitement in the auditory should lead to an attack on the bench. There was, however, no bitterness in that outpouring of thankfulness, and when order had been at last restored, the judges directed that the prisoner should be led back to the Tower. If there was any intention of trying him for some lighter offence, the idea was abandoned, and on November 8 the Council of State gave orders for his liberation. On the same day his three companions in misfortune, Walwyn, Prince, and Overton, were also set at liberty. [2]

Popular applause.

Nov. 8.
Lilburne liberated.

---

[1] *An Outcry of the Young Men* (E, 572, 13), p. 1.

[2] Warrants, Nov. 8, *Interr.* I, 63, pp. 234–236.

The cry of the citizens in Guildhall was substantially identical with the cry which eleven years later was to call for a Free Parliament, and thereby to bring about the Restoration. In the meanwhile it might be permitted to those who had to face the immediate dangers of the situation to ask how the government was to be carried on. It is certain that few, if any, of the men in possession of power contemplated a permanent tenure of it at the will of the military commanders. They imagined it possible that at no distant time they would be able to retire in favour of another Parliament chosen by a new constituency, as free, if not quite as democratic, as that which Lilburne declared to be the sole legitimate representative of the nation.

How was the government to be carried on?

A new Parliament looked for.

To prepare the way for this result, the existing Parliament was anxious to win the hearts of the masses to the new Commonwealth by popular legislation. Of such legislation they had already given a specimen by the Act for poor prisoners, passed on September 4. The condition of insolvent debtors was most unequal.

Popular legislation proposed.

Sept. 4. Act for poor prisoners.

To a man with property who was unwilling or unable to meet his creditors, the imprisonment to which he was subjected brought with it the enjoyment of a riotous life under sordid conditions. To a poor man it brought untold misery. Unable to pay the fees required for food and maintenance, he was thrust into the beggars' ward, where his sole means of existence was the charity of passers-by, who might chance to be touched by his doleful appeals. Amidst dirt and vermin, disease spread fast. Vice added its scourge, and the life of the insolvent debtor of this class was seldom prolonged. By the new Act he was enabled to obtain his liberty, if he could show that he did not possess more than the value of 5*l.* in addition to the necessaries of life. On December 21 it was re-enacted with amendments which placed the whole transaction under the safeguard of a jury. With unwise narrowness all persons who had taken the

Dec. 21. It is re-enacted with amendments.

King's side in the late war were excluded from the benefit of
this law.[1]

An attempt to remedy another evil was less successful than
it deserved. Since the end of the war highway robbery had

Highway
robbery.

been on the increase, as disbanded soldiers,
especially from the Royal army, found in it a con-
genial occupation. In the first year of the Commonwealth it
assumed alarming proportions. The roads round London had
become notoriously unsafe, and robbery was not unfrequently

Nov. 14.
Soldiers to
put it down.

accompanied by murder. On November 14 Fairfax
was directed by the Council of State to employ his
soldiers in clearing the roads, while power was given
to the officers to search inns and ale-houses, and to require
from the landlords a strict account of their guests.[2] Unfortunately experience shows that a regular army is little calcu-
ated for the suppression of crime, and the experience of the
Commonwealth was no exception to the rule.

However desirous Parliament may have been of initiating
generous legislation, it was constantly thrown back upon its

Religious
liberty
considered.

own defence by the necessities of its position. Though
a body mainly consisting of Independents could
hardly avoid attempting to legalise religious liberty,
it was often driven to bethink itself of contriving limits to the
excesses of its opponents. The Presbyterian clergy gave special

July 9.
Resolution
against
political
sermons.

annoyance. On July 9 Parliament, stung by these
attacks, passed a resolution declaring all ministers to
be delinquents if they preached or prayed against
the present Government, publicly mentioned Charles
or James Stuart, or refused to keep days of public humiliation,
or to publish Acts and Orders of Parliament. It is to the
credit of Cromwell and Ireton, who were at that time still at

[1] *Scobell*, ii. 87, 99. See *The Œconomy of the Fleet*, edited by Dr.
Jessopp, for the Camden Soc. Before May 25, 1653, one hundred and
thirty persons took the oath, and were liberated under the Act. *A
Schedule . . . of the Prisoners in the Fleet*, E, 698, 13. At that date two
hundred and thirty-four were still in prison.

[2] **C. of St.** Order Book, *Interr.* **I,** 63, p. 258.

Westminster, that they acted as tellers against a scheme which would place restrictions on their own bitterest enemies; but they only secured sixteen votes, whilst those given on the other side amounted to twenty-eight.[1]

On August 6 the House took into consideration a declaration on the government of the Church, and it was significant

Aug. 6. Tithes not to be compulsory. of the feeling which prevailed, that a proposal to declare the payment of tithe compulsory was rejected by twenty-five to sixteen.[2] Other questions were

Aug. 16. Petition of the Council of Officers, referred to a committee, and on the 16th, before its report was given in, a petition was presented from Fairfax and the Council of Officers asking that penal laws in matters of religion might be swept away, yet that the liberty so accorded might not 'extend to the toleration of popery, prelacy, the Book of Common Prayer, public scorn or contempt for God and His Word.' The petitioners also asked for the punishment of all who committed 'open acts of profaneness, as drunkenness, swearing, uncleanness, and the like.'[3] A similar request was made by Cromwell, writing from

and of Cromwell. Milford Haven, but it was remarked at the time that he omitted any mention of restrictions to full religious liberty.[4] On the 21st, on the receipt of Cromwell's letter, Parliament to some extent responded by the appointment

Aug. 21. A committee on ordination. of a committee to consider how persons who had scruples about the Presbyterian form of ordination might be admitted to the ministry.[5] As far as Roman Catholics were concerned, the House soon showed that it agreed with Fairfax. On August 31 it ordered the arrest of Sir John Winter, who, in the teeth of an order of Parliament,[6] was still in England, and the banishment of Sir Kenelm Digby and Walter Montague.[7] If Cromwell still differed, his experience in Ireland would soon bring him to concur in this matter with Fairfax.

---

[1] *C.J.* vi. 257.   [2] *Ib.* vi. 275.
[3] *Ib.* vi. 279 ; *The Petition of His Excellency,* E, 569, 22.
[4] *The Moderate,* E, 572, 1.   [5] *C.J.* vi. 282.
[6] See p. 82.   [7] *C.J.* vi. 289.

On Sunday, September 9, a practical attempt to secure liberty of worship was made in London, when the service enjoined by the Book of Common Prayer was freely read in many London churches. In one a troop of horse intervened, stopped the service, and inflicted severe injuries on some of the congregation who rallied round the minister. In another place a lawyer's clerk, attempting to preach, was interrupted by a number of people said to have been Presbyterians or Royalists, and it was only owing to the assistance of soldiers that he was able to continue his sermon.[1]

Sept. 9. The Common Prayer Book used in London.

A lawyer's clerk preaches.

Parliament seems to have been alarmed at the course matters were taking. An Act for the Relief of Tender Consciences, which was at this time in the hands of a committee, was allowed to sleep, and on September 28 the House ordered the issue of a declaration in which strong language was used against the Levellers, and an attempt was made to win over the moderate Presbyterians by a protest that Parliament entertained no intention of 'countenancing a universal toleration,' and that it would proceed effectually against all who abused the liberty granted.[2]

Act for tender consciences proposed.

Sept. 28. A declaration ordered.

Liberty of religion to be limited.

It was not only in respect to religious matters that Parliament had convinced itself that liberty to be worth having must be regulated. The virulence of Lilburne's pamphlets and of the Royalist newspapers had led to the preparation of a measure for the restriction of the Press, and an Act for that purpose was finally passed on September 20.[3] The Act was directed not against opinion, but against false news and misrepresentation of the proceedings and intentions of the Government. No 'book or pamphlet, treatise, sheet or sheets of news' was to be published without a licence. The penalty for spreading abroad scandalous or

Sept. 20. Act for restricting the liberty of the Press.

---

[1] *The Moderate Intelligencer*, E, 573, 19.

[2] *A Declaration*, E, 575, 9. Thomason's date of publication is Oct. 3. See p. 172.

[3] *Scobell*, ii. 88.

libellous books was to be 10*l.* or forty days' imprisonment for the author, 5*l.* or twenty days' imprisonment for the printer, and 2*l.* or ten days' imprisonment for the seller, whilst the purchaser was to forfeit 1*l.* if he did not give information within four and twenty hours.[1]

It was easier to pass such an Act than to enforce it. With London hungry for writings which would turn the laugh against the Government, unlicensed presses easily kept themselves in existence. Of the three principal Royalist newspapers, one, *Mercurius Elencticus*, disappeared after November 5. The other two, *Mercurius Pragmaticus* and *The Man in the Moon*, were still in full swing at the end of the year. Nor was it easy to stop the flow of political pamphlets directed against the Commonwealth. Clement Walker, for instance, issued, under the title of *Anarchia Anglicana*, a second part of his *History of Independency*, in which he virulently attacked the existing Government. On October 24, Parliament ordered the arrest of the author, and on November 13, undeterred by its failure in Lilburne's case, sent him to the Tower and ordered him to be tried for High Treason.[2]

The attempt thus made to suppress false news was accompanied by an effort to replace it by news more favourable to the Government. On October 2 appeared the first number of *A Brief Relation*,[3] published by authority under the superintendence of Gualter Frost, the Secretary of the Council of State. On October 9 appeared the first number of *Several Proceedings*, with the licence of Henry Scobell, Clerk of the Parliament. Both papers were eminently respectable, and are amongst our most valuable sources of information.

The un-licensed press.

Oct. 24. Order for the arrest of Clement Walker.

Nov. 13. Walker sent to the Tower.

Oct. 2. A Brief Relation.

Oct. 9. Several Proceed-ings.

---

[1] See Masson's *Life of Milton*, iv. 118, where it is pointed out that only newspapers and political pamphlets were aimed at.

[2] *C.J.* vi. 312, 322.

[3] *A Brief Relation.* The first number (E, 575, 6) is 'published by authority.' The second number (E, 575, 15) is 'licensed by Gualter Frost, Esq., &c.'

Without any distinct line being traceable between them, *Several Proceedings* [1] devoted itself principally to domestic affairs, whilst *A Brief Relation* is for the most part filled with news from foreign countries, and especially with those which concerned the exiled family. Transactions in Scotland and Ireland furnished a common ground to both.

Amongst the literary defenders of the Government must be counted Milton, whose *Eikonoklastes* appeared on October 6.

Oct. 6.
Milton's
Eikono-
klastes.

It is barely more than a Miltonic piece of hack-work. Even if Milton had thrown into it his heart and soul, the method adopted, perhaps adopted by order, was fatal to the production of a great work. The provision of a counterpart to each separate division of the *Eikon Basiliké*, showing that Charles under each heading was despicable rather than admirable, makes toilsome reading, and, however much it accorded with the literary fashion of the day,[2] was not the way to win adherents. With all its faults the *Eikon Basiliké* went straight to the hearts of thousands. The picture of the Royal sufferer would not be erased from their memories by an exaggerated display of his despotism, or even of his personal failings. In such a case mere negative criticism avails but little. What was needed was the development of a higher loyalty to the nation in the place of the lower loyalty to the King, and the quickening of a sense of the exuberant vitality of the collective life of the people in the place of devotion to the head of the national organisation. Time had been when Milton had struck that key, and gazed on the vision of a ' noble and puissant nation rousing herself like a strong man after sleep and shaking her invincible locks.' He could not speak in that strain of a Commonwealth supporting itself on an armed force, though he still might hope that, under the guidance of the statesman who now watched over its destinies, the time would

---

[1] *Several Proceedings* (E, 575, 14) is not said to be printed by authority, but has the name of ' Hen. Scobell, Cleric. Parliamenti,' printed under the title.

[2] Chillingworth, for instance, adopted this method in his *Religion of Protestants*.

yet come when such glories would again present themselves as realities.

Parliament itself was not without hopes that this vision would some day be realised. On October 11, it resolved that 'the committee for regulating elections and their equal distribution' should meet from day to day, and report to the House on the 30th. Yet it was impossible for the members to prepare for fresh elections without misgiving. In a declaration recently issued[1] they had accused the Levellers of urging a dissolution, though they knew 'that, as the present distemper of the people was the violence of faction, and activity of their secret enemies, either these elections could not be free, or the people must have lost their liberty by it.' To provide, in some way, against the choice of a Royalist Parliament, the House resolved that every member then sitting, or hereafter chosen, should sign the engagement which had been taken by most of the members of the Council of State : " I do declare and promise that I will be true and faithful to the Commonwealth of England as the same is now established, without a King or House of Lords."

On the following day the obligation of signing this engagement was extended to officers of the army and navy, to all soldiers and sailors under their command, to judges and officials of the Courts of Law, to members of the Inns of Court, as well as to all who held municipal offices, or sat in municipal councils ; to all graduates and officers in the Universities, and to the masters, fellows, schoolmasters, and scholars of the Colleges of Eton, Winchester, and Westminster ; to all ministers admitted to a benefice, and finally to all who received pensions from the State.

The intention of the Legislature was evidently to create a state within the nation, upon which authority could rest securely, thus following, in one respect at least, the *Agreement of the People.* Yet though the engagement was freely taken by officials during the following

Oct. 11. Committee for regulating elections.

Misgivings felt.

The engagement to be taken by members

Oct. 12. and by officials generally.

A state to be created within the nation.

[1] See p. 173.

weeks, the attitude of the London citizens after Lilburne's acquittal gave cause to suspect that even this test would be insufficient to keep out the enemies of the Commonwealth at the election of Common Councillors which was to take place

Dec. 14.
Act for
elections
in London.

on December 21. Accordingly, on the 14th, Parliament passed a new Act disabling from holding office or from voting at elections in the City during the ensuing year, any person who had 'been imprisoned,' or had 'had his estate sequestered for delinquency,' had 'assisted the late King against the Parliament,' had taken part in bringing in the Scots, had subscribed 'the treasonable engagement' which had led to Hamilton's invasion, or had abetted the tumults in London and the neighbouring counties in the year 1648. Further, all who had supported any engagement for a personal treaty with the late King in London, or who now refused to sign the new engagement, were disqualified from holding office in the City.[1]

The net had been spread widely enough to exclude Presbyterian Royalists, as well as Cavalier Royalists, but there was nothing in it to exclude Levellers. Lilburne had,

Dec. 21.
Lilburne
elected
a Common
Councillor.

since his trial, taken up his abode in the City, and when the day of election arrived, he was duly chosen to a seat in the Common Council. Being challenged

Takes the
engagement
with a quali-
fication.

to take the engagement, he at once expressed his readiness to do so, but accompanied his unusual compliance with a declaration that by the Commonwealth to which he promised fidelity, he understood 'all the good and legal people of England to be meant,' not 'the present Parliament, Council of State, or Council of the Army.'[2]

Action of
the Lord
Mayor and
aldermen.

Scandalised at this evasion, the Lord Mayor and aldermen committed to prison Lilburne's chief supporters, Chetwin and Caverly, and on the 26th

Dec. 26.
Lilburne's
election
quashed.

brought the matter before Parliament. Parliament at once quashed Lilburne's election, as well as that of Lieutenant-Colonel Fenton of whom no particulars

[1] *An Act Disabling the Election of Divers Persons*, E, 1,060, No. 72.
[2] *The Engagement Vindicated and Explained*, E, 590, 4.

are known. Chetwin was disfranchised and sent prisoner to
Windsor Castle. Caverly received no further punishment, and
it is therefore probable that he had in the meantime made his
peace with the City authorities.[1]

Even this last affront did not rouse Lilburne to break the
silence which he had maintained since his acquittal. " I have
Lilburne's
temporary
silence. been judged by man," he is reported to have said,
"but God and men will have to judge between
Cromwell and me." [2] Yet he was in no haste to
appeal to the tribunal of public opinion. For the present he
betook himself to the occupation of a soap-boiler,[3] leaving
politics alone for a time, unless, indeed, he took part in the
overtures which his comrades were at that time making to
Charles on the ground that more was to be expected from a
Royalist restoration than from the oligarchy which had usurped
the name of a Commonwealth.[4]

That Lilburne, consciously or unconsciously, was playing
into the hands of the Royalists was the best justification of the
Danger
from
abroad. high-handed measures employed against the Levellers. It was fortunate for the Commonwealth that
the relations between the continental Governments

---

[1] *C.J.* vi. 337.

[2] He said 'qu'il avoit esté jugé par des hommes, mais qu'il falloit
que Dieu et les mesmes hommes fussent encore juges entre Cromwell et
luy.' Croullé to Mazarin $\frac{Oct. 29}{Nov. 8}$, *Arch. des Aff. Étrangères*, li. fol. 303.

[3] The project of 'the wild levelling representative,' writes *Merc.
Politicus*, on June 12, 1650, 'is at an end since John Lilburne turned off
the trade of State-mending to take up that of soap-boiling.'

[4] " During the time of his attendance at Court, and especially since
John Lilburne was acquitted upon his trial, there came several overtures
from the people that go under the notion of Levellers to the King of
Scotland." Their letters ' did contain a demand from the King of some
assurance for a full and general liberty, or to that purpose, and an offer
upon those terms to give him assistance for the suppression of the present
power.' Coke's examination, *Hist. MSS. Com.* Rep. xiii. App. i. 591.
That Lilburne was likely to share the opinions of other Levellers in this
matter is shown by the extract from *An Impeachment of High Treason*,
quoted at p. 162.

were such that even those most ready to take umbrage at the apparition of a military republic in England were in no case

Improbability that continental Governments will interfere. to give armed assistance to the claimant of the throne. Mazarin had on his hands not only a war with Spain, but a revolutionary movement in France itself. Charles's brother-in-law, the Prince of Orange, had entered on an embittered controversy with the Provincial States of Holland, whilst the King of Spain had enough to do in making head against the armies of France. There were, however, elements enough of disorder in Europe—disbanded soldiers, unemployed officers, and discontented princes—which Charles might turn to account, if only he could find a basis of operations to substitute for the one which he had lately hoped to secure in Ireland. Every fresh victory of Cromwell hastened the day when Charles would, however much against his will, be driven to capitulate to the Covenanters at Edinburgh.

As far as the continental Governments were concerned, the leaders of the Commonwealth knew better than to assume a tone of weakness. In the Netherlands their agent, Strickland, was directed to protest against the refusal of the States General to admit him to an audience, and to return to England if the

Strickland's recall. refusal was repeated.[1] For the present, however, the order was suspended, perhaps because Strickland was needed to give warning of the movements of the Royalists in Holland, and it was not till the following July that he actually left the Netherlands.[2]

The attitude of the English Government towards France and Spain was no less decided. Croullé, the French agent, and

France and Spain required to recognise the Commonwealth. Cardenas, the Spanish ambassador, were told that no business would be transacted with them till they recognised the Commonwealth. With France the Independents had long been on bad terms, and the seizure in the Mediterranean of eight ships of the Levant Company, valued, together with their cargoes, at 300,000*l.*, by French

---

[1] C. of St! Order Book, *Interr.* I, 63, pp. 196, 561.

[2] *Ib.* 64, p. 171 ; Admiralty Committee Day Book, *Interr.* I, 123, pp. 376–379.

men-of-war, had caused considerable indignation in England.[1]
On August 23, on the plea that the French Government had
in the preceding year forbidden the importation of
English draperies, Parliament prohibited the importation of French wine, as well as of French woollen
and silken manufactures.[2] So hostile was the feeling at Westminster that it was believed that France and England were on
the brink of war.

Aug. 23.
Commer-
cial reprisals
on France.

Towards the end of October it was reported that Cromwell
had declared that if he were ten years younger every king in
Europe would tremble before him. He had a better
cause than the late King of Sweden, and he thought
himself able to do more for the good of the peoples
than Gustavus had done for his own ambition. Such words
were most unlikely to have been Cromwell's,[3] but they gave expression to an opinion which was beginning to take root in the
minds of the more ardent supporters of the new system.

A saying
attributed
to Crom-
well.

With Spain the Council of State was, outwardly at least,
on a better footing. Though nothing could exceed the detesta-

[1] A petition of the Levant Company to the Council of State in
February 1649 (*S. P. Dom.* i. 10) complains of having suffered 'by the
injurious and hostile attempts of the French fleet within the Streights,
who continue to seize upon your petitioners' ships and estate to a great
value ; not only to their heavy loss, but to the unspeakable prejudice of
this Commonwealth ; by the decay of shipping, diminution of custom,
and in conclusion a total loss of this ample trade into the Levant which
had been so advantageous and honourable to this land. A list of the
ships already taken by them, together with a valuation of their lading,
being hereto annexed.'

The list gives the names of eight ships 'that have been lately surprised and sunk or taken by the French fleet within the Straits, whereof
seven (besides others also of smaller value) have been taken within twelve
months past ; which ships with their lading amount to 300,000*l.* and
upwards.' This French fleet must have been a fleet of the French king's,
which explains the resolution of the authorities of the Commonwealth to
hold the French king a special wrong-doer, and bound to make com-
pensation in his own name above such as might be due for the action of
privateers.   [2] *C.J.* vi. 285.

[3] Croullé to Mazarin, Nov. $\frac{1}{11}$, *Arch. des Aff. Étrangères*, lix. fol. 306.
Croullé did not himself believe that the saying was Cromwell's.

tion with which Philip IV. and his advisers regarded a regicide
republic, they knew that those who directed its course were

Spain and
the Com-
monwealth.

hostile to their French enemies, and though Cardenas
was not instructed to give it formal recognition, he
was authorised to hold secret communications with its
leading statesmen.   Early in August he informed his Government that they were anxious to despatch an ambassador to

August.
A proposed
embassy.

Oct. 19.
Cottington
and Hyde
in Spain.

Madrid.[1]   In the winter this desire was strengthened
by the news that Cottington and Hyde had crossed
the frontier on October 19, and that though the
Spanish Government had done everything in its
power to interpose delays, they had reached Madrid
on November 26.[2]   Philip indeed showed no readiness to
comply with their demands for pecuniary assistance ; but it
was manifestly undesirable in the eyes of the English Government that their diplomacy should remain uncounteracted.

In one quarter especially the Council of State might fairly
calculate on the goodwill of Spain.   Since his escape from

Rupert
makes
prizes, and
carries them
to Lisbon.

Kinsale, Rupert had been making prizes of English
shipping and had been permitted by the King of
Portugal, John IV., to bring them into the Tagus
and to dispose of them at Lisbon.   To be the
friend of Portugal was to be the enemy of Spain, and the
English Government was not unreasonable in hoping that
Philip might be induced to make common cause with them

1650.
Jan. 16.
Mission of
Ascham
and Vane.

against Rupert, or at least to refuse him permission
to enter a Spanish harbour.   Accordingly, on
January 16, Anthony Ascham was appointed to go
as English Agent to Madrid, whilst Charles Vane was
to go in a similar capacity to Lisbon to remonstrate with the

Blake to
command
against
Rupert.

King.   It was hoped that their mission would be
the more efficacious as they were to be conveyed in
a powerful fleet about to sail against Rupert under
the command of Blake.[3]

[1] Cardenas to Philip IV., *Guizot*, i. App. ix. 4.
[2] Edgeman's Diary, *Clarendon MSS.*   They were detained at St.
Sebastian nineteen days.   [3] C. of St. Order Book, *Interr.* I, 63, p. 525.

CHAPTER VIII

THE CONFERENCE AT BREDA

FIRM as was the attitude of the Commonwealth towards
domestic enemies and foreign rivals, its leaders could not but
watch with anxiety the development of events in
Scotland. They were well aware that efforts were
being made to renew the negotiation which had
been broken off at the Hague. Argyle, though he would
doubtless still have preferred an alliance with the
English Commonwealth, had recognised it to be impracticable, and was now doing everything in his
power to remove the difficulties in the way of an understanding with Charles. At a conference held at Edinburgh early in July between five ministers and five
of the leading statesmen, Johnston, Chiesley and one
of the ministers argued in favour of the English alliance, whilst
the others who were present, including Argyle and Loudoun,
came to the conclusion that, if only the King would give satisfaction about religion and the Covenant, they were bound to
shed the last drop of their blood in his cause.[1] It is hardly
likely that Argyle at least was blind to the difficulties in the
way of such a policy,[2] but it was enough for him that any

1649.
Danger
from
Scotland.

July 1.
Argyle's
policy.

July.
A conference
at Edin-
burgh.

---

[1] *Balfour*, iii. 416.

[2] According to Graymond, the Covenanters considered the English as
enemies of the Covenant, and Charles ' comme une personne qui n'est
pas beaucoup portée pour luy.' The Covenanters, he adds, were ' generale-
ment tous les ministres et le parlement excepté environ sept ou huict des

attempt on his part to stem the popular current would be the signal for his own expulsion from power.

A few days after this decision had been taken Will Murray arrived in Edinburgh with letters from Charles to Argyle and *July 15.* his principal colleagues. Argyle gathered from their *Letters from Charles.* contents that it was still possible to continue the negotiation, if only the extreme demands of the Covenanters were relaxed. He therefore seized an opportunity when the warmest partisans of the Kirk were absent from Parliament, to obtain the consent of that body to a scheme for *Proposed mission of Lothian.* sending Lothian to the King, Lothian being, like himself, desirous of paying some consideration to Charles's feelings. So loud, however, was the outcry *Aug. 7. Winram substituted for him.* raised that Lothian refused to go. On August 7, the name of George Winram of Liberton was substituted for that of Lothian. Winram, like Lothian, belonged to Argyle's following, and when he found that Parliament intended to entrust him with a letter in which Charles was asked to acknowledge the legality of the existing truncated Parliament, and also to meet commissioners who would expect 'a full agreement upon the grounds contained in the former desires,' he too declined to set forth on a hopeless errand.[1] Argyle was taught that he had no power to make his party more reasonable than it was.

Winram's objection to undertaking the mission was, however, not one of principle, and when the news of Cromwell's

principaux qui, pour se conserver absolument le maniement des affaires en ce pays, ne feroient jamais difficulté de recognoistre la republique pretendue des Independans.' Graymond to Brienne, Aug. $\frac{7}{17}$, *Harl. MSS.* 4,551, fol. 414.

[1] *Balfour,* iii. 417 ; *Baillie,* iii. 99 ; *Acts of Parl. of Scotl.* vi. part ii. 538, 739, 740. The letter, says Baillie, was 'drawn by Sir John Chiesley,' and was, 'though much smoother than the Church's, drawn by Mr. James Wood, yet so harsh, and the instructions so scabrous, that there was no hope of doing any good with the King thereby.' Chiesley was, as has been seen, in favour of the English alliance, and therefore inclined to throw difficulties in the way of an understanding with Charles.

success at Drogheda came to convince him that Charles was more likely to prove flexible, he consented to set out. On October 11 he sailed from Leith.[1] Taking Holland on his way [2] he opened communications with a knot of English Pres-

Oct. 11.
Winram
sails from
Leith.

byterian exiles, amongst whom Lord Willoughby of Parham, Massey, Graves, and Alderman Bunce were the most notable. With them was Colonel Silas Titus,

The Eng-
lish Pres-
byterians in
Holland.

who had at one time fought in the Parliamentary ranks, but who had transferred his allegiance to the late King, in whose service he had been during his

Silas Titus.

captivity at Carisbrooke. He now offered himself as a medium of communication between the Queen's ministers, Jermyn and Percy, in whom the Scottish alliance found warm supporters, and the London Presbyterians who were working in the same direction. When Titus set out for Jersey in Winram's company, he had with him a list of eighty London citizens favourable to a restoration of monarchy, and asserted boldly that if only Charles would 'agree with the Scots, he should want neither men nor money.' [3]

For a disciple of the Kirk, Winram may be regarded as a moderate man. He did not wish to push matters to extremities

Winram's
principles.

against the Engagers.[4] Yet, though he had been unwilling to undertake a bootless mission, he was incapable of comprehending that there could be any valid

His hope
to win
Charles.

objection to the acceptance of the Covenant. "Now," he wrote to a clerical friend, "is the time to pray that the Lord would prevent the King with His tender mercies, for indeed he is brought very low, when he has

---

[1] *Balfour*, iii. 432.

[2] According to Balfour, the Committee thought that Charles was still at Brussels. In any case, Winram's route lay through the Nether-lands and France, unless he was to run the risk of being seized by an English cruiser.

[3] *State Trials*, v. 43; Coke's Examination, *Hist. MSS. Com.* Rep. xiii. App. i. 585. Compare the papers in the Appendix to Hillier's *Narrative of the Attempted Escapes of Charles I.*

[4] Winram to Douglas, Oct. 31 (? Oct. $\frac{21}{31}$); *Baillie*, iii. 522.

not bread both for himself and his servants, and betwixt him and his brother not one English shilling, and worse yet, if I durst write it. I am confident no ingenuous spirit will take advantage of his necessities; but, for all this, use him princely. . . His case is very deplorable, being in prison where he is, living in penury, surrounded by his enemies, not able to live anywhere else in the world unless he would come to Scotland by giving them satisfaction to their just demands; yet his pernicious and devilish council will suffer him to starve before they will suffer him to take the League and Covenant. I am persuaded no rational man can think he will come that length at first; but if he could once be extricate from his wicked council, there might be hope." [1]

Winram and those who sent him were right in supposing that Cromwell's successes would have great influence over

Oct.
Charles
anxious for
news from
Ireland.

Charles's resolutions. Yet though Henry Seymour had been despatched to Ormond in October to inquire into the truth of conflicting rumours,[2] some

Seymour's
mission.

time must elapse before an answer could be received. Uncertainty about the progress of his cause in Ireland did not as yet breed in Charles any desire to relax his opposition to the Covenant. On October 31 he issued a manifesto, in which he called on

Oct. 31.
Charles's
manifesto.

Englishmen to rally round him as their lawful king, and to free themselves from a tyrannical usurpation,

Nov.
His mes-
sage to the
Queen of
Sweden.
Feeling
in Jersey
against the
Scots.

without implying by a single word any intention to make the slightest concession to the Presbyterians.[3] In November he sent a messenger to Sweden 'chiefly to satisfy the Queen of the unreasonableness of the Scots.'[4] Among Charles's younger followers the feeling against the Scots was very strong. "I had

---

[1] Winram to Douglas, Nov. $\frac{8}{18}$; *Baillie*, iii. 522.

[2] See p. 144. Seymour was descended from the elder branch of the family of Protector Somerset.

[3] *His Majesty's Declaration*, Oct. 31, E, 578, 2.

[4] Trethewy to Edgeman, Nov. $\frac{12}{22}$, Hoskins, *Charles II. in the Channel Islands*, ii. 348.

forgot to tell you," wrote one of Hyde's correspondents, "that Winram was expected at Jersey before my coming from thence. I believe he will think he hath made a good voyage if he escape with a broken pate : the gallants talked before I came away of throwing him over the wall." [1]

Diplomatic proprieties were too strong for such a practical solution. Winram on his landing was received with all due Winram's respect, and as only three of Charles's councillors reception. were at that time in Jersey, the propositions of the envoy were laid before a body in which all the lords then in the island were included. Charles spoke Winram fairly, but he delayed giving him a definite answer in the hope that Seymour's return with a favourable report would relieve him from the necessity of placing his neck under the Scottish yoke.

Dec. 27. On December 27, Seymour at last arrived with the Seymour's worst of tidings. [2] Charles learnt from his lips that news from Ireland. Munster had revolted, and knew that, unless he could bend himself to accept the Scottish terms, he would have to wait, as an impoverished exile, the day on which a victorious Montrose might summon him to reascend his ancestral thrones.

It is not strange that Charles hoped to find a way out of the hideous dilemma. Might not the Scots even yet be induced to desist from their harsh requirements? Charles His Council, like himself, resolved that 'a treaty on hopes to escape from honourable terms' with those by whom Winram had his dilemma. been sent would probably lead to an agreement with 1650. Scotland by which Ireland might be saved and An advice of the Council. England recovered. Nicholas was alone in proposing to declare that honourable terms were inconsistent with the abandonment of Ormond or Montrose. [3] To await events and to avoid all definite resolutions was the course which most commended itself to Charles's mind.

[1] Berkeley to Hyde, $\frac{\text{Nov. 23}}{\text{Dec. 3}}$, *Charles II. and Scotland*, I.

[2] Intelligence from Jersey, Jan. $\frac{1}{11}$, *Clarendon MSS.* ii. No. 213; Seymour to Ormond, March $\frac{5}{15}$, *Carte MSS.* ccxiii. fol. 12.

[3] Proceedings in Council, Jan., *Nicholas Papers*, i. 160.

On January 11, taking no notice of the Parliament's preliminary request for the recognition of its legality further than by addressing his letter to the Committee of Estates, Charles expressed a wish to receive commissioners at Breda on March 15, to treat of the just satisfaction of his subjects in Scotland, and of assistance to be given for bringing his father's murderers to punishment, and for the recovery of his own rights. To this Charles added a strong hint that he expected the Committee to be guided by a 'just and prudent moderation.' He then referred to the earnest desire which he himself entertained to oblige all his subjects in that kingdom. A junction of the existing Government with the Engagers, and if possible even with Montrose, in defence of his own rights in England, would evidently have been most in accordance with his wishes.[1] Two days later he gave Titus a reply to an address from the English Presbyterians, in which he urged them 'to send presently into Scotland to prevail with them to bring such reasonable demands to the treaty as, meeting with our inclinations and resolution to accord all just and reasonable things, may, by the blessing of God, produce a full and happy agreement.'[2]

Jan. 11. His letter to the Committee of Estates.

Jan. 13. Charles's reply to the English Presbyterians.

If Charles's quest after moderation in Scotland was not a hopeful one, he was at least shrewd enough not to trust solely to the equity of the Committee of Estates. "To the end," he wrote to Montrose, "you may not apprehend that we intend, either by anything contained in these letters or by the treaty we expect, to give the least impediment to your proceedings, we think fit to let you know that as we conceive that your preparations have been one

Jan. 12. His letter to Montrose.

---

[1] Charles II. to the Committee of Estates, Jan. 11, Carte's *Orig. Letters,* i. 355.

[2] Message sent by Titus, Jan. $\frac{13}{23}$, Hillier's *Narrative of the attempted escapes of Charles I.,* 321. In a letter to Robert Douglas of Feb. $\frac{5}{15}$, Charles wrote in the same strain : " I entreat you, therefore, to use your credit amongst the ministers to persuade them to reasonable moderation." *Baillie,* iii. 524.

effectual motive that hath induced them to make the. said address to us, so your vigorous proceeding will be a good means to bring them to such moderation in the said treaty as probably may produce an agreement and a present union of that whole nation in our service. We assure you therefore that we will not, before or during the treaty, do anything contrary to that power and authority which we have given you by our commission, nor consent to anything that may bring the least degree of diminution to it. . . . We require and authorise you therefore to proceed vigorously and effectually in your undertaking. . . . Wherein we doubt not but all our loyal and well-affected subjects of Scotland will cordially and effectually join with you; and by that addition of strength either dispose those that are otherwise minded to make reasonable demands to us in the treaty, or be able to force them to it by arms in case of their obstinate refusal."

In a private letter written at the same time Charles assured Montrose that he would never fail in his friendship towards him, and bade him to proceed in his business with all alacrity.[1] As a further token of the warm feeling he entertained towards his chivalrous champion, he sent him the insignia of the Order of the Garter.[2]

Charles's private letter.

He sends Montrose the Garter.

That there was thoughtlessness in forgetting that the mere existence of a negotiation with the Covenanting Government would make Scottish Royalists unwilling to compromise themselves by joining Montrose is not to be denied. Apart from this, however, the scheme is not deserving of censure, especially as it was known that Montrose was about to sail for Scotland from Sweden, and as rumour credited him with the possession of supplies and forces which would be sufficient to enable him to hold his own, even if not a single Scotsman declared in his favour.[3]

---

[1] Charles II. to Montrose, Jan. $\frac{12}{22}$, Carte's *Orig. Letters*, i. 356; Charles II. to Montrose, Jan. $\frac{12}{22}$, Napier's *Memoirs of Montrose*, ii. 752.

[2] *Ib.* 753.

[3] Proceedings of the Marquis of Montrose, Jan. $\frac{20}{30}$; Nicholas to Ormond, undated ; Carte's *Orig. Letters*, ii. 345, 359. These exaggerated

In real earnest Montrose's position was by no means so satisfactory as was supposed in Jersey. In the preceding July,

1649.
July.
Montrose
and the
Elector of
Branden-
burg.

before he left the Netherlands, he learnt that the Elector of Brandenburg—the great Elector as he was afterwards called—who had promised to borrow for him 10,000 rix-dollars, professed himself unable to obtain the money.[1] Sending off the Earl of

Aug.
Kinnoul
sent to the
Orkneys.

Kinnoul to the Orkneys with about 100 Danish and other recruits and with eighty officers [2] who were to raise and train the islanders, Montrose addressed himself to tread the weary round of Courts profuse in promise

Montrose
pleads in the
northern
Courts.

and slack in performance, where his breath would be wasted in warning rulers exhausted by the wasting calamities of the long war from which they had but recently escaped, that they had a common interest in relieving from misfortune a disinherited king.

Kinnoul indeed landed safely in the Orkneys, and was well received by his uncle, the Earl of Morton, who encouraged the

Sept.
Kinnoul's
preparations.

islanders to enlist in the Royal cause. On the day after his landing a Captain Hall arrived with a ship laden with arms and ammunition sent by Argyle

Captain
Hall's
ship.

to his own clansmen in the West Highlands, all of which he cheerfully made over to the representative of the King. In October, indeed, David Leslie hurried north-wards, but the Committee of Estates had no navy, and being

Oct.
Leslie in the
North.

unable to cross the Pentland Firth, Leslie contented himself with leaving a few garrisons behind him, and retired into winter quarters in the south. Beyond the reach of attack by an enemy without a fleet, the Orkneys formed an impregnable fortress for the Royalists, within reach

---

accounts are later than the date of Charles's letters to Montrose, but the news may have arrived earlier ; and even before the end of November good news arrived in Jersey. See Berkeley to Hyde, $\frac{\text{Nov. 23}}{\text{Dec. 3}}$, *Charles II. and Scotland*, 3.

[1] Montrose to the Elector of Brandenburg, July 22 ; the Elector to Montrose, July 27 ; *Deeds of Montrose*, App. iv.

[2] *Balfour*, iii. 431.

of that Celtic part of Scotland where Montrose's earlier victories had been won. Unluckily for Montrose, Morton died in November, and a few days later Kinnoul followed him to the grave.[1] There was no one left in the Orkneys capable of taking up their work.

Montrose himself met with but scanty success. From Hamburg he could gain nothing, and though the King of Denmark, Frederick III., spoke him fair, he could not compel the Danish nobles, with whom all real authority lay, to disburse a penny.

Oct.
Montrose in
Denmark.

Towards the end of October Montrose was enlisting men secretly at Copenhagen, but with his scanty supply of money he failed to obtain more than 200 recruits.[2] It was time for him to seek his fortunes elsewhere. Early in November, before leaving Denmark, he published a Declaration in which he demanded the aid of all who had ' any duty left them to God, their king, country, friends, homes, wives, children, or would change now, at least, the tyranny, violence and oppression of those rebels with the mild and innocent government of their just prince.'[3] About November 12 he arrived at Gothenburg, where he hoped great things from Queen Christina. Christina, however, did but close her eyes to his presence, and though she sold him a small vessel, she had no further help to give. One friend at least Montrose found in John Maclear, a wealthy Scottish merchant settled at Gothenburg, who not only hospitably entertained him, but advanced him 60,000 rix-dollars, a sum equivalent to 13,500*l*., and also made over to him a considerable quantity of arms, forming half of those which had been begged from Christina by Brentford in the spring, the other half having been destined for Ormond.[4] Before the end of the year, therefore,

Nov. 12.
Montrose at
Gothenburg.

---

[1] Captain Gwynne's *Memoirs*, 83–88 ; Gordon's *Geneal. Hist. of the Earls of Sutherland*, 551 ; *Balfour*, iii. 433.

[2] *Deeds of Montrose*, 259–266. Letter from the Swedish Resident, *ib.* 264, note 61, where ' in al stilhed ' is mistranslated.

[3] *Ib.* 267.

[4] There is frequent mention of these arms in the *Carte MSS.*

Montrose had before him the prospect of reaching Scotland with a force not altogether contemptible, at least as a nucleus for the native troops which he expected to rally round him. On December 15 he made ready to sail on the morrow with two ships,[1] but some cause now unknown detained him, possibly his expectation of being joined by Lord Eythin, who hoped to gather in Sweden a notable reinforcement to Montrose's numbers. On January 10, Montrose was on board, this time with some 1,200 men. A strong frost, however, set in, and on the 18th his vessels were frozen in about two leagues from the shore, and only regained the port with some difficulty.[2] In the middle of February, there being still no news of Eythin, he succeeded in despatching his remaining force. He himself travelled through Norway, and sailing from Bergen reached Kirkwall at some time before March 23.

Dec. 15. Montrose talks of sailing.

1650. Jan. 10. Montrose on board with 1,200 men.

Jan. 18. Is driven back by the ice.

It was thus under the sense of an impending but not very imminent danger that, on Winram's return on February 2, the Scottish Committee of Estates addressed itself to consider their future relations with the young King. Eager as every party was to have the King amongst them, his sentiments were sufficiently known to give pause to all except the extreme Royalists. Charles had authorised Montrose 'to communicate and publish his letter to all whom he thought fit,' apparently in order to make it known that his very tentative acceptance of the Scots' proposals did not imply the abandonment of the true Royalists.[3] This letter, together with the

Feb. 2. Winram arrives in Scotland.

[1] Montrose to Seaforth, Dec. 15, *Deeds of Montrose*, 274.

[2] Ribbing to Torstenson, Dec. 16, Jan. 11, 1618. *ib.* 511, 513, 514; Letter from Stockholm, $\frac{Jan. 26}{Feb. 5}$, *Charles II. and Scotland*, 5. This letter is the foundation of the paper which appears in *Balfour*, iii. 437, where the detention by the ice is mixed up with the story of the wreck of some of Montrose's vessels. As Ribbing's letters contain no information of any wreck, it is possible that it took place nearer the Orkneys, if it took place at all.

[3] Charles II. to Montrose, Jan. $\frac{12}{22}$, Carte's *Orig. Letters*, i. 358.

other letter to the Committee of Estates,[1] had fallen into the hands of a certain Wood, Montrose's agent in Paris, and by him both were translated into French and published. They afterwards appeared, on February 19, in an English re-translation in a London newspaper,[2] and already copies in the French form were in the hands of members of the Committee of Estates when they met to discuss the steps to be taken in consequence of Winram's tidings.

That meeting took place on February 21. So stormy was the debate that an Englishman, who reported the proceedings,

Feb. 21. A meeting of the Committee of Estates. could only compare them 'to those in England in the reign of Holles and Stapleton.' Argyle, Loudoun, and all the lords present, with the exception of

Two parties. Cassilis, were for sending commissioners to treat at Breda without further question. Cassilis and John-

Commissioners to be sent to Breda. ston of Warriston were for merely repeating to Charles the demand that he should acknowledge the legality of the existing Parliament, and should give a safe-conduct for commissioners.[3] In a committee, numbering nearly fifty, only nineteen votes were given for this last proposal. Argyle's view of the case, therefore, prevailed. Then came a long struggle over the instructions to be given to the Com-

Harsh instructions. missioners. Here, the party opposed to Argyle gained the upper hand, and it was resolved to require of Charles the same absolute surrender which had been required of him at the Hague.[4]

In the selection of the Commissioners both parties were

The Commissioners represent the two parties equally. equally represented. Cassilis, Alexander Brodie, and Alexander Jaffray would have preferred no negotiation at all. Lothian, Winram, and Sir John Smith were attached to Argyle, and would be ready, so far

---

[1] See p. 187.   [2] *A Brief Relation*, E, 593, 14.   [3] See p. 183.

[4] *Balfour*, iv. 2 ; a Letter from Scotland, Feb. 19 ; Intelligence from Scotland, Feb. 26 ; *Milton St. P.* 3, 4. Balfour gives the date of the meeting as Jan. 12, the figures having been transposed. That the Commissioners were taken equally from the two parties appears from the Life of Livingstone in the Wodrow Society's *Select Biographies,* i. 172.

as it was possible, to make some concessions to the young King. They were, however, bound by their instructions to conclude nothing of their own authority. There were also Commissioners sent independently by the Kirk, three ministers, Livingstone, Wood, and Hutchinson being associated with Cassilis and Brodie, who sat in both bodies.

Commissioners of the Kirk.

As might have been expected, the negotiation between Charles and the Scots caused no slight alarm at Westminster ; all the more because it seemed probable that the English Presbyterians, who had stood aloof from the Royalists in 1648, might throw in their lot with them in 1650. On December 25, upon the reading of a letter from Strickland—doubtless containing information about Winram's conferences with the Presbyterian exiles in Holland—Parliament ordered the sequestration of the estates of Willoughby, Massey, and Bunce.[1] On the 28th, a proposed Act for compelling the whole population to take the engagement to be faithful to the Commonwealth, without King or House of Lords, was taken into consideration.[2]

1649. Dec. Alarm at Westminster.

Dec. 25. Sequestration of estates.

Dec. 28. Proposal to make the engagement compulsory.

As originally drafted, the Act directed that the Courts of Law should refuse justice to all persons who had not taken the engagement. An attempt to exempt those who had constantly adhered to Parliament from its operation if they would promise to live peaceably was rejected, and the only amendment of importance admitted was one which saved women from persecution by the substitution of 'men' for 'persons' in the enacting clause. This amendment was moved by Marten in a speech in which he expressed a hope that 'though they baited the bull, they would not bait the cow too.'[3] Thus altered the Act became law on January 2.

[1] *C.J.* vi. 337. [2] *Ib.* vi. 339.
[3] *Merc. Pragm.* E, 587, 8. The story is confirmed by the use of the word 'persons' in an amendment rejected on the 28th, and by its occurrence in every part of the Act except in the enacting words.

The new Act,[1] as foolish as it was tyrannical, was admirably calculated, as Algernon Sidney had said of a former attempt to force a similar test on the Council of State, to 'prove a snare to every honest man, whilst every knave would slip through it.'[2]   How real was the alarm felt by those who passed it, was shown by their vote on January 8, recalling Cromwell to England in the midst of his career of victory.[3]   Further intelligence, however, convinced them that the danger was less immediate than they supposed, and the order was tacitly allowed to remain unexecuted for a time.

It was, in fact, perfectly clear that no Scottish invasion and no English insurrection need be feared till Charles and the Scots had actually come to terms.   On February 13 Charles left Jersey.[4]   On the 21st[5] he reached Beauvais, where he was met by his mother and remained in consultation with her for nearly a fortnight.   Henrietta Maria, now that her hope of Irish assistance had been disappointed, was distinctly in favour of an understanding with the Scots ; but she placed too high a value on the English Cavaliers to make her willing to alienate them by extreme concessions to the Presbyterian clergy.   She therefore urged Charles not to take the Covenant, abandon the Irish, or give up his own faithful supporters.   When Henrietta Maria left Beauvais she had reason to believe that he intended to follow her advice.[6]

Even amongst those Englishmen who most eagerly pressed Charles to agree with the Scots, there were few, if any, who thought otherwise than the Queen.   The Earl of Cleveland threatened to cane any one who called him a Presbyterian.[7]   In truth not a man at Charles's Court

Margin notes:
1650.
Jan. 2.
Passing of the Act.

Its tyrannical character.

Jan. 8.
Cromwell recalled.

Feb. 13.
Charles leaves Jersey,

Feb. 21.
and holds a conference with his mother at Beauvais.

Feeling at his Court.

---

[1] *An Act for Subscribing the Engagement*, E, 1,060, No. 77.

[2] See p. 5.   [3] *C.J.* vi. 344.

[4] Trethewy's Intelligence, *Clarendon MSS.* ii. No. 254.

[5] Letter from Paris, $\frac{\text{Feb. 27}}{\text{March 9}}$, *Charles II. and Scotland*, 15.

[6] Henrietta Maria to Charles II., May $\frac{16}{20}$, *ib.* 106.

[7] Watson to Edgeman, April $\frac{12}{22}$, *ib.* 60.

contemplated a straightforward acceptance of any terms likely to be advanced by the Scots. The only point on which his advisers differed was that some of them counselled him to make promises which he had no intention of performing, whilst others urged him summarily to reject the monstrous claim of his northern subjects to force upon Englishmen an uncongenial religion.

When, on March 16, Charles arrived at Breda,[1] he had leisure before giving audience to the Scottish Commissioners

March 16. Charles at Breda. to take into consideration the proposals of his partisans in England. One report, at least, that

March 18. He receives Keane's report. of Colonel Keane, his agent for London and the Western Counties, was submitted to him on the 18th, and it is probable that advices from other agents reached him about the same time. The chief

The London Royalists. London Royalists, it seemed, urged a union with Montrose rather than with 'the contrary faction,' suggested the appointment of a special agent in London, and recommended that a private assurance of liberty of conscience should be given to the Catholics. They also asked that they might themselves be allowed to take the engagement without prejudice to their loyalty to the King, as it would be necessary for them to do so 'for their preservation in order to his service.'

The Cornish Royalists. In Cornwall the Arundells asked that Sir Richard Grenvile might be sent to Scilly with 1,000 foot and 300 horse. If the King were to land in some other part of England, and the Parliamentary forces had been withdrawn from Cornwall, Grenvile, if he brought with him a sufficient quantity of arms, would not only be able to secure the county, but would be joined by 3,000 foot and 200 horse ready to follow him in any direction. A further force of 4,000 foot and 1,000 horse would be provided by Devon, Somerset, Hants, and Dorset. An attempt was to be made to secure the co-operation of the Levellers,[2] who, ever since

---

[1] Letter from Breda, March $\frac{20}{30}$, *Charles II. and Scotland*, 39.

[2] Colonel Keane's Memorial, March $\frac{18}{28}$, *ib.* 36. Compare T. Coke's Confession, *Hist. MSS. Com.* Rep. xiii. App. i. 577.

Lilburne's trial, had been deeply dissatisfied with the Government of the Commonwealth, and had already made frequent overtures to the King.[1]

Whatever Charles may have thought of the prospect of a rising in England, he at least showed what were his feelings

March
19, 20.
Warrants
to Eythin. towards Montrose. On March 19 he signed a warrant appointing Eythin Montrose's lieutenant-general, and on the following day he enlarged Eythin's powers, giving him full authority to command in case of Montrose's absence.[2]

Nor was it to Montrose and the English Cavaliers alone that Charles was looking for help. In March, Meynell, the

Charles
applies to
the Pope, agent whom he had unavowedly sent to Rome in the preceding summer,[3] had, by his orders, been urging Pope Innocent X. to impress upon the whole Catholic world the duty of assisting the young King to recover his throne.[4] About the same time Charles himself applied to

to the
Duke of
Lorraine, the Duke of Lorraine, as his father had done before, begging him to lead an army into England. On the duke's refusal, the hopes of the exile were placed on Von Karpfen, formerly a general in the service of the Landgrave of Hesse, who had engaged to levy 4,000 men in his service, and who was now sent to extract money from the impoverished

to the
German
princes, German princes assembled in Diet at Nüremberg. In the absence of Von Karpfen, overtures were entertained from Count Waldemar, a son of

and to
Count
Waldemar. Christian IV. of Denmark by a morganatic marriage, who offered to raise at least 8,000 men if 50,000l. could be placed in his hands.

March 25.
The Scot-
tish terms. Such were the schemes with which Charles's head was full, when, on March 25, he received from the Scottish Commissioners a complete statement of their

---

[1] Coke's Confession, *Hist. MSS. Com.* Rep. xiii. App. i. 591.

[2] Warrants, March 19, 20, *Charles II. and Scotland*, 38, 39.

[3] See p. 70.

[4] Many of Meynell's letters are printed in the *Clarendon State Papers*.

terms. As in the preceding year, they asked him to swear to
the two Covenants, to assent to Acts establishing the Presbyterian system in England and Ireland, to observe the
Presbyterian discipline in his own person and household, and to engage never to make opposition thereto.
Secondly, he was to acknowledge the legality of the late
sessions of the Scottish Parliament, and to agree that
all civil matters in Scotland should be determined by the parliaments of that kingdom, and matters ecclesiastical by the general
assemblies of the Kirk. Finally, he was to put in operation all
Acts made 'against the liberty or toleration of the Popish
religion' in any of his dominions, and to make void all treaties
contrary to those Acts, besides recalling all declarations issued
in his name, and making void all commissions issued by himself,
in case that such declarations or commissions were prejudicial
to the Covenant. In other words, he was to abandon both
Ormond and Montrose. Even if Charles bowed himself under
the yoke, he was to receive no promise of armed assistance.
All that the Commissioners had to say on this head was that
they were confident that, if their proposals were accepted, God
would 'shine upon his counsels and affairs.'

Of these demands the first alone was repeated by the Commissioners of the Kirk, as the only one dealing with purely
ecclesiastical matters, but they added a warning against
the sin of the young King in 'granting to the Irish
rebels the liberty of the Popish religion,' and in giving
a commission 'to that justly excommunicate rebel,
James Graham, to raise new troubles' in Scotland.[1]

We may well believe that, on listening to these outrageous
demands, Charles's thoughts turned to Montrose. It is said
that he now intended to carry out a plan formed at
Beauvais, and to offer—if the Commissioners refused
to modify their terms—to take shipping to plead his
cause in person at Edinburgh. Once on board ship, he was to

Demands of the Commissioners of Parliament.

Demands of the Commissioners of the Kirk.

Charles thinks of joining Montrose.

---

[1] The Commissioners of Parliament to Charles II., $\frac{\text{March } 25}{\text{April } 4}$; The
Commissioners of the Kirk to Charles II., $\frac{\text{March } 25}{\text{April } 4}$; *Clar. St. P.* ii.
App. li. liii.

direct his course—not to Leith, but to some northern port in which he would be under the protection of Montrose.[1]

Closely connected with Montrose's preparations for a descent in Scotland were the plans for a rising of the English Cavaliers.

March 29.
Instructions to Keane.
On March 29 Charles instructed Keane to urge the London Royalists to collect money for his service. Cavaliers might take the engagement without forfeiting their character for loyalty, and those of them who were Catholics were to be promised liberty of conscience. The Cornishmen were to be told that arms and ammunition had been despatched to Scilly, and they were, therefore, to be in readiness to seize Pendennis, Plymouth, and even Weymouth. Even the discontented Levellers were to be encouraged to declare for the King.[2]

Four days later Charles drafted a letter for the Queen of Sweden, in which he assured her that he had little hope of being

April 2.
A draft letter to Queen Christina.
able to satisfy the demands of the Scots, and begged her to do her uttermost to support Montrose and Eythin. Though the letter was never sent, it is none the less significative of the thoughts of the writer.[3]

April 5.
A letter to Lord Napier.
On April 5 a letter actually sent by Charles to the young Lord Napier tells the same tale. " I pray," he wrote, " continue your assistance to the Marquis of Montrose." " It is certain," observed one who had his eye on the game, " some good news from Montrose . . . would soon spoil the treaty." [4]

For all that, Charles came to no open breach with the Commissioners. He indeed accentuated his desire to come to an

----

[1] Letter from Breda, $\frac{\text{March } 28}{\text{April } 7}$, *Charles II. and Scotland*, 45. The newswriter is corroborated by Livingstone's language, "It is like the King come to Scotland whether we agree or not." Livingstone to Johnston of Warriston, $\frac{\text{March } 26}{\text{April } 5}$, *Deeds of Montrose*, 300.

[2] Answer to Colonel Keane's Paper, $\frac{\text{March } 29}{\text{April } 8}$, *Charles II. and Scotland*, 48.

[3] Charles II. to Christina, Draft, April $\frac{2}{12}$, *ib.* 50.

[4] Letter from Breda, April $\frac{4}{14}$, *ib.* 51 ; Charles II. to Napier, April $\frac{5}{15}$; Napier's *Memoirs of Montrose*, ii. 756.

understanding with them by ordering their chief opponents, Nicholas and Hopton, to absent themselves from the Council Table, whilst Hamilton, Newcastle, and Buckingham, all of them supporters of an understanding with the Scots, were nominated Privy Councillors and entrusted with the conduct of the negotiation.[1] The Commissioners were approached privately in the hope that they would agree to a modification of their terms. Charles indeed had reason to believe that, but for their instructions, at least three of them would gladly comply with his wishes. They themselves suggested that Montrose, whose arrival in the Orkneys was now known in Holland, should be employed against Cromwell in Ireland.[2]

Charles continues his negotiation with the Scots.

Proposal to employ Montrose in Ireland.

Under these circumstances the Prince of Orange offered his mediation. Coming to Breda on the 8th he urged the Commissioners to yield to a compromise. Charles was to accept the Presbyterian system in Scotland and to approve of the taking of the Covenant in England by those who voluntarily came forward to do so. He was also—not indeed to assent to the Bills establishing Presbyterianism in England which his father had rejected, but to accept such Bills as might be presented to him with the same object by a Parliament freely elected after his restoration.[3] To this reasonable compromise the Commissioners refused to listen. Even such of them who were contented to accept Charles's assent to Bills hereafter to be presented, wished those Bills to be prepared by the existing Parliament reinforced by the admission of the Presbyterian members excluded by Pride's Purge.[4] No Scottish Presbyterian could be brought to admit that the religion of England must be left to the decision of Englishmen themselves.

April 8. Mediation of the Prince of Orange.

[1] Nicholas to Ormond, April $\frac{3}{13}$, May $\frac{2}{12}$, Carte's *Orig. Letters*, i. 375, 378.

[2] Letter from Breda, April $\frac{4}{14}$, *Charles II. and Scotland*, 51.

[3] See two undated papers published by Dr. Wijnne, *De Geschillen, &c.*, 93, 114 ; and *Charles II. and Scotland*, 55, 56.

[4] See Coke's examination, *Hist. MSS. Com.* Rep. xiii. App. i. 596.

Vexed at the stubbornness of the Commissioners the Prince of Orange abandoned his self-imposed task. When he left

April 11.
Its failure. Breda on the 11th 'he told them plainly that he thought they intended little peace, and would so declare it to the world on behalf of his brother, to whom, he added, he would be no mediator for a dishonourable peace, whatsoever were his hazard.' So irritated were Charles's confidants that 'scarce one would profess himself a Presbyterian.' In vain Lothian and Lauderdale whispered 'up and down that the Covenant would not be pressed.' When Newcastle visited Cassilis to seek an explanation of these words, all that he could draw from him was a pious rebuke 'for his customary swearing.'[1]

The less Charles was able to count on Presbyterian Scotland the more inclined was he to rely on the English Cavaliers.

Charles
thinks of
sending a
foreign
army to
England. The notion of sending a foreign army to form a rallying point for their risings had for some time occupied his mind.[2] Finding it still hopeless to gain the co-operation of the Duke of Lorraine, he was anxiously expecting the result of Von Karpfen's mission to Nüremberg, and in the meanwhile opened a negotiation with

A loan
proposed on
the security
of the Scilly
Isles. some merchants of Amsterdam for the loan of the 50,000*l.* which had been required by Count Waldemar for his expenses in raising an army for the invasion of England. Charles offered the Scilly Isles as a security for the repayment of the money.

By the middle of April it was evident that there was small probability of these schemes ending otherwise than in failure.

Approach-
ing failure
of Charles's
projects. At the same time Charles was warned by Bunce that the Presbyterian Londoners would keep back their contributions unless they were assured of

Bunce's
warning. Charles's intention to co-operate with the Presbyterian Scots and not with Montrose and the English Cavaliers.[3]

Under these discouraging circumstances Charles was the

[1] Watson to Edgeman, April $\frac{12}{22}$, *Charles II. and Scotland.*

[2] See p. 196.

[3] Coke's Confession, *Hist. MSS. Com.* Rep. xiii. App. i. 594 ; Peti-

more ready to listen to a suggestion made by some of the
Commissioners which would at least postpone the
evil day when he would be compelled to break with
his supporters in England. " If in any particular,"
they wrote on the 15th, " our answers be not fully
satisfactory to his Majesty's desires, we humbly conceive it
more expedient that his Majesty, putting himself on the affec-
tions of his people, should refer them to his Parliament, where
his Royal presence will obtain more than we are warranted to
grant." [1] Though two out of the three signatures appended to
this letter were those of members of the austere party, there is
some reason for thinking that the suggestion emanated from
Argyle. His special agent, Will Murray, had recently arrived at Breda, charged to warn Charles
against too close a dependence on the Hamiltons,
and to offer him the hand of Argyle's own daughter, Ann
Campbell, as a means of strengthening his interest in Scotland.
What is more likely than that Argyle should also have wished
to transfer the negotiation itself to Edinburgh, where his own
influence would be better felt ? [2]

The temptation to procrastinate was too alluring
to be readily dismissed from Charles's mind. Yet
baser arguments urged him in the same direction.

April 14.
A sug-
gestion of
the Com-
missioners.

Will
Murray's
mission.

Charles
tempted
to comply.

tion of Von Karpfen, Declaration of Charles II., *Charles II. and Scotland*,
92, 94. See also Letters from Breda, $\frac{\text{April 26}}{\text{May 6}}$, May $\frac{9}{19}$, *Charles II. and
Scotland*, 77, 88. The affair of the Scilly Isles is treated of in a paper
printed by Dr. Wijnne, *Geschillen, &c.*, 106 ; but we learn from Coke's
confession that the matter had been under consideration for some time.
See also Instructions to Berkeley concerning the business of Scilly, *Carte
MSS.* cxxx. fol. 222. Count Waldemar was at Breda on April $\frac{4}{14}$,
Charles II. and Scotland, 54.

[1] Cassilis, Lothian, and Jaffray to the Prince of Orange, April $\frac{15}{25}$, *ib.* 67.

[2] We do not know the day on which Murray arrived at Breda, but
Graymond, writing on April $\frac{9}{12}$, notices that he was then about to leave
Scotland (*Harl. MSS.* 4, 551, fol. 493). The marriage scheme is connected with him in Livingstone's Life (Wodrow Soc. *Select Biographies*,
i. 170). See also letters from the Hague, May $\frac{20}{30}$, *Charles II. and Scotland*, 114, and Nicholas to Hatton, May $\frac{8}{18}$, *Nicholas Papers*, i. 172.

The Duke of Lorraine, the Queen of Sweden, and the Prince of Orange are said to have combined in urging him to promise anything with the direct intention of breaking his word whenever he was strong enough to do it with impunity.[1] That time, he may well have thought, would not be long postponed, perhaps only till he had secured the opportunity of showing himself to his Scottish subjects.

Not without hesitation, Charles yielded to the tempters. On April 17 he made one more appeal to the Commissioners,

April 17.
Charles
again asks
for con-
cessions. begging that there might be 'a reconciliation of all parties, and a union of them in his Majesty's service,' and that 'the Lords and others of the late engagement might be restored to their votes in Parliament and all other capacities for public trusts in that kingdom, and that all censures, civil and ecclesiastical, be taken off them.'[2] Whatever else the Commissioners might concede to Charles's

Refusal of
the Scots. personal wishes, they refused to concede that,[3] and in the course of the day Charles gave way almost

Charles
gives way. entirely. The only point on which he made any difficulty was that, though he was willing to promise to put in execution the penal laws against the Roman Catholics, he objected to annul treaties made with them; that is to say, Ormond's treaty in which, as far as Ireland was concerned, the Roman Catholics were exempted from the operation of those laws.[4]

As might have been expected, the Parliamentary Commissioners took umbrage at Charles's omission of the words

The con-
demnation
of the
Irish
Treaty
urged. condemning the Irish Treaty. He struggled hard, and for a few days he even threatened to throw up the whole negotiation rather than submit.[5] As the end of April drew nigh, his prospect of receiving

---

[1] Coke's Confession, *Hist. MSS. Com.* Rep. xiii. App. i. 595 ; Letter from Breda, $\frac{\text{April 26}}{\text{May 6}}$, May $\frac{1}{11}$; *Charles II. and Scotland*, 77, 80.

[2] His Majesty's Demands, April $\frac{17}{27}$, *Clar. St. P.* ii. App. lv.

[3] The Scottish Commissioners' Answers, undated, *ib.* ii. App. lvi.

[4] Reply of Charles II., April $\frac{17}{27}$, *Clarendon MSS.* ii. No. 291.

[5] Dean King to Ormond, Oct. 15, *Charles II. and Scotland*, 140.

help from other quarters than Scotland grew desperate. Von Karpfen arrived with information that no money was to be expected from the German princes, whilst the negotiation for the mortgage of the Scilly Isles was no nearer a conclusion than it had been at the beginning of the month. Count Waldemar withdrew his offer to raise an army and returned to Germany.[1] Accordingly, a few days before the end of the month, Charles, in a private note placed in the custody of Cassilis, promised to insert the required form of words after his landing in Scotland, if the Parliament should require him so to do.[2] That he should have fancied for a moment that a Scottish Parliament could be induced to pass over his alliance with Irish Catholics is unanswerable evidence of his confidence that the party of the Kirk would melt away in his presence.

April 28.
A private engagement on the Irish Treaty.

The Commissioners now professed themselves satisfied, and on the 29th they formally invited Charles to Scotland. The Engagers, they said, would be admitted to the enjoyment of their personal rights, though it might be that Parliament would take exception to the return of some of them. On this point, however, they assured Charles that his presence and desires would have great weight.[3] Fortified by these assurances, Charles, on May 1,[4] appended his signature to the draft of an agreement which usually goes by the name of the Treaty of Breda.[5] Even now he was not left in peace. Between him and the Commissioners of the Kirk there was still a long wrangle upon the

April 29.
Charles invited to Scotland.

May 1.
A draft agreement.

A form of oath discussed.

---

[1] Letter from Paris, $\frac{\text{April 24}}{\text{May 4}}$, *Charles II. and Scotland*, **77**.

[2] *Clar. St. P.* ii. App. lviii., note.

[3] Paper of Invitation, $\frac{\text{April 29}}{\text{May 9}}$, *ib.*

[4] This is the date given in J. P.'s letter of May $\frac{4}{14}$, *Charles II. and Scotland*, 83. For the date of May 3, usually given, see *ib.* 85, note 1.

[5] The official phrase at the time is the Treaty at Breda, meaning the whole negotiation carried on there, and its final result signed on board ship off Heligoland.

form of the oath by which he was to signify his acceptance of the Covenant.[1]

That Charles was now playing a double game is beyond dispute.   He had but lately assured Nicholas that he would never consent to anything prejudicial to the Irish Treaty.[2]   Even now he found it hard to dissemble, and those about him had no difficulty in divining his true feelings.   There were bickerings between him and the Commissioners on the subject of his English chaplains, whose services he wished to retain in Scotland, and on one occasion he is said to have broken out 'into a great passion and bitter execration.'   " It is easy to see," continues the reporter of this scene, " that the Scots' edge is much taken off from him.   They say they find nothing but vanity and lightness in him, and that he never will prove a strenuous defender of their faith ; and 'tis evident still that he perfectly hates them, and neither of them can so dissemble it but each other knows it ; and 'tis a matter of pleasant observation to see how they endeavour to cheat and cozen each other.   The King strokes them till he can get into the saddle, and then he will make them feel his spurs for all their old jade's tricks they have played his father and for their present restiveness, and they know it, and therefore will not agree that he shall back them with his heels armed.   They hate the thing monarchy, but they must have the name of it, and they care not for the person of the man but his relations.[3]   They must make a property of him ; no other will serve them to stalk their ends by." [4]

Charles playing a double game.

Ill will between Charles and the Commis-sioners.

Anger of the Cavaliers,

It was an ill-natured, but probably fairly accurate, view of the situation.   To Charles's cavalier sup-porters, ignorant of his secret intentions and too honest to approve them even if they had been admitted to his

[1] The Commissioners of the Kirk to Charles II., $\frac{April\ 23}{May\ 3}$, May $\frac{13}{23}$, *Clar. St. P.* ii., App. lvii. lxii.

[2] Nicholas to Ormond, May $\frac{2}{12}$, Carte's *Orig. Letters*, i. 378.

[3] *I.e.* his being the representative of the monarchical idea.

[4] Letter from Breda, May $\frac{1}{11}$, *Charles II. and Scotland*, 80.

confidence, this bowing down to the Presbyterian idol was but as gall and wormwood. " Our religion," wrote one of them, " is gone, and within few days is expected the funeral of our liturgy which is dead already. . . . To call the greatest abetter of this whole business yet a Presbyterian, breeds a mortal quarrel, so much ashamed are they of themselves." [1]   Even Charles's own mother was shocked by his promise to accept the Covenant. She told him that though she would never cease to love him as a son, she would never again be his political adviser. [2]

and of
Henrietta
Maria.

---

[1] Watson to Edgeman, May $\frac{2}{12}$, *Charles II. and Scotland*, 81.   See also Hatton to Nicholas, May $\frac{11}{21}$, *Nicholas Papers*, i. 173.

[2] Henrietta Maria to Charles, *ib.* 106.

CHAPTER IX

THE LAST CAMPAIGN OF MONTROSE

CHARLES was too thoroughly disgusted with the Covenanters to lose sight of Montrose. There can be no doubt that before he signed the draft agreement, he had received assurances that if Montrose would lay down his arms, not only he and his troops, but the Scottish Royalists in Holland should receive complete indemnity.[1] Though the evidence is far from complete, there are reasons for thinking that these assurances were given, not by the official commissioners, but by Will Murray acting as Argyle's agent.[2]

An indemnity for Montrose.

It seems to have been Charles's intention to employ Montrose against the English, probably to supply the place of Count Waldemar in the projected landing on the East Coast.[3] Sir William Fleming, the confidential agent of the Engagers, was to be sent to acquaint Montrose with the arrangement; but he was directed to consult Murray on certain points, a course which would hardly have been taken unless Argyle had been privy to the transaction.[4]

Scheme for his employment.

[1] Long's Notes, May $\frac{5}{15}$, *Charles II. and Scotland*, 126. On May $\frac{6}{16}$ Charles told his mother that he had made provision for the royal party. J. P. to -- ? *ib.* 86.

[2] For a discussion on Argyle's share in the matter, see *Edinburgh Review*, Jan. 1894, p. 154.

[3] On May $\frac{3}{13}$ Charles instructed Sir W. Fleming to assure Montrose that ' we shall shortly have an honourable employment for him in our service against the rebels in England.' He can hardly have intended to subordinate Montrose to Leslie.

[4] It is possible that Argyle had agreed to the employment of Montrose in Ireland, and that Charles hoped to obtain his assent to his employ-

On May 3, Charles instructed Fleming to inform Montrose of the reasons which had induced him to accept the terms of the Covenanters. The European powers were un-willing or unable to assist him. He had been dis-appointed in his hopes from Ireland, and the force which Montrose had brought across the sea was, through no fault of his own, far smaller than had been expected. More-over, even if Montrose succeeded in gaining the upper hand, it would only drive the Covenanters into the arms of the English rebels. If Montrose would now disband his men and leave the kingdom, he had hopes 'upon good grounds' to 'be able in a little time to make his peace in Scotland.' Fleming also carried two letters addressed to Montrose, ordering him to carry the substance of these instructions into effect.[1] On May 8, Charles wrote to the Scottish Parliament, requesting that suitable conditions might be made for the disbandment of Montrose's troops.[2]

*May 3.
Fleming's
instructions.*

It is no wonder that the young man's mind misgave him. It might be that these elaborate arrangements had, after all, been made in vain, and that the gulf between Mont-rose and the Covenanters was too wide to be bridged over. It was not impossible that 'the prevailing party now in Scotland' had no intention of accepting the con-cessions made to them, and had only entered on the negotiation at Breda in order to wrest Montrose's arms out of his hands. If that appeared to Fleming to be the case, he was, as he was told by fresh instructions delivered to him on the 9th, to see that Montrose continued on his guard. So, too, if the Scottish Royalists thought it desirable that he should remain armed, they were to be encouraged to place themselves under his orders. If, however, Montrose did lay down arms—the con-dition, though not expressed, is plainly intended—Fleming was,

*May 9.
Hesitation
of Charles.*

ment in England. See Letter from Breda, April $\frac{12}{22}$, *Charles II. and Scotland*, 65.

[1] Instructions to Fleming, May $\frac{3}{13}$, $\frac{5}{15}$; Charles to Montrose, May $\frac{3}{13}$, $\frac{5}{15}$; Wigton Papers, in *Maitland Club Miscellany*, ii. 472.

[2] Charles to the Scottish Parliament, May $\frac{8}{18}$, *ib.* ii. 478.

if Montrose proved to have a considerable force, to do his best, with the advice of Murray, ' to get them not to be disbanded.' If the men were few ' they might be disbanded, but if possible entertained in other troops,' evidently in the Scottish service. There was—it may be supposed—to be an understanding with Argyle that the men might be made useful for the further designs with the execution of which Charles hoped to entrust Montrose.[1]

Fleming's well-intended mission was all too late to effect the object for which it was designed. It was as easy to check a cannon ball in its course as to hold back Montrose. When Montrose reached the Orkneys in March, he learned, if he did not know it before, that Kinnoul had died in November, leaving no one to carry on his task of bringing the levies of the islands under military discipline. It was, however, the letter written by the King from Jersey,[2] which cut him to the heart. Announcing Charles's intention to treat with the Covenanters, and assigning to Montrose the task of frightening them into the acceptance of reasonable conditions, it in reality landed him in a situation from which there was no escape. Montrose was too experienced a soldier not to be aware that few, if any, of the professing Royalists of Scotland would rally round the King's standard in the hands of a man whom the King might at any moment disavow.

When, therefore, Montrose sat down on March 26 to reply to the letter which had reached him three days before, he was weighed down by visible emotion. " I have received," he wrote with touching dignity, " your Majesty's of the 12th of January, together with that mark of your

Marginal notes:

March. Montrose in the Orkneys.

March 23. He receives Charles's letter from Jersey.

March 26. Montrose's last letter to Charles.

---

[1] Further instructions to Sir W. Fleming, May $\frac{9}{15}$, Wigton Papers, *Maitland Club Miscellany*, ii. 479. It will be observed that it is only on the last point that Murray was to be consulted, not on the possible retention of an armed force by Montrose. I believe that the explanation I have given to it is the true one, but the language is obscure. It must be remembered that Charles gave verbal instructions to Fleming, who would be able to clear up all doubtful points.   [2] See p. 187.

Majesty's favour wherewithal you have been pleased to honour me,[1] for which I can make your Majesty no other humble acknowledgment, but with the more alacrity and bensell[2] abandon still my life to search my death for the interests of your Majesty's honour and service, with that integrity and dearness as your Majesty and all the world shall see that it is not your fortunes in you, but your Majesty, in whatsomever fortunes, that I make sacred to serve. . . . If I may make bold to let fall to your Majesty a part of my humble thoughts, it should be my wish and humble desires your Majesty would be pleased, from all former experiences, to have a serious eye, now at last, upon the too open crafts are used against you chiefly in this conjuncture, and that it would please your Majesty to be so just to yourself as ere you make a resolve upon your affairs or your person, your Majesty may be wisely pleased to hear the zealous opinions of your faithful servants who have nothing in their hearts, nor before their eyes, but the joy of your Majesty's prosperity and greatness." [3]

Having written these words of warning, the last ever addressed by him to his Sovereign, Montrose turned to his great enterprise as calmly as if he had known nothing of the *Montrose's chances.* malign influences which threatened to blast his career. It is true that, apart from the dangers revealed in Charles's letter, his prospects might seem hopeful even to one less sanguine than himself. The Act of Classes and the exclusiveness of the Kirk party had irritated considerable numbers of the Lowland gentry, to whom Montrose had despatched Colonel Sibbald—his faithful companion in his first hazardous ride out of England—to warn them to be ready for his coming. Further north, the new Marquis of Huntly—the Lord Lewis Gordon of Montrose's earlier campaign—promised to bring with him the Gordon following. Montrose's greatest danger lay in Leslie's disciplined army, a very different body of men from the half-trained burghers and peasants who had fallen

---

[1] The Order of the Garter.   [2] *I.e.* force or vigour.
[3] Montrose to Charles II., $\frac{\text{March 26}}{\text{April 5}}$, *Charles II. and Scotland*, 42.

before his sword at Tippermuir and Kilsyth. Yet even here hope was not wanting. Middleton, who had commanded the horse in Hamilton's expedition, was in ill odour with the Kirk, and he now professed to have such influence over Leslie's cavalry that he could bring them over to the Royal cause.[1] If Middleton was as good as his word, Leslie would be disarmed, and all Scotland would be at Montrose's feet.

For Montrose, therefore, the one thing needful was to find a district in the Highlands where he could be safe from the attack of disciplined cavalry till Middleton's entice-

State of the northern Highlands.

ments had time to work. Such a district might seem to be offered him by the Mackenzies, who spread over the western coast from Kintail on the south to the borders of Assynt on the north. That the Macleods of Assynt would declare in his favour was at that time expected by Montrose, and further north were the Mackays, whose chief, Lord Reay, was an undoubted Royalist. Nor did Montrose entertain any doubt that the Mackenzies could be trusted, as their chief, Seaforth—uncertain as his allegiance had been in the former war—had given Montrose every possible assurance of fidelity, though in his safe retirement in Holland he avoided running any personal risk in the approaching campaign. His brother, however, Thomas Mackenzie of Pluscardine, who had taken a leading part in the Royalist insurrection of the preceding year,[2] had remained in Scotland, and was probably expected to supply the place of the chief.

On April 9, Montrose gave orders to his old adversary Hurry—who, with his usual readiness to attach himself indis-

April 9. Montrose's orders to Hurry.

criminately to either side, was now serving as his Major-General—to conduct part of the forces to the mainland. Hurry landed at Thurso, whence he was to make his way as rapidly as possible to the Ord of Caithness,

---

[1] "Middleton . . . can take off the most part of all their horse, to go along with him any way that he pleases to command them, but chiefly in the King's service." Ogilvy of Powrie to Montrose, March 3, *Deeds of Montrose*, 286–7. Compare May to Charles, March 30. *Charles II. and Scotland*, 49.   [2] See p. 63

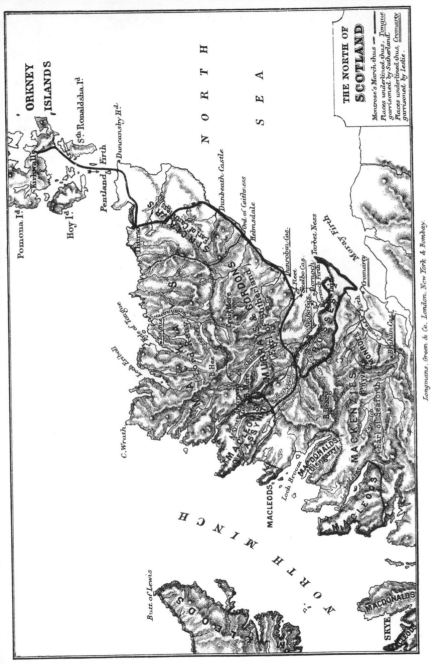

THE NORTH OF SCOTLAND

Montrose's March thus —
Places underlined thus, *Tongue*
garrisoned by Sutherland
Places underlined thus, *Cromarty*
garrisoned by Leslie.

ORKNEY ISLANDS

Pomona I.ᵈ
Hoy I.ᵈ
St.ʰ Ronaldsha.I.ᵈ
Kirkwall
Pentland Firth
Duncansby H.ᵈ

NORTH SEA

Dunbeath Castle
Ord of Caithness
Helmsdale
Dunrobin Cas.
Fleet
Skelbo Cas.
Dornoch
Dornoch Firth
Tarbet Ness
Moray Firth
Cromarty

C. Wrath
Kyle of Tongue
Loch Eriboll
B. Hee

MACLEODS
Loch Broom
MACDONALDS
Dingwall

MACKENZIES
Earl of Seaforth

Butt of Lewis
LEWIS
NORTH MINCH
MACDONALDS
MACLEODS
SKYE

SUTHERLAND
SUMMORE
GORDON'S
ASSYNT

Longmans, Green, & Co. London, New York & Bombay.

a high hill overhanging the sea, over the precipices of which
lay the only track by which an advancing army could make its
way into Sutherland,[1] a district held for the Covenanters by the
Earl of Sutherland. Hurry on the way captured
Dunbeath Castle, which was sacked by his men
contrary to the terms of the capitulation.[2] Then pushing
rapidly on he seized the important position of the Ord, where
after no long delay he was joined by Montrose himself.

Hurry in Caithness.

Montrose, having been compelled to leave parties of his
followers behind to hold Dunbeath Castle and to raise troops
in Caithness, now found himself at the head of
about 40 mounted officers and some 1,200 footmen,
of whom about 450 were Danes or Germans, and the
remainder peasants from the Orkneys. Above him waved the
standard of the King, of the dead King rather than of the living
one. It was ' of black damask with three pair of hands folded
in each other,' representing doubtless those of the three
kingdoms, ' and on each side of them three hands and naked
arms out of a cloud with swords drawn.' To the foot was
designed a standard of black taffety, in the middle of which
was a man's head 'bleeding as if cut off from a body.'
Montrose's own characteristic device showed a lion about to
spring across a rocky chasm, with the motto of *Nil Medium.* No
mean intrigue, no thought of personal interest lurked in that
gallant heart.

He is joined by Montrose.

Once over the Ord, Montrose [3] pushed on along the coast
till he was confronted by the works of Dunrobin Castle,

[1] Order to Hurry, April 9, *Deeds of Montrose,* 294.

[2] Gordon of Sallagh's *Continuation of the Geneal. Hist. of the Earls of
Sutherland,* 552.   So far from Gordon's political bias making him
' a doubtful authority ' on the charge of plundering, as the editors
of the *Deeds of Montrose* suggest (297, note 32), the language of Gray-
mond's despatch of $\frac{\text{April 30}}{\text{May 10}}$ (*Harl. MSS.* 4,551, fol. 504) is far stronger
than his.

[3] The only contemporary accounts of the movements which follow
are those of Gordon of Sallagh, noticed above, and a despatch, perhaps
Strachan's, on which is based an account printed in Balfour's *Annals*
(*Hist. Works,* iv. 8).   For these and for a criticism of the evidence on

P 2

garrisoned by Sutherland's tenants, as were also the neighbour-

Montrose in Suther-land. ing fortresses of Skelbo, Skibo and Dornoch. To avoid these garrisons, as well as those which had been placed in Brahan Castle and Cromarty by Leslie, Montrose turned aside up Strath Fleet, making his way

He makes for Strath Oykell. slowly towards Strath Oykell, where he might expect to receive intelligence that Pluscardine and the Mackenzies were ready to welcome him to their glens. Pluscardine was far away on the lands of the abbey [1] from which he derived his title,[2] and without him the Mackenzies showed no signs of a disposition to rise. Was it merely that Pluscardine, having made his peace with the Covenanting Government, was unwilling to endanger his own safety, or was it that Seaforth himself had sent secret orders to his clansmen to keep aloof from Montrose? Not a particle of evidence exists on the subject, but from all that is known of Seaforth's character, it seems probable that he would prefer a return to Scotland as the result of an agreement between Charles and the Covenanting Government, to a hazardous enterprise which would expose him to the implacable hostility of the latter. Whatever the explanation may be, Montrose's ruin can be indirectly traced to Charles's resolution to play fast and loose with diplomacy and war. The defection of the Mackenzies forced Montrose back upon the eastern coast where cavalry charges were possible, and where therefore his deficiency in that arm would expose him to almost certain destruction.

No one knew better than the victor of Philiphaugh how formidable a body of disciplined cavalry was against Montrose's

April 25. A rendezvous at Brechin. infantry. When therefore Leslie heard of Montrose's landing, he did not content himself with ordering a general rendezvous at Brechin on April 25. He also

which this account of the battle is based, I would refer my readers to an article in the *Edinburgh Review* for January 1894.

[1] A few miles from Elgin.

[2] When Montrose was led as a prisoner through that part of the country Pluscardine came to greet him.

gave special directions to Lieutenant-Colonel Strachan, who was nearer the scene of action,[1] to push rapidly forwards and to gather round him the garrisons—almost entirely composed of cavalry—of the posts occupied by the Covenanters in the neighbourhood of the Dornoch Firth.

Strachan indeed was admirably fitted for the work on hand. He had served as a Major in the English army against Hamilton in 1648, and had been entrusted by Cromwell with the message to Argyle which resulted in their combination against the Engagers.[2] He had been the first to bring to Edinburgh the news of the execution of Charles I.[3] He not unnaturally became an object of suspicion to the commission of the Kirk, which, on February 5, 1649, directed a committee to examine the scandals arising from his conduct. It was not till March 14 that, after considerable discussion, he was allowed to sign the League and Covenant and admitted to the Presbyterian fold.[4]

*1649.
Feb. 5.
Strachan
examined,
March 14,
and allowed
to sign the
Covenant.*

Whatever may have been Strachan's hesitation on points of discipline, on points of practice he counted amongst the strictest of Presbyterian zealots. He would have the State and army purged of all malignants and Engagers, and the work of the Lord done by the godly alone.[5]

*Strachan's
position in
the army.*

---

[1] We do not know where Strachan was posted, but it is certain, as the editors of the *Deeds of Montrose* (p. 303, note 45) remark, that he cannot have started with Leslie from Edinburgh so as to reach Brechin on the 25th, and yet have fought at Carbisdale on the 27th.

[2] *Life of Blair*, 206.

[3] Graymond to Brienne, Feb. $\frac{13}{23}$, *Harl. MSS.* 4,551, fol. 302. See p. 15.

[4] *Minutes of the Commission of the General Assembly*, Feb. 8, March 1, 8, 13, 14, 1649.

[5] For Strachan's views, see his letter published in the *Deeds of Montrose*, 302. The date is torn away, but is given in Wodrow's Index as June 3. The editors, seeing that June 3, 1650, is obviously impossible, assign it to Jan. 3, 1650, which is also impossible, as it is addressed to Guthrie as minister of Lauder, from which place he removed to Stirling in November 1649. I believe the real date to have been June 3, 1649. This view is confirmed by Strachan's language about purging the army, in

Though accepted by the Kirk, he got into difficulties with
Leslie, who objected to allow a companion of sectaries to
serve in his ranks. Leslie's scruples, however, gave way
before the arguments of Mungo Law, one of the notable
preachers of the day, who told him that if he cashiered
Strachan he 'would want the prayers of 10,000 of the saints
and godly of Edinburgh.'[1]   Not long afterwards the part
taken by Strachan in the dispersal of Pluscardine's forces
at Balvenie gave him an assured position. Leslie now knew
his man. It might be doubtful whether Strachan could be
trusted to fight against the English. It was certain that he
could be trusted to fight against Montrose.

When, therefore, on the morning of April 27, a Council of
War at which Strachan and the Earl of Sutherland were
present was held at Tain, it was resolved that
Sutherland and his followers should be sent off to
guard their own district in Montrose's rear, and to prevent him from receiving reinforcements from the extreme north.
The debate then turned on the question whether it was
desirable to march at once with the remainder of the troops
against Montrose, who was supposed to be still in Strath
Oykell. Those who opposed an immediate advance, did so
on the ground that, as it was Saturday, and they could not
expect to come up with the enemy till the morrow, it was
unseemly to make preparations for a battle to be fought on
the Lord's day. Before a resolution was taken news arrived
that Montrose had moved down by the side of the Kyle of
Sutherland, where the united waters of the Oykell and the
Shin flow through a chain of lakelets into the Dornoch Firth.
On the reception of this intelligence it was determined to
bring on a conflict without further delay.

Of Montrose's movements during the week before the

which he takes no notice of the Act relating to the subject passed on
June 21, 1649. *Acts of Parl. of Scotl.* vi. part ii. 446.

[1] *Balfour*, iii. 413, 414. Balfour puts this at the beginning of May, a
month too late. See Graymond to Brienne, April $\frac{10}{20}$, *Harl. MSS.* 4,551,
fol. 341.

battle, whether he spent one day or six in Strath Oykell, it is
impossible to speak with certainty.[1] There can, however, be no
doubt that on the 27th he mustered his little force
at Carbisdale, at the foot of the glen through which
the Culrain burn bursts out of the hills to mingle
with the waters of the Kyle of Sutherland about a mile and a
half lower down. The ground on which the Royalist
army was posted was rugged enough to present difficulties to assailants on horseback, and it rose gradually up to the foot of the steep side of Craigcaoinichean—the
Mossy Hill—the lower part of which was clothed with a thinly
planted wood of stunted birch. As Montrose commanded a
view reaching for about a mile and a half in the direction from
which any enemy was likely to approach, he might calculate,
apparently with safety, that if any cavalry advanced to attack
him he would have time to draw back his men into the wood,
where, if they climbed sufficiently high, they ought to be able
to defend themselves with ease. He could dispose, as had
been said, of 1,200 foot and forty horse. He was the more
confident as he had been told that the enemy had no more
than a single troop of horse in the country, and it is probable
that he expected the Rosses and Monros who were settled in
those parts to join their forces to his own, though they were in
reality prepared to take the part of the winning side, whichever
it might prove to be.

Strachan, on the other side, had with him about 220 horse
and thirty musketeers, to say nothing of 400 Rosses and
Monros upon whom no dependence could be placed.
When he arrived at Wester Fearn he had still the
Carron to cross, and by way of the ford, by which alone the
river was at that time passable, he had about eight miles to
cover to reach Montrose. Of these eight miles
more than six were thickly overspread with broom,
which still grows profusely by the sides of the rail-

Montrose's move-ments.

His posi-tion at Carbisdale.

Strachan's force.

The lie of the ground.

---

[1] Gordon of Sallagh says that he had been six days at Carbisdale. I
incline to believe the despatch printed by Balfour (see *ante,* p. 211,
note 3), that he only arrived there on the 27th.

way and the road.   Even if the broom had not been there, the levels were such as to render an advancing force invisible from Carbisdale till a little before the Culrain burn was reached.[1] It is therefore safe to conclude that Strachan was able to reach

Advance of Montrose's horse.

this point unobserved, and that it was somewhere near it that he received intelligence that Montrose's little band of forty horse was galloping towards him.[2]

If Strachan had been so minded it would have been easy for him to overwhelm Montrose's horse, but he was too good

Strachan unwilling to attack it.

a soldier to think of giving the alarm to the enemy's foot, who would at once slip up the hill and thereby protract the war amongst the Highlands.   The clans would then, it might be feared, again rally round Montrose, and there might well be another Inverlochy and another Kilsyth.

With this fear before him Strachan, acting on the advice of

He forms an ambuscade.

his scoutmaster, Andrew Monro, concealed his men in a gully overshadowed by broom, with the exception of a single troop.   The stratagem took effect. Montrose's reconnoitring party—for it was no more than that— drew rein at sight of the enemy and hastened back with the tidings that his numbers were by no means formidable.   On receiving the news Montrose made what must have appeared

Montrose's preparations.

to him to be adequate preparations.   Placing himself at the head of the main body, he gave the command of the van to Hurry.   Occupied with these cares, he allowed—such at least is the most reasonable explanation at hand—some minutes to pass before he was aware that the enemy had crossed the Culrain burn in unexpected numbers,

[1] This I ascertained when walking along the road in 1893.

[2] I have assumed that Montrose occupied the rising and rugged ground which is traditionally pointed out as the site of the battle, and which is marked by cross swords in the accompanying map.   Broom alone would not have hidden horses.   There is no direct evidence that Strachan aimed at catching the infantry, but if it had not been so he would have made a dash at the reconnoitring horse.   Moreover, at the council at Tain, when Montrose was supposed to be in Strath Oykell, it was considered 'that it was very probable, the enemy's strength being in foot, they would take the hills upon the advance of more of our horses.'

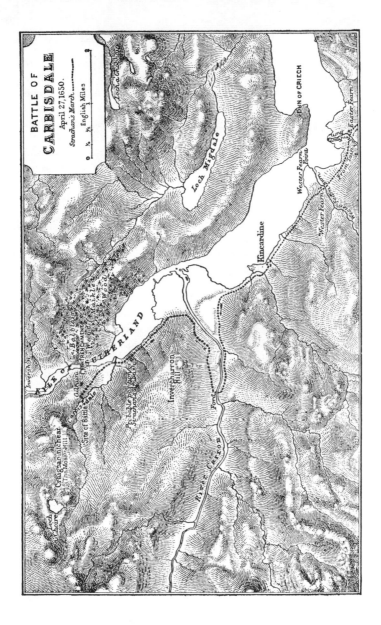

BATTLE OF
CARBISDALE
April 27, 1650.
Strachan's March. ....
0   ¼   ½   ¾   1
English Miles

Loch a' Ghriama

DUN OR CREICH

Loch Migdale

Wester Fearn Point

Kincardine

Wester Fearn

From Tain

Wester Fearn Farm

R. Euster

R. Euster Farm

KIRK OF SUTHERLAND

Invershin

Probable Positions
Strachan's Horse

Southern
Entrenchment

Wood

Gulley

Site of Battle

Probable Positions
Newton's Horse

Inveran Hill

Ford

Creag an riachea
The Moss-Hill

River Carron

Loch a' Choire

and was sweeping down at full charge upon his still
disordered ranks.   Grasping the danger in an instant, Mont-
Montrose's
defeat,   rose gave orders to his whole force to seek shelter
amongst the birches on the hill side.[1]   It was all
too late.   In spite of the inequalities and roughness of the
ground Strachan's horse broke in upon his array before the
manœuvre was accomplished.   The forty horsemen were soon
broken.   Down went the Royal standard with its avenging
arms, and down went the gallant men who guarded it.   The
Orkney levies, unused to war, fled at the first sign of danger,
whilst the Danes and Germans, old soldiers as they were,
retreated into the fringe of the wood, where the trees did not
grow thickly enough to protect them.   At the first assault [2] they,
too, broke and fled.   The superiority of cavalry over infantry
had vindicated itself in face of unusual obstacles.   In the pursuit which followed, all of Montrose's following, with the
exception of about a hundred scattered men, were slain or
taken.   Eighty of the Rosses, who had taken no part in the
fight, were in time to share in 'the execution.'

Montrose himself succeeded in effecting his escape.   Young
Lord Frendraught, it is said,[3] persuaded him to accept his
and flight.   horse.   Once at a safe distance Montrose dismounted,
and stripping off his belt and sword, his coat and the jewel of
the Garter which scarcely more than a month before he had received from Charles, he donned a peasant's garb.   As the way
by which he had come was blocked by Sutherland, his only
chance of escape lay in his being able to reach the western sea,
where some fisherman's bark might take him back to Kirkwall
to raise anew the standard of his King.   In company with the

---

[1] The two movements—first, the ordering of the army, and secondly,
the retreat 'to a wood and craggy mountain which was not far distant'—
are both placed by Gordon after ' the intelligence of the approach of some
horse,' this being shown by words in the preceding paragraph to refer to
intelligence brought by the reconnoitring party.

[2] In the despatch given by Balfour it is called a charge, but, at least in
the usual sense of the word, it would be impossible for cavalry to charge
on such ground.   [3] See the *Deeds of Montrose*, 308, 309.

new Earl of Kinnoul [1] and a few others whom he had gathered round him, he made his way up Strath Oykell, doubtless keeping high up on the hillside to avoid the peril which lurked in human habitations. Progress under these conditions would be laborious even for a well-equipped traveller. To wanderers without guides and without the means of procuring food it threatened to be fatal. One by one the members of the little band dropped behind. Kinnoul, worn out by toil and famine, lay down to die on the mountain side. Montrose himself, accompanied by Major Sinclair alone, staggered on, having lighted on a cottage where bread and milk was given them. After three days the pair descended into Assynt, on the western slope of the hills. [2]

Here Montrose might at least expect to be among friends. When he was last in Scotland, the Macleods of Assynt had Macleod been dependants of Seaforth, and their chief, of Assynt. Neil Macleod, had, as a boy, served for a short time under Montrose himself on one of those rare occasions when Seaforth attempted to redeem by act his professions of loyalty to the King. Montrose was unaware that since that time Macleod had quarrelled with Seaforth, had transferred his allegiance to Sutherland, and had been by him appointed sheriff depute of Assynt. That in this change of front Macleod was inspired by any wide political principles is extremely unlikely. The clan-feeling was predominant in the Highlands, and by accepting the protection of Sutherland he bound himself, especially now that a civil office had been given him, to serve that Covenanting party to which Sutherland gave his support.

Macleod was also attached to the Covenanters by marriage. His wife was a daughter of Andrew Monro, who had scouted for Strachan at Carbisdale, and whose first thought after the

---

[1] A brother of the one who died in the Orkneys (see p. 208). The existence of this earl has been questioned on very insufficient grounds. I have stated my view of the case in a letter to the *Athenæum* of Nov. 11, 1893.

[2] Gordon's *Cont. of the Hist. of the Earldom of Sutherland*, 555.

victory had been to send a message to his son-in-law, bidding
him to arrest Montrose if he came in his way.   Accordingly,
either Macleod himself, or, according to some accounts, his young wife in his absence, sent out search
parties to arrest the wanderer.   One of these parties
fell in with Montrose, and bore him to their master's
castle of Ardvreck.   It is of little importance whether
the deed was done by the master or the mistress of that abóde.
If Macleod himself was absent at the time, he returned whilst
Montrose was still in custody, and must, therefore, be held
responsible for his detention.

Macleod
receives a
message.

Capture of
Montrose.

Montrose himself found it difficult to realise that all chance
of deliverance was at an end.   He pleaded hard with Macleod
to accompany him to the Orkneys, where he probably believed that the reinforcements which he expected to accompany Eythin had already landed.
Macleod was obdurate, and when Major-General
Holborn, a Scot who, before the days of the New
Model, had been in the service of the English Parliament,[1] arrived with orders to fetch away the prisoner, he
delivered him up without compunction.

Montrose
pleads for
liberty.

May 4
Montrose
given up
to Holborn.

That Macleod's conduct should lend itself to hostile comment was natural enough.   Though there is not a shadow of
evidence that he had acted treacherously, or had done
anything more than his duty to the Government of
which he was a servant, the plain fact that he had
delivered up a hero who believed him to be a friend militated
against him, and the ill-opinion entertained of him was
strengthened when, a few weeks later, he appeared in Edinburgh to claim the blood-money which he had earned.[2]   Macleod would have won fame if he had ruined himself by protecting the fugitive who had taken refuge with him under a mistaken belief, but he was not the man to risk his own fortunes
by such an heroic disregard of consequences.   It is unlikely
that he ever conceived the idea that it was possible for him to
act otherwise than he did.

Character
of Macleod's
action.

[1] See *Great Civil War*, ii. 94, 98, 183.   [2] Gordon, 555.

The thoughts of posterity are with the captive, not with the captor. Montrose's sword had at last been shattered in his hand. The cause of the ideal monarchy for which he had stepped into the lists had been too heavily weighted by the very unideal monarch who was seeking to re-establish himself in power and comfort by sacrificing every principle for which Montrose was exposing his life. The hero's work, as an active restorer of a system of government which the progress of events had rendered for ever impossible, was now at an end. His work as a sufferer was beginning. The simplicity of aim which marred his career as a factor in the complex web of political life gave inspiration to his martyrdom, and appealed to hearts which beat, not for wise arrangement of the affairs of the world, but for nobility of character coupled with absolute forgetfulness of self. Behind the successful warrior, behind the utterer of crude political opinions, stood revealed the man.

Montrose's military career at an end.

His career as a martyr beginning.

On or about May 8 Holborn handed Montrose over to Leslie at Tain. The prisoner was at once despatched southward, together with other captives taken at Carbisdale. An onlooker, who saw him on his way through Lovat, described him as mounted on a Shetland pony with ' a quilt of rags and straw ' by way of a saddle and pieces of rope for stirrups. His feet were ' fastened under the horse's belly with a tether.' His upper garment was ' a ragged old dark reddish plaid,' probably the same as that in which he had disguised himself after his defeat. On either side of him marched a musketeer, and behind him followed the train of his fellow-prisoners, trudging along the road. He was at that time suffering from a burning fever, but his look was calm and high. " Montrose," cried an old woman as he crossed the bridge at Inverness, " look above ; view those ruinous houses of mine which you occasioned to be burnt down when you besieged Inverness ! "[1] It is ever so.

May 8 (?) Montrose delivered to Leslie. He is carried south.

May 9. His appearance at Lovat.

May 10. He passes through Inverness,

---

[1] The editors of the *Deeds of Montrose*, 315–321, have collected all available information on Montrose's progress, and have given references to

What to the captain is a necessary operation of war is ruin to the peasant.

The magistrates of Inverness showed kindness to the unhappy prisoners, offering wine as they passed. The others drank heartily of it, but Montrose would not taste it till he had mingled it with water. " My lord," said an aged citizen, himself a prop of the Covenanting cause in the north, as he watched the captive passing out of the gate, " I am sorry for your circumstances." "I am sorry," replied Montrose, "for being the object of your pity." During the next few days he received visits from the Royalist gentry, who came to condole with him in his misfortune ; amongst them Mackenzie of Pluscardine, whose failure to appear in Strath Oykell had been the main cause of that misfortune. Pluscardine would hardly have appeared unless he had been personally free from blame.

May 10. and receives visits from his friends.

Harsher voices were soon heard. At Keith on Sunday, May 12, a minister chosen to preach before Montrose chose for his text the words spoken by Samuel to Agag : " As thy sword hath made women childless, so shall thy mother be childless among women." The invective which followed disgusted even the Covenanters present. Montrose listened patiently for a time, and then with the words " Rail on, Rabshakeh," turned his back to the preacher. It is said that further on, at Grange House, the lady of the mansion made the guard drunk, in hope that Montrose might escape disguised in her clothes, but that he was detected by a soldier and brought back in custody.

May 12. A sermon on Agag.

Montrose attempts to escape.

At last, on May 18, the sad and wearisome pilgrimage reached its end at Edinburgh. As Montrose had already been declared a traitor by Parliament, no formal judicial proceedings were required to condemn him, nor was any consideration for the master whom he

May 18. His arrival at Edinburgh.

the sources from which it has been drawn. Of course the old woman did not give vent to her feelings in this literary form.

served likely to stand in the way of his doom. On the day
before his arrival Parliament had appointed a committee to
give directions for his reception and execution. It was,
therefore, by the order of this committee that Montrose was
met at the Water Gate Port at the lower end of the Canongate
He is placed in a cart with his hands tied. by the magistrates, who placed him in a cart driven
by the hangman. His hands were tied to the sides
of the cart, in order, as it was said, that he might
not be able to protect his face against stones or dirt thrown at
him by the crowd which lined the street. It was also said
that, with the object of provoking the people to violence,
many widows of men slain by his followers had been hired to
appear in the throng. If this tale be true, those who had
Progress through the street. organised this cruel plot were grievously disappointed. So calm and majestic was the aspect of
the captive that hands prepared to strike hung
down, and hostile eyes were bedewed with tears. The
Countess of Haddington, venturing to laugh, was silenced by
a rude voice telling her that it would better become her to ride
in the cart as an adulteress. Argyle, too, had not thought it
Argyle's retreat. shame to seat himself in a balcony, together with his
son Lord Lorne and Lorne's newly married wife, to
gloat over the misfortunes of the great enemy of their house,
but they dared not meet the eye of Montrose. As they
caught his unabashed gaze, they stealthily crept back into the
house. "No wonder," cried an Englishman who witnessed
their retreat, "they start aside at his look, for they durst not
look him in the face these seven years bygone."

At last the cart stopped at the door of the Tolbooth.
"Fellow," said Montrose to the hangman, after his hands had
Montrose in prison. been loosed, "there is drink-money for driving the
cart." Once inside the prison doors he was accosted
by commissioners from the Parliament. Before he would
consent to answer them, he inquired on what terms they stood
with the King. When he was told that Parliament and the
King were agreed, he contented himself with asking to be
allowed to rest. He was weary, he said, of the day's journey,

'and the compliment they had put upon him that day was somewhat tedious.' The next day was a Sunday, but it was to be no day of Sabbath rest for Montrose. He was baited by ministers and laymen all equally urgent with him to acknowledge his sin. No word of submission could they drag from him.

May 19.
He is baited by his visitors.

Early on Monday morning he was again exposed to assault. Four ministers came to urge him to penitence in the name of the General Assembly. Had he not come into the land 'with a commission from the King to fight against his country, and raise a civil war within our bowels?' Had he not taken Irish and Popish rebels by the hand? Had not his men spoiled and ravaged the country through which their path had been marked by bloodshed? Montrose urged that it was impossible to restrain unpaid troops from plundering, and that as far as bloodshed was concerned 'he would rather it had all come out of his ówn veins.' As for the charge of employing such troops at all, he replied to it in characteristic fashion. " No wonder," he said, " that the King should take any of his subjects who could help him, when those who should have been his best subjects deserted and opposed him. We see what a company David took to defend him in the time of his strait." Montrose, in short, saw the nation in the King, whilst his antagonists had some idea of the value of constitutional forms and national rights, even when they strained them to suit their own purposes.

May 20.
Montrose questioned by four ministers.

The same spirit animated Montrose when he answered a complaint that he had broken the Covenant. " The Covenant which I took," he cried, " I own it, and adhere to it. Bishops, I care not for them, I never intended to advance their interest ; but when the King had granted you all your desires, and you were every one sitting under his vine and under his fig-tree—that then you should have taken a party in England by the hand and entered into a league and covenant with them against the King, was the thing I judged my duty to oppose to the yondmost." It was lawful, in short, for the King's servant to ally himself with predatory

Montrose and the Covenant.

Highlanders and 'Irish Papists' to maintain the King's authority; it was unlawful for the Scottish Parliament to fight against a King whose victory would have rendered Parliamentary right nugatory in Scotland as well as in England.

Happily, in this world of mingled motives, the correctness of a religious or political creed does not form a test by which Montrose prepares to appear before the Parliament. to distinguish the noble from the ignoble man. They little knew Montrose who imagined him likely to seek escape from his persecutors by suicide, and consequently denied him the use of a razor. He had made up his mind to treat the Parliament, before which he was now summoned, as the High Court of his Sovereign, and when he entered the hall in which it sat, pale and worn as he was, and with the comeliness of his face marred by his untrimmed beard, the splendour of the dress he had chosen was significant of the attitude which he had assumed towards the enemies who filled the benches. He was clothed in a suit of black cloth thickly overlaid with costly lace, whilst his upper coat was of scarlet trimmed with silver. Round his hat was a silver band. His stockings, his garters, and the roses in his shoes were of carnation silk.

When Montrose was admitted to the Parliament House he had to listen to an harangue from Loudoun of the usual Loudoun's charge. condemnatory character. As soon as he was allowed to speak, he explained the reason why he appeared bareheaded before those whom he had little occasion to respect. "Since," he said, "you have agreed with the King, I look upon you as if his Majesty were sitting amongst you, and in that relation I appear with this reverence —bareheaded." Then he told the story of his life, much as he had told it to his clerical tormentors. He had been faithful to the first Covenant. For the Solemn League and Covenant, 'he thanked God he was never in it, and so could not break it.' He had, in 1644, entered Scotland by his Majesty's commission to make a diversion against a faction which had assisted the English rebels.

"What my carriage was in this country, many of you may

bear witness. Disorders in arms cannot be prevented ; but they were no sooner known than punished. Never was any man's blood spilt but in battle ; and even then, many thousand lives have I preserved. And I dare here avow, in the presence of God, that never a hair of Scotsman's head that I could save fell to the ground. My coming at this time was by his Majesty's just commands, in order to the accelerating the treaty betwixt him and you ; his Majesty knowing that, whenever he had ended with you, I was ready to retire upon his call. I may say that never subject acted upon more honourable grounds, nor by so lawful a power as I did in these services." If they would judge justly it would be well. "If not," he ended by saying, "I do here appeal from you to the righteous Judge of the world, who one day must be your judge and mine, and who always gives out righteous judgments."

From the stern enemies who sat on the judgment-seat, Montrose had neither justice nor favour to expect. They had Montrose's too many wrongs to avenge, and many of them had sentence. too bitter recollections of their own dastardly flight before his avenging sword, not to clothe themselves in the comforting vesture of patriotic sentiment. The sentence, prepared in advance, was pronounced by Johnston of Warriston as Clerk Registrar. Montrose was to be hanged for three hours on a gibbet erected near the Cross in the High Street, with a copy of Wishart's History and of his own Declaration [1] about his neck. His corpse was then to be beheaded and dismembered. [2] The head was to be fixed to the Tolbooth at Edinburgh, the legs and arms to the gates of Stirling, Glasgow, Perth and Aberdeen ; the body to be buried, if the condemned man repented, in the Greyfriars' Church ; if he did not repent, on the Burroughmoor, in the place where criminals were interred. In the eyes of the modern reader the strangest part of the sentence is that which treated the carrying of Wishart's History as an addition to the disgrace of the hero whose valour it

[1] See p. 190.

[2] The word quartered used in the sentence cannot mean anything but this, as the trunk still remained.

commemorated. To the contemporary Presbyterian Scot it was a record, not of heroic achievements, but of causeless slaughter.

Montrose had hoped for a more honourable form of death by the headsman's axe. " It becomes them." he said, as he was removed from the Parliament House, "rather to be hangman than for me to be hanged." Parliament had given him permission to see his friends, but either he refused to avail himself of it, or the favour was intercepted. That night he slept, according to the acknowledgment of his guards, as calmly as ever they had themselves. On the morning of the 21st he dressed himself with care, this time in a scarlet mantle trimmed with gold lace. In such guise he passed along the few steps which parted the prison from the lofty gibbet, thirty feet high, which now stood up in the midst of the street. When he reached the place of execution he forgave his enemies. " I blame no man," he said. " I complain of no man. They are instruments, God forgive them." What he had done, he reiterated, had been done in obedience to the just commands of his lawful sovereign, 'for his defence in the day of his distress against those that did rise up against him.' He knew nothing, but to fear God and honour the King, according to the commandments of God and the laws of nature and nations. The late King had 'lived a saint and died a martyr.' " For this king never people were happier of a king. His commandments to me were most just ; in nothing that he promises will he fail ; he deals justly with all men. I pray God he be so dealt with that he be not betrayed under trust,[1] as his father was." Then after a few more words and an interval of silent prayer, Montrose submitted to have his hands bound ; and protesting that he counted this more honourable than the jewel of the Garter, he bent his neck to receive the book and the declaration. Then stepping up the ladder he met his death as calmly as he had been

Margin note: May 21. Montrose's execution.

---

[1] That is to say, by those who had given him reason to trust them with his person.

accustomed to watch the wavering fortunes of the battle-field. The remainder of the grim sentence was duly carried out.[1]   A hero had passed to his rest.   For him it was better that a veil should be cast over the future of his beloved country, and of his idolised Sovereign.   A few more weeks of life would have revealed to him a Charles who was neither great, good nor just, veiling his honour before the Covenanting crew, and seeking to gain his ends by walking in the crooked paths of deceit.

[1] For references to the evidence on which this narrative rests, see Napier, *Memoirs of Montrose*, ii. 777–809.

CHAPTER X

THE TREATY OF HELIGOLAND

IT is depressing to turn from the death-scene of the pure-souled champion of monarchy who had set his life upon the cast to the Argyle's strength and weakness. plots of the intriguers who, on either side of the sea, were making their game to win ease or power. Amongst this baser class Argyle was pre-eminent. Far superior to Montrose in political insight, Argyle had early recognised that government could only be firmly established in Scotland with the goodwill of the Presbyterian middle classes, and that it was folly for the smaller kingdom to dream of imposing its will upon the larger. Unhappily this statesmanlike insight into the realities of the situation only served to bring into relief the shiftiness of his character. As in 1648 he had attached himself to Cromwell, in 1650 he attached himself to Charles, and in taking up Charles's cause he had set himself to forward what he knew to be the hopeless task of forcing Presbyterianism on England, a task all the more hopeless because the young King in whose name the effort was to be made regarded the attempt with aversion, and would find his natural supporters amongst those very nobles who had been the chief antagonists of Argyle. Whether Charles lost or won Argyle was ruined. To balance between Charles and the Presbyterians, to attempt to convince Charles that the Kirk was less opinionative than it was, and to attempt to convince the Kirk that Charles was devoted to its interests, was now the height of wisdom for the Achitophel of his generation. He had schemed and intrigued, but no word of honest warning to his countrymen had sprung to his lips as he followed the multitude turning aside to what he knew to be stupendous folly.

On May 15 [1] Fleming reached Edinburgh with Charles's order for the disbandment of Montrose's force. If Argyle was

—as surely must have been the case—a party to the bargain to which Charles had assented,[2] there is no difficulty in understanding why he ostensively with-

drew from all participation in the proceedings which led to the execution of his own personal enemy.[3] His partisans in Parliament were slow to imitate this fine-drawn diplomacy. They had now before them the agreement to which Charles had with great reluctance

consented. On May 18, the day on which Charles's noblest champion was borne as a captive through the streets of Edinburgh, the Scottish Parliament resolved to send additional instructions to its Com-

missioners at Breda, directing them to insist on far more stringent terms than those which had been originally presented. At the beginning of the negotiations Charles had been asked to declare void all treaties and agreements contrary to the laws against toleration of ‘the Popish religion.’ He was now asked to declare void ‘ all treaties or agreements whatsoever with the bloody rebels in Ireland, and to declare that ’ he ‘ would never allow nor permit any liberty of the Popish religion in Ireland or any other part of ’ his dominions. His plea for postponing his oath to the Covenants was summarily rejected. He was to take it whenever the Commissioners chose to demand it, and the Commissioners were told to demand it either before or at his landing in Scotland. Charles's entreaty for permission to be given to the Engagers to return to their native land was met by the reply that, if the Engagers wished to return, they would have first to give satisfaction to the Kirk, and then security to the kingdom not to trouble its peace. Even then they would

---

[1] This is the date given in a letter from Edinburgh in *A Perf. Diurnal*, E, 777, 5. A letter of May 9 in *A Brief Relation* (E, 601, 12), which makes him land on the 8th, can only embody a false report.

[2] See p. 206.   [3] *State Trials*, v. 1,427.

not be suffered to come within the verge of the Court. It must be distinctly understood that Parliament had no intention of repealing a single clause of the Act of Classes.[1]

The determination of Parliament to show even this modified grace to the Engagers was soon put to the test. On May 24 [2]

May 24. Arrival of Will Murray and Callander.

Will Murray arrived, bringing with him Callander, one of the least obnoxious of the Engagers. It is indeed probable that Callander had been sent over to try the ground. If so, it soon appeared that the feeling in Parliament against granting him permission to remain

Callander expelled from Scotland.

was too strong to be resisted. The most that his friends dared to ask was that he should be allowed fifteen days to settle his affairs. The proposal was, however, defeated, and he was ordered to quit the country in

The lords deserted by the other orders.

three days. It was significant that whilst the barons [3] and burgesses voted in the majority, the lords, presumably including Argyle himself, voted in the minority. The middle classes which Argyle had raised to power would have nothing to say to the politic compliances of their leader.[4]

The difficulty of reconciling Charles to Callander's expulsion was nothing in comparison with the difficulty of reconciling

May 25. A letter from Charles.

him to the execution of Montrose. Yet a letter which Will Murray brought from the King to the Parliament may have served to convince the latter that the task was not altogether hopeless. The letter itself, written on May 12, on the first vague news of Montrose's defeat,[5] has unfortunately not been preserved. According to a

[1] Instructions from Parliament, May 18 ; Draft of Explanation to be given to the Commissioners, May 15 ; *Clar. St. P.* App. lix. ; Propositions to be offered to the King, May 18 (?), *Thurloe*, i. 147.

[2] Graymond to Brienne, $\frac{\text{May 28}}{\text{June 7}}$, *Harl. MSS.* 4,551, fol. 513.

[3] *I.e.* the country gentlemen.

[4] *Acts of Parl. of Sc.* vi. part ii. 568 ; *Balfour*, iv. 25 ; Graymond to Brienne, $\frac{\text{May 28}}{\text{June 7}}$, *Harl. MSS.* 4,551, fol. 513.

[5] In a letter from Breda, written on May 9, we read that there were then some rumours of Montrose's defeat, *Charles II. and Scotland*, 89.

report of the substance of it given out in Parliament, Charles merely expressed himself as 'heartily sorry that James Graham had invaded this kingdom, and how he had discharged him from doing the same, and earnestly desires the estates of Parliament to do himself that justice as not to believe that he was accessory to the said invasion in the least degree.' Possibly if we had the letter itself before us it might be found that Charles simply dissociated himself from Montrose's invasion on the ground that he had countermanded it by orders sent through Fleming, and this supposition obtains support from the fact that it was accompanied by a copy of the letter in which he gave orders to Montrose to lay down his arms.[1]

A few words added by Argyle himself put a still worse construction on the relations between Charles and Montrose. He announced that he had received a letter from Lothian, telling him 'that his Majesty was no ways sorry that James Graham was defeated, in respect he had made that invasion without and contrary to his command.[2] Charles was neither truthful nor high-minded, but it is at least improbable that he should have intended to say that he had never at any time ordered Montrose to invade Scotland when his own letter to Montrose urging him to persist in his undertaking had long been in print,[3] and was known as familiarly to Argyle and Lothian as to himself. On the other hand, there is evidence that Argyle was anxious to clear Charles of what was conceived amongst the Covenanters to be the disgrace of instigating Montrose to invade the country. " James Graham," he had written to Lothian three days before this scene in Parliament, " . . . was warned to be sparing in speaking to the King's disadvantage, or else he had done it ; for before the Parliament, in his own justification, he said he had several commissions from the King for all that he did ; yea, he had particular orders, and that lately, for coming to the mainland of Scotland." [4]

Argyle's additional charge.

On the whole, therefore, the most likely explanation is that

[1] *Balfour,* iv. 24.   [2] *Ib.* iv. 25.   [3] See p. 192.
[4] Argyle to Lothian, May 22, *Ancram and Lothian Correspondence,* ii. 262.

Argyle, trusting to Charles's eagerness to be received in
Scotland and his well-known easiness of character, did not
scruple to distort or exaggerate phrases which, as
spoken, bore a comparatively, though only a comparatively, innocent meaning. It can hardly be doubted
that Will Murray brought with him another letter
from Charles to Argyle himself, and it may well be that it contained words expressing confidence that the understanding
about the indemnity for Montrose would, in spite of the conflict
at Carbisdale—of which alone Charles had as yet any knowledge
—be carried out without delay. At all events, it was not
thought well to publish Charles's letter to the Parliament, a
watery account of it, in which he was made merely to ask for
further information, being put into circulation.[1] It was
enough, it would seem, if the lines were traced out in Parliament, within which Charles would be expected to bear himself
in his relations with the leading Covenanters when at last he
landed in Scotland. Before that time he would know that he
was expected to repudiate Montrose, and there was little likelihood that, being the man he was, he would do otherwise than
repudiate one who long before that time arrived would be
counted amongst the dead.

Was Charles misrepresented by Argyle?

If the lesson had been doubtful, it would be strengthened
by the measure served out to Montrose's principal followers.
On May 29, Hurry, who had served all causes with
impartiality, and Spottiswoode, who had taken a
leading part in the murder of Dorislaus, were beheaded. On June 7, Hay of Dalgetty together with
Sibbald, who had been sent before Montrose to rouse the
gentry to take arms for the King, underwent the like sentence.
If the French Agent is to be trusted, Sibbald had been put to
the torture, and had acknowledged a design for seizing the
Castle of Edinburgh. A fifth victim, Colonel Charteris, was
executed on the 21st.[2] Of the common soldiers who had been

May 29-June 21. Execution of five of Montrose's followers.

---

[1] *Charles II. and Scotland*, 103.

[2] Graymond to Brienne, $\frac{May\ 28}{June\ 7}$, *Harl. MSS.* 4,551, fol. 513; *Balfour*,
iv. 32; *Acts of the Parl. of Sc.* vi. part ii. 572, 573; Nicoll's *Diary*, 16.

taken prisoners, the foreigners received passes to enable them to return to the Continent. The Orkney men had been already

Treatment of the prisoners.

disposed of. About forty, who had wives and children or aged parents depending on them, were restored to their homes. Of the remainder, who numbered 241, six fishermen were presented to Argyle, and six to David Leslie, whilst six others were given to Sir James Hope to work in his lead-mines. All the rest were presented to the Earl of Angus and Sir Robert Moray as recruits for regiments in the French service.[1]

Punishments were accompanied by rewards levied on the fines payable by those who had shown sympathy with Mont-

Rewards.

rose. First on the list of the favoured recipients of

Gift to Macleod.

the bounty of Parliament was Macleod of Assynt, who was to have 20,000 Pounds Scots—equalling 1,666*l*. 13*s*. 4*d*. in English money—and 400 bolls of meal. Celtic tradition persistently maintained that two-thirds of the meal was sour.[2]

The victory over Montrose appears to have convinced Parliament that it could afford to dispense with the support of the leading Engagers, and we may be sure that its action in this respect fully commended itself to Argyle. On June 4 an

June 4. Banishment of sixteen persons.

Act was passed declaring that sixteen persons high in Charles's confidence were to be excluded from the kingdom till Parliament chose to remit the sentence. Amongst these were the Royalists Brentford,[3] Napier, and Eythin, alongside of the Engagers, Hamilton, Lauderdale and Callander. Besides this, no person comprehended in the first and second class of the Act of Classes[4] was to be allowed to come into the young King's presence.[5]

What did the Parliament expect of Charles?

Had the Covenanting Parliament so taken the measure of Charles's capacity for yielding as to expect him to accept in good faith such treatment as this? If so, it must have been badly served by its Commis-

---

[1] *Acts of Parl. of Sc.* vi. part ii. 566 ; *Balfour*, iv. 18.

[2] *Deeds of Montrose*, 523, 525.

[3] Earl of Forth in the Scottish peerage.

[4] See p. 14.   [5] *Balfour*, iv. 41.

sioners at Breda, who had good means of knowing what his temper really was. The ministers at least who had been deputed by the Kirk to wait upon Charles, could not close their eyes to his deficiencies as a Covenanting King. On one occasion he denied that the Scriptures were a perfect rule to settle all controverted questions, and even asked how ' people knew that it was the Word of God, but by the testimony of the Church.' As long as he remained at Breda 'he continued the use of the service-book and his chaplains, and many nights he was balling and dancing till near day.' At last, on May 25, the Commissioners of the Kirk were horrified by the news that he meant to communicate on his knees on the following morning. In writing and by word of mouth they protested against the scandal which, as they said, was ' against that which he had granted in his concessions, and would confirm some to think he was dallying with God and with us.' Charles stubbornly refused to give way, and not only received the Communion on his knees, but allowed a bishop—Bramhall of Derry—to pronounce the benediction.[1]

Whilst the Scots deplored Charles's ecclesiastical aberrations, the more stalwart Englishmen at Breda were thrown into despair by the knowledge that they could not count on him — as they could have counted on his father —to stand by the teaching of his own Church whenever his private interests were concerned. Hopton retired in dudgeon to Utrecht. " Our religion," wrote Hopton's chaplain, "is gone, and within a few days is expected the funeral of our liturgy which is gone already." [2]

On May 29,[3] if not earlier, Charles was at Honslaerdyck

Marginal notes:
Charles's language about religion.

May 25. Protest of the Commissioners.

May 26. Charles receives the Communion kneeling.

Discontent among the Cavaliers.

Charles's reluctance to accept their ecclesiastical standard.

---

[1] Commissioners of the Kirk to Charles, $\frac{May\ 25}{June\ 4}$, *Clar. St. P.* ii. App. lxiii.   [2] Watson to Edgeman, May $\frac{2}{12}$.

[3] An extract from a letter of Nicholas, printed in the *Nicholas Papers*, i. 185, from Birch's transcripts, says, in a letter dated $\frac{May\ 29}{June\ 8}$, ' that the King goes the day before, being Whitsunday,' to Honslaerdyck. Whitsunday O.S. was June 2, 'the day on which Charles embarked. But he had been at Honslaerdyck to see the Prince of Orange some days earlier. *Charles II. and Scotland*, p. 112.

preparing for his passage to Scotland.   On that day he first
heard of the execution of the most loyal of his servants by

May 29.
Charles
hears of
Montrose's
execution. those into whose hands he was about to trust his
person and his crown.   A letter to Montrose's eldest
son, written by him after hearing the terrible news,

His letter
to Mont-
rose's son. bears no impress of that indignation which would
have been aroused in most other men.[1]   To the end
of his life Charles was incapable of noble passion.
With him what was past was soon out of mind, and he trusted
for the future to lucky chance and his own skill.   The day
fixed for his embarkation in three Dutch vessels awaiting him

Charles at
Honslaer-
dyck. at Terheiden was June 2.   During the greater part
of the preceding day he remained under the impres-
sion that the agreement which he had come to with
the Commissioners at Breda would be ratified in Edinburgh.

He learns
the addi-
tional
demands
of the Par-
liament. It was only late in the evening that he learnt the
truth.   He now knew that the Scottish Parliament
not only rejected all the modifications he had proposed, but required him to take his oath to both
Covenants with the smallest possible delay, to condemn in express words Ormond's treaty with the Irish, and to forbear to
bring with him those of his councillors whom he trusted most.[2]

Against such exigencies Charles at last rebelled.   On June 2

June 2.
Charles
sails for
Scotland. he embarked, taking with him a whole train of the
men who were most obnoxious to the ruling party in
Scotland.   Amongst them were Hamilton, Lauderdale, Brentford, together with English noblemen and gentlemen, Buckingham, Cleveland, Widdrington.   Above all there
were his English chaplains, Goffe and Harding.   Nor was
Charles more yielding in other respects.   He would not hear of
signing the articles of the treaty which the Commissioners presented to him.

Time, however, and his own lonely position brought
counsel.   Contrary winds, or the fear of meeting English

---

[1] Charles to the second Marquis of Montrose, $\frac{\text{May 29}}{\text{June 8}}$, Napier's *Memoirs of Montrose*, ii. 766.

[2] Livingstone's Life in Wodrow Soc. *Select Biographies*, i. 178.

cruisers, drove him out of his course, and he could not but bethink himself of the risk he would run in landing in Scot-

Charles driven out of his course. land in defiance of the governing powers. He struggled long—longest, as he himself afterwards asserted, against the clause in which Ormond's treaty was condemned.[1] The more lukewarm amongst the Commissioners justified their own moderation to their more resolute brethren, on the ground that if the King were provoked it would drive him ' to take some other course, and not to go to Scotland at all.'

At last, on June 11,[2] when the little squadron was anchored in the roads of Heligoland, just as the Commissioners were

June 11. The Treaty of Heligoland. about to declare the negotiations broken off, Charles unexpectedly gave way, and signed the treaty without making any further difficulty. The only thing left uncertain was when and where he should take the oath to the two Covenants to which he was now engaged. If he was to bend his neck beneath the yoke, it was better to humiliate himself with as few witnesses as possible, and he accordingly elected to rid himself of the hateful obligation before he stepped

June 23. Charles swears to the Covenants. on shore. On the 23rd, as soon as the ship in which he sailed had cast anchor at Speymouth, he professed his willingness to do what was expected of him. One feeble attempt, indeed, he made to save his credit in the eyes of his English subjects on board, by asking permission to protest that in taking the oath he had no intention of infringing the laws of England, and that the Bills which he promised to confirm were not those which, though they had already passed the English Parliament, had never received the Royal assent and had consequently expired at the death of the late King.[3] What Charles asked for, in short, was to be allowed to promise to confirm future Bills presented by a future English

---

[1] Message delivered to Ormond by the Dean of Tuam, August 1, *Charles II. and Scotland*, 143.

[2] That this is the correct date and not June 21 is shown by *Acts of Parl. of Sc.* vi. part ii. 601.

[3] The Bill abolishing Episcopacy was passed on January 30, 1643. See *Great Civil War*, i. 34.

Parliament which might possibly be very moderately Presbyterian, if indeed it was Presbyterian at all.   He gained nothing by his pleading.   In the original form of the confirmation of the Covenants he was asked to engage to give his ' Royal assent to the Acts of Parliament enjoyning the same ' in his dominions outside Scotland.   Additional words were now inserted in the margin pledging him to assent to ' Bills or ordinances passed or to be passed in the Houses of Parliament,' thus binding Charles to give a legal position to the Presbyterian system in England and Ireland immediately upon his restoration in England.   Charles at once accepted the position, initialled the marginal correction after he had signed the main body of the document, forswearing himself before God and man.[1]

---

[1] The original document signed by Charles is amongst the *Clarendon St. P.* ii. No. 346.   See also the Commissioners of the Kirk to Charles, June $\frac{11}{21}$; The Commissioners of Parliament to Charles, June $\frac{12}{22}$; *Clar. St. P.* ii. App. lxiii. lxv.   (The above are the true dates.)   Livingstone's Life in Wodrow Soc. *Select Biographies*, i. 178–183.   According to a statement in *The Hind Let Loose* (ed. 1797), p. 95, to which Mr. H. F. Morland Simpson has called my attention, the negotiation which led to Charles's arrival in Scotland was at one time nearly broken off.   "They sent Commissioners and concluded a treaty with him at Breda ; during which treaty the commissions which he had sent to that bloody villain Montrose and his cut-throat complices to raise an army and waste and invade the country with fire and sword the second time were brought to the Committee of Estates, discerning what sort of a King they were treating with.   Whereupon after serious consulting not only together but with the Lord ; and after many debates what to do in such a doubtful case wherein all was in danger, the Estates concluded to break off the treaty and recall the Commissioners.   To which intent they sent an express with letters to Breda which, by providence falling into the hands of Liberton a true libertine, a false betrayer of his trust and country, was by him without the knowledge of the other Commissioners, delivered unto the King ; who consulting the contents of the packet with his jesuitical and hypocritical cabal, found it his interest to play the fox—and so sending for the Commissioners," &c.   Some such story seems to have been current at the time, as there is a hint of it in an English newspaper.   The difficulty is to fix its date.   If there is any truth in it, it may probably be referred to the second week in April, and in that case Will Murray's mission (see p. 201) may have been a

Charles had not yet fully drained the cup of humiliation. As he was conducted slowly southwards he saw the arm of

June 27.
Charles at
Aberdeen.

July 6.
He arrives
at Falkland.

Most of his
followers
banished.

Montrose suspended over the gate of Aberdeen, and when at last, on July 6, he reached the palace at Falkland, he was there informed that Parliament on the one hand had confirmed the treaty of Heligoland, and on the other hand had voted that, with the exception of nine persons, all the followers who had accompanied him from Holland were to leave the country.[1] Of the nine, however, four or five who were pledged to give support to Argyle rather than to the Hamiltons, of whom Buckingham was one, were allowed to remain at Court, whilst the remainder, amongst whom was Secretary Long, were informed that they might remain in Scotland, provided that they kept at a distance from the King. Of those on whom sentence of banishment was pronounced, an exception was subsequently made in favour of Hamilton, who was allowed to remain in the Isle of Arran, whilst Lauderdale was included amongst those who, though excluded from Court, were allowed to remain in Scotland. What modifications had been introduced into the original list of proscription may be traced to the energy of Argyle, who would fain have extended the exemptions further, and have rallied the two parties in the common defence of the King, at least so far as it could be done without admitting his personal rivals to power.[2]

counterplot of Argyle's, and it may have been Murray who placed the despatch of the Committee of Estates in Winram's hands. The recall may also have been only conditional in case of Charles's continuing to refuse acceptance of the terms offered.

[1] *Acts of Parl. of Sc.* vi. part ii. 603. Nine names are given in the vote, but in the subsequent instructions only eight appear. The missing name is that of Lord Wentworth, which appears on the list of those who were to leave the country. Balfour also gives nine names, substituting that of Mr. Pouliey [Pooley], but there is nothing to show whether he was allowed to stay at Court or not.

[2] Balcarres to Lothian, June 28, *Ancram and Lothian Papers*, ii. 269; *Acts of Parl. of Sc.* vi. part ii. 603; Walker's *Hist. Discourses*, 159–163; *Balfour*, iv. 58–77.

When Parliament broke up on June 5, leaving, as usual, its authority to a Committee of Estates, Charles had little reason

June 5.
End of the session.

to congratulate himself on the success of his plan for winning the Scottish nation to his side to the detriment of its Government. He might console himself as best he might with the sparkling talk which Buckingham always had at his disposal, and to which he could look as an antidote to the dreary Presbyterian sermons and the no less dreary conversation of the Presbyterian ministers by whom he was afflicted. If his thoughts strayed beyond the interests of

Charles looks to England.

the moment, the only part of the horizon which gleamed brightly was England. Before he left the Netherlands he had laid his plans for a Cavalier rising, and a Cavalier rising, if it could be brought about whilst the army of Fairfax and Cromwell was engaged on the Scottish border, would not only dislocate the forces of the enemy, but would loosen the bonds in which he had been confined by his professing friends. Once restored to Westminster by his English subjects, Charles would laugh in the faces of the baffled Covenanters, if they ventured to recall to his mind that oath which sat so lightly on his conscience.

Every preparation had indeed been made for a rising in England, to take place as soon as the movement of the English army towards the Scottish border made a rising feasible. Early

May.
Preparations for a rising in England.

in May the commands of the insurgent armies had been allotted, though, unfortunately for the Royalist cause, to men who had little but their titles to recommend them for a service which needed the highest military

Generals named.

qualifications. Buckingham was to be General of the Eastern Association, Newcastle of the Northern Counties, Willoughby of Parham of Lincolnshire, Derby of Lancashire, Cheshire, and the neighbouring counties. In the West the gentry bound themselves to rise the moment that the Parliamentary troops, no more than three hundred in all, were removed from their midst, and they gave assurances of being able to seize Exeter, Weymouth, and Poole for the King. There can be little doubt that the gentry of the other counties were equally forward, but it was in the West, as the part of the country most distant from Scotland, and therefore from the main body of the English army, that the movement was to begin. All that was asked of Charles was that, when the proper moment arrived, he would send 2,000 foreign troops under Sir Richard Grenvile to land in Torbay, bringing with them horses, arms and ammunition, to distribute amongst the King's partisans. As for the Engagement, it 'was by most refused, and resolved to be broken by those who took it.'

For the necessary supply of money Charles looked mainly to the City of London. His agent, Colonel Keane, was assured that many of the wealthy citizens would give liberally, if only no questions were asked as to the names of those who sent the money. Not long after his arrival in Scotland, Charles was able to write to the Prince of Orange, not only asking him to levy the 2,000 men required for the West of England, but also assuring him that the money needed for the purpose would be forthcoming.[1] Nor were Charles's financial hopes even now confined to his own subjects. Before he left Holland he had commissioned Newcastle to attempt what Montrose had attempted in vain—to persuade the King of Denmark to supply men, money, and arms for the coming war.[2]

Money expected from London.

It is true that the rising was not to be exclusively one of Cavaliers. The money which went to support it was drawn mainly from the Presbyterians, and much was expected from the action of Presbyterian London, but it is evident that Charles wished the Cavaliers to be as strong as possible. About the end of July he wrote to Lord Beauchamp telling him what he had done in the matter of the 2,000 men. Beauchamp was to assure the Catholics, who were asking for the remission of their penalties, that he was ready to grant their wishes as soon as it was in his power to do so.

Promises to the Catholics.

---

[1] Second Report of Colonel Keane, May $\frac{10}{20}$, *Charles II. and Scotland*, 94; Confessions of J. Coke, *ib.* 154, *Portland MSS.*, *Hist. MSS. Com. Rep.* xiii. part i. 576–604; Charles to the Prince of Orange, *Clar. St. P.* ii. 546; Beauchamp to Charles, May 31, *Nicholas Papers*, i. 178, 179.

[2] Long's Notes, *Charles II. and Scotland*, 124.

As to the Presbyterians he had a cautious word to give.   " I pray you," he wrote, " be careful to link yourself as much with the Presbyterians as you can, and to give them all possible satisfaction ; for though I desire that as many of my own party should be in arms as can be drawn together, yet if it pass for an army of Royalists, and do not move upon the Presbyterian interest, or at least with their consent and concurrence, I have reason to believe that the Scots will not only not join with you, but even declare and fight against you." [1]   Charles, in short, was ready to be all things to all men.   The scruples which had weighed heavily with his father were without significance for the son.

It is hardly necessary to say that all who took part in the government at Westminster were eager to penetrate the secret

Anxiety at West-minster. details of a plan of which the general scope was patent to the world.   The first news of Winram's arrival in Jersey had, as has been already seen,[2] given rise to a spasmodic effort to detect the enemies of the Commonwealth by a general enforcement of the Engagement.   Yet there was an uneasy feeling that mere police measures would be insufficient to meet the crisis, and that it would be well to appeal to the patriotism of the English nation against a threatened invasion from Scotland, and to seize the opportunity of building up the Commonwealth upon a broader basis.

Accordingly, on January 9, Vane at last made his report from the committee appointed nearly eight months before [3] to

Jan. 9. Vane's report on a new Parliament. consider the question of elections to future Parliaments.   In the first place there was to be a sweeping redistribution of seats.   As in the Agreement of the People presented by the officers shortly before the King's execution,[4] the number of members was fixed at 400. Of these a certain number were allotted to each county, leaving it to Parliament to distribute that number between the county

---

[1] Charles II. to Beauchamp, June (?), *Nicholas Papers*, i. 180.
[2] See p. 193.   [3] On May 15, 1649 ; see p. 57.
[4] *Great Civil War*, iv. 295.

itself and the towns within its limits.[1] The question of the franchise to be adopted was also left to the House, though the committee distinctly recommended that, in lieu of a general election, the existing Parliament should direct partial elections to be held to fill up vacancies in accordance with the new scheme of redistribution, the sitting members for each county retaining their seats as 'part of the said proportion.'[2]

Parliament at once adopted the proposed number of 400. All other questions were referred to a Committee of the whole

The plan discussed. House, which sat usually once a week for some time to come. Of the debates which took place in

Committee of the whole House. this committee scarcely a word has reached us, but it is improbable that many of its members were pre-

Reluctance to proceed to a dissolution. pared to go beyond the scheme for partial elections which had been submitted to them. With a Scotch war impending over their heads, it may be believed

that the majority was unwilling to go even as far as this. If desire of gaining popular support had made them hold out to the electors the prospect of filling up the vacant seats, fear of danger to the Commonwealth and of loss of their own power

Feb. Marten compares the Commonwealth to Moses. was the more powerful influence. " The Commonwealth," said Marten one day in February, " seems to me to be much like Moses." After pausing for a moment to attract attention, he added that, as

Pharaoh's daughter seeking for a nurse for the infant she had raised from the ark of bulrushes found its own mother, 'so they themselves were the true mother to this fair child the young Commonwealth,' and they ' themselves, therefore, were the fittest nurses.' " This," adds the Royalist reporter of the story, " was disliked afterwards by the sages. They would

---

[1] In the Agreement of the People only 341 seats were allotted, the remainder being left to be filled up by the first Parliament elected under the scheme. In accordance with the present proposal 396 were allotted. Probably the four seats wanting were assigned to Carmarthenshire, as that county is unnoticed, probably by a slip of the pen or an error in the press.

[2] Here is the germ of the proposal to continue them as members of the next Parliament which roused Cromwell's anger in 1653.

not have their meaning so clearly opened." [1]   There can be
no stronger evidence of the prevailing alarm caused by the
renewal of Charles's negotiations with the Scots than is furnished by the accession of Marten—hitherto so closely connected with Lilburne and the Levellers—to the ranks of the
The subject   champions of the existing Parliament.   The meet-
dropped.   ings of the committee continued for many weeks,
but as the prospect of a war with Scotland became plainer,
what little chance there was of their leading to a practical conclusion vanished for the time.

The reasoning which made for the retention of the existing
House, made also for the retention of the existing Council of
Feb. 11.   State, the powers of which were to expire on
Election of   February 16.   On the 11th, 37 out of the former 41
the second
Council of   were re-elected.   Of the four whose names were no
State.   longer to be found on the list, [2] Pembroke had
recently died, Mulgrave and Grey of Warke had refused to sit
Rejection of   in the outgoing Council.   The fourth, Sir John Dan-
Sir John   vers, had unadvisedly suggested that the new Council
Danvers.   might be more independent, 'and not expect the
tediousness of the House's debates and resolutions.'[3]   "Since
that gentleman," replied Marten, "likes not the tediousness of
Feb. 20.   the House's debates, it were best let him alone," and
The Council   Danvers's name was rejected by a smart majority.[4]
finally com-
pleted.   On the 20th the House chose five successors to

---

[1] News from England, $\frac{\text{Feb. 27}}{\text{March 9}}$, *Clarendon MSS.* ii. No. 250.

[2] Mrs. Everett Green writes (Preface to *Calendar of S. P. Dom.* 1649–
1650, p. xix) that the Earl of Denbigh 'was not continued upon the second
Council.'   "The reason for his expulsion," she adds, "will be found in
papers of Dec. 19, showing him in his true character of a cowardly trimmer,
rather than a conscientious partizan on either side."   Denbigh in reality
was re-elected to the second Council, and the papers in question consist of
charges against him of misconduct in the early part of the Civil War, which
cannot be accepted as evidence in the absence of a reply from the accused
person.

[3] *I.e.* not have to wait, before taking action, for orders from the
House.

[4] News from England $\frac{\text{Feb. 27}}{\text{March 9}}$, *Clar. MSS.* ii. No. 250.

the four vacant seats, thus raising the number of the members of Council to 42.[1]

The views of Danvers as to the necessity of strengthening the executive were not confined to himself. On February 15 a pamphlet appeared under the title of *A Word for the Commonweal*.[2] Its author was the younger Isaac Pennington, the son of the Isaac Pennington who had once been Lord Mayor and was now a member of the Council of State. Pennington warned his father's colleagues that they had still much to do to satisfy public opinion. Men complained, he said, of three evils, ' multitude of affairs, prolixity in your motions, and want of an orderly government of your own body.' Nor was he without a remedy to propose. The executive and legislative functions should not remain in the same hands. " It seemeth to me," he wrote, " improper for Parliaments to intermeddle with matters of government farther than to settle it in fit hands and within just bounds, because they [3] are entrusted with an arbitrary power which is absolutely necessary to the work whereunto they are called ; they are to redress things at present for which there is as yet no law, and to provide future remedies for things amiss which the law did not foresee." When such words could be written the Protectorate was already in the air. Lilburne's democratic theory had been met by a counter-theory. The demand for government by the people was confronted by a demand for a strong executive, dependent indeed in the long run upon Parliament or the people, but sufficiently independent to keep clear of the rapid fluctuations of opinion to which all large bodies of men

Marginal notes: Feb. 15. A pamphlet by Isaac Pennington the younger.

Marginal note: Lilburne's theories answered.

---

[1] *C.J.* vi. 360, 369. A committee had suggested the name of the elder Vane, who had remained in Parliament after the King's execution, but the House rejected it.

[2] *A Ward for the Commonweal*, E, 593, 10. The author's name is given on the title page as Isaac Pennington without the addition of Junior, which appears in his other works. A comparison with *The Fundamental Right, Safety, and Liberty of the People*, published by the younger man in 1651, leaves no doubt of the authorship.

[3] *I.e.* Parliaments.

are subject in dealing with affairs of which they have no special knowledge.

Even if it had had the will, Parliament had far too much on its hands to undertake so serious a reform. Dropping all

Attitude of
Parliament
towards the
Presby-
terians.

specially Independent legislation, it pushed on measures for the propagation of the Gospel and the suppression of Sabbath-breaking, swearing, and drunkenness, which would appeal to both sections of the great Puritan party and might tend to weaken the alliance which was suspected to exist between the Royalists

Difficulty in
enforcing
the Engage-
ment.

and the Presbyterians.[1] On the other hand the enforcement of the Engagement was accompanied with grave difficulties. The penalties for refusing it were sufficiently serious to secure its acceptance by that vast majority to which all forms of government are equal if only they provide for the security of life and property ; but the Presbyterian clergy preached and argued against it, and the Royalists either abstained from taking it or took it only with

Fairfax
refuses to
take it,

a resolution to break it. What was most annoying was that Fairfax, who a year before had refused to take it as a member of the Council of State,[2] repeated his refusal now. Parliament could not, as yet, afford to dis-

Feb. 20.
and is ex-
cused.

pense with his services, and on February 20 it had to content itself with informing its general that the promise which he had already given as Councillor to maintain and defend the resolutions of Parliament in the settlement of the Commonwealth would be accepted as equivalent to the new Engagement.[3] Fairfax was too loyal to

Feb. 23.
Further
time given
to those
who refuse
the Engage-
ment.

betray his trust, but it was evident that he had no heart in the service of the Commonwealth. That Fairfax's example was likely to be followed appears from the fact that on February 23 an Act was hurried through Parliament to suspend till March 25 the exaction of penalties from recalcitrant officials.[4]

[1] These measures are set forth chronologically in Masson's *Life of Milton*, iv. 123.

[2] See p. 7.   [3] *C.J.* vi. 369.   [4] *Ib.* vi. 370.

To secure obedience and detect conspirators by the enforcement of an oath was plainly a difficult and probably a useless process. Parliament therefore fell back on a simpler way of disarming opposition. On February 26,

Feb. 26.
Delinquents
expelled
from
London. before Charles's arrival at Breda, an Act was passed ordering all Papists, soldiers of fortune, and delinquents to leave London by March 20. Not only were they forbidden to come within twenty miles of it after that date, but on October 20 they were to report themselves in the parishes in which they resided, in order that they might be confined within a radius of five miles.[1] So great was the

March 30.
The large-
ness of their
numbers. number of those affected, that we were told, doubtless with considerable exaggeration, that on the appointed day no fewer than thirty or forty thousand persons quitted London.[2]

Even this dispersion of suspected persons did not allay the disquietude of Parliament. On March 26 it established a new

March 26.
A new High
Court of
Justice. High Court of Justice 'for the preservation of the common peace and for the better preventing of the miseries of a new and bloody war.' The new court, which sat without a jury, had power to condemn to death all who betrayed towns, fortresses, or ships, stirred up mutinies in the army, took up arms against the Commonwealth, or being soldiers or sailors deserted their trust and adhered to the enemies of the Commonwealth. The penalties to be meted out to those who corresponded with Charles Stuart, his relatives, or councillors, were left to the discretion of the Court, whilst persons who harboured or relieved enemies, or, being officers of a prize taken at sea, suffered prisoners of war to escape, were to be condemned to minor punishments. The Court was also to sit in judgment on cases of treason.[3]

---

[1] *Act for the Removing of Papists*, E, 1,060, No. 83. Did the last-named clause suggest the idea of the more celebrated Five Mile Act?

[2] *A Perfect Diurnal*, E, 534, 21. The Presbyterian Royalists, it must be remembered, were not delinquents, and would therefore remain in London.

[3] *Act for Establishing a High Court of Justice*, E. 1,060, No. 89.

The existence of this new Star Chamber with powers of life and death was limited to the 29th of the following September.

Appointed for six months. The justification of those who created it was neither more nor less than the justification of every government whose existence is imperilled. A special weakness of the Court as originally constructed was that of its

Few lawyers on it. sixty-four members only three were lawyers, Keble, a commissioner of the Great Seal, the Recorder of London, and one Serjeant. A few days later, however, Parliament remedied this defect by adding six of the

April 2. Six judges added. Judges.[1]

Such a proceeding indicates the alarm into which the leaders of the Commonwealth had been thrown by Charles's

April. Reported saying of Bradshaw. threatened conjunction with the Scots. "I wonder much," Bradshaw was reported to have said about the end of April, "that, all the fair or foul means we can use, yet not any one Cavalier is heartily converted to us." Vane was no less despondent. He was at

Vane's despondent language. least reported to have said that 'they were in a far worse estate than ever yet they had been ; that all the world was and would be their enemies ; that their own army and general were not to be trusted, that the whole kingdom would rise and cut their throats upon the first good occasion ; and that they knew not any place to go unto to be safe.' Another Independent who was present when this conversation was held, added 'that they should find London also their greatest enemy when their army was drawn north, and wished it burnt to ashes to be secured of that fear.'[2]

---

[1] *C.J.* vi. 392.

[2] Colonel Keane's Second Report, May $\frac{10}{20}$, *Charles II. and Scotland*, 98.

CHAPTER XI

FAIRFAX AND CROMWELL

THAT the words attributed to Vane and his associates were to some extent coloured by the Royalist medium through which they passed, is probable enough ; but it is not likely that they were altogether invented by the reporter, and least of all those relating to the general and the army. No one could tell what hold the Levellers still had upon the soldiers, and it was known that some at least of the Levellers had been trying to come to an understanding with Charles. That Fairfax was not heart and soul with the Commonwealth there could be no doubt whatever. Though it is in the highest degree improbable that, as a Royalist agent some months afterwards declared, he had acknowledged himself to be 'bound in conscience to give the King some assistance and that upon good terms he would comply with him to that purpose,'[1] his refusal to take the Engagement to the Commonwealth [2] left no doubt in which direction his mind was tending. Charles, at least, was moved by what he heard of him to offer him the Earldom of Essex, 'what place he pleased in England,' and an estate worth 10,000*l.* a year, on condition that he should 'bring in with him any considerable

May.
Position of Fairfax and the army.

The Levellers and Charles.

Position of Fairfax.

Charles's offers to Fairfax.

---

[1] T. Coke's Confession, March 31, 1651, *Charles II. and Scotland*, 154. Coke was then trying to save his life by making revelations, and this story he only professes to have had at second or third hand.

[2] See p. 246.

part of the army to the Scotch interest.'[1] The offer never reached Fairfax, and it is most unlikely that if it had come to his knowledge he would have consented to betray his trust. He was, however, thoroughly dissatisfied with the course of events, and in this he was but the voice of large numbers of those who had not only taken part against the King at the beginning of the Civil War, but had even opposed the imprudent efforts of the Presbyterian party to come to terms with Charles.

It had for some time been evident that Fairfax would be called on before long to make his choice. Every week which

Impending war with Scotland. passed brought conviction with it that, whether there were internal commotions or not, a war with Scotland could not be averted. On April 9 Parliament had

April 9. The Council of State to provide against invasion and tumults. directed the Council of State to provide against invasions from abroad and tumults at home.[2] The Cavaliers were by this time regarded as enemies who must be held down with a strong hand, and Parliament was hardly likely to be beguiled into the folly with which the simple-minded Western gentry had credited it, of removing all its troops from the most disaffected district in

May. New regiments for the West. England.[3] Before the end of May Parliament had ordered the raising of two regiments of foot and one regiment of horse for special service in the West;[4]

Barkstead's regiment increased. in the same way provision was made for keeping in check the London Presbyterians, orders being given on May 15 for making up Barkstead's regiment, by

June 4. Horse to be raised for the City. which London and Westminster were guarded, to 2,000 men,[5] and, on June 4, authority was given to strengthen the militia by raising horse.[6]

Such measures as these, in addition to the far greater burden of a war with Scotland, were very costly, and as there

Financial needs. was in Parliament a general agreement that it would be impolitic, if indeed it were practicable, to increase

---

[1] T. Coke's Confession, April 11, 1651. *Hist. Com.* Rep. xiii. App. part i. 587.   [2] See p. 195.

[3] *C.J.* vi. 394.   [4] *Ib.* vi. 411, 415.   [5] *Ib.* vi. 412.

[6] *An Act . . . to raise Horse*, E, 1,061, No. 1.

the burden of taxation, the members were at their wits' ends to discover new sources of revenue. The lands of the late King and the Royal family, of the bishops, and of deans and chapters, found buyers, though not quite as rapidly as was hoped, and it was possible to raise money on loan by assigning the security of future sales. Yet even this was insufficient, and more money was ordered to be raised by the sale of delinquents' lands.[1] The exigencies of the time, combined with the belief that Cavaliers were not to be enticed into more than nominal submission, undoubtedly led Parliament into harsh dealing with individual delinquents. On April 15 it refused to entertain a proposal for freeing delinquents whose offences were prior to some unnamed day in the year 1644.[2] At a later period of the year, when there was an Act for the sale of delinquents' estates before Parliament, there was a suspicious eagerness to add names to the list which had been already drawn up.[3]

Sales of land and loans.

April 15. Proposed sale of delinquents' lands.

The Commonwealth, therefore, had at its disposal money as well as arms. How far it had any hold on the hearts of the people is a question more difficult to answer. It was easy, on the one hand, for Royalists to assert that all England, save a few fanatics, were yearning for a restoration ; and it was equally easy for the newswriters who supported the existing Government to refer to the crowds which flocked in from country districts to take the Engagement as proof of the popularity of the Commonwealth. The truth lay probably between the two extremes. We shall hardly be wrong in supposing that for every hundred convinced Royalists or Republicans, there were at least a thousand who were ready to accept whatever Government was actually in existence, rather than risk disturbance of the peace by a fresh civil war. Every acre of land sold was a bond attaching the purchaser to the Commonwealth. Nor was the amount of sales regarded from this point of view at all despicable. Of fee farm rents, for instance—or permanent ground rents,

Was the Common-wealth un-popular?

Sale of fee farm rents.

[1] *C.J.* vi. 393.   [2] *Ib.* vi. 399.   [3] *Ib.* vi. 442, 446.

formerly in possession of the Crown—of which the sales began on April 1, the sales in ten months amounted to 273,000*l.*, and of this no less than 120,000*l.* was brought in in the course of the first three months, when the danger to the Commonwealth appeared to be the greatest.[1] Every man who effected a purchase of this kind—and the same may be said of those who bought the lands of the clergy or of the Royal family—not only was interested in the defence of the Commonwealth, but must have already convinced himself that there was little danger of a restoration of monarchy which would wrest from him the property which he had acquired by the payment of hard cash.

It was doubtless with a view to increasing the number of its supporters from amongst the class not yet committed to any special policy, that the Government resolved to proceed a step farther in the line which it had taken when, in the preceding winter, it resolved to issue two newspapers to represent its views. For some months *Several Proceedings* and *A Brief Relation* had poured forth news, both domestic and foreign, with such scanty comments as appeared to be needful. Their decorous sheets, however, necessarily failed to enter into competition with the Royalist products of the unlicensed press, *Mercurius Pragmaticus*, or *The Man in the Moon*, which set themselves not to instruct, but to amuse, with scant regard for the virtues of truthfulness and decency. The Government woke to the consciousness that it might be worth while to turn the laugh on their opponents, and no doubt would fain have discovered some one in their own ranks with the faculty of being amusing. If they searched at all, their search was in vain. Puritans had many virtues, but neither wit nor humour was amongst them.

The Government and the Press.

A lively newspaper in request.

If the Government could not discover a lively writer amongst their own supporters, the next best thing was to steal one from the enemy. Of the scurrilous scribes on the Royalist side, the ablest was Marchamont Needham, whose *Mercurius Pragmaticus* was widely

Marchamont Needham.

[1] *Augmentation Office Miscellaneous Books*, *R.O.* cxi.

read, and who consequently suffered imprisonment in the summer of 1649.[1] He was, however, discharged in November,[2] probably in expectation that he might be induced to transfer his services to his former opponents. At all events, on May 8 His *Case* he published a pamphlet, *The Case of the Common-*
of the *wealth of England Stated,* frankly acknowledging his
Common-
wealth. political conversion, but ascribing it entirely to the weight of reason. His arguments were marshalled in two parts, in the first of which he sought to convince ' the conscientious man ' that the cause of the Commonwealth was equitable, whilst in the second he strove to impress ' the worldling ' with the belief that it was to his own interest to stand by the existing Government instead of courting the dangers which would attend any attempt to unsettle it.

Needham's appeal to the conscientious man was indeed a strange one to find favour in the eyes of a Puritan Govern-
Nature of ment. No Government, he urged, lasted for ever, and
the argu- the success of the present Government was a sign
ment. that divine Providence intended it to last for its allotted time, especially as the tendency in Europe—the events in France had taken an extraordinary hold on the English imagination—was distinctly against monarchy. What if the present Government rested its claims on victory ? The power of the sword was the foundation of all Governments. To resist an existing Government on pretence of oaths taken to one which had been thrust aside was treason. Private persons had ' no right to question how those came by their power that are in authority over them ; for, if that were once admitted, there would be no end of disputes in the world touching titles.' It was enough to say that the King, having exceeded the bounds of his authority, had been lawfully resisted, and being vanquished had lost his own proper authority by the law of arms. The whole power therefore now resided in that part of the people which had prevailed over him. No popular

---

[1] Warrant for his arrest, June 18, 1649, *Interr.* I, 62, 449.
[2] Warrant, Nov. 14, 1649, *ib.* I, 63, 257.

consent was required; 'the whole right of kingly authority being by military decision resolved into the prevailing party; what Government so ever it pleases them next to erect, is as valid *de jure* as if it had the consent of the whole body of the people.' Nor was any objection on the ground that the present Parliament was but a remnant of that which had been originally elected, to be listened to for a moment. The secluded members, 'in adhering to the conquered party even after the victory, and favouring the invaders,[1] were justly deprived of their interest, and the supreme authority descended lawfully to those members that had the courage to assert their freedom, secure their own interest, themselves and their adherents from future inconveniences, and take the forfeiture of those prerogatives and privileges of the King, lords, and secluded commons, as heirs apparent by the law of arms and custom of nations to an investiture in the whole supremacy.'[2]

After reading this audacious defence of the rights of force addressed to the conscientious man, it is unnecessary to pry into the arguments with which Needham essayed to capture the worldling. Yet the piece has an historical importance which its reasoning does little to deserve. Crude as the production was, it was the first open notice given to Puritanism to quit the stage—the first definite revolt against idealism— idealism of religion, idealism of law and precedent, idealism of government. What were the divine right of kings, the sanctity of the reformed religion, or the unassailable fortress of the fundamental laws in the eyes of this light-hearted champion absolutely detached from the theorists of his day, who saw in force alone the basis of human society without thinking of looking deeper to search for those elements of human nature upon which force rests, and by which its exercise is directed to beneficent ends?

So blind was the Council of State to the tendencies of Needham's pamphlet, or, as is more probable, so eager in its

---

[1] *I.e.* the Scots.
[2] *The Case of the Commonwealth*, E, 600, 7.

depressed condition to welcome any ally who promised to be serviceable, that, on May 24, they voted him a gift of 50*l.* and

May 24.
A gift and
pension for
Needham.

a pension of 100*l.*[1] The condition on which the pension was granted was made public by the appearance, on June 13, of *Mercurius Politicus*, written for

June 13.
*Mercurius
Politicus.*

the most part by Needham, in which the cause of the Government was temperately and, at least in comparison with the existing official journals, interestingly advocated. If it cannot be said that *Mercurius Politicus* kept itself altogether free from scurrility, it was decency itself as compared with Royalist journals such as *The Man in the Moon*, and even with Needham's earlier Royalist ventures.

Whatever might be tolerated in so serviceable a champion, the founders of the Commonwealth had no intention of

Puritan
legislation.

abandoning the almost Presbyterian legislation on which they had proposed to enter in the preceding autumn.[2] The Acts for the Propagation of the Gospel in Wales[3] and in various parts of England might indeed be regarded by adverse critics as so many parts of a scheme for gaining political support, or as an appeal to those Presbyterians who were wavering on the brink of Royalism to rally to the standard of a common Puritanism. It was this common Puritanism, too, which the Parliamentary statesmen attempted to fan into life by a series of well-intentioned efforts to coerce Englishmen into the observance, not merely of the outward

April 19.
Act for the
observance
of the Lord's
day.

marks of religion, but of the very moral law itself.[4] On April 19 an Act was passed directing the seizure of all goods cried or put to sale on the Lord's day, or on days of humiliation and thanksgiving, and imposing a fine of ten shillings on all persons travelling and all innkeepers entertaining travellers on the Lord's day without

---

[1] C. of St. Order Book, *Interr.* I, 63, p. 385. The whole of the facts about Needham's change of politics have been set forth in Masson's *Life of Milton*, iv. 149, 226.   [2] See p. 173.

[3] *Act for the Propagation of the Gospel in Wales*, Feb. 22, E, 1,060, No. 80.

[4] See the remarks of Professor Masson, *Life of Milton*, iv. 178.

urgent cause.[1] On May 10 came a fierce Act, declaring incest and adultery to be felonies punishable with death, whilst simple fornication was punishable with three months' imprisonment.[2] On June 28 another Act inflicted a series of fines, graduated according to rank, upon profane oaths.[3] Yet the zeal of the House for protecting morality by legislation was not without its limits. A proposal made on June 7 to pass 'an Act against the vice of painting and wearing black patches and immodest dresses of women,'[4] was never heard of again, probably because the wives and daughters of members were resolved on following the fashion, however ridiculous it might be, whilst they had no interest in protecting their erring sisters from the utmost peril of the law.

May 10.
Adultery Act.

June 28.
Act against swearing.

June 7.
Proposed Act against immodest dress.

Whether legislation conceived in this spirit was likely to gain recruits amongst moderate Presbyterians or not, those from whom it emanated were well aware that something sharper than legislation was required to quell the rising storm. Uncertain as they were of the steadfastness of Fairfax, it was with real joy that they learnt that Cromwell had landed at Bristol. Parliament had already, on February 25, voted that he should have the use of the house opposite Whitehall, known as the Cockpit, of St. James's House, and Spring Gardens, as well as that he should have the command of St. James's Park.[5] On May 31 they added a grant of lands sufficient to bring in a yearly income of 2,500*l.*

An impending struggle.

Cromwell's landing.

Feb. 25.
Grant of houses to Cromwell,

May 31.
and of lands.

On June 1 Cromwell was received with a hearty welcome on Hounslow Heath. Fairfax himself was there to congratulate him on his Irish victories, attended by members of Parliament and of the Council of State, as well as by many officers of the army and a large throng eager to do honour to the hero of the day. On the 3rd Cromwell visited Fairfax, with

June 1.
His reception on Hounslow Heath.

June 3,
Cromwell with Fairfax and the City.

---

[1] Scobell, ii. 119.   [2] *Ib.* ii. 121.   [3] *Ib.* ii. 123.

[4] *C.J.* vi. 21.   [5] *Ib.* 371.

whom he is said to have exchanged friendly communications,
and then passed on to the City, where the official
heads accorded him a hearty welcome. On the
4th he received the thanks of Parliament.[1] On
the 11th he made a report on the situation in Ireland,
adding sundry recommendations which were promptly
adopted by the House.[2]

June 4.
*He is
thanked by
Parliament.*

June 11.
*His report
on Ireland.*

It was not on Ireland that the thoughts of Parliament were
anxiously fixed. By this time there could be no reasonable
doubt that the Scots were preparing to invade England in the
name of the King. That an army must be sent
against them was beyond question. It was more
doubtful who was to be named to the command.
Distrust of Fairfax's hesitations conflicted with confidence in his honesty of purpose. Some proposed,
while Cromwell was still in Ireland, that Fairfax
should be superseded, and Cromwell, with the title of Protector
or Constable, entrusted with the defence of the country. Others
desired that Fairfax should be sent to suppress the Royalists in
the West, whilst Cromwell marched against Scotland ; whilst
others again proposed that Fairfax and Cromwell should both
go against Scotland in their old capacities of General and Lieutenant-General.[3] All schemes which had been formed for
depressing Fairfax and elevating Cromwell at his expense found
a determined opponent in Cromwell himself, and for the present
were abandoned even by their promoters.[4] On June
12 Parliament voted that both Fairfax and Cromwell
should go on the Northern expedition.[5] Both Fairfax
and Cromwell accepted their respective commands, and on the

*A war with
Scotland
certain.*

*May.
Who is to
command
the Eng-
lish army?*

*June 12.
Fairfax
and Crom-
well to go.*

[1] *Merc. Politicus*, E, 603, 6 : *A Perf. Diurnal*, E, 777, 10 ; *Ludlow*
(ed. 1751), i. 269.   [2] *C.J.* vi. 422.

[3] Croullé to Mazarin, June $\frac{3}{15}$, $\frac{10}{20}$, *Arch. des Aff. Étrangères*, lix·
fol. 389, 394.

[4] "Il s'est montré si esloigné d'en vouloir, et d'endeurer, que depuis son
retour il n'en a plus esté parlé." Croullé to Mazarin, June $\frac{17}{27}$. *Arch. des
Aff. Étrangères*, lix. fol. 398.

[5] *C.J.* vi. 423.

14th orders were given to draw up a new commission for Fair-

June 14.
A new
commis-
sion for
Fairfax.

fax, in the name of the Commonwealth of England, in lieu of the one which had been granted him by the two Houses.[1]

For some days it appeared as if the crisis had been entirely surmounted. On the 20th, however, the Council of State

June 20.
The Coun-
cil of State
resolves
that Scot-
land shall
be invaded.

adopted a resolution that an English invasion of Scotland was the only means of preventing a Scottish invasion of England, but directed that its decision should only be reported to Parliament after a delay of six days, a resolution hardly explicable, except on the supposition that opposition was expected which it was desirable to smooth away.[2] There was, in fact, a likelihood that Fairfax, who had hitherto supposed that he would have to conduct a defensive war in the North of England, might shrink from leading an invading army into Scotland, and, whatever private negotiations may have taken place, it was probably on

June 22.
Fairfax
objects.

the 22nd that Fairfax informed the Council of the scruples which he entertained,[3] and of his resolution to take no part in the proposed invasion of Scotland.

He is
urged to
reconsider
his ob-
jections.

The other members of the Council having vainly urged him to reconsider his determination, Cromwell proposed that the precedent of the Irish war should be followed, and that Fairfax should retain the Generalship without any obligation to command in Scotland. Such a solution, however, found no support in the Council, where, as may be supposed, the danger of leaving Fairfax to deal with a possible Presbyterian rising in England would be keenly felt, and it was resolved to appoint a committee to make a further attempt to induce Fairfax to take the command of the invading

A Com-
mittee ap-
pointed to
meet him.

army.[4] For this purpose three members of the Council, Cromwell, St. John, and Whitelocke, were to be combined with two officers, Lambert and Harrison.

---

[1] *C.J.* vi. 424.

[2] C. of St. Order Book, June 20, *Interr.* I, 64, p. 465.

[3] The Council Books show that Fairfax was present on the 22nd and not again till the 25th.   [4] *Ludlow*, i. 243.

The meeting of the Committee with Fairfax took place on the 24th. Fairfax's position was that it would be a breach of the Solemn League and Covenant to invade Scotland, and that there was no certainty that the Scots intended to invade England. The position of the Committee was that the Scots had already broken the Solemn League and Covenant by invading England in 1648, and that it was morally certain that they intended to invade it again. "I say, my Lord," argued Cromwell, "that upon these grounds I think we have a most just cause to begin or rather to return and requite their hostility first begun upon us, and thereby to free our country—if God shall be pleased to assist us, and I doubt not but He will—from the great misery and calamity of having an army of Scots within our country. That there will be war between us I fear is unavoidable. Your Excellency will soon determine whether it is better to have this war in the bowels of another country or of our own, and that it will be one of them I think it without scruple."

June 24. Discussion between them.

Cromwell's argument.

To this, and to all other appeals made to him by the other members of the Committee, Fairfax's reply was singularly weak. First came a demand for assurance that the Scots actually intended to invade England, after which, having received a pertinent reply from Harrison, Fairfax fell back on the assertion that human probabilities were not sufficient ground to make war upon a neighbour nation.

Fairfax's reply.

The fact was that Fairfax's determination to take no part in an invasion of Scotland lay beyond the reach of argument. It was a moral repugnance rather than an intellectual persuasion, and, without troubling the members of the Committee to produce evidence of that which they asserted and he denied, he intimated his intention of laying down his commission, from which resolution no pleadings of Cromwell or of anyone else were able to move him.[1]

Fairfax's repugnance to the proposed invasion.

He resolves to lay down his commission.

That Cromwell pleaded with Fairfax in all resolute honesty

---

[1] *Whitelocke*, lix. foll. 398, 460, 461.

of purpose will be denied by those alone who believe him to
have been actuated by the meanest personal ambition. The
Cromwell's withdrawal of Fairfax was the severest blow which
protest. could be dealt to the policy which, with Cromwell's
Cromwell's full approval, Parliament had recently been pursuing
reason for
protesting. —the policy of conciliating the moderate Presbyterians by an appeal to a common Puritanism.[1] In a Declaration which had been drawn up by the Council of State for the
acceptance of Parliament, a passage occurs of which Cromwell
may possibly have been the author. "We cannot but think,"
Parliament was asked to say in justification of the proposed
invasion, " that an interest of dominion and profit under a pretence of Presbytery and the Covenant, is by these men of more
value and esteem than the peace and love of the Gospel, to
which all that may be called discipline or government in the
Church is, and ought to be, subordinate ; and for which the
least violation of the love and peace before mentioned ought not
to be."[2] Cromwell might favour the use of such words as these,
but he was too pronounced an Independent to obtain credence
from his adversaries. Fairfax stood on the border-land between
the two religious parties. His wife was a Presbyterian, and so
too was his secretary Rushworth. He was himself fond of
listening to Presbyterian sermons, and had friends amongst the
Presbyterian clergy, whilst he still cherished the Independent
Danger in- opinion on the virtue of toleration. His retirement
volved in
Fairfax's would be an intimation to all Presbyterians that the
resignation. army as well as the State was passing under hostile
influences, and might lead many who, with Fairfax in command,
could be reckoned on as indifferent if not friendly, to rally to
the enemy's standard.[3]

[1] According to Croullé's despatch of June $\frac{17}{27}$, Cromwell's reconciling
tendencies had even gone beyond this, and had led him to advocate a
diminution of the rigour with which Cavaliers were hunted out of London,
on the ground that they were less dangerous there than in the country.
Arch. des Aff. Étrangères, lix. fol. 398.

[2] *A Declaration of the Parl. of England*, E, 604, 4.

[3] This is evidently pointed out in Lambert's words : "If your Excel-
ency should not . . . continue your command . . . I am very fearful of

As Fairfax persisted in his resolution there was nothing for it but to persuade him to couch it in terms expressing as little

June 26.
Fairfax's
resignation
sent in.

ill-will to the Commonwealth as possible. Fairfax was too loyal to his old comrades to refuse, and on the following day he penned a letter to Lenthall, in which he grounded his resignation on ' debilities both in body and mind, occasioned by former actions and businesses.' [1]

On receiving this intimation Parliament at once hurried through an Act appointing Skippon to command in

Skippon to
command
in London.

London. The order kept by him in 1648 in the City, then, as now, swarming with Presbyterians, was not forgotten. [2]

On the 26th the Council of State's Declaration of the justice and necessity of an invasion of Scotland [3] was adopted

June 26.
Declara-
tion
against
Scotland.

by Parliament without a dissentient voice. Then, after Fairfax had taken the formal steps for the surrender of his commission, Parliament appointed Cromwell ' Captain-General and Commander-in-Chief

Cromwell
appointed
General.

of all the forces raised or to be raised within the Commonwealth of England.' Evident as might be the danger of superseding a commander whose very presence was a symbol of conciliation, it was still more evident that when an invasion was actually impending the conduct of the national defence could only be entrusted to one who was eager with all his heart and soul for a successful issue.

Everything that could possibly be done was done to make the change appear as slight as possible. In a sermon preached

June 27.
A sermon
in Somerset
House.

on the 27th, Cromwell and Fairfax were compared to Abraham and Lot, separating from one another without anger. This sermon was almost immediately published with a preface in which the preacher, Henry Walker, pointed to a popular explanation of Fairfax's resignation.

the mischiefs which might ensue, and the distraction in the public affairs by your laying down your commission." *Whitelocke*, 461.

[1] Fairfax to Lenthall, June 25, Slingsby's *Diary* (ed. Parsons), 340.

[2] *C.J.* vi. 431.

[3] *Ib.* ; *A Declaration of the Parl. of England*, E, 604, 4.

"What," he wrote, "though your old Lord General be not with you, he is not against you. . . . You have his heart still in the camp, though his spouse hath persuaded his weary body to take rest in her bosom."[1]

Neither this nor any other single explanation can be accepted as an adequate account of Fairfax's motives; still less is it

Fairfax's own explanation.

possible to trust to the narrative[2] in which, some thirteen or fourteen years after the events recorded, he explained his conduct, not as it had actually been, but as he fancied it ought to have been. Few men are to be trusted to throw themselves dramatically into their dead selves, and Fairfax at least was not one of those few.

So far as it is possible to draw a conclusion from the past conduct of Fairfax, it would seem that up to a certain point

His political views compared with those of Cromwell.

his political views were identical with those of Crom-well. Both had set out with the idea of winning by arms a constitutional settlement in which as much as possible of the old Constitution should be preserved in order to secure the safe establishment of the new. Both were from time to time convinced that one or other portion of the old system must give way, because it had been shown to be incompatible with the new. There, however, the resemblance ends. When a forward step had been taken, Cromwell regarded it not only as irrevocable, but as one of which the justice ought never to be called in question. His mind, in short, was so filled with the next problem that presented itself to him that he forgot that he had ever had any difficulty over any steps which had gone before. Fairfax's mind was cast in a different mould. Gradually, in 1647 and in 1648, he had broken first with the Presbyterian majority and then with the King. At each step

Fairfax probably satisfied with each of his actions,

he convinced himself, just as Cromwell had done, that constitutional government was impossible if either the Presbyterian majority or the King were allowed to triumph. The expulsion of the eleven

[1] *A Sermon preached in the Chapel at Somerset House*, E, 604, 5.
[2] *The Short Memorial.*

members, the crushing of the Royalists at Maidstone and Colchester, even Pride's Purge itself, commended themselves to him as things necessary to be done if a worse calamity was to be averted.   That in all this the persuasions of Cromwell and Ireton counted for something is hardly to be denied.   It was, however, one thing to be satisfied with each act at the time when it was done, and quite another thing to be satisfied with their tendency when taken together.   Strong indications are not wanting that by the end of 1648 Fairfax was dissatisfied with the general result of the work which he had reluctantly approved in detail.

but dissatisfied with their tendency.

If this is anything like a true explanation of Fairfax's behaviour in 1647 and 1648, his subsequent conduct cannot be difficult to explain.   The tendency of the recent actions of the military power was presented to him in the clearest light by the trial and execution of the King, and after the first day's meeting of the High Court of Justice he stood entirely aloof from its proceedings, though it is possible that he might have approved of them if the sentence had been one of dethronement or banishment.   After the King's death his action is equally intelligible.   On the one hand he was ready to do his duty in defending the Commonwealth, the only possible form of government at the time, against its enemies.   On the other hand he refused to bind himself by taking the Engagement to oppose the restoration of a constitutional monarchy in the future.

His conduct at the King's trial,

and on the establishment of the Commonwealth.

Such a view of political duty may be logically defensible, but is certain to lead to practical inconsistencies which, if persisted in, are fatal to the self-respect of him who gives rise to them.   Inconsistencies of this kind are sure to reveal themselves in speech, and it is therefore easy to understand how Fairfax may at one time have used language capable of being interpreted as acknowledging an obligation to do something for the King,[1] and at another time

Inconsistency of his position.

[1] See p. 249.

have explained his unwillingness to attack the Scots on the
ground that the English army was split into factions, and there-
Mental
doubt. fore likely to break asunder in his hands.[1]   A mind
divided against itself easily falls under the sway of
others, and the absence of Cromwell and Ireton left the field
open to his Presbyterian wife and to the Presbyterian ministers
whose counsel he sought.   For a moment it seemed as if there
would be opportunity for him to persist in his old course, and
that he might defend England loyally from a Scottish invasion.
The resolution of the Council of State to invade Scotland put
an end for ever to the delusion.   To invade Scotland was to
attack the person of the young King and to shatter those hopes
of a future constitutional understanding which Fairfax had
never at any time wholly thrown aside.   It is of little consequence to enquire whether Fairfax rightly drew the line
between that which was permissible to him and that which
was not permissible.   The line drawn by the most honest of
men is always to a certain extent arbitrary, and its choice is
determined by considerations many of which have nothing to
do with logic.   It is enough to say that Fairfax retired with
dignity, carrying with him in his retirement at Nun Appleton
the respect of all honourable men.

Fairfax's best memorial, save in the deeds which he
achieved, is to be found in the lines with which his son-in-
Bucking-
ham's
epitaph
on Fairfax. law, the Duke of Buckingham, recorded the main
features of his character in days when a Restoration,
to the success of which he had contributed, had
placed men in power with whom he had little in common.

> Both sexes' virtues were in him combined ;
> He had the fierceness of the manliest mind
> And all the meekness too of womankind.
>
> He never knew what envy was, nor hate ;
> His soul was filled with worth and honesty,
> And with another thing, quite out of date,
>   Called modesty.

---

[1] Croullé to Mazarin, $\frac{\text{June 24}}{\text{July 4}}$.   *Arch. des Aff. Étrangères*, lix. fol. 404.

> He ne'er seemed impudent but in the field, a place
> Where impudence itself dares seldom show its face.
> Had any stranger spied him in a room
> With some of those whom he had overcome,
> And had not heard their talk, but only seen
> Their gesture and their mien,
> They would have sworn he had the vanquished been ;
> For as they bragged, and dreadful would appear,
> Whilst they their own ill-luck repeated,
> His modesty still made him blush to hear
> How often he had them defeated.[1]

If Cromwell was to march into Scotland it was necessary to make arrangement for the conduct of military affairs in Ireland

June 26. Ireton to be continued as Lord Deputy. and in England. As for Ireland, the Council of State reported on the 26th that Ireton should continue to exercise the powers of a Lord Deputy under Cromwell, and that two commissioners—a number afterwards enlarged to four—should be sent to Ireland to give their assistance in civil affairs. One of the two first-

June 27. Commissioners to be sent to Ireland. named was Ludlow, who accepted the post with some reluctance, though in his case it was combined with the office which had been vacant since the death

Ludlow to be Lieutenant-General. of Michael Jones, that of Lieutenant-General, carrying with it the command of the Horse.[2] These nominations were as a matter of course confirmed by Parliament.[3]

Cromwell had been, in a special sense, the author of Ludlow's appointment. Ludlow was one of those stern

Cromwell and Ludlow. Republicans who had blamed Cromwell for his attempt made in 1647 to come to terms with the King, and even for his shooting the trooper Arnold,

---

[1] *Somers Tracts,* v. 397.

[2] C. of St. Order Book, *Interr.* I, 64, p. 490. Ludlow is here styled a Member of Parliament, a title which had often been given before when members of the two Houses had to be placed under a common designation, and which was now naturally used for a member of a single House. After the Restoration it came to be the designation of a member of the House of Commons. [3] On July 2. *C.J.* vi. 435.

the ringleader of the mutiny on Corkbush Field. Cromwell, therefore, now sought an interview with him, and, assuring him that he was convinced of his error in negotiating with the King, justified the execution of Arnold on the ground of military discipline, and declared that he himself desired nothing more than the establishment of a free and equal Commonwealth, as the only 'probable means to keep out the old family and government from returning upon us.'

It was, however, no merely theoretical republicanism that had taken possession of Cromwell's mind. A Commonwealth Cromwell's was in his eyes nothing unless it brought with it the hopes. removal of grievances endured by those who had no one to help them. For a whole hour he discoursed on tl e 110th Psalm. Confidently believing that the Lord was about 'to strike through kings in the day of his wrath,' Cromwell doubtless dwelt even more strongly on the prediction, "Thy people shall be willing in the day of Thy power." Cromwell hoped to see a voluntary obedience founded on a sense of loving service, the new order taking the place of servile submission to the sword which he had himself wielded so freely. "He looked," he said, "on the design of the Lord in this day to be the freeing of the people from every burden." He acknowledged, however, that there were difficulties in the way other than those interposed by a reigning family. The lawyers —those sons of Zeruiah—had as yet been too strong for him, crying out that those who wished to reform the law were bent on the destruction of property. The law, as constituted, served only to maintain lawyers and to encourage the rich to oppress the poor. It had been found possible to do justice in Ireland, in 'a summary and expeditious way,' and perhaps the example might tell even in England. After this, Cromwell sounded Ludlow as to the possibility of his accepting the vacant post, raising objection to any other name which was brought forward either by Ludlow or himself.[1] There was always a vein of shrewdness mingled with Cromwell's most fervid enthusiasm, and it is not impossible that he urged Ludlow to go to Ireland because he feared that he might give trouble in England.

[1] *Ludlow.* i. 2 5 247.

Cromwell was no less sharp-sighted in his selection of Harrison to command the forces left in England in his own absence.[1] A vigorous soldier and a fanatic in religion, Harrison might be counted on to do the utmost that man could do to repress Royalists and Presbyterians with an equal hand. To give him a force adequate to the danger, the regiments under his command were to be supplemented by a reorganised militia in every county. On July 11 a new Militia Act, which had been for some time under consideration, was finally passed.[2] As far as the levy of money was concerned, the old principle of the obligation of holders of property to contribute proportionately to the defence of the country was adhered to. Those who had at least 200*l.* a year derived from land were charged with the horse and arms of a cavalry soldier; those who had at least 200 marks, or 133*l.* 6*s.* 8*d.*, with a horse and arms for a dragoon; and those who had at least 20*l.*, with arms for a foot soldier. In each case the possession of goods or money amounting to ten times as much as the income fixed was to qualify for these respective obligations. No one who had less than 10*l.* a year was to be charged at all, but those who had more than 10*l.* and less than 20*l.* might furnish the arms required by a common contribution.

June 21. Harrison to command in England.

July 11. A Militia Act.

When it came to personal service, the obligation was far less general. Commissioners with control over the militia in each county were to be nominated by Parliament or the Council of State, subject to the obligation of taking the Engagement. These commissioners were not only to supersede the Lords Lieutenant in the command of the militia, but were to have full powers to disarm and imprison disaffected persons as well as to take examinations on oath for the discovery of their plans. The force put at their disposal was the new militia, consisting of 'well affected' persons selected by themselves. In arms as in council, the party organisation of the men of the Commonwealth was to be supreme.[3]

Selection of the Commissioners.

[1] *C.J.* vi. 428.   [2] *Ib.* vi. 441.
[3] An Act for Settling the Militia, E, 1,061, No. 8

Moral weapons were supplied to the defenders of the Commonwealth by Charles himself. Neither Cavalier nor Presbyterian was without compunction in accepting the assistance of the other, whilst most Cavaliers and all Presbyterians loathed the very idea of resting for support upon the Pope. On July 16 the cause of the Commonwealth was admirably served by the publication of an address made four months before to Innocent X. by one of Charles's agents, probably by Meynell. In this address, Meynell, whose chief object was to induce the Pope to lend money to his master, not only boasted of the peace made in Ireland, but asserted that Charles himself 'while his father yet lived was known to have good and true natural inclinations to the Catholic faith,' and had therefore promised to the Irish Catholics not only the free exercise of their religion, but to restore to them, " whether lay or ecclesiastic, their lands, estates, possessions, or whatever other rights did at any time belong unto them.' [1] Whether such a policy in Ireland were good or bad, it sorted ill with the character of a Covenanted King. Many a sober Presbyterian, who had been half persuaded to attach himself to the Royalist enemies of a sectarian army, would hesitate to give aid in recalling to the throne a youth who was indifferent whether he gained his ends with the help of Presbyter or Pope.

Moral weapons.

Publication of an address to the Pope.

---

[1] *A Brief Relation*, E, 607, 15. The publication was so opportune that suspicions of forgery would seem natural. There is, however, a copy of the address in the Simancas Archives, with a note ' Para embiar à su Mag^d. Cat^ca., 18 de M^co. 1650,' showing by the date that it was sent direct from Rome, and not a mere copy of the publication in England. Neither in the *Brief Relation* nor in the Simancas copy is the name of the speaker mentioned. The speech was republished on Sept. 6 (E, 612, 6), the French translation being ascribed to Father John Roe. An English note, however, argues that this is impossible, as Roe was not in Rome at the time. If the signature, P[ère] I[ean] R[oe], C[armelite], were genuine, it would settle the matter, but the English editor points out that no copy in any other language than French has any mention of Roe. It is therefore to be supposed that Meynell, Charles's ordinary representative (see p. 70), was the speaker.

CHAPTER XII

DUNBAR

WHEN on June 28 Cromwell set out to take up his command in the North, he had under him Fleetwood as Lieutenant-General and Lambert as Major-General. He was anxious to find a post for Monk, whose military abilities he fully appreciated, and, soon after the army had passed Alnwick, he selected him for a colonelcy which had been vacated by the resignation of Bright. Fearing, however, lest discipline might suffer if an officer with such a past as Monk's were forced on an unwilling regiment, he directed his officers to feel the pulse of their men. "Colonel Monk!" was the prompt reply. "What! To betray us? We took him not long since at Nantwich prisoner. We'll none of him." Cromwell knew better than to persist, and Lambert's name, having been next suggested, was received with general applause. Ultimately a new regiment was formed for Monk out of five companies serving under Hazlerigg, the governor of Newcastle, and five companies serving under Fenwick, the governor of Berwick. The men thus brought together without regimental tradition cheerfully acquiesced in the new arrangements.

June 28. Cromwell sets out. Fleetwood and Lambert.

Attempt to find a command for Monk.

On July 19 Cromwell halted near Berwick, where he mustered 16,000 men, of whom about 5,500 were cavalry.[1] Before crossing the Tweed he sent forward

July 19. A rendezvous near Berwick.

---

[1] *Perf. Passages*, E, 777, 20; *A Perf. Diurnal*, E, 778, 7; Hodgson's *Memoirs*, 159; C. of St. Order Book, *Interr.* I, 8.

a trumpeter with the Parliament's declaration,[1] and with a second addressed by the army ' to all that are saints and partakers of the faith of God's elect in Scotland.'[2] Yet a third declaration, bearing unmistakable traces of Cromwell's own pen, was called forth by statements alleged to have been circulated by the Scottish clergy to the effect that the English army intended ' to put all men to the sword, and to thrust hot irons through the women's breasts.' Cromwell now assured all peaceable Scotsmen of his protection, warning them against the designs of those who had taken the bitter enemy of the English nation for their king, and were making war against 'the very power of godliness and holiness.'[3] This declaration was not sent to Edinburgh, but retained to be dispersed amongst the people as soon as the army crossed the Border.

In the meanwhile the Scots had not been idle in preparing for defence. Though old Leven was left in nominal command
The Scottish preparations. with the title of General, it was upon David Leslie, the Lieutenant-General, that the direction of the army virtually devolved. The existing force was far too small to meet the invaders, and on June 25, and again on July 3, Parliament gave orders[4] for the raising of levies which, it was calculated, would bring the whole Scottish force up to at
Numbers of Leslie's army. least 40,000. As a matter of fact Leslie by the end of July was unable to dispose of more than 27,000 foot and 5,000 horse,[5] a force, however, numerically far superior to that which was approaching under Cromwell. It is doubtful, however, whether even these numbers were kept up, and, at all events, the men of whom the Scottish army was
Its quality. composed were decidedly inferior to the English in quality. The greater part of the men having been drawn, or even dragged, from their homes, had very little of

[1] See p. 261.   [2] The Perf. Weekly Account, E, 778, 2.
[3] A Declaration of the Army, E, 608, 5.
[4] Acts of the Parl. of Sc. vi. part ii. 588, 597.
[5] See Mr. Firth's Battle of Dunbar in the Hist. Society's Transactions, 1900.

the military instinct and still less of military discipline. The finest regiment—one levied by means of voluntary contribution from the clergy—was commanded by Strachan.[1]

If Scotland had been united, it is possible that David Leslie might have succeeded in reducing even these unpromising materials to some kind of order. Unfortunately for Scotland her leaders were not united. In the debates which had preceded the votes for the levies, the antagonism between the nobility and the other orders had again made itself manifest. The nobility urged that the levies should be made without delay, whilst the barons and burgesses urged that means must first be taken to purge out all who had shared in the Engagement or had shown signs of deflection from the acknowledged standard of piety and morality.[2] The barons

June 21.
Commis-
sion for
purging it. and burgesses had their way, and on June 21 a Commission for purging the army was appointed four days before the first vote for levying soldiers was adopted.[3]

Whatever might ultimately be the numbers of the Scottish army, it did not need Leslie's knowledge of war to convince

The Scots
to take the
defensive. him that, for some time to come, it would be necessary for him to stand on the defensive. The time

July 22.
Cromwell
enters
Scotland. was rapidly approaching when his skill would be put on trial. On July 22, Cromwell entered Scotland from Berwick. On his line of march the whole of the male population, except a few decrepit persons, had either been drafted into the army or had fled to escape the cruelties of the invaders. Some of the women, 'pitiful sorry creatures, clothed in white flannel in a very homely manner . . . bemoaned their husbands,' who had been forced by the lairds ' to gang to the muster.' Though stores of corn, wine, and beer were occasionally found in the deserted houses, the army would have been starved but for the supplies landed by the fleet which accompanied its march. Without the command of the sea

[1] *Baillie*, iii. 113.   [2] *A Brief Relation*, E, 607, 1.
[3] *Acts of Parl. of Sc.* vi. part ii. 586.

Cromwell could no more have ventured to invade Scotland, than Wellington could have ventured to defend Portugal if Nelson's fleet had been destroyed at Trafalgar.

On July 28, Cromwell reached Musselburgh, and on the following morning, perceiving that Leslie had entrenched his army in a line stretching from Leith to the foot of the Canongate, advanced by way of Restalrig and Jock's Lodge. Finding the enemy too strongly posted to be assailable with advantage, he detached a force to occupy St. Leonard's Hill on the south of the eastern extremity of the city ; the possession of which would have given him an advantageous position for an attack on the not very strong fortifications of that side. As the eminence was not strongly occupied, the assailants succeeded in forcing their way up the rising ground, but were subsequently dislodged by a Highland regiment under Campbell of Lawers, which, pursuing the retreating English on to the lower ground, succeeded in capturing two of Cromwell's cannon, though not in retaining its prize.[1] After this repulse Cromwell could hardly venture to renew the attack on the same lines. The day, moreover, was wet, and in the night the English troops were exposed shelterless to the pouring rain.

Cromwell, therefore, fearing the effect of exposure on his troops, and perceiving that nothing was to be gained by persistence, drew back to Musselburgh. The Scottish horse, attacking the rear of his retreating columns, gained some temporary success, and at one time Lambert was a prisoner in their hands. Lambert, however, was soon rescued, and this attempt to throw the English army into disorder ended in failure. On the 31st the Scots made a fierce attack on Musselburgh, but this too was repulsed without much difficulty.[2]

July 28. Cromwell at Musselburgh.

July 29. A fight before Edinburgh.

July 30. Cromwell draws back to Musselburgh.

July 31. An attack repulsed.

[1] The topography of this affair has been cleared up by Mr. Douglas, *Cromwell's Scotch Campaigns*, 43–47.

[2] Cromwell to Bradshaw, July [31], *Carlyle*, Letter cxxxv. ; Hodgson's *Memoirs*, 131 ; *A True Relation*, E, 608, 23 ; *A large Relation of the Fight at Leith*, E, 609, 1.

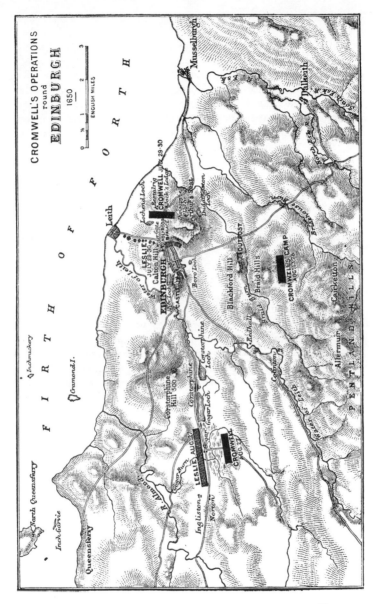

CROMWELL'S OPERATIONS
round
EDINBURGH
1650

ENGLISH MILES

In his despatch to Westminster, Cromwell naturally made
the most of the enemy's failures, but, for all that, the advantage

The advan-
tage on the
Scottish
side.

was on Leslie's side. For the Scottish commander
fighting in his own country it was enough that he
had not been defeated. His own difficulties were
more political than military. On the 29th, the day on

July 29-
Aug. 2.
Charles at
Leith.

which Cromwell's attack was made, Charles, invited by the Earl of Eglinton and the officers of the
army, had ridden into Leith. At the same time a
proclamation in which he announced his determination to
grant the propositions of Newcastle and Hampton Court was
issued in his name, though his assent had never been given to
it.[1] His own ardent desire was to make himself popular with
the soldiers, not to carry out the wishes of the Kirk. The time
for which he had looked when he had lied so unblushingly at
Breda appeared to have come at last. Surrounded by a faithful
army, he would shake off the yoke of the Kirk. The nobles
would surely be on his side, and he could hope to find officers
enough to secure obedience. For the present, however, circumstances did not lend themselves to such an enterprise.
The Committee of Estates took alarm, and urged him to
depart on the plea of danger to his person. On August 2,
Charles gave up the game and withdrew to Dunfermline.[2]

The clergy had no mind to expose themselves again to the
danger of a military uprising. At their urgent entreaty the

Aug. 3-5.
The Scot-
tish army
purged.

Commissioners for Purging[3] applied themselves to
their task. In three days they dismissed eighty
officers and more than 3,000 soldiers.[4] The army of
the Kirk, thus purified from Malignants and Engagers, was

---

[1] The King's Declaration, Walker's *Hist. Discourses*, 163. Walker
says it was in his Majesty's name published in the army, which his Majesty
disapproved as not being according to his order. A note on a copy
amongst the *Clarendon MSS*. No. 380, 5, runs as follows :—" This is the
proclamation that was put forth in his Majesty's name, which he never saw
till 't was printed, and which was disavowed by him."

[2] Walker's *Hist. Discourses*, 164.

[3] See p. 271.   [4] *Balfour*, iv. 89.

fondly believed to be invincible, and there was at any rate less chance of its falling under the influence of Charles.[1]

What Cromwell thought of the self-sufficiency of the Scottish clergy is easily seen. "I beseech you in the bowels

*Aug. 3.
Cromwell's
warning to
the clergy.*

of Christ," he had written to them, "think it possible you may be mistaken." Communications from either side, urging the righteousness of one or other cause, passed frequently between the armies, Cromwell laying especial stress on the argument that Charles was no fitting king for a godly people.[2]   He, for one, was anxious that the cloud between the two peoples should pass away, and it was not in word only that his anxiety was shown. In testimony of his goodwill he sent back sixty wounded prisoners, lending his own coach as a conveyance for as many as it would hold.[3]

Cromwell's main difficulty lay in his commissariat. So strong was the westerly gale, that though his store-ships were

*Aug. 6.
Cromwell
goes to
Dunbar,*

at no great distance to the eastward of Musselburgh they were unable to fetch the little port, and he was therefore compelled to lead back his army to Dunbar, where they could easily drop down before the wind to join

*Aug 11.
but returns
to Mussel-
burgh.*

him.[4]   On the 11th Cromwell, having first given food to the famished poor at Dunbar,[5] returned to Musselburgh, where he found that the women, who during the first stay had baked and brewed for his army, had been drawn away by Leslie's orders. As Leslie showed no sign of willingness to accept battle, Cromwell determined to do his best to compel him to fight. On the morning of the

*Aug. 12.
Preparations
for a start.*

12th every regiment received not only a supply of provisions for three days, but tents as a protection against the weather. They were to march round Edinburgh on its southern side and push on for Queensferry. Once there, with the assistance of the English fleet, Cromwell would have no difficulty in operating on either side of the

---

[1] Loudoun to Charles II., Aug. 12, *Charles II. and Scotland*, 130.

[2] Cromwell to the General Assembly, Aug. 3, *Carlyle*, Letter cxxxvi.

[3] Nicoll's *Diary*, 22.   [4] *Perf. Diurnal*, E, 778, 20.

[5] *Ib.* E, 778, 22.

Forth.   Edinburgh was already short of provisions, and if the supplies received by the town from Fife were cut off, Leslie would have no choice but to come forth and try the issue of a battle.   On the evening of the 13th Cromwell's tents were pitched on Braid Hill, where he was safe from attack, whilst his outposts were stationed on Blackford Hill.[1]

Aug. 13.
Cromwell on
Braid Hill.

If on the following morning Cromwell abstained from pushing on, the motive of a delay hard to account for on military grounds is probably to be traced to a message received from Leslie, which enabled him to gather that there were serious differences of opinion in the enemy's camp.   His argument that it was unfitting for those who boasted the purity of their covenanting zeal to harbour a malignant king had struck home.

Cromwell
remains on
Braid Hill.

Effect of
his argu-
ments.

The stricter Presbyterians grew suddenly anxious to clear themselves of the reproach ; but they were men of words rather than of deeds, and, instead of examining what truth there might be in Cromwell's reproaches, they contented themselves with an effort to extract from the young King an assertion that the facts were otherwise than they really were.   Charles was accordingly besieged with urgent demands that he should sign a Declaration in which he was not only to avow himself sensible of his own duty, but to acknowledge that he was humbled in spirit by his father's opposition to the work of reformation and by his mother's idolatry.

Aug. 10.
Charles
asked to sign
a Declara-
tion.

[1] *Several Proceedings*, E, 778, 21.   Compare Rushworth's letter in *Merc. Pol.* E, 610, 7.   Rushworth speaks of the camp being on the Pentland Hills, a little above a mile from the castle.   If he is correct in his distance, Blackford as well as Braid Hill must have been occupied by the English army.   Both hills appear to have been spoken of at that time as forming part of the Pentlands.   Moreover, Blackford Hill is so good a look-out, that it is unlikely to have been neglected by Cromwell.   For a discussion on the objects of Cromwell's march and the difficulties in his way, see *Douglas*, pp. 54–57.   Mr. Douglas suggests as a possibility that Cromwell may have 'got wind of a Scots design to slip past him and carry the war into England.'

As might have been expected, Charles struggled with all his might against this unseemly test, and on the 13th, when Cromwell was moving towards Braid Hill, the Declaration was still unsigned. The Commissioners of the Kirk, therefore, with the approval of the Committee of Estates, resolved that until it had been signed they were not bound to defend the King's cause. A copy of this resolution accompanied the message from Leslie which reached Cromwell on the morning of the 14th.[1]

Cromwell had nothing but scorn for this miserable subterfuge. He ordered the resolution to be read in the hearing of his officers. In his reply to Leslie he told him that as he and his countrymen had chosen to make themselves a centre of malignant action, the war could not end till security had been given that it should be so no longer. That security, he added, ' we conceive will not be by a few formal and feigned submissions from a person that could not tell otherwise how to accomplish his malignant ends.'

Whilst Cromwell was writing his reply a conversation sprang up between some English officers and a few of the stricter Presbyterians on the other side, Colonel Gilbert Ker, a close ally of Strachan, being the most notable amongst them. Much, however, as they distrusted Charles, they could not bring themselves to see that he and the covenanting system were by nature incompatible. It was only on the ground that he had refused to sign the Declaration that they allowed themselves to have ' thoughts of relinquishing him and ' of acting ' upon another account.'[2] That this other account did not imply an accommodation with Cromwell appears from a remonstrance which the officers addressed on the 15th to the Committee

---

[1] Argyle was charged after the Restoration with having stirred up the Commissioners to draw up this resolution. He replied that he had had nothing to do with it, but had urged Charles to draw up an answer which, while omitting the clauses dishonourable to himself, would yet have given satisfaction. *State Trials*, v. 1416, 1476.

[2] Cromwell to Leslie, Aug. 14, *Carlyle*, Letter cxxxvii. *The Lord General Cromwell's Letter*, E, 610, 4.

of Estates, in which, after asserting that they did not ' own any malignant quarrel or interest of any person or persons whatever,' and asking that the Court and army might be further purged ; they declared their resolution ' to fight merely upon the former grounds and principles in defence of the cause, Covenant, and kingdom.' [1]

Aug. 15.
Remon-
strance of
the Scottish
army.

After this the only choice before Charles was to see himself abandoned by the army or to make a base and hypocritical surrender. So far as Covenanters were concerned, Charles had come to the conclusion that in the game which he was playing, falsehood carried with it no dishonour. On the 16th he signed the Declaration with some modifications.[2] The religious officers were now at liberty to persuade themselves, if they could, that they were fighting for a man whose whole soul was in the cause of the Covenant.

Aug. 16.
Charles
signs the
Declaration.

Having signed the Declaration, Charles rode off to Perth hoping to gather round him the reinforcements coming up from the North, in order that he might have an army of his own. As might have been expected, this move was met by a peremptory order to the northern forces to march to Edinburgh.[3] Charles can have gained little comfort from the assurances of Argyle that he would be in greater liberty when he was once in England, coupled as they were with the admission that it was neces- sary for the present ' to please these madmen.' [4]

He tries to
gather an
army at
Perth.

Argyle's
cold com-
fort.

In his private conversation with friends whom he could trust, Charles, as might have been expected, did not mince his words. " I . . . give you assurance," he said to the Dean of Tuam, whom he was despatching to Ireland to assure Ormond of his constancy in the matter of the Irish peace, " that, however

[1] Remonstrance of the Officers, Aug. 15, *Ancram and Lothian Cor-respondence*, ii. 284.

[2] Walker's *Hist. Discourses*, 170 ; *Balfour*, iv. 90–94.

[3] Loudoun to Argyle, Aug. 16 ; Loudoun to Charles, Aug. 16; *Ancram and Lothian Correspondence*, ii. 289.

[4] Radcliffe to Nicholas, $\frac{\text{Aug. 28}}{\text{Sept. 7}}$, *St. Dom.* ix. 152. Radcliffe derived his information from two persons who left the King ' nine days ago.'

I am forced by the necessity of my affairs to appear otherwise,

Charles declares himself a Cavalier. yet that I am a true child of the Church of England, and still remain firm unto my first principles.   Mr. King, I am a true Cavalier." [1]

For the time Charles's discreditable signature of the Declaration frustrated Cromwell's expectations of gaining a party amongst the Scots.   He had now no choice but to

Aug. 15-18. Cromwell fetches provisions from Mussel- burgh. carry on the war vigorously.   Having on August 15 conducted his army back to Musselburgh to fetch provisions, he returned on the 18th to his camp on Braid Hill,[2] with the resolution to march upon Queensferry in accordance with the plan conceived by him some days before.   This prolonged negotiation had, however, cost precious time, and he now found that Leslie, taking advantage of his central position in Edinburgh, had removed his artillery from the works in which he had resisted the English attack in the beginning of the month to the northern side of the town, and had also sent a party with two great guns to occupy Corstorphine, and command the road between Edinburgh and Queensferry.[3]   For some days, however, Cromwell abandoned his design of marching westwards, and contented himself with fresh efforts to bring

Aug. 18. Colinton occupied. on an action in front of Edinburgh.   On the 18th he occupied Colinton House.   Everything he learnt convinced him that the greatest distress prevailed in Edinburgh.   Hungry women straggled out to regain their homes, hoping that more food was to be had outside than

Aug. 20. Interview between Strachan and Lam- bert. inside the walls.   No fight, however, was to be had from the cautious Leslie, and though on the 20th Strachan had an interview with Lambert which inspired the English officers with the hope of a division in the ranks of the enemy, it led to no result.[4]

[1] Conference with his Majesty, Carte's *Orig. Letters*, i. 391.

[2] *A True Relation*, E, 610.   Cromwell is there said to have returned on Sunday, the 17th.   The 17th was, however, a Saturday.

[3] *The Lord General Cromwell's Letter*, E, 610, 4.   The name of the post is not here given, but is filled in from the Scottish accounts.

[4] *A True Relation*, E, 610, 8.

On the 21st Leslie made a fresh move. Marching his
army out of Edinburgh, he took up a strong position on a
Aug. 21. rising ground behind Corstorphine. In front of him
Leslie at
Corstor-   spread out two lakes, one on each side of the village,[1]
phine.   whilst further to the west bogs made the approaches
almost impossible. In such a post Leslie, himself unassailable,
had all the forces of the North and West of Scotland behind
him. Everything depended on his being able to support his
army where it was. Loudoun wrote pressingly to the magistrates of Edinburgh for bread and cheese. "You are desired,"
he added, "to stand to your arms; ply the Lord and His
throne with strong prayers and supplication for us and for His
cause."[2] So short indeed did provisions run, that there had
been for some time talk of slipping past Cromwell to carry the
war into England.[3] The objections to this scheme were
numerous enough, and it was resolved to abandon it, at least
till the probabilities of an English rising in favour of the King
were better known. Loudoun, indeed, in a letter of the 22nd,
professed his eagerness for a battle,[4] but it is hardly likely that
Leslie shared the civilian's ignorant impetuosity.

Cromwell, in fact, had been thoroughly out-generalled.
Partly perhaps through the difficulty of carrying provisions so
far from his ships, partly through his desire to avoid
Cromwell
out-   bringing his conflict with his brother Protestants to
generalled.   the arbitrament of battle, he had shown himself, for
once in his career, halting and irresolute, whilst Leslie had on
every occasion known his own mind, and had carried out his
designs with promptness and resolution. Cromwell, however,

---

[1] Both of them have now disappeared. They will be found in Adair's
map of 1680. There is a facsimile of it in Selway's *A Midlothian
Village*, 6.

[2] Loudoun to the Lord Provost, Maitland's *Hist. of Edinburgh*, 89.
The letter is undated.

[3] Loudoun to Charles II. Aug. 10, 12, *Charles II. and Scotland*,
130, 131.

[4] Loudoun to Argyle and Lothian, Aug. 22 [not, as printed, Aug. 2],
Ancram and Lothian Correspondence, ii. 276.

had not yet given up the game. On the 24th he stormed
Redhall, a fortified house commanding the passage over the
Water of Leith.[1] After a delay of forty-eight hours,
caused, perhaps, by the necessity of replenishing his
provisions,[2] he crossed the Water of Leith on the
27th and advanced westwards, inclining towards the
left to clear the lakes which had hitherto sheltered
Leslie's army. Leslie on his part, perceiving Cromwell's aim, made a corresponding movement towards his own
right, taking up a position on a rising ground behind Gogar
right in the line of Cromwell's march. In the English army it
was firmly believed that the long-desired battle was at last at
hand. So exhilarating was the prospect to the soldiers that
many of them cast away their tents and biscuits, in the firm
belief that a speedy victory would put an end to their toils.

Aug. 24.
Surrender
of Redhall.

Aug. 27.
An ex-
pected
battle.

This sanguine temper did not last long. When the army
reached the place where they had hoped to find a field of
battle, it was easy to see that no battlefield was
there. The bogs stretching in front of Leslie's
army in its new position protected it from cavalry,
and wherever a piece of hard ground was to be found it was
cut up by stone walls, presenting no less obstacles to the
English horse. There was a cannonade, and a few men fell on
either side, but Cromwell had no wish to prolong a useless
slaughter, and he ordered a retreat to his old position on Braid
Hill.[3]

A disap-
pointed
army.

Now that Cromwell had been taught that it was no longer in
his power to reach Queensferry, he had no motive for
remaining in this advanced position. Dysentery and
other diseases incidental to exposure had been telling
on his ranks, and had left 500 sick men on his hands.
He fell back on Musselburgh, where he shipped his
sick, and on the 31st he continued his retreat by

Aug. 28
Cromwell
falls back on
Mussel-
burgh,

Aug. 31.
on Hadding-
ton,

[1] *A Perfect Diurnal*, E, 780, 1 ; Nicoll's *Diary*, pp. 24, 25.

[2] This is suggested by Mr. Douglas, *Cromwell's Scotch Campaign*, 77.

[3] Hodgson's *Memoirs*, 140 ; *Several Letters from Scotland*, E, 612, 8 ;
A Brief Relation, E, 612, 10.

way of Haddington, where he drove off a small force of the
enemy, after which he pushed on to Dunbar, which
he reached on September 1.

Sept. 1.
and reaches
Dunbar.

The day was a Sunday, and according to one
account the Scottish officers refused to engage in the battle
which Cromwell ardently desired to bring on, because they were
warned by their ministers not to stain the Lord's day with the
shedding of blood.[1]   Leslie, therefore, instead of pushing the
retreating English hard, followed leisurely at a distance
of some two miles.   When Cromwell entered Dunbar
the Scottish general sent forward a force to seize a defile at
Cockburnspath, on the road to Berwick, whilst he himself with
the bulk of his army occupied the Doon Hill, an
outlying ridge of the Lammermuir Hills, from which
he could look down upon the enemy's regiments sprinkled
over the peninsula of Dunbar.

Leslie's
movements.

Leslie on
Doon Hill.

As far as numbers went the Scots had an immense
superiority.   Lumsden, with those northern reinforcements
which Charles had been anxious to retain as a guard
for his own person,[2] had recently joined Leslie,[3]
whose army could now be reckoned at little short of
23,000,[4] whilst Cromwell commanded but 11,000—less than
half the number.   In quality the Scots were even more inferior
than when they first faced Cromwell behind their entrench-
ments in front of the Calton Hill.   The English may have
been, as was afterwards said of them, 'a poor, shattered,
hungry, discouraged army ;'[5] but they were war-worn veterans

Comparison
between the
armies.

---

[1] Cadwell's Narrative in Carte's *Orig. Letters*, i. 380 ; Walker's *Hist.
Discourses*, 179, 180 ; Cromwell to Lenthall, Sept. 4, *Carlyle*, Letter cxl. ;
A Brief Relation, E, 612, 10.   [2] See p. 278.

[3] Cromwell says that Leslie had been joined by three new regiments.
These may be taken to be the northern reinforcements, as their commander,
Lumsden, was in the battle.

[4] Walker gives 23,000, and Cromwell calculates them as at least
22,000.

[5] Hodgson's *Memoirs*, 143.   It must be remembered that an account
written some time after the victory would be apt to exaggerate the weakness of the victorious army.

under trusted leaders, whereas the Scots were not only for the
most part new to war, but were split asunder in heart and
mind by the wedge of faction. Only a day or two
before the Committee of Purging had summoned
Lord Eglinton from his post at the King's side and
compelled him to discharge some of his officers. The work of
purging went merrily on, and soldiers who might have fought
well for their country were driven from their ranks on the
plea that their covenanting principles were not sufficiently
pure.[1] That strictness of this kind was not conducive to
military discipline needs no proof. Wherever the veil is lifted
the Scottish army is seen to be cleft asunder by the spirit of
party, the clergy and the members of the Committee of
Estates who sympathised with them distrusting the more
worldly-minded soldiers as Malignants and Engagers ; whilst
the more worldly-minded soldiers writhed under the yoke of
the fanatics and, bearing in mind the interviews of the strictly
covenanting officers with the English commanders, even suspected them of a settled intention to betray the army to the
enemy.[2]

The army again purged.

It is hardly likely that Cromwell was aware of these chances
in his favour. That he felt the full difficulties of his position
appears from a letter which he despatched to Hazlerigg on the
2nd. "We are," he wrote, "upon an engagement
very difficult. The enemy hath blocked up our way
at the pass at Copperspath,[3] through which we cannot
get without almost a miracle. He lieth so upon the hills that
we know not how to come that way without difficulty ; and our
lying here daily consumeth our men, who fall sick beyond
imagination." Cromwell hardly knew what to do. Hazlerigg,
however willing, had no forces at his disposal capable of setting
him free. "Wherefore," continues Cromwell, "whatever becomes of us, it will be well for you to get what forces you can
together, and the South to help what they can ; the business

Sept. 2. Cromwell's letter to Hazlerigg.

[1] Walker's *Hist. Discourses*, 179.
[2] *Life of R. Blair* (Wodrow Soc.), 237.
[3] The local pronunciation of Cockburnspath.

nearly concerneth all good people ; but the only wise God knows what is best ; all shall work for good ; our spirits are comfortable, praised be the Lord, though our present condition be as it is ; and indeed we have much hope in the Lord, of Whose mercy we have had large experience." [1]

Cromwell's religious confidence never failed him, and his military instincts recoiled from any such confession of failure as would be implied in an escape by sea, even if shipping sufficient to convey his whole force could be provided. At a Council of War held before the army left Musselburgh, it had been resolved to fortify Dunbar, and to use it as a basis of operations [2] where provisions might be stored and the army await reinforcements. If, for a moment, as appears from his letter to Hazlerigg, the thought of pushing on to Berwick had crossed his mind, such a plan was now rendered impossible, and it was necessary to revert to the original scheme.

Cromwell's plans.

Yet, even before Cromwell had time to form a definite conclusion, there were signs that his difficulties would be solved in a way more to his taste. A night's experience of its exposed quarters on Doon Hill had been sufficient for the Scottish army. The season was wet, and to remain in the open in that exposed position was, even if famine could be averted, to court an outbreak of the disease which had wasted the English regiments. The Lammermuirs grew no corn, and the rich lands between Dunbar and Edinburgh had been for weeks the spoil of opposing armies. It was no light matter to feed 23,000 men on that bleak, waterless height. What passed in the Council of War that evening will never be known with certainty. There is, however, reason to believe that whilst the Committee of Estates, and especially those members of it who were most under clerical influence, were for falling on the English with as little delay as possible,

Quarters on Doon Hill.

A Council of War.

---

[1] Cromwell to Hazlerigg, Sept. 2, *Carlyle*, Letter cxxxix. The letter must have been sent off very early in the morning, as there is no hint in it of Leslie's movement down the hill.

[2] Cromwell to Lenthall, Sept. 4, *ib.*, Letter cxl.

David Leslie and old Leven, who was present in the camp, were on the side of caution, apparently wishing to remain on the hillside till Cromwell's army had marched on, and then to fall on its rear when entangled in the blocked defile at Cockburnspath.[1]

[1] "Burnet," writes Mr. Hill Burton (*Hist. of Scotl.* vii. 24, Note 2), "is the authority generally cited for the interference : ' Leslie was in the chief command, but he had a Committee of the Estates to give him his orders, among whom Warriston was one. These were weary of lying in the fields, and thought that Leslie made not haste enough to destroy those sectaries, for so they came to call them. He told them ·by lying there all was sure, but that by engaging in action with gallant and desperate men all might be lost ; yet they still called on him to fall on. Many have thought that all this was treachery done on design to deliver up our army to Cromwell, some laying it upon Leslie and others upon my uncle. I am persuaded there was no treachery in it, only Warriston was too hot and Leslie too cold, and yielded too easily to their humours, which he ought not to have done.' It has recently become a sort of historical canon that Burnet is ever to be discredited. . . . He had good means of knowing what he speaks of here, for the ' uncle ' referred to was Warriston. Burnet was a child seven years old when the battle was fought ; he was eighteen years old when his uncle Warriston was executed."

Burton then shows that in the main Burnet is confirmed by Baillie. In a letter of Jan. 2, 1651, Baillie writes that the descent of the army was a consequence of the Committee's order, contrary to his, *i.e.* Leslie's, mind (*Baillie*, iii. 111). A statement made by Major White on Sept. 10 to the English Parliament, and no doubt gathered from prisoners, helps to clear up the matter. "The General [and] Lieutenant-General of the Scots were of opinion to have let our army retreat till they came to their last pass, and so to fall upon their rear, but the ministers did so importune them that they could not rest quiet until they had engaged." *C.J.* vi. 464. This renders Leslie's wish to stay on the hill intelligible. If he thought that Cromwell meant to pursue his march the next day, he might well think that the best place for the Scottish army was on the hill. It would not be so under other conditions, unless, indeed, for the present Leslie intended simply to look on whilst Cromwell re-embarked his army by instalments, or to wait till part of it had disappeared and then to fall on the remainder. Cromwell, too (*Carlyle*, Letter cxlii.), says : ' I hear, where the enemy marched last up to us, the ministers pressed their army to interpose between us and home, the chief officers desiring rather that we might have way made, though it were by a golden bridge ; but the clergy's counsel pre-

It was only, it seems, on a formal order from the Committee that Leslie gave the order to descend the hill on the following morning. If this was the case, before the day was far spent he became as confident as the Committee itself.[1] The grounds of this change of mind are not difficult to conjecture. Morning revealed no sign of any intention of Cromwell to march further. If, then, the English army tarried at Dunbar, it could only be with the intention, Leslie may fairly have reasoned, of effecting its escape—so far as escape was possible —by sea. Under any circumstances the embarkation of an army affords chances which an active enemy, superior in numbers as the Scottish army was, can easily turn to his profit. In the present case the circumstances were most unfavourable. It was hardly likely that the commissariat vessels by which the English invaders had been accompanied could have found room for anything like the whole number of men of which Cromwell's army was composed, and it was certain that they could not have found room as well for the horses of his cavalry. Cromwell, therefore, if he really intended to make use of his shipping, could only do so either by dividing his force or by abandoning his horses. Nor was this all. Leslie appears to have been under the impression that the division of Cromwell's army had already taken place, and that the vessels which had borne away the sick from Musselburgh had in reality conveyed away the whole of Cromwell's artillery and some at least of his fighting men.[2] No wonder that before his own army had reached the bottom of the hill Leslie had cast away all thought

Sept. 2. Leslie moves down the hill.

Leslie hopeful of success.

vailed.' The phrase about the 'golden bridge' can only mean that Leven and David Leslie would have been willing to give Cromwell money to retreat. Mr. Douglas (pp. 96, 97) has entirely misunderstood it to signify that they were ready to take bribes from Cromwell, which, to my mind, is unthinkable.

[1] This is shown by his language to an English prisoner. See p. 289.

[2] See again Leslie's conversation with the prisoner noted at p. 289. Compare Rushworth to Lenthall, Sept. 3, *Several Proceedings*, E, 780, 5.

of reluctance to carry out the manœuvre which had been imposed on him the evening before.[1]

Yet, though Leslie had evidently made up his mind to
attack on the following day, he appears not to have altogether
lost sight of the chance that Cromwell might still
attempt—like Essex's lieutenant at Lostwithiel—to
cut his way out at the head of his horse, an operation which would undoubtedly have played into the hands of
the Scottish general. It must have been with this object in
view that he made no attempt to block up the issues from the
English camping-ground, though the nature of the ground had
furnished him to a marvel with the opportunity of so doing.
At the foot of the hill flows the Broxburn, meandering at the
bottom of a natural trench some forty or fifty feet deep, the
sides of which are so steep as to render it easily defensible.
The upper part of this trench ran immediately under the steep
slopes of the hill, whilst lower down there is a passage near
Brant's mill across which a few troops could be pushed, and
about a furlong lower the stream is crossed by the road to Berwick, which then, as now, was crossed about a mile and a half
from Dunbar, at a point above that at which the stream enters
the grounds of Broxmouth, belonging to the Earl of Roxburgh.
Almost immediately above this point the trench comes to an
end, and though at that time the stream was crossed by no
bridge, it was shallow enough to be easily forded, whilst the
ground sloping gently down on either side offered a fair passage
for cavalry. Between this road and the shore, the course of
the stream lies for about half a mile through the grounds of
Broxmouth House, at that time in the possession of the
English. If Leslie's design had been merely to force Cromwell's evidently strong position, his obvious course would have

*The
Scottish
position.*

[1] "I know," wrote Leslie two days after his defeat, "I get my own
share of the salt by many for drawing them so near the enemy, and must
suffer in this as many times formerly ; though I take God to witness we
might as easily have beaten them as we did James Graham at Philiphaugh,
if the officers had stayed by their own troops and regiments." Leslie to
Argyle, Sept. 5, *Ancram and Lothian Correspondence,* ii. 297.

been to occupy in strength the ground opposite the three exits, and to prepare for an attack on the following morning. What he did was to leave open the way to Cromwell to make that mad dash for liberty which could hardly fail to end in surrender or annihilation.

With this object, it is to be presumed, in view, he stationed his army, not parallel with the Broxburn, but on the slope of the hill facing northwards, in all probability some little way south of the road, whence a downward slope affords good charging ground for cavalry upon an enemy insane enough to pass along the road at the foot in line of march.[1]   It was in

---

[1] It will be seen that I accept the evidence of Mr. Firth's map as to the direction in which the Scottish army faced.   In addition to the arguments he adduces, I would add that Cadwell's statement that ' our brigade of horse gave way a little, being charged by the enemy coming down the hill upon them,' may be quoted in his favour.   The descent from the highest point in the road to the bridge, where this charge must have taken place if the Scots had been planted astride on the road, is no more than 35 feet in half a mile, whereas the ground above the road drops some hundred feet in less than half a mile.   It is only, then, by placing the army where it stands in Mr. Firth's map that Cadwell's statement becomes intelligible. At the same time I am unable to accept the extreme length of line attributed to the Scots in the map.   It is made to reach to the point at which the hills behind descend to the east—that is to say, to the Dryburn, giving to the army a front of at least two miles.   Hodgson's account is quite clear. " A great clough was betwixt the armies, and it could be no less than a mile of ground betwixt their right wing, near 'Roxburgh," *i.e.* Broxmouth, " House, and their left wing ; they had a great mountain behind them." Hodgson, no doubt, did not write till thirty years after the event, but he had evidently a good memory, and was in a position to know where the Scottish right wing was.   I do not want to take the expression about the proximity of that right wing to Broxmouth House too literally ; but it is absolutely inconsistent with placing it near the Dryburn, especially as he shows himself to be in the right in placing the mountain ' behind' the Scots. Another point in his narrative deserves attention.   He says that if the Scottish right wing were beaten their whole army would be hazarded " in regard they had not great ground to traverse their regiments betwixt the mountain and the clough "—that is to say, he treats the Scottish foot as being on narrow ground between the hill and the Broxburn.   In Mr. Firth's map the foot reaches beyond a house which he holds to be Meikle

consonance with this idea that the Scottish general massed the greater part of his horse on his right, whilst leaving a smaller force of cavalry on his left to shield the foot, which, as usual, was placed in the centre, against any danger on that side. One thing remained to be done, to post an advanced guard on the road to give warning of any attempt to break out in that direction ; and it was probably with that object that in the course of the afternoon the Scots attacked and overpowered a small English force posted in a cottage on the right bank of the stream.

When the combat was at an end, a prisoner—a one-armed man who had been one of the defenders of the post--was

An English prisoner. brought before Leslie. " Do the enemy," asked the Scottish general, "intend to fight ? " " What," was the prompt reply, " do you think we came here for ? We came for nothing else." " Soldier," said Leslie, still incredulous, " how will you fight when you have shipped half of your men and all your great guns ? " The prisoner knew better than that. " Sir," he answered, " if you please to draw your army to the foot of the hill you shall find both men and great guns also." " How durst you," said a bystander, " answer the General so saucily ? " " I only," replied the man, " make answer to the questions demanded of me." Leslie gave him his liberty. The soldier, when he made his report to Cromwell, told him that he had lost twenty shillings when he was taken. Cromwell gave him more than double the amount, and sent him on his way rejoicing.[1] Leslie appears to have thought that he had to do

Pinkerton. If so, there is about a mile and a half between that farm and the sea, affording plenty of ground for the regiments to manœuvre in. Hodgson's narrative hangs well together, and I find it easier to accept it than to take the map as literally correct so far as the extension of the Scottish line is concerned. If we take the house in the map as Little, and not Meikle Pinkerton, and the extension eastwards to be imaginary, all difficulty vanishes, and map and narrative are brought into substantial agreement.

[1] Cadwell's Relation, in Carte's *Orig. Letters*, i. 382. Mr. Douglas (p. 107, note) thinks that Leslie merely asked the question about shipping the men and guns to worm the truth out of the prisoner. He would, how-

with a braggart. He is said to have told his soldiers that by seven o'clock the next morning they would have the English army dead or alive.

All through that day the eye of Cromwell had been on the Scottish army. It was not till four in the afternoon that

Cromwell watches the Scots.

Leslie's intention was revealed beyond dispute. By that time, horse, foot, and artillery were drawing down towards the right, and taking up a position on the lower ground. Fixing his eye on the movements of the

Thinks he sees an advantage.

enemy he turned to Lambert. He 'thought,' he told his Major-General, 'it did give us an opportunity or advantage to attempt upon the enemy.' "I had thought," replied Lambert, "to have said the same thing to you." Monk was then called and agreed with his superior officers. Late in the day others expressed themselves in the same way.

But for the immense superiority of the English army in point of discipline, and for the absence of the veteran officers, purged

Grounds of his belief.

out of the Scottish army for insufficiency of religious zeal, Cromwell's flash of insight would have been of little worth. No doubt Cromwell could see that if once he succeeded not only in beating the Scottish horse now massed on Leslie's right, but also in turning their flight up the narrowing gorge, the routed horse would trample down their own comrades and convert a defeat into a disaster. The really important question was whether he could, by any tactical manœuvre, succeed in what might well have seemed the impracticable operation of directing the bulk of his army along the front of the enemy's line. It was from the consciousness that in his army he possessed an instrument of war unequalled in its day, that Cromwell's heart drew that inspiration of chastened confidence, to which an unsupported tradition has given expression in the words attributed to him : " The Lord hath delivered them into our hands."

ever, hardly have asked it unless he had had some suspicion, to say the least of it, that the thing had actually happened. Otherwise, what did he want to know?

It was difficult for Cromwell to make all his officers share this confidence of his. At a last council of war in the evening some at least of the colonels proposed to ship the foot and let the horse cut their way through the enemy, thus inviting a repetition of the disaster which had befallen Essex at Lostwithiel. Against this poltroonery Lambert— surely at Cromwell's instigation—protested, bidding the officers be of better cheer, and predicting a victory for the morrow. At the prayer of one of the officers Cromwell entrusted to Lambert the command of the force which was to make the attack.[1]

A last council of war

It was a dripping night, but by four in the morning of the 3rd the moon shone out. By that time Lambert was hurrying regiment after regiment to the brink of the ravine. As one of the officers was speeding past, his ear caught the voice of prayer sounding in the night from the lips of a cornet. Halting awhile to listen he gathered courage. " I met," he afterwards explained, " with so much of God in it as I was satisfied deliverance was at hand." [2] Everything that human ingenuity could devise had been done by Cromwell to distract the enemy whilst his audacious plan was put in execution. The bulk of the English army, indeed, was stationed on the Berwick Road, where the passage of the brook was the easiest. To his right he threw out a small body of horse, which by crossing the ravine near Brant's mill might create an impression on the enemy that his weakened left was about to be the subject of the attack. At the same time, Pride's brigade, consisting of three regiments of foot, supported by the General's own regiment of horse, was to cross below Broxmouth House, thus not only relieving the crowded passage higher up the stream, but, taking a wide circuit so as to fall upon the enemy's right wing, without exposing itself to the danger of an attack in flank. In this way the attention of the main body of the Scottish horse would be distracted from the scene of action at the ford over which the greater part of

Sept. 3. Cromwell's preparations.

---

[1] Hodgson's *Memoirs*, 144.　　　　[2] *Ib.* 148.

the English army was to be led. Each infantry regiment was accompanied by two field-pieces, whilst the heavy guns were placed at the edge of the ravine to gall the left wing and centre of the enemy.

Meanwhile Cromwell, already at his post, was impatiently waiting for Lambert, fearing lest the enemy should begin the

Cromwell impatient. attack. He had no need to be so disquieted. Leslie's army had been ruined by its many purgings.

Condition of the Scottish army. Though it was probably untrue, as an English Royalist asserted, that the new officers were all ' ministers' sons, clerks and such sanctified creatures, who hardly ever saw or heard of any sword but that of the Spirit,' [1] they were at least for the most part unknown to their men, who had been bound to the old officers by the force of local attachment so strong at that time with the Scottish peasant. Not a few of those in command shrank away in the darkness of the night to seek refuge from the rain. About two in the morning Major-General Holborn, going his rounds amongst the foot, bade all except two in a company extinguish their matches, probably in order to avoid drawing the enemy's fire upon them. The weary men took advantage of the permission to cower under the shocks of corn and to fall asleep. [2]

Lambert had been busy bringing up the guns, and when he reached Cromwell, a little before sunrise, [3] a trumpet on the

Lambert arrives. other side of the stream had already called to horse. By this time Cromwell had completed his preparations.

At last the moments of suspense were at an end. With the rush of Lambert's cavalry the battle opened. Gallantly did such

The battle. parties of horse as could be gathered together at a moment's notice from the smaller body on the Scottish left wing withstand their onset in the narrow pass. It

---

[1] Walker's *Hist. Discourses*, 162.   [2] *Ib.* 180.

[3] Cromwell speaks of the fight as not beginning till six, whereas on Sept. $\frac{3}{13}$ the sun rises at 5.33. Cadwell, however, talks of fighting by moonlight, and Cromwell's well-known words, ' Let God arise, &c.,' spoken after the tide of battle turned, coincided with sunrise.

took an hour's hard fighting to clear the way. Happily for Cromwell the main bodies of the opposing force had been slow to stand to arms, and were still in the positions which they had occupied during the night. Lambert's first attempt to assail the cavalry of the right wing was repulsed, the Scots having the advantage of the ground and charging down the hill upon him,

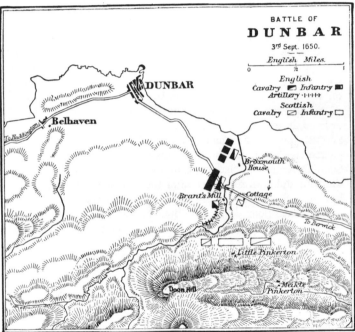

G. Philip & Son.

whilst the same good fortune attended the Scottish infantry in the centre, where, when it was attacked by the foot regiments under Monk, its superior numbers were here, too, favoured by the sloping ground. Once at the foot of the hill this advantage was lost, the slope being no longer considerable, and when Lambert had been joined by his supports he was able to recover himself, and, charging once more, he drove the masses of cavalry opposed to him off the field.

Difficult as it is to unravel the detail of the action, there can be little doubt that the main body of the English army would have been unsuccessful in establishing itself on the front of the battle, if the attention of the Scottish cavalry on the enemy's right had not been occupied by the greater part of the English regiment of horse sent across the lower course of the Broxburn, so as to fall unexpectedly on its quarters before it had time to put itself in array. Somewhat later two at least of the three foot regiments of Pride's brigade must have appeared in support of the horse. . The third regiment, Lambert's, was somewhat late on the field, and was preparing to join the attack on the Scottish infantry, by that time denuded of the support of cavalry, when Cromwell himself, appearing on the scene, ordered it to take ground to the left, and, passing round the Scottish infantry, to attack it on the flank. Though this was a picked regiment, it found its efforts unavailing against one Scottish regiment—that of Campbell of Lawers—which continued a stubborn resistance after the rest of the line had been broken, till a troop of horse had charged through it. The infantry then poured into the breach, and Monk, returning to the charge, brought the battle to an end. The Scottish [1]

---

[1] The main difficulty is to reconcile Hodgson's statement that Lambert ordered the brigade in which he was 'to march about Roxburgh House, towards the sea,' and so to fall upon the enemy's flank, with the entire silence both of Cromwell and other witnesses on the existence of such a manœuvre. Mr. Firth, too, points out that in Fisher's picture plan these regiments are represented as 'coming up in the rear of the infantry already engaged, and rather to the left, but hardly on the flank.' He has also reminded me that Hodgson does not speak of the whole brigade, but only of his own regiment, being moved to the left by Cromwell. This, too, he tells after, not before, the rout of the Scottish infantry regiment. Looking again over the whole evidence, I incline to think that Hodgson's memory was at fault in supposing that orders had been given for an attack on the Scottish flank. It could never have entered into the head of a general in those days to order infantry regiments to attack cavalry, and therefore the supposed order would not have been given till after the

retreat soon became a rout, and, at the moment that the sun rose out of the sea, Cromwell, crying, as his rough face lighted up with the joy of victory, " Let God arise, let His enemies be scattered ! " remorselessly pushed on the flying horsemen over the ranks of their own infantry, scarcely roused from sleep as they lay above the stream. Trampling down in their headlong flight all that were in their path, they fled towards Haddington, the victors following hard with the avenging steel. Such of the foot as escaped rushed aside towards Dunbar, and surrendered themselves as prisoners without resistance. Of the whole Scottish army, about three thousand had perished in the fight and the pursuit. Ten thousand prisoners, the whole of the artillery and baggage, 15,000 arms, and nearly 200 colours, fell into the hands of the conquerors. On the English side, the slain —so at least Cromwell avouched—did not exceed twenty men.[1]

In disposing of the prisoners Cromwell did what he could, without destruction of their lives, to prevent their ever again serving in the enemy's ranks. On the morning after the battle he issued a proclamation allowing the inhabitants of the country round to carry away all such as were severely wounded. The remainder, some 5,000 in all, were sent off to Hazlerigg at Newcastle to be forwarded to the South. " I pray you," he wrote to Hazlerigg a few days later, " let humanity be exercised towards

Sept. 4.
The dis-
posal of
the pri-
soners.

Scottish cavalry was beaten. Still, the fact that Hodgson thought such an order had been given is enough to justify us in assuming that a flank attack was really made, but probably only by the regiment in which Hodgson was personally serving. On these assumptions I have substituted the story as told above for that which appeared in former editions. I hope to be able to discuss the difficulties of the battle in greater detail in the *Historical Review*.

[1] Hodgson's *Memoirs* (p. 147) are the only authority for the flank march of the infantry, but as he himself took part in it, his account cannot be set aside. There is nothing in Cromwell's own despatch (*Carlyle*, Letter cxl.) to contradict it, and the manœuvre is just what one would have expected from Cromwell's power of seeing into the possibilities of a battlefield. Compare Cadwell's Relation in Carte's *Orig. Letters*, i. 380, and Leslie's letter quoted at p. 287, note 1.

them ; I am persuaded it will be comely." [1] Unhappily the
fate of most of the prisoners was determined before they came
into Hazlerigg's hands. The conductors were probably short
of provisions, or at all events they took no trouble to supply
the helpless men under their charge. When the prisoners
arrived at Morpeth after an eight days' march, in which they
had been half-starved,[2] they were thrust into a large walled
garden. The hungry men threw themselves voraciously on the
cabbages growing in it, and devoured them raw. Dysentery
set in, and though Hazlerigg gave them rest at Durham, and
did all that man could do to feed and nurse the sick, they died
like flies.[3] The survivors were ultimately sent to New
England, where they met with as much kindness as was
compatible with their lot. After a term of servitude they were
set at liberty, and in many cases established as landowners on
an equal footing with the rest of the community.[4]

The victory of which those poor peasants bore the brunt
would never have been won but for the command
of the sea which enabled the English Government
to pour in the supplies by which alone their army

Causes
of the
victory.

[1] Proclamation, printed by *Carlyle* before Letter cxl. Cromwell to
Hazlerigg, Sept. 5, *ib.* App. No. 19.

[2] " They," wrote Hazlerigg, " having fasted, as they themselves said,
near eight days." They could not have marched so far if they had been
left absolutely without food.

[3] Hazlerigg to the Council of State, Oct. 31, *Merc. Pol.* E, 616, 1.

[4] " The Scots whom God delivered into your hand at Dunbar, and
whereof sundry were sent hither, we have been desirous, as we could, to
make their yoke easy. Such as were sick of the scurvy or other diseases
have not wanted physic and chirurgery. They have not been sold for
slaves to perpetual servitude, but for 6 or 7 or 8 years, as we do our own ;
and he that bought the most of them, I hear, buildeth houses for them, for
every four a house, layeth some acres of ground thereto, which he giveth
them as their own, requiring 3 days in the week to work for him by turns,
and 4 days for themselves, and promiseth as soon as they can repay him
the money he laid out for them he will set them at liberty."—John
Cotton to Cromwell, 28, 5—*i.e.* July 5, 1651. *Hutchinson Papers* (Prince
Society), ii. 264. This mode of dating was coming into use with the
extreme Puritans.

was preserved from starvation. From a purely military point of view Cromwell's success was owing to his own tactical skill and the disciplined valour of his army, though he piously ascribed it to the direct intervention of Providence against a hypocritical nation. Dunbar ranks with Naseby as one of the two decisive battles of Cromwell's career. As Naseby rendered

Effect of Dunbar on the international relations, for ever impossible the re-establishment of purely personal government in England, Dunbar struck down the Solemn League and Covenant,[1] and rendered it for ever impossible that Scotland should attempt to impose upon England a form of ecclesiastical or political government against the will of Englishmen. Nor was

and on the domestic affairs of Scotland. Dunbar less decisive in its influence on the domestic affairs of Scotland herself. Never again would the stricter Covenanters grasp the reins of government and mould armies at their pleasure. Their impracticable zeal, their intolerance of contradiction, would still produce martyrs, in some of whom it is hard to draw the line between the criminal and the hero; but they could no more produce men who claimed to be statesmen and generals. The sword of Cromwell at Dunbar was wielded on behalf of two nations, and, as is often the case, his transcendent service was requited with the gratitude of neither.

[1] The 'word' of the Scottish army was appropriately 'The Covenant:' of the English 'The Lord of Hosts.'

CHAPTER XIII

THE SEA POWER OF THE COMMONWEALTH

THE naval supremacy which had contributed to Cromwell's victory at Dunbar could not long be maintained without the protection of the maritime commerce on which it was based. It would little profit the masters of the State to control Scotland and Ireland unless they could protect the shipping which drew wealth to the shores of England and gave exercise to the hardy breed of mariners on whom, in times of emergency, reliance might be placed. As matters stood, a merchantman, leaving an English port in quest of gain, was in danger almost immediately after it had put to sea. The Isle of Man under the Earl of Derby, the Scilly Isles under Sir John Grenvile, and Jersey under Sir George Carteret, were nests of Royalist privateers, the two latter ports lying in the very track of navigation. Even in Guernsey, which had sided with Parliament, Castle Cornet was held by a garrison for Charles.

The naval supremacy of the Commonwealth.

Its commercial marine.

The Royalist privateers.

Dangerous as these enemies were, the Council of State was compelled, at the beginning of the year 1650, to take measures against an enemy more dangerous still. When Rupert escaped from Kinsale [1] he made his way with a string of prizes to Lisbon, where he was hospitably received by John IV., the first sovereign of the House of Braganza, who allowed him to refit his vessels and to make, in the name of Charles II., preparations for fresh attacks

Rupert at large.

Rupert at Lisbon.

[1] See p. 137.

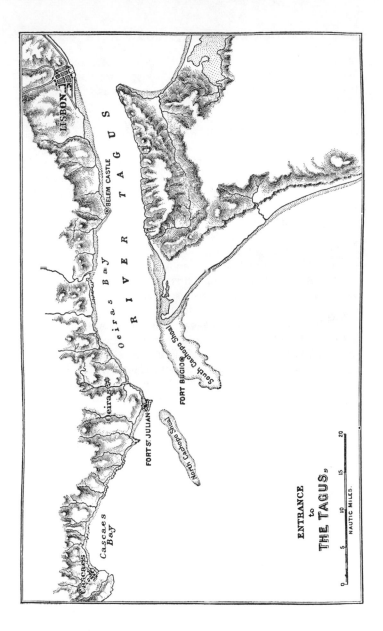

LISBON

BELEM CASTLE

Oeiras Bay

R I V E R T A G U S

Oeiras

FORT ST. JULIAN

North Cachopo Shoal

FORT BUGIO

South Cachopo Shoal

Cascaes Bay

Cascaes

ENTRANCE
to
THE TAGUS,

0   5   10   15   20
NAUTIC MILES.

on the property of English rebels. It was quickly perceived at
Westminster that the question was no longer whether Rupert's
fleet or the Scilly privateers were more dangerous. If the King
of Portugal were allowed to give shelter to ships, held at Lisbon
to be duly commissioned warships of the King of England, but
in London to be no better than pirates, every ruler in Europe
French might do the like. Already French cruisers, know-
piracy. ing that their own Government had hitherto refused
to recognise the Commonwealth, had fallen on English merchantmen wherever they could find them, though English warships
were prepared to retaliate in kind. It was therefore not with
Danger from Rupert alone, but with a hostile Europe as well, that
hostile the statesmen of the Commonwealth had to do.
Europe. Self-preservation drove England to become a maritime
power such as she had never been before.

The King of Portugal had first to be coerced, and Blake,
who was entrusted with the task, cast anchor on March 10 in
Mar.–May. Cascaes Bay, outside the forts which guard the
Rupert and entrance to the Tagus. King John was inclined to
Blake in the
Tagus. temporise, and, though by a cannonade from the
forts he frustrated an attempt of the English admiral to advance
up the river against Rupert, he subsequently, on the 18th,
allowed him to seek safety from a heavy gale by anchoring in
the Bay of Oeiras, inside the forts, and about two miles below
the position of Rupert's fleet. In numbers the fleets commanded respectively by Blake and Rupert were not very
unequal, but Blake was somewhat superior in guns, and
immensely superior in the quality of his crews.

Blake, who had engaged himself to return to Cascaes Bay
as soon as the weather moderated, retreated before long to the
April 13. outer anchorage. On April 13 the Vice-Admiral's
An attempt ship, the 'Leopard,' was exposed to an unexpected
on the
'Leopard.' danger. Rupert had contrived an explosive machine
placed inside a barrel of oil, and made so as to blow up at the
pulling of a string which passed through the barrel. This
ostensible barrel of oil was entrusted to an Englishman disguised as a Portuguese, who took it with him in a fruit boat for

sale to the crew of the ' Leopard,' with instructions to pull the string as soon as it had been hoisted on board. Unluckily for the success of his craftily devised plan, the Englishman gave vent to some ejaculations in his own tongue before the critical moment arrived. The man was arrested, and the plot discovered. On the same day some of Rupert's men fell upon a watering party from the ' Bonaventure,' killed one of the sailors, wounded several more, and took three prisoners. Rupert excused the deed by alleging that he was himself to be kidnapped by the boat's crew.

All this while Blake's attitude towards the Portuguese Government was one of friendly warning. By messages conveyed through the English resident, Charles Vane,[1] Blake fails to persuade the Portuguese to expel Rupert. he urged the King to be wise in time and to expel the pirates. Rupert, on his part, had the Queen's influence on his side, and he did not disdain to stir up the passions of the priests and the populace against the English heretics. The King hesitated for some time, but gave way at last, and declared in Rupert's favour.[2]

On this Blake showed his strength. On May 16[3] May 16. English ships in the Portuguese service seized. the annual fleet bound for Brazil dropped down the Tagus, nine of the eighteen ships of which it was composed being owned by English merchants resident at Lisbon, and manned by English seamen. These nine ships were seized by Blake, upon which the greater

---

[1] See p. 181.

[2] *A Letter from Lisbon*, E, 598, 3 ; *Prince Rupert's Declaration*, E, 598, 7 ; *Warburton*, iii. 300–305 ; Agreement between Vasconcellos and Charles Vane, March $\frac{18}{28}$, *Hist. MSS. Com.* Rep. xiii. App. part i. 520 ; C. Vane to the King of Portugal, April $\frac{15}{25}$, *Thurloe*, i. 141. The best description of the explosive machine is in a Letter from the Fleet of May 31, *Perf. Diurnal*, E, 777, 10, where, however, the date is incorrectly given.

[3] The date is fixed by a statement that Popham, who arrived on the 26th, came ten days after the seizure of the ships. *S.P. Dom.* xi. 91. A later date is indeed given in a Letter from the Fleet, June 12, *Perf. Diurnal*, E, 777, 21, but other dates in this series of letters are demonstrably inaccurate, and little weight can, therefore, be given to this assertion.

part of the crews gladly took service under the Commonwealth. As yet Blake had no instructions to meddle with the actual property of the subjects of the King of Portugal. The defect was soon supplied. On the 26th Popham arrived with eight ships and instructions to treat the Portuguese

May 26. Popham's arrival.

Open hostilities.

as enemies. Charles Vane escaped from shore with some difficulty, whilst English merchants, refusing to declare for Charles II., were themselves thrown into prison and their goods sequestered.[1] Blake had now before him a long blockade with its attendant risks. Neither food nor water was any longer obtainable from the shore, and it therefore became necessary from time to time to despatch ships for supplies to Vigo or Cadiz. At last, on July 26, when

July 26. Rupert comes out,

Blake had with him but nineteen sail—nine of which were the captured merchantmen—Rupert attempted to break out with twenty-six ships and eighteen smaller vessels, the greater part of his fleet having been supplied by the Portuguese and by some French merchants then at Lisbon. Rupert's crews, however, having no stomach for the fight, hugged the shore under the guns of the forts, and on

July 27. but draws back.

the 27th, perceiving that Blake had been reinforced by seven or eight ships which had returned from Cadiz, the whole fleet drew back to the safe anchorage in Oeiras Bay.[2]

As Rupert had slipped back, the weary blockade had to be commenced afresh. But for the friendly disposition of the

Resumption of the blockade.

Spaniards, who regarded an enemy of Portugal as a natural ally, Blake would have found no port at which to revictual and water his ships nearer than

Sept. 3. Blake sends ships to Cadiz.

those of his own country. On September 3, the day on which Cromwell was dashing the Scots into ruin at Dunbar, the English Admiral had again to send off eight of

[1] Letter from the Fleet, June 12, *Perf. Diurnal*, E, 777, 21.
[2] Blake and Popham to the Council of State, Aug. 15, *Hist. MSS. Com.* Rep. xiii. App. part i. 531 ; Letter from the Fleet, Aug. 15, *Several Proceedings*, E, 780, 2. There is a slight difference in the reckoning of the numbers of the ships. I have adopted Blake's account.

his ships to Cadiz for supplies.[1] Having long ago dismissed his prizes homewards as being no longer able to remain at sea, he had but ten vessels remaining with him to keep up the blockade. On the 7th Rupert, supported by the Portuguese Admiral, came out to try his fortune once more, this time with thirty-six ships. That morning a heavy fog lay upon the water, and when at last it lifted Rupert found himself near Blake's own ship, two of her consorts being not far off. Rupert, as he had so often done on shore, made straight for the enemy, bidding his gunners to reserve their fire until they were alongside. Blake, on the other hand, made full use of his artillery. Down came Rupert's fore top-mast, but before advantage could be taken of the disaster the fog once more enveloped the combatants and put an end to the engagement. On the following morning the Portuguese Admiral—so at least Rupert averred— showed no inclination to challenge the supremacy of the sailors of the Commonwealth, and the whole of the combined fleet drew back to its anchorage within the forts.

Sept. 7.
A futile engagement.

Sept. 8.
Rupert returns to port.

Blake now resumed his watching, no longer for the exit of Rupert—which was hardly to be expected after his last failure— but for the Portuguese fleet approaching from Brazil. Early in the morning of the 14th twenty-three sail topped the horizon. Blake at once dashed at the prey. Laying himself alongside of the Vice-Admiral's ship, he fought her for three hours, whilst a gale, which made it impossible to work the guns of the lower tier, was howling over the tumbling sea. When, at length, the Portuguese commander struck his flag, flames were gaining the mastery over his ship, which sank at last, though the greater part of the crew was saved by the English sailors. When the gains were counted it was found that seven prizes remained in the hands of the victors, having on board no less than 4,000 chests of sugar and 400 men.[2]

Blake looks out for the Brazil fleet.

Sept. 14.
His fight with the Vice-Admiral.

[1] On their way home they took six French vessels. Reference of Petitions, Sept. 28, *S.P. Dom.* xi. 35.

[2] Blake to the Council of State, Oct. 14, *Hist. MSS. Com.* Rep. xiii. App. i. 536.

Having thus taught the King of Portugal a lesson, Blake had no longer any reason to remain on the coast.   The time Blake makes for Cadiz. was approaching after which no sailor would, in those days, think of prolonging a blockade.[1]   As soon as the fight was over Blake made for Cadiz, where he was received with all honour by the Admiral of Spain.   He had his prizes to send home under convoy, and no brief delay on his part off Lisbon could prevent Rupert from coming out sooner or later if he were disposed to do so.   Blake had now but six ships left, and with these he resolved to remain at sea a month or two longer.[2]   Perhaps he may have thought that if Rupert put to sea there was the more likelihood of capturing him.[3]

On October 12, whilst Blake was still at Cadiz, Rupert, with the sea open before him and a Portuguese Court now Oct. 12. Rupert puts to sea, anxious to be rid of him, put out from the Tagus; this time with no more than six sail.[4]   With these he made for the Straits, and entering the Mediterranean

---

[1] Thus in a letter of July 13 from the Council of State to the generals at sea (*Thurloe*, i. 156) we find : " The time of year wastes apace in which you can there ride without danger."   On Aug. 14 (*ib*. i. 157), after ordering that certain ships shall be detached on special service, ' we conceive it convenient to send home the rest.'   On Aug. 16 (*ib*. i. 158) they wrote that they have sent money to Cadiz to be paid to them or to their order ' at any time when you shall call for the same between the beginning of October next and the end of December.'

[2] Blake to the Council of State, Oct. 14, *Hist. MSS. Com*. Rep. xiii. App. i. 536.

[3] " I beg to inform your Lordship," said Nelson to the Lord Mayor, " that the port of Toulon has never been blockaded by me ; quite the reverse ; every opportunity has been offered the enemy to put to sea, for it is there we hope to realise the hopes and expectations of our country."

[4] The date and number of the ships are given in Stokes's Narrative, *Clarendon MSS*. ii. No. 436.   Stokes was an officer on board one of Rupert's ships, and his statement must be accepted as conclusive against the date of Sept. 29 given in the account of Rupert's voyages printed in *Warburton*, iii. 313, of which the original MS. is amongst the Fairfax Papers in the Bodleian Library.   Probably Rupert had to sell some of his ships to fit out the others.

ranged along the Spanish coast on the look-out for English merchantmen. Emboldened by the seizure of two which he met at sea, he audaciously attempted to cut out some English vessels under the guns of the Spanish forts at Estepona and Malaga. Failing in this he appeared off Velez-Malaga, where, in spite of the remonstrances of the Spanish officer in charge of the coast, he sent a fireship into the harbour and destroyed two English ships.[1] At Motril three more were captured and burnt in the teeth of armed Spaniards who had come down to the coast to protect the neutrality of their harbour.

By this time Blake was on Rupert's track. On November 2 the crew of the 'Henry,' perceiving the English Admiral's approach, broke out into mutiny and surrendered the ship. On the 3rd Blake captured the 'Roebuck.' The next day five more of Rupert's fleet were sighted, two of them being prizes taken by him since his departure from Lisbon. One of these five, the 'Black Prince,' was run ashore and burnt by her own crew. The other four took refuge under the guns of Cartagena. Blake attempting to follow them up was checked by shots from the castle, and by an announcement made by the Alcalde that the vessels of which he was in pursuit were under the protection of the King of Spain. Unlike Rupert, Blake curbed his zeal, and made no further attempt to violate the neutrality of the Spanish harbour. On the following day it blew a gale, and Rupert's four vessels were driven ashore. One became a total wreck, and the others were in little better condition.

On the 7th Blake despatched a letter to the King demanding the cables and anchors from the wrecked men-of-war, and the goods from the two prizes. Philip, indignant at Rupert's violation of his harbours, promptly granted the request. The destruction of Rupert's fleet was almost complete. Rupert and his brother Maurice,

Side notes:

and makes prizes of English merchantmen.

Nov. 2. Surrender of the 'Henry.'

Nov. 3-5. Capture or destruction of six more of Rupert's fleet.

Nov. 7. Blake writes to the King of Spain.

---

[1] This is the Spanish account. According to the narrative in *Warburton*, iii. 316, one ship here was fired by its crew before the fireship reached it.

with two ships and a prize, had indeed been separated from their consorts a few days before, and though Blake pursued them as soon as he was able to leave Cartagena, they effected their escape to Toulon. Blake having accomplished everything in his power returned to Cadiz.[1] Before long he was recalled home, Penn having been despatched with eight ships to relieve him.

Rupert escapes to Toulon.

The reception of Rupert at Toulon was but one more of the offences given by France to the English Commonwealth. At the end of October it was calculated that during the twenty-one months which had elapsed since the King's execution, and therefore in addition to the seizure of the Levant Company's vessels by ships belonging to the French navy, French privateers had made off with 5,000 tons of English shipping, 400 pieces of ordnance, and goods valued at 500,000*l.* So necessary did it appear to guard against further ravages that on October 31 an Act was passed adding 15 per cent. to the Customs, and directing that the money thus gained should be used in paying the expenses of men-of-war employed to convoy merchantmen.[2] Hitherto, though successive governments had acknowledged it to be their duty to protect trading vessels in the immediate vicinity of the English coast—a duty which they had frequently omitted to perform—they had never held themselves under any such obligation to guard commerce in the Atlantic or Mediterranean. Captain Hall was now directed to place himself at the head of a squadron destined to act as convoy to vessels engaged in the Mediterranean trade.[3]

Maritime losses by French privateers.

Oct. 31. Act for securing trade.

Dec. 11. Hall to convoy ships.

---

[1] Blake to the Governor of Cartagena, Nov. $\frac{5}{15}$; Blake to Philip IV. Nov. $\frac{7}{17}$; Philip IV. to Fernandez de Marmoleso, Nov. $\frac{14}{24}$; Saltonstall to Coytmore, Nov. 22 ; A Relation presented by Cardenas, Dec. 26 ; *Hist. MSS. Com. Rep.* xiii. App. part i. 539–548 ; Stokes's Narrative, Nov. $\frac{5}{15}$ (?), *Clarendon MSS.* ii. No. 436 ; Philip IV. to Blake, Nov. $\frac{14}{24}$, *S.P. Dom.* xi. 89 ; Blake to —— (?), Dec. 21, *The Weekly Intelligencer*, E, 621, 14.

[2] *Scobell*, ii. 143.

[3] C. of St. Order Book, *Interr.* I, 14, p. 74.

On February 13 Blake received the thanks of Parliament for his achievements.[1] He had done more than successfully

1651.
Feb. 13.
Blake
thanked by
Parliament.

blockade Lisbon or break up Rupert's piratical fleet. He had completed the revolution in naval warfare which had set in since the victory over the Armada—the revolution which substituted fleets

1650.
Change in
naval war-
fare. Blake's
merit.

entirely composed of ships permanently in the service of the State for ships most of which were the property of merchants impressed or hired for the occasion. The navy of the future which had been sketched out in the ship-money fleet of Charles I. was brought into working order in the hands of Blake. That much of his success was due to the Council of State and to the Admiralty Committee in which Vane was the leading spirit, it is impossible to deny; but it is to Blake that the credit is due of keeping in high efficiency the delicate organisation entrusted to his care. Of the miseries to which sailors were compelled to submit in the days of Charles I.[2] no trace remained. Officers and crews co-operated heartily under a chief whom they trusted, and the loyalty which resulted showed itself in the efficiency which can never be produced by mechanical means.

Though Blake was not the first English admiral to pass the Straits, his appearance was the first sign that England was

England's
Mediterra-
nean power.

about to claim influence in the Mediterranean. With no seaports of her own in that sea, her fleets could effect nothing without the support of some power in possession of harbours in which her vessels could be refitted and revictualled. It is remarkable that the power to which she had recourse was Spain, long her enemy and soon to be her enemy again. Yet, without the help of Spain, Blake could never have blockaded Lisbon or have been in case to pursue his foes to Malaga and Cartagena. When Penn entered the Mediterranean in 1651 it was to the Spanish ports, not

[1] *C.J.* vi. 534.

[2] See Mr. Oppenheim's article on the Navy of Charles I. in the *Eng. Hist. Review* for July 1893.

only in Spain itself, but in Sicily, in Naples and Sardinia, that he looked for a basis of operations. The animosity of the heroes who had fought against Spain with Drake and Raleigh appeared to have died out in the hearts of the sailors of the Commonwealth.

The fact was that the understanding with Spain was merely political, and in no way bound the nations together after existing conditions had passed away. It was doubtless in Blake's reply to a taunt of some Spaniard that Blake, when he was last at Cadiz, expressed an opinion 'that monarchy is a kind of government the world is weary of ; that it is past in England, going in France, and that it must get out of Spain with more gravity; but in ten years' time it would be determined there likewise.'[1] It is easy to understand that Philip IV. and his subjects loathed the very notion of paying court to the standard-bearers of a form of government under which such things could be said. Yet it was impossible any longer to keep at arm's length the men whose fleets dealt destruction to the marine of Spain's deadliest enemies, Portugal and France, and, on November 23,[2] not long after Blake's proceedings at Cartagena were known at Madrid, Philip had instructed his ambassador to take the long-deferred step of recognising the revolutionary Government, and Cardenas had accordingly, on December 26, presented his credentials to the Speaker.[3] Yet, in spite of the pressure of political requirements, the two nations were too discordant in manners and religion to make easy the task of the reconciler, and already a question had arisen between the Governments on which it was hard for the best-disposed negotiations to find common ground.

Ascham, who had been sent out in Blake's fleet as resident at the Spanish Court,[4] had landed near Cadiz, and on May 26 had reached Madrid. On the

Marginal notes:

Blake's language about monarchy.

Nov. 23. Philip orders Cardenas to recognise the Commonwealth.

Dec. 26. The Commonwealth recognised.

May 26. Ascham at Madrid.

---

[1] Hyde to Nicholas, $\frac{\text{Jan. 30}}{\text{Feb. 9}}$, *Clar. St. P.* iii. 27.

[2] *I.e.* $\frac{\text{Nov. 23}}{\text{Dec. 3}}$, Cardenas to Philip IV., Jan. $\frac{14}{24}$, *Simancas MSS.* 2,527.

[3] *C.J.* vi. 515.   [4] See p. 181.

following day six young English Cavaliers, who had resolved to
deal with him as Montrose's Scottish followers had dealt with
Dorislaus, entered the inn room in which he was
dining. Taking advantage of the low bow with which
Ascham returned their salute, one of the conspirators,
a Monmouthshire gentleman, Captain Gwilliams, seized him
by the hair and stabbed him to death. The others fell upon
a renegade Genoese friar, who acted as interpreter to the
embassy, and slew him also. Of the six, one succeeded in
effecting his escape. The other five sought refuge in the house
of the Venetian Ambassador. Being refused admission, they
fled into a neighbouring church, from which they were taken
by the Spanish authorities and lodged in prison. The King
and his Ministers expressed their eagerness to bring the
assassins to justice, but the Church, on the other hand, laid
claim to them as having been dragged from a consecrated
building, and nowhere was it harder to resist a claim made by
the Church than it was in Spain. In the meanwhile Ascham's
corpse was buried upright in a hole dug behind the inn in
which he had been killed.[1]

At Westminster the news roused bitter indignation. It
was resolved to make reprisals on the Royalists in
the hands of Parliament, and on July 9 an Act was
passed authorising the new High Court of Justice to
proceed against six persons, one of whom was the
poet Davenant.[2] The Government of the Commonwealth, however, was not bloodthirsty, and contented
itself with keeping them as hostages for the safety
of Ministers of the State on the Continent.

As month after month passed away without justice being

Marginal notes:
May 27.
Murder of
Ascham.

June 20.
Effect of
the murder
at West-
minster.

July 9.
Six Royal-
ists to be
tried in
retaliation.

---

[1] Fisher to the Council of State, $\frac{\text{May 30}}{\text{June 9}}$; A Relation of what hath been
done, &c., *Thurloe*, i. 148, 149 ; Cottington and Hyde to Long, $\frac{\text{May 28}}{\text{June 7}}$,
Lister's *Life of Clarendon*, iii. 56. Where there is any discrepancy be-
tween the narratives, I have followed Fisher, who derived his information
from Griffin, Ascham's servant, the only surviving witness of the murder
except the murderers themselves.

[2] Act for the trial of Sir John Stowell and others, E, 1,061, No. 5.

done at Madrid, Parliament grew impatient. On January 22, less than a month after the Commonwealth had been recognised by Spain, Philip was informed in a letter turned into Latin and perhaps actually drawn up by Milton, that, however much the English Government might desire to cultivate his friendship, it must insist on prompt justice upon Ascham's murderers.[1]

1651.
Jan. 22.
A demand
for justice.

Philip was indeed in a dilemma. Reasons of State had induced him to hold out a hand to a regicide republic, the principles of which were detested alike by his subjects and by himself.[2] Yet, how could he rescue from the hold of the Church criminals who had taken sanctuary? In one way only could he intimate his desire to remain on friendly terms with the Commonwealth. He directed representations to be made to Cottington and Hyde that their presence at his Court was no longer desirable. Their reply was that it was impossible for them to travel without money, and that they must therefore insist upon receiving the present customarily made to ambassadors at their departure. In the end, after some haggling, the King presented them with the equivalent of 500*l.* in cash, and bills of exchange for 2,000*l.* payable at Antwerp. Cottington, who had been re-admitted into the Roman communion, was allowed to remain at Valladolid, where he died in the course of the following year.[3] Hyde, who earlier in the year had been baffled in an attempt to witness an *auto de fé*, had now to leave without an opportunity of adding so edifying a spectacle to his memories of travel.[4]

Philip's
dilemma.

Cottington
and Hyde
requested to
leave
Madrid.

Feb. 24.
March 6.
Their
departure.

[1] The Parliament to Philip IV., Jan. 22, *Hist. MSS. Com.* Rep. xiii. App. part i. 554 ; Milton's *Prose Works* (ed. Symmons), v. 396.

[2] See Fisher's letters in *Thurloe*, i. 152–181.

[3] *Clarendon*, xiii. 25–29; Hyde's Report, July $\frac{3}{13}$; *Clarendon MSS.* ii. No. 540.

[4] " The same day my Lord Hyde should have been at Toledo to have seen the *Auto* there of the Inquisition ; but being thought of too late, and the accommodations there too scarce, the journey was put off, to my great

Unluckily for Philip, the dismissal of Charles's ambassadors gave no satisfaction to the English Parliament. Fisher, who acted as its agent in Spain after Ascham's death, was recalled on the pretext of being needed to give an account to his employers of the progress of his negotiation about the punishment of the murderers.[1] On July 2 he left Madrid on his homeward journey.[2] Some time before he had expressed an opinion that Philip cared for neither of the English parties. He would 'govern himself according to the successes that the Parliament have this year in Scotland.'[3] Cromwell and Blake, it seems, had taught the King that it was worth while to be on friendly terms with the Commonwealth ; but if Cromwell failed to follow up his victory at Dunbar, the Spanish Ministers would think it worth while to be on friendly terms with Charles. In the meanwhile nothing serious was done to convince Parliament of the intention of the Spanish Government to proceed to extremities against the murderers. In the end, indeed, the

June 9.
Fisher recalled.

July $\frac{2}{12}$.
He leaves Madrid.

regret ; for there had been no *Auto* before since the year 1634, and then it was kept here at Madrid, so that there was now seventy persons in that delinquency for Jews, witches, and heretics, of which number only one was burnt, and he was a Calabrese, a poor mechanic fellow that gained a livelihood by tagging of points, and was rather mad than otherwise infected, and in that frenzy denied the immortality of the soul, and because he did in no degree recant (for the custom is that if they express any penitence for their heresy before the instant of death, they shall have the favour to be strangled first and then cast into the fire) the cords with which he was tied yielding presently to the flame, he leapt out several times, insomuch that some of the spectators ran him through with their swords, so that he died *à stocadas*." Edgeman's Diary, Jan. 1, 1651, *Clarendon MSS.* The writer goes on to say that some have been 'reserved for a general *Auto de fé* which is to be held at Madrid in May next for the entertainment of the Queen, who, it seems, desires to see the fashion of it ; and to make the sport the better, they have kept a priest and some other great delinquents who are sure to be burnt.' The 'tagging of points' was also Bunyan's occupation in prison.

[1] C. of St. Order Book, *Interr.* I, 20, p. 48.

[2] Fisher to the C. of St., Aug. 6, *S. P. Dom.* xvi. 20.

[3] *Id.* May $\frac{5}{15}$, *Thurloe,* i. 181.

Spaniards allowed one of the number, Sparks, who was a Protestant, to be hanged. The other four being Catholics were restored to sanctuary, from which they all ultimately succeeded in effecting their escape.

If the Commonwealth stood on its rights with Spain, it was not likely to deal leniently with Portugal. On April 10 Gui-

April 10.
A Portuguese ambassador learns the extent of the English demands.

maraes, who had been sent to England by John IV. to obtain, if possible, restitution of the ships and goods captured by Blake, was confronted with the demands of Parliament. He was informed that if his master wished to have peace with England he must set at liberty his English prisoners, restore all ships, money, and goods seized by him, and also do justice on those who had murdered Englishmen, and on those who had contrived the explosive machine for the destruction of the 'Leopard.' Besides all this, he must pay 180,000*l*. towards the expenses of the fleet sent against Rupert, as well as the value of all English prizes sold in Portugal, though, on the other hand, the value of the Portuguese prizes taken by the English would be

May 16.
The ambassador dismissed.

allowed as a set-off to these demands.[1] The answer given by Guimaraes being held to be unsatisfactory, he was, on May 16, ordered to leave the country within fourteen days.[2]

The military and naval strength of the Republic, together with the possibility of its alliance with Spain could not fail to

1650.
Oct. 28.
A despatch from Croullé.

produce an effect upon French politicians. On October 28, when the victory at Dunbar had had time to produce an impression, Croullé, who still remained in England as an unrecognised agent, warned Mazarin that the time was come to enter into relations with the Commonwealth. To the virtues of those who governed in its name he bore ample testimony. " Not only are they powerful," he wrote on Nov. 14, " by sea and land, but they live without ostentation, without pomp, without emulation of one another. They are economical in their private expenses, and prodigal in their devotion to public affairs, for which each one toils as if for his private interests. They handle large sums of money, which they administer honestly, observing a severe discipline. They reward well, and punish severely." Croullé's evidence is the more trustworthy, as he was in some sort an unwilling witness. He was aware, he continued, that the men whose virtues he had been describing were aiming at the destruction of all monarchies, and that it was for the interest of all princes to root them out as criminals. In England, he added, a war with France was regarded as unavoidable, and men were betting that an English army would be fighting in France before the end of the spring. Would it not be worth while, in order to avoid such a danger, at least temporarily to condone the wicked deeds of these republicans?

Croullé's subsequent despatches were still more alarming. He had been assured on good authority, he wrote, that a close alliance with Spain was being discussed, that it was probable that Philip would invite an English army to land in Flanders, that the combined forces were to proceed to besiege Dunkirk, and that that fortress when it had been captured would be made over to the English Government.[1]

Nov.
A projected attack on France.

Whether this tale were true or not—and it is probable that it had at least some foundation of truth—Mazarin, who could hardly make head against his own domestic antagonists, and who could not make head at all against the arms of Spain, had every reason to avoid war with the Commonwealth beyond the Channel. As both he and the Queen Mother shrank from entering into open relations with the regicides, he directed or permitted the Viscount Salomon de Virelade to propose to visit England as a private personage, in order to urge on behalf of the French merchants that it was desirable to put an end to the

Mazarin's advances.

Mission of Salomon de Virelade.

---

[1] Croullé to Mazarin, $\frac{Oct. 28}{Nov. 7}$, Nov. $\frac{4}{14}$, $\frac{18}{28}$, *ib.* lix. foll. 470, 478, 485. The belief in the project of a joint attack on Dunkirk can be traced to an earlier date. It is to be found in a letter written by the Prince of Orange on Feb. $\frac{14}{24}$, 1650. Groen van Prinsterer, *Arch. de la Maison d'Orange-Nassau*, Sér. II. tom. iv. 352.

mutually destructive war upon commerce. The Council of State refused even to answer his demand for a passport, and ordered Secretary Frost to reply in his own name that they would never treat except with a public Minister.[1] On December 25 they followed up this announcement by ordering Croullé, who had been detected in allowing Mass to be said in his house, to leave the country in ten days.[2]

Dec. 11.
A passport
refused to
him.

Dec. 25.
Croullé
dismissed.

In February, when it was known in France that Spain had recognised the Commonwealth, Mazarin resolved to take a further step in advance. A new agent, Gentillot, was now authorised to proceed to England, where he was to assure the Council of State that the French Government would recognise the Commonwealth as soon as a scheme for the restoration of commercial peace had been accepted.[3] Gentillot reached England, but had no better success than Salomon. On March 14 he was summoned before a Committee of the Council of State and ordered to leave London within three days, and the territory of the Commonwealth at the next opportunity. Recognition must precede any attempt at negotiation.[4]

1651.
Feb.
Mission of
Gentillot.

March 14.
Gentillot
dismissed.

The English Government could the better leave France out of account, as the authority of Mazarin and the Queen Mother had for the time crumbled away. In France every conflict ultimately resolved itself into a struggle between the Crown and the nobility, and by the beginning of 1651 the question at issue was no longer whether a law court should assume the constitutional functions of an English Parliament, but whether the nobility with Condé at its head should break loose from the fetters imposed on it by Richelieu. On January 27, Mazarin was driven from Paris. On February 3, Condé, who

The posi-
tion in
France.

Jan. 27.
Feb. 6.
Mazarin
driven
from Paris.

[1] Guizot, *Hist. de la Rép. d'Angleterre*, App. **xiv.**

[2] C. of St. Order Book, *Interr.* I, 15, p. 49.

[3] Instructions to Gentillot, *Guizot*, App. xvii.

[4] C. of St. Order Book, *Interr.* I, 65, p. 100; Gentillot to Servien, March $\frac{16}{26}$, *Arch. des Aff. Étrangères*, lx. fol. 414.

had been Mazarin's prisoner for more than a year, regained his

Feb. $\frac{3}{13}$.
Condé at
liberty. liberty. It was unlikely that either party would have leisure to resent the dismissal from England of the agents of the French Government.

In the meanwhile French commerce continued to suffer. In the Mediterranean Penn's fleet [1] snapped up what French

Penn's fleet
in the Medi-
terranean. prizes it could come by, and carried off French goods laden in neutral vessels. As far as the main object of his voyage was concerned—the destruction of Rupert's remaining force—Penn accomplished nothing. Misled by a report that Rupert had gone eastward to the Levant, Penn cruised up and down between Sicily and the African coast, seeking for intelligence and finding none. Even when as late in the year as the early part of September he was convinced that Rupert had passed out into the Atlantic, he considered that he was doing enough by waiting in the Straits of Gibraltar to intercept him on his return. [2]

The report that Rupert had sailed for the Levant had been spread by himself in order to deceive Penn. In point of fact,

Rupert
in the
Atlantic. he made with five ships [3] for the Atlantic. His own purpose was to establish himself in the West Indies, and from that vantage ground to set the Commonwealth at defiance. He had to learn that his crews looked to immediate gain and not to distant political aims. They in-

He is de-
tained at
the Azores. sisted on his tarrying by the Azores, the old cruising ground of the Elizabethan heroes. English ships bound from the East Indies, Spanish ships bound from America, would alike be good prize to them. Rupert had chosen to be virtually a captain of pirates, and by the laws of piracy he found himself strictly bound. [4]

Rupert's eagerness to carry his crews to the further side of

---

[1] See p. 306.

[2] Penn's Journal, in Granville Penn's *Memorials of Sir W. Penn*, i. 317.

[3] The three he and Maurice brought with them, one he bought, and another whose captain volunteered to join him.

[4] *Warburton*, iii. 318.

the Atlantic requires little explanation. Virginia, Bermuda, and the West Indian colonies, of which the principal were Barbados and Antigua, had shown Royalist inclinations, and Charles before leaving Breda in 1650 had despatched a commission to Sir William Berkeley, the Governor of Virginia, to continue to act in his name. As far as the West Indies were concerned there could be no doubt in whose hand Charles should place authority so far as his own powers extended. The proprietor of the Caribbean Islands, as they were then styled, was the Earl of Carlisle, and in 1647 Carlisle had leased his rights to Lord Willoughby of Parham. Early in 1650 Willoughby set sail for his new province fortified with commissions from Carlisle and from the King himself.

1650. Royalism of Virginia, Bermuda, and Barbados.

Willoughby sails for the West Indies.

Willoughby made straight for Barbados. The condition of that island was somewhat peculiar. Lying apart from the main chain of the Windward Islands, it took no concern in the spread of colonisation amongst them. Of late years it had developed a great sugar industry kept on foot by the labours of negro slaves and of Christian 'servants,' of which latter class the Scottish prisoners, sent out after the Preston campaign, formed no inconsiderable part. By the custom of the colony the term of service of these 'servants' was limited to five years, and their treatment, therefore, except when they found an unusually kind master, was far harsher than that of the slaves in the maintenance of whose health the owner had a permanent interest.

State of Barbados.

Slaves and 'servants.'

As for the masters themselves, they long lived in harmony in spite of the distracting influence of the English Civil War. For some time anyone calling another either Cavalier or Roundhead was bound to give a dinner of pork and turkey to all within hearing when the offence was committed. Of late, however, this happy agreement had been brought to an end. Young English Royalists, smarting from defeat and sequestration, had flocked to the island, where, headed by two Devonshire brothers named Walrond, they made themselves masters of the colony by a combination of

Cavalier and Roundhead in Barbados.

force and intrigue. The Governor and Assembly were reduced
to do their bidding, and when, on April 29, 1650, Lord
Willoughby put into Carlisle Bay, he found a strong

Willoughby's arrival.

Act against holding conventicles passed, and every
preparation made not only to proclaim Charles II.

Violent proceedings.

but to banish the Roundheads, amongst whom were
some of the wealthiest proprietors in the island. So
determined was the dominant party to carry out its design, that it
insisted on Willoughby's absenting himself for three months on
the transparent pretext of visiting Antigua. Scarcely had he
left the harbour when an Act was passed banishing ninety-
seven persons from the island, some of the number being also
heavily fined as partakers in an imaginary conspiracy. When
Willoughby returned, though he could do nothing as far as the
banished men were concerned, he ousted the Walronds from
authority, and putting the island in a state of defence threw
himself mainly on the support of the moderate Royalists who
had viewed the late violent proceedings with dissatisfaction.[1]

Some of the banished men made their way to England,
where they filled the ears of members of Parliament with their
outcries. The victory of Dunbar had now inspired the statesmen of the Commonwealth with fresh confidence, and on

*Oct. 3.
Act prohibiting trade with Royalist colonies.*

October 3 an Act was passed prohibiting trade with
the Royalist colonies, Virginia, Bermuda, Barbados,
and Antigua. At the same time Parliament gave
instructions to prepare a fleet of seven ships to sail

*1651.
Jan. 22.
Ayscue's fleet to go to Barbados;*

under Ayscue for the reduction of Barbados,[2] and
before the end of January it was reported as ready
for sea.[3] On February 1 Ayscue was directed to
proceed at once upon his mission.[4] The Common-

*Feb. 1.
his instructions;*

wealth had resolved to grasp the whole of the
inheritance of the Stuart kings, and to rule it far
more vigorously than they had ever done.

[1] The whole story is given in full in Mr. Darnell Davis's *Cavaliers and Roundheads in Barbados.*

[2] *C.J.* vi. 478.   [3] *Ib.* vi. 526.

[4] Instructions to Ayscue, C. of St. Order Book, *Interr.* I, 45, p. 21.

Many months were, however, to pass away before Ayscue was able to set sail. Wide as was the sweep of Commonwealth

his sailing
delayed. politics there were dangers nearer home than those arising beyond the Atlantic, and those dangers were likely to be accentuated by any risk of a misunderstanding with the Dutch Republic, hitherto beyond compare the greatest naval power of the time. Whilst Charles was at Breda, indeed,

1650.
England
and the
Dutch
Republic. the hostility of the Prince of Orange to the new Commonwealth had become notorious, but it had been counterbalanced by the evident disinclination of the merchant princes of Holland to expose their commercial marine to the depredations of English cruisers. In May 1650, as the States General under Orange influence persisted in their refusal to enter into diplomatic relations

May.
Schaef's
mission. with the Commonwealth, the Provincial States of Holland despatched an agent—Schaef—to negotiate at Westminster on matters of commerce.[1]

Such independent action on the part of the Provincial States could not but exacerbate the irritation already prevailing

The Prince
of Orange
and the
States of
Holland between them and the energetic and ambitious William II., whose authority had already been gravely diminished by the peace with Spain. It was by heading the national defence that his family had risen to power, and it was unlikely that, when the national defence ceased to be the main object of consideration, he would be able to maintain the high position which he had inherited. The Provincial States of Holland had, not unnatu-

The reduc-
tion of the
army. rally, clamoured for the reduction of the army in time of peace. William II., whose dream it was to renew the heroic achievements of his predecessors against Spain, looked on with dissatisfaction whilst regiment after regiment was disbanded by the States General. In the spring of 1650 an army which in time of war had counted 60,000 men was reduced to 29,000.

---

[1] His arrival was noticed in the Council of State on May 20, C. of St. Order Book, *Interr.* I, 64, p. 387.

The States of Holland held even this reduction to be insufficient. On March 30 they resolved to disband part of

March 30
April 9.
Holland
resolves to
disband
part of its
contingent.
their own contingent without waiting for permission from the States General. William II. had thus the excuse—probably in his eyes it was no mere excuse —of regarding the States of Holland as aiming at the disruption of the Union. Supported by a majority of the States General, he had recourse to violence.

July 20/30.
Seizure of
the leaders
of the
States of
Holland.
The Prince
fails to sur-
prise Am-
sterdam.
On July 20 he invited six leading members of the States of Holland to a conference at the Hague, arrested them in his own ante-chamber and threw them into prison in the Castle of Loevesteen. Though baffled in an attempt to make himself master of the great city of Amsterdam, William II. did not despair of attaining his object. The army was on his side, and he calculated on wearing out the resistance of his opponents before the summer came to an end.[1]

All this while the Prince's relations with Mazarin were most intimate. He even offered to mediate between France and Spain, hoping, in the very probable event of the refusal of Spain to repose so great a trust in a notorious enemy, to induce the States General to renew the war against Spain in alliance with France, and if possible to replace thereby his brother-in-law Charles on the throne of Great Britain. Visions of dynastic greatness filled his mind.[2] If he had lived and prospered, a

[1] Wijnne, *De Geschillen over de Afdanking van 't Krijgsvolk*. See also Lefèvre-Portalis, *Jean de Witt*, ch. i.

[2] In *Lettres, memoires et negociations de M. le Comte d'Estrades*, i. 101, is printed a draft treaty between the Prince of Orange and D'Estrades, agreeing that there shall be an alliance with France for a joint attack on the Spanish Netherlands, &c. The treaty is so manifest a forgery that I can only express my surprise that many historians of repute have accepted it as genuine. Such a sentence as this for instance, " Que le Roi et M. le Prince d'Orange rompront en même temps le 1 Mai 1651 avec Cromwell," could only have proceeded from some one who forgot that Cromwell was not the ruler of England in 1651. In the following letter, moreover, D'Estrades is supposed to write twice of Cromwell as Protector in 1652. The treaty besides is said to be dated at the Hague on October 10/20, 1650.

warlike alliance between England and Spain would have been inevitable. No wonder that in the summer of 1650 Blake's ships were hospitably received at Vigo and Cadiz.

These ambitious designs were destined never to be fulfilled. On October 27 the Prince of Orange, possessed of all the

Oct. 27
Nov. 6
Death of
the Prince
of Orange.

qualities to make or mar a great career, fell a victim to the ravages of the small-pox, that terrible disease which in those days filled so many houses with mourning. Eight days after his death his widow, the daughter and sister of kings, brought into the world a sickly

Nov. $\frac{4}{14}$.
Birth of a
posthumous
son.

infant who was one day to raise still higher the glories of his race, to restore the fallen Stadtholderate, and to encircle his head with the triple crown of the British Isles.

The effect of the death of William II. was to produce a sweeping revolution in the political character of the Union.

Effect of
the death of
William II.

The army, which had recently counted for so much, found itself without a head. Count William Frederick, descended from a brother of William the Silent, held, it is true, the Stadtholdership of two provinces, Friesland and Groningen, but he was not inclined to support the claims of the new-born infant to the succession in the other five, whilst as a chief adviser of William II. in his unconstitutional proceedings, he was not likely to be permitted to gain possession of the vacant office in his own person. The States of Holland lost no time in claiming for themselves all the powers which had hitherto been exercised by the Stadtholder, and nearly all the powers which had been exercised by the States

1651.
Jan. $\frac{8}{18}$.
Meeting of
a Grand
Assembly
at the
Hague.

General. The deputies of the remaining provinces meeting on January 8 at a Grand Assembly had no choice but to follow suit as far as the confederation was concerned. The tie which united them, loose enough before, was now made looser still. Each province was master, not only of the administration of justice

We know, however, from a despatch of Brasset's dated October $\frac{9}{19}$ (*Groen van Prinsterer*, Série II. tom. iv. 422) that the Prince had left the Hague a few days before on the excursion from which he never returned.

within its frontiers but, what was of far more importance, of its own contingent to the common army. The powers of the States General were, for external purposes, reduced to a shadow.

Disintegration of the Dutch Republic.
Not only was no new Stadtholder named for any one of the five provinces, but no Captain-General nor Admiral-General was appointed to command the armies and fleets of the Republic. Such disintegration, impossible in time of war, could only be projected in time of peace.

Ascendency of Holland.
Yet even in time of peace some practical corrective of so centrifugal a system was certain to be found, and that corrective was ultimately found in the ascendency of the wealthy and powerful province of Holland.

Nowhere, except in Spain, was the news of the death of William II. more heartily welcomed than at Westminster. For

1650. The news of the death of the Prince welcome at Westminster.
some time there had been little doubt that if he succeeded in his enterprise his energies would be directed against the English Commonwealth. On June 21, Strickland, finding the refusal of the States General to admit him to an audience unalterable, had been definitely recalled. On September 26, the Council of State ordered Joachimi, the ambassador of the Netherlands, to quit the country.[1]

The revolution which took place in the Netherlands upon the death of the Prince of Orange kindled new hopes at West-

Hopes raised in England by the Revolution in the Netherlands.
minster. Why, it was thought, should not the two Protestant and commercial Republics ally themselves against all other States? Why, too, should not this alliance be so managed as to secure the assistance of the Netherlands in the dangerous times through which England was now passing? Why even—the thought, impracticable as it was, appears to have passed through the minds of some at least of the Council of State— might not some form of political union be achieved strong enough to render permanent what might otherwise prove but a transitory bond?

[1] C. of St. Order Book, *Interr.* I, 64, p. 471. C. of St. to Joachimi, Sept. 26, *Add. MSS.* 17,677, T, fol. 518.

With these ideas in the minds of the leading statesmen, Parliament on February 1 instructed Chief Justice St. John and Strickland to negotiate a close alliance with the Grand Assembly of the States General, then in session at the Hague. They were to do all in their power to bring about the closest possible alliance, whilst as far as existing evidence reaches, the wild scheme of political union was only to be proposed in the event of satisfactory assurances being given on the more practical demands. At all events it was never actually proposed, and its details are entirely unknown at the present day.[1]

1651.
Feb. 14.
St. John and Strickland to go to the Hague.

Their instructions.

The negotiation thus opened with the States General was

---

[1] The instructions printed in *Hist. MSS. Com.* Rep. xiii. App. i. 557, are insignificant, and the Private Instructions have not been preserved. My account of the aims of Parliament is derived from the known proceedings of the ambassadors. The relation between the intended proposal and those actually made appears from St. John's speech in taking leave, where he says that if he had had opportunity he would have propounded ' matters tending to a nearer union which the Parliament had thereupon commanded us to do' (Ambassadors' Narrative, *S.P. Holland*), and partly from a paragraph in the additional instructions given on May 3 (C. of St. Order Book, *Interr.* I, 19, p. 95). " And for that this said paper . . . intimates a more strict union than formerly, and yet restrains it as we conceive, to the matter of that and other former treaties as by mutual consent they shall be settled, corrected, amplified, you are to demand of them whether besides the confederacy perpetual therein proposed to be agreed upon with the corrections and amplifications mentioned, they do not intend a further and more intrinsical union, which, if they do declare they do intend, and shall also have consented unto the matter of the six first articles in the second of these instructions mentioned ; you shall then declare unto them the nature of that more intrinsical union mentioned in your instructions from Parliament and contained in the sixth article of your private instructions from the Council of the 28th of February, 165$\frac{0}{1}$." That this last proposal was for a political union is shown not only by the use of such words as 'coalescence' in its description by contemporaries, but by the fact that the clause thus referring to it in the instructions of May 3 is preceded by a clause offering to waive in favour of the Dutch the prohibition against aliens holding real property in England. Nothing but a political union can have gone beyond this.

the first serious diplomatic business undertaken by the founders of the Commonwealth. Unfortunately their very conception
of the relations which ought to prevail between the two States showed their unfitness to direct a delicate negotiation in which firmness and patriotic zeal would avail them little unless it were safeguarded by that most dearly acquired of all knowledge, the knowledge of the interests, the feelings, the very prejudices of those with whom they had to deal. What they sought was to utilise the power and vigour of the Dutch Republic to assist them out of the dangers in which they were involved, and this purpose they veiled, probably from themselves, in vague desires for confederation and intimate union between the States. If, as a Dutchman observed, they had acted in the spirit of the English saying, " Love me little, love me long," [1] and had contented themselves with demanding what might readily have been granted by a high-spirited nation proud of its long years of struggle against alien tyranny, this abortive attempt might have led to a good understanding between the two peoples which it would not have been easy to interrupt.

Nor was there anything in the character of the ambassadors selected to counterbalance the defects of their principals. St.
John, on whom the burden of the negotiation fell, was an able political lawyer who had never shown a symptom of interest in foreign affairs, whilst Strickland, whose superior knowledge should have stood him in good stead, had been irritated by the persistent hostility of those very States General with which he was now about to treat, and could hardly fail to remember that for many a long month they had closed their doors against him.

Pomp and ceremony at least was at the command of the new ambassadors, and when on March 17 they passed through
the streets of the Hague, their suite consisted of no less than 246 persons. The town swarmed with English Royalists, many of them in a state of desti-

---

[1] Aitzema, *Saken van Staet en Oorlog*, iii. 658.

tution, and the representatives of the victorious party were greeted, in their own tongue, with shouts of 'King-murderers, Cromwell's bastards, English hangmen, Fairfaxes,' and the like. It was found impossible to accommodate so vast a retinue in the house usually provided for ambassadors, and most of their attendants had to seek lodgings elsewhere. Many of these, fearing the worst, slept in their clothes, and on the following day none of them ventured abroad except in large parties, carrying their swords in their hands.[1]

Their reception by the English Royalists.

A proclamation issued by the States of Holland quelled the disturbances for a time. A few days later there were fresh complaints. Prince Edward, Rupert's younger brother, called the ambassadors 'Rogues' to their faces. James Apsley, Lucy Hutchinson's Royalist brother, sought an interview with St. John, with the intention of assassinating him, as there is every reason to believe. A mob of Englishmen beset the ambassadors' lodging, threatened or ill-treated their servants, and broke their windows. The Provincial States appear to have done their best to punish the offenders, but both Prince Edward and Apsley got away unpunished, and the ambassadors complained that the penalties inflicted on others were by no means commensurate with their offences.[2]

March 19. Quiet restored.

Fresh attacks on the ambassadors.

The truth probably was that the States of Holland had not to deal with the English exiles alone. They had attained authority less by their own inherent strength than by the coincidence of a time of peace with the infancy of the Prince of Orange. The Orange party had always been the popular party even in Holland, and the populace of the Hague, unable to throw off the yoke of the oligarchy by which they were governed, took pleasure in abet-

Position of the States of Holland,

---

[1] *Aitzema,* iii. 638 ; *Joyful News from Holland,* E, 626, 18 ; The Ambassadors to Lenthall, March $\frac{20}{30}$; Grey's *Impartial Examination,* iv. App. li.

[2] *Aitzema,* iii. 657, 659 ; *Merc. Pol.* E, 626, 22 ; *The Faithful Scout,* E, 785, 10.

ting the violence of the English Royalists who had been under the protection of the House of Orange.

It was not, however, with the States of Holland that the ambassardors would have to negotiate. The States General,

and of the States General. weakened as they were by the abeyance of the Stadtholderate, still directed the foreign affairs of the Republic. They accordingly appointed Commis-

March 25. Opening of the nego-tiation. sioners to treat, to whom, on March 25, St. John and Strickland expressed, in vague and guarded language their desire for a more intimate alliance than had

hitherto existed, though they refused to state their terms definitely till this general offer had been accepted. As might be expected, the States General hung back from adopting so elastic a proposal. They were afraid, as well they might be, of being dragged into the war in Ireland and Scotland. There was much consultation with the provinces, and the ambassadors set down to wilful design a delay in reality incidental to the defects of the Dutch constitution.

Whilst the ambassadors were impatiently waiting for an answer, news arrived at the Hague which must have convinced

March. Tromp off the Scilly Isles. the Dutch negotiators that a complete rejection of the English overtures might possibly be attended with danger to themselves. The piracies of Sir John

Grenvile's cruisers sent forth from the Scilly Isles had been carried on irrespective of the nationality of the prizes, and the Dutch Government, smarting under losses to its commerce, had despatched Tromp with a fleet to claim redress. Failing to obtain justice from Grenvile, Tromp declared war against him.[1] Whether the Council of State was at this time aware of the bargain discussed in the previous year for a mortgage of the Scillies by Charles to the city of Amsterdam[2] we have no means of knowing, but even if they were in complete ignorance

April 1. Blake sent against the islands. of this, the prospect of seeing the Scillies in Dutch hands was sufficiently alarming. On April 1, the Council simultaneously ordered its ambassadors to

---

[1] *Whitelocke,* 491.   [2] See p. 200.

remonstrate at the Hague, and directed Blake to prepare for an attack on the islands,[1] borrowing for the purpose Ayscue's fleet destined for Barbados. In consequence of the remonstrance the States General promised to abstain from all interference. Blake lost no time in fulfilling his appointed task, and on May 23 Grenvile, on promise of freedom of retreat for himself and the garrison, engaged to surrender the islands. The commerce of all nations would profit by the change.[2]

May 23.
Grenvile's
surrender.

It is possible that the remonstrance of the ambassadors quickened the proceedings of the Dutch Commissioners. At all events, on April 17 they replied to the English demands made on March 25,[3] that the States General were prepared to enter into 'a nearer and more intimate alliance and union.' The ambassadors replied by asking 'that the two Commonwealths may be confidential friends, joined and allied together for the defence and preservation of the liberty and freedoms of the people of each against all whomsoever that shall attempt the disturbance of either State by sea or land, or be declared enemies to the freedom and liberty of the people living under either of the said governments.'[4] The Dutch negotiators, knowing as they did that there was far more likelihood that England would require their help against Charles than that they would require the help of England against the infant Prince, hung back from accepting the proposal.

April 17.
Reply of
the Dutch.

Demand of
the ambas-
sadors.

It is therefore the more surprising that, on April 22, the Dutch Commissioners produced, as a basis of negotiation, the

----

[1] Instructions to Blake, April 1, *Interr.* I, 96, pp. 95, 96.

[2] Remonstrance of the Ambassadors, *Thurloe*, i. 177 ; C. of St. to Blake, April 17, *Int.* I, 96, p. 130 ; Articles of surrender, May 23, *S.P. Dom.* xv. 80.   [3] See p. 325.

[4] Ambassadors' Narrative, *S.P. Holland.* Mr. Geddes, in his *Hist. of the Administration of John de Witt*, has anticipated me in most of my inquiries into this embassy. He does not seem, however, to have examined the *Intercursus Magnus.*

Intercursus Magnus, the treaty which had bound together Henry VII. and the Archduke Philip in 1495, the year in which Henry had reason to anticipate the landing of Perkin Warbeck on the English coast. That treaty, after guaranteeing the freest commercial intercourse between England and the Netherlands, stipulated not only that neither of the contracting parties should give aid to the enemies of the other, but also that each should lend military aid to suppress them at the expense of its ally; and that neither should receive or support rebels or fugitives of the other, but that each should expel them if they had already found a refuge on its soil.

April 22.
The *Intercursus Magnus* produced.

St. John, it seems, had thus obtained an offer of everything he could reasonably desire. He had, however, now no mind to treat at all. Irritated by the indignities to which the embassy had been exposed, and perhaps aiming at that visionary union which he now knew to be far beyond his reach, he had obtained from Parliament an order of recall, and he therefore informed the astonished Commissioners that the negotiation was at an end. It was only at the urgent entreaty of the Dutch that the ambassadors consented to despatch their secretary, Thurloe, to England to ask for a prolongation of their powers, and on his return they were able to announce that the negotiation was to continue for forty days.[1]

The ambassadors announce their recall.

The negotiation prolonged.

It was all to no purpose. On May 10 the ambassadors delivered in a paper in which what, from their point of view, were the most important clauses of the *Intercursus Magnus*, were slightly amplified and adapted to existing circumstances.[2] It was now the turn of the Dutch Commissioners to be startled. Clauses which looked innocent enough when applied to a world in which the Archduke Philip and Perkin Warbeck were living forces, were regarded with suspicion when applied in the days of the English Common-

The English demands.

---

[1] Narrative, *S.P. Holland*. The Treaty is printed at the end of Selden's *Mare Clausum*, ed. 1636.

[2] English proposals, May 10, *Thurloe*, i. 182.

wealth. It was one thing to read about a pledge to confiscate under certain circumstances the property of the Duchess of Burgundy, the sister of Edward IV., and quite another thing to give a pledge to confiscate, under precisely similar circumstances, the property of the Princess of Orange and her infant son, the sister and nephew of Charles II., in case of her affording protection to Royalist conspirators. The States General could but refer these exacting proposals—which had virtually originated with themselves—to the Provinces for consideration.

A reference to the Provinces.

As week after week passed away without bringing a reply to his demands, St. John grew more and more convinced that the States General were but spinning out time till they learnt the event of the year's campaign in Scotland. When at last, on June 14, the reply took the shape of a counter-proposal, his suspicions were confirmed. The States General professed their readiness to consent that each Power should assist against the enemies of the other at the expense of the party benefited, and also that each should take care that no assistance was given by persons within its territory to the rebels of the other. The demand that they should banish each other's rebels, that is to say, in plain language, that the Dutch should expel the English Royalists, though it was implied in one of the clauses of the *Intercursus Magnus*, was now passed over in silence, as was the special proposal that the Princess of Orange and her son should be held answerable for proceedings of English Royalists on their estates·

St. John chafes under the delay.

June 14. The Dutch counter-proposal.

In their offers of commercial union the Dutch were far more explicit. Colonies of either nation in the West Indies and on the coast of North America were to be open to the commerce of both. The fleets of the two Republics were to co-operate against pirates. The subjects of each Government were to pay no higher taxes in the territory of the other than were paid by the natives. There was to be liberty of fishing for both, and free access to the harbours of either.[1] These

---

[1] The full propositions are given in the Ambassadors' Narrative, *S.P. Holland.* A shorter draft is in *Hist. MSS. Com.* Rep. xiii. App. i. 605.

and other propositions of somewhat similar import fairly disclose the intentions of the Dutch negotiators. Whilst the English ambassadors were set upon an assurance that the Netherlands should not again be made the basis of attacks upon the Commonwealth, the Dutch, conscious of the vastness of their commerce, were ready to offer equal terms in matters of trade, in all probability believing that—to use language which had once been applied to a political contract— the greater would draw the less, and that with a commercial marine superior in numbers and, as they fully believed, in energy, they would gain far more than they would lose by the projected bargain.

Aims of the two parties.

The English ambassadors treated this answer as a rejection of their proposals. All efforts to revive the negotiation failed, and on June 18 St. John and Strickland took their leave. In his parting speech to the States General, St. John expressed his regret that the rejection of the English terms had prevented the bringing forward of 'matters tending to a nearer union,' and politely added a hope that the negotiation might be conducted to a successful end at some future day.[1] In speaking to the Commissioners he used haughtier language, telling them that they had an eye upon the events in Scotland. "In a short time," he continued, "you will see our dispute with Scotland at an end, and you will then send envoys to ask what we have now offered you cordially ; but, believe me, you will then repent of having rejected our offers." [2]

The negotiation drops.

June 18. The ambassadors take their leave.

In after years the great Dutch statesman, John de Witt, attributed the failure of the negotiation to the activity of the Orange party, which had resisted the re-enactment of the *Intercursus Magnus*, at least till, as St. John alleged, it was known that Charles's case was desperate in Scotland.[3] Yet it is impossible to throw the blame entirely upon any Dutch party. The English ambassadors had

Causes of the failure of the negotiation.

---

[1] Narrative, *S.P. Holland.*

[2] *Histoire de la vie et de la mort des deux illustres frères, C. et J. de Witt*, i. 63.   [3] *Ibid.*

stepped on the scene in ignorance of the weight which the Orange party still possessed in the Netherlands, and in ignorance of the practicability of imposing their own will upon a neigh-bouring nation, however friendly its rulers might be. It is most unlikely that if the demands of the English Parliament had been granted permanent friendship would have been the result. There would have been widespread irritation in the Netherlands if the English Royalists had been expelled and the tradition of Dutch hospitality broken. There would have been still more widely spread irritation if hands had been laid on the Princess of Orange.

Alienation between the Republics.

For the time there was nothing to be done. The attempt to bring two peoples into over-close relationship had resulted in fostering ill-feeling between them. The evident desire of the Dutch to increase facilities of commercial intercourse led to a belief that the interest of England lay rather in diminishing them. When these views were spreading it could not pass out of sight that, however much the Dutch commercial marine might outstrip that of England, England could now, for the first time since the accession of the Stuarts to the throne, dispose of a fleet of warships as numerous, as well found, and as well commanded as those at the disposal of the Republic which had rejected the desired terms of friendship.

A quarrel averted for the present.

For the present, however, all such thoughts were rigorously repressed. It was not only at the Hague that men's eyes were fixed on Scotland. Whether the English Common-wealth were to live or die depended more upon the sword of Cromwell than upon the seaman-ship of Blake.

All eyes fixed on Scotland.

CHAPTER XIV

SCOTLAND AFTER DUNBAR

It was natural that all continental Powers having dealings with the English Commonwealth should watch anxiously the course of events in Scotland. With apt prevision Cromwell had placed his finger on one at least of the results of Dunbar. " Surely," he had written on the day after the great rout, " it's probable the Kirk has done their do. I believe their King will set up upon his own score now, wherein he will find many friends." [1] This view of the situation was not likely to escape the notice of Charles. The disaster which had befallen the extreme Covenanters cannot have caused him unqualified regret. It is even said that when the news of disaster reached him he fell on his knees and gave thanks to God ' that he was so fairly rid of his enemies.' [2] However this may have been, he decorously assured Argyle of his wish still to be guided by his counsels. Yet the extreme Covenanters refused to acknowledge defeat. Strachan and Ker—still as before the favoured champions of the Kirk—charged Leslie, who with a shattered force of 4,000 men had taken refuge at Stirling, with being the principal cause of the loss of the battle. Leslie, nettled by the accusation, threw up his command, and it was only at the urgent entreaty of the

Side notes:
General anxiety for news from Scotland.

1650. Cromwell's anticipation.

Charles's conduct on hearing of Dunbar.

Leslie attacked.

---

[1] Cromwell to Hazlerigg, Sept. 4. *Carlyle,* Letter cxli.

[2] The story was told to Cromwell by a messenger from Strachan, *Merc. Pol.* E, 613, 1. Did Charles really fall on his knees?

Committee of Estates that he consented to withdraw his resignation. It was finally resolved to find occupation for

Strachan, Ker, and Chiesley to command in the West.

Strachan and Ker by appointing them, in conjunction with Sir John Chiesley, to levy troops in the West. The three men gladly accepted the commission, hoping to lead a new Whiggamore Raid[1] to the discomfiture of the politicians who professed to stand up for the Covenant in the name of a lukewarm, if not a hostile King.[2]

The party of the extreme Covenanters was strong in the Commission of the General Assembly, having for its leading clerical champions James Guthrie, minister of Stirling, and

Sept. 12. A Short Declaration.

Patrick Gillespy, minister of the High Church at Glasgow. On September 12, the latter body issued *A Short Declaration* calling to repentance, and especially requiring Charles to mourn for his own and his father's faults, ' and to consider if he has come to the Covenant and joined himself to the Lord upon politic interests for gaining a crown to himself rather than to advance religion and righteousness.' To this Declaration was appended *Causes of*

Causes of humiliation.

a solemn public humiliation,[3] calling on the nation to humble itself for the neglect of a thorough purge of the King's household and guard, the confidence placed in a numerous army rather than on the protection of God, the bringing home malignants with the King, the worldly policy of

---

[1] *Great Civil War*, iv. 228.

[2] Walker's *Hist. Discourses*, 183.

[3] *Balfour*, iv. 98. Burton says that ' the report on the causes of the Lord's dealing at Dunbar, resembles a report on a railway accident or the explosion of a powder manufactory, explaining how it has been caused by neglect of the regulated precautions,' *Hist. of Scot.* vii. 34. He, however, misnames this paper ' *The Causes of the Lord's Wrath*,' which was a different document, prepared in 1651 and published in 1653. It is said to have ' been agreed upon by the Commission of the General Assembly, 1650.' This, however, as Mr. Paton, who has transcribed the records of that Commission for publication by *The Scottish History Society*, informs me, merely means that Guthrie and others who drew up the paper in 1651 claimed to be themselves the Commissioners appointed in 1650, though many of their colleagues held aloof from their proceedings.

some of the Commissioners at Breda, and the tendency of judges and officers to serve their own interests. There was a

Protests in Fife against the exclusion of reconciled Engagers. ring of fanatical sincerity in these complaints, but Scotland had been taught by bitter experience that she could not be saved by the party of religious exclusiveness. Even in Fife—the home of rigid Presbyterianism—ministers had been asking whether it was necessary to shut out from military service those Engagers who had given satisfaction to the Kirk.[1]

By this time Cromwell was assuming a threatening attitude. After his victory at Dunbar he had occupied Edinburgh and

Cromwell at Edinburgh. Leith without meeting with resistance, the Castle of Edinburgh alone holding out. The inhabitants who remained behind were well treated, but empty houses, whose owners had fled, were mercilessly plundered. Leaving behind him a force to block up the Castle and complete the fortifications of Leith, Cromwell marched on the 14th to assail

Sept. 14. He marches against Stirling. Leslie's shattered forces at Stirling. The weather was wild and stormy, and the roads were little suited for military operations. On the 18th Cromwell found

Sept. 18. Reaches Stirling. Leslie, now at the head of some 5,000 men, too strongly posted to be attacked with advantage, and he had nothing for it but to return to Edinburgh and

Sept. 19-21. Returns to Edinburgh. push on the siege of the Castle.[2]

In the meanwhile the divisions at Stirling were widening daily. Strachan, before departing for the

Dissensions at Stirling. West, took it upon himself to write a letter to Cromwell offering that if the English army would leave Scotland he would undertake that England should suffer no harm. The letter was intercepted, and Leslie being refused permission to punish the captain who carried it, again resigned his command. Leslie, too, necessarily looked on the question of the employment of reconciled Engagers from a military point of view, and accordingly resisted the harsh solution which would

[1] Lamont's *Diary*, 23 ; Walker's *Hist. Discourses*, 187.
[2] *The Lord General's March to Stirling*, E, 613, 16.

deprive him of the services of qualified officers. On the other hand, the watchword of the stricter party, in which the ablest politician was Johnston of Warriston, was 'No association with Engagers.' Much as these stern Presbyterians disliked an alliance with the English sectaries, it was already becoming clear in what direction they would ultimately drift. A proposal to admit moderate Engagers having been made in the Committee, Chiesley laid his hand on his sword. "I would rather," he said, "join with Cromwell than with them."[1]

At last Chiesley together with Strachan and Ker departed for their commands in the West, and Leslie, freed from their *Argyle's* opposition, once more resumed his post. In his *desperate* desire for a reconciliation with the moderate En-*policy.* gagers, Leslie was supported by Argyle, with whom he was notoriously in close personal relations. Argyle, in truth, whose position was already desperate, was clutching at any means of escape from the dilemma in which he had placed himself. Subordinating his convictions to his interests, he had tried to unite in an unholy wedlock the zealots of the Kirk with the zealots of Monarchy. Now that Cromwell had forbidden the banns, Argyle's statecraft had become foolishness. To gratify the Covenanters was to alienate Charles, and he could not gratify Charles without admitting all the Engagers, including his own rivals, Hamilton and Lauderdale. He therefore declared for the admission of moderate Engagers in the vain hope that he would still be able to exclude his personal enemies from the list of the reconciled.[2]

Charles was not yet shaken in his belief that Argyle had at least the desire to serve him. After a violent speech from *Sept. 21.* Johnston of Warriston, in which all the misfortunes *Violence* of the country were traced to the sins of the late *of John-* King's house in opposing the work of reformation, *ston of* *Warriston.* Charles turned to Argyle with brilliant promises— all that he had it in his power to bestow. He would, he said,

---

[1] Walker's *Hist. Discourses*, 187.

[2] On the state of Scottish parties, see a letter from Edinburgh of Oct. 10, in *The Weekly Intelligencer*, E, 615, 8.

make him a duke and a gentleman of his bedchamber, and as
soon as he regained his rights in England, would pay him the
40,000*l.* due to him out of the money promised to
Scotland by the English Parliament when Charles I.
was delivered up at Newcastle.[1]

Sept. 24.
Charles's
offers to
Argyle.

Charles, however, did not wholly trust Argyle. He had
recently been alarmed by a report that Strachan had formed the
design of making a dash on his quarters at Perth in
order to deliver him up to Cromwell, and he had
in consequence been anxious to secure wider support than any that Argyle was capable of giving. With this

Charles
tries to
unite all
parties.

object in view he was eager to revive that project of uniting all
reasonable parties in his defence which he had cherished before
he left Jersey on his way to Breda. Through the medium of
his physician Dr. Fraser and of two of his attendants he had
succeeded in forming a combination of Royalists and Engagers
on which he now resolved to fall back.

October 3 was fixed as the day on which Charles's new
supporters were to appear in the field to protect him against
Strachan's alleged design. On that day, under pretence of hunting, Charles was to cross the Bridge of
Earn, and to ride forward into Fife, where he would

A Royalist
rising pro-
jected.

be joined by many of the gentry, and by his own life-guard
then quartered at Kinross. In the meanwhile Perth was to be
secured by some Highlanders secretly introduced within the
walls, who were to be reinforced on the following morning by a
thousand men sent down from Athol. A centre of resistance
being thus formed, Charles's more immediate partisans were
expected to gather round him. The old Earl of Airlie and his
son Lord Ogilvy, the companions of Montrose, were ready to
rally the Royalists of Forfarshire, whilst Lord Dudhope was to
secure Dundee, of which place he was hereditary constable.
The gentry of Kincardineshire were expected to follow the Earl
Marischal, with whom was Middleton, who, having hitherto
resisted the threats and blandishments of the Kirk, was marked
out as the military chief of the enterprise. It was calculated

[1] *Appendix to Echard's History.*

that Charles, on the day after his escape, would find himself at the head of 1,500 mounted gentlemen, to say nothing of the infantry which might be levied amongst their tenants. It was also believed that when once the King's standard had been raised the greater part of Leslie's army would accept it as its own.[1]

The one thing needed for success was that Charles should keep counsel, and this was precisely what he failed to do. On

Oct. 2.
Charles
divulges
the plan
to Buck-
ingham,

the 2nd, as he was riding with Buckingham, whom he knew no reason to distrust, he thoughtlessly chatted about his plans. Buckingham made an excuse for returning to Perth and told the story to Wilmot.

and aban-
dons it.

The pair had been too much in Argyle's confidence to hope for good treatment from the Royalists if they got the upper hand, and before the evening was over they persuaded Charles to abandon his design and send off messengers to warn the conspirators against appearing in arms on the following day.[2]

There can be little doubt that one or other of the persons admitted into the secret had already given information to the

Oct. 3.
Balfour
ordered to
purge the
King's
house.

Committee of Estates at Stirling. On the morning of the 3rd Sir James Balfour received instructions drawn up a week before, but hitherto kept back, to tell Charles that his household was again to be purged.

No less than twenty-four of his attendants were to leave him within twenty-four hours, and all of these except two were to quit the kingdom within twenty days. To give effect to these instructions the King's life-guard of horse was at once to be thoroughly purged, and orders were given to Sir John Brown to employ the foot-guard, on which dependence could be placed, to enforce the dismissal of the suspected members of the household.[3]

---

[1] Walker's *Hist. Discourses*, 196.

[2] *Ib.* 197. A letter from Nash (*Charles II. and Scotland*, 148) says that Lauderdale also knew of the plan and dissuaded him from it. If so, it must have been talked of some time before, as Lauderdale was not at Perth.

[3] *Balfour*, iv. 109. There is some uncertainty about the date of the original resolution of the Committee. Balfour puts it on Sept. 27, whilst

At noon Balfour delivered his message. Charles could think of no better resource than to beg that nine at least of his followers might be spared till he could receive an answer from Stirling to a plea on their behalf. On the morning of the 4th Loudoun, to whom Charles had appealed, appeared with an announcement that the Committee of Estates refused to modify their order. By this time Charles had received from some at least of those who had engaged to rise on his behalf strong remonstrances against the abandonment of their well-concerted project. Asking Lothian, who accompanied him as secretary, whether an indemnity would be granted to the men who were prepared to support him in arms, and receiving a negative answer, Charles flung himself on his horse, and with seven or eight attendants rode off at full speed to Dudhope's house hard by Dundee.

Charles pleads for his household.

Oct. 4. His request rejected.

He rides off.

Scarcely was the King out of sight when those members of the Committee of Estates who happened to be in Perth secured the town against attack, and sent off Colonel Montgomery to follow up the runaway. At the same time they sent a message to Charles himself, urging him to return and assuring him that none of his supporters should be harmed.

Perth secured by the Committee.

The adventure was too inconsiderately undertaken to have a successful ending. The young King no doubt showed considerable physical endurance. Having covered some forty-two miles, he took refuge for the night in a cottage at Clova high up in the glen of the South Esk. When morning came the spirit of adventure had gone out of him. The squalid hut which sheltered him, the unclean rushes on which he lay were by no means to his taste. Two mountain ranges separated him from Huntly, whose protection he sought. The appearance of the messengers of the Committee with loyal

Charles at Clova.

he assigns a letter in which the existence of this resolution is implied to Sept. 26. Why the order, whenever given, was kept back does not appear. It reached Balfour at Kinnaird, near Newburgh in Fife, about nine in the morning of Oct. 3.

assurances shook his purpose, and when Montgomery rode up at the head of six hundred horse, he threw all the blame on Dr.

He agrees to return. Fraser, and agreed to return under Montgomery's protection. On October 6 he was back at Perth.[1]

Oct. 6. Returns to Perth. Such was Charles's escapade, to which Scottish writers give the name of 'The Start.' By his conduct

Charles's failure. on this occasion Charles had demonstrated that he was an unfit leader in any enterprise which demanded secrecy and decision. Nevertheless the situation of the Committee of Estates was not ameliorated. The Earl of Athol was up in arms, resolved to maintain the King's cause even if the King

Oct. 10. Position of the Committee of Estates. took refuge amongst his enemies. On the 10th the Committee, thinking it prudent to treat Charles at least with the outward signs of courtesy, for the first time assembled in his presence. On the following

Oct. 11. Charles excuses himself. day he responded by an acknowledgment that he had been deluded by wicked counsel. As he was a Christian, he ended by saying, 'when he went first out he had no mind to depart, and he trusted in God' it would be a lesson to him all the days of his life.

It was easier to humiliate Charles than to overpower his followers in arms. For some days negotiations with the latter

Oct. 21. The surprise at Newtyle. as to the terms of indemnity were in progress. On October 21, however, Sir David Ogilvy, a younger son of the Earl of Airlie, fell in the night upon Sir John Brown's regiment at Newtyle, killed four of his men and captured twenty prisoners.[2]

It was in vain that the more fiery ministers excommunicated Middleton, and that Leslie was sent to carry on war against the

Oct. 24. Leslie sent for. insurgents. Middleton met him with a bond signed by the leading Royalists and Engagers—Huntly,

The Northern bond. Athol, Seaforth, Sir George Monro, and Middleton himself amongst them—exhorting to national unity in defence of the country against the invader.[3] On the

[1] *Balfour*, iv. 112 ; Walker's *Hist. Discourses*, 199.

[2] *Balfour*, iv. 116-127.

[3] Middleton to Leslie, Oct. 24, *Balfour*, iv. 130.

26th Charles with the concurrence of the Committee of Estates published an act of pardon and indemnity. On November 4

Nov. 4.
The agree-
ment at
Strathbogie.
the indemnity was accepted at Strathbogie by the insurgents in the presence of Leslie.[1] In appearance a surrender, the acceptance of the indemnity was in reality a coalition between all parties except one. It was a substitution of the national for the covenanting cause.

On all these perturbations Cromwell had kept his eye. He was loth to abandon the hope that the Scots would yet

Oct.
Cromwell's
hopes.
listen to reason and expel the youthful King who had come amongst them on false pretences. Being himself debarred from distant enterprises by the necessity of covering the siege of Edinburgh Castle, a siege which since September 29 had been carried on by the long process of mining, he was unable to repress the hope that the Western leaders would be amenable to argument. About October 8 or 9

Oct. 9.
Cromwell
starts for
Glasgow
he had received a letter from Strachan, which was sufficiently encouraging to induce him to start for Glasgow. Despatching from Linlithgow an appeal

Oct. 11.
and enters
Glasgow.
to the Committee of Estates,[2] he entered Glasgow on the 11th. On the 13th, which was a Sunday, the preacher, Zachary Boyd, thundered from the pulpit against the English sectaries, who with exemplary patience received his hard words without a murmur. The strong language of the clergy had more effect upon their own people, who fled from their dwellings 'not so much,' as a Scottish diarist acknowledged, 'for fear of the enemy, for their conduct was indifferent good, but because they feared to be branded with the name of compliers with sectarians.'[3] The yoke of the Kirk was not an easy one.

On the 14th, Cromwell, hearing that Leslie was about to interrupt the siege, hurried back through miry ways to Edin-

[1] *Balfour*, iv. 132, 160.

[2] Cromwell to the Committee of Estates, Oct. 9, *Carlyle*, Letter cl.

[3] Nicoll's *Diary*, 30. Compare Letter from Edinburgh in *Merc. Pol.* E, 615, 10. Carlyle makes Cromwell enter Glasgow on Oct. 18, a week too late.

burgh.[1] If he had not won over Strachan and Ker openly to
join his cause, he had the satisfaction to find that they were

Oct. 14.
He returns
to Edin-
burgh.

not likely to give much assistance to his enemies.
At Dumfries, on October 17, in conjunction with
Patrick Gillespy and others of the stricter clergy,

Oct. 17.
The Remon-
strance.

these officers—now at the head of three or four
thousand men—issued a Remonstrance in which
they defined their position towards the national cause.

In this remarkable manifesto all intention of fighting for the
King until he had given satisfactory evidence of sincere repent-

Its cha-
racter.

ance and of honest intention to abandon the company of Malignants was entirely repudiated.   Still
less was assistance to be given to him to force upon England
a government which Scotland herself ought never to endure.
There was, moreover, much sharp criticism of the worldly
wisdom and self-seeking with which men in high places, for
purposes of their own, had closed their eyes to the hypocrisy of
the King.   Until sins such as these were repented of, and
assurances of an entire abstinence from an alliance with Malignants given, the Western army must stand aloof.[2]

In these visionaries the Kirk of John Knox—narrow and
intolerant indeed, but inspired with a lofty zeal for moral recti-

The Re-
monstrants
stand for
morality.

tude and purity—raised its head once more.   The
pervading influence of her organisation, the severity
of her judgments, and her sustained conflict with
men in high position, sprang from her perception of the strength
of the elements arrayed in Scotland against the upholders of
any high moral standard whatever.

It was not, in fact, merely against pleasure-loving nobles that
the Kirk had to contend.   A large part—possibly the larger

Moral con-
dition of
Scotland.

part—of the population was unwilling to be coerced
into purity of conduct.   The testimony of English
invaders to the prevalence of immorality may have
been exaggerated—it is not likely to have been without founda-

---

[1] *Merc. Pol.* E, 615, 10.

The Remonstrance, in Peterkin's *Records*, 604.   Compare *Baillie,*
iii. 110.

tion. "I thought," wrote Cromwell himself, "I should have found in Scotland a conscientious people and a barren country : about Edinburgh it is as fertile for corn as any part of England, but the people generally given to the most impudent lying and swearing as is incredible to be believed." [1] Still more outspoken was an officer or soldier whose name has not reached us. "I believe," he wrote, "the people have as much of profession, as any people that call themselves Christians . . . and not so much as the least appearance of power in any one man, that I have discoursed withal of this nation. It is usual with them to talk religiously and with a great show of piety and devotion for a time, and the very next moment to lie, curse and swear without any manner of bounds or limits. . . . For the sins of adultery and fornication, they are as common amongst them as if there were no commandment against either. They call those only broken women that have had but six bastards. For the committing of adultery, the Kirk Books of some of the ministers which we have found will show the names of their parishioners who have stood in the stool from time to time, and many have fallen into relapses after they have undergone that punishment." [2]

Modern thinkers may doubt whether the strong hand of ecclesiastical coercion was the best way of checking immorality, but there can be no doubt that the struggle was a very real one —as real in the eyes of the Scottish ministers of those generations as was the struggle against supposed witchcraft which cost so many innocent lives. It was only to be expected that the men on whom the battle against sin had left its mark most strongly, should have been the first to be repelled by the hypocrisy of Charles and his leading supporters, and the first to drop out of sight the claims of national defence against an invading enemy. It boded ill for Scotland that it should be so. In 1638 the national feeling and the religious feeling had been fused into one. In 1650 they were separated by an impassable gulf, rendering mutual assistance impossible.

[1] Cromwell to Bradshaw, Sept. 25, *Carlyle*, Letter cxlix.
[2] Letter in *Charles II. and Scotland*, 134.

For some time the Western army abode by the neutrality it had avowed. Strachan indeed, finding his position untenable between Cromwell and the Government at Perth, withdrew from his military command. Ker, on whom authority now devolved, refused to entangle himself with the English, but also refused to take orders from the Committee of Estates. They were the more anxious to secure his services as a partisan warfare had broken out in the counties subjected to the English, and the owners of fortified houses were giving support to their countrymen who ranged the hills. Cromwell's summons to Borthwick Castle produced an order to Ker to hasten to its relief.[1] Ker's reply was a profession of inability to undertake the task, and an uncompromising refusal to accept any favour from Charles till he became 'a servant to the King of kings.' "I desire," he wrote, "to love the King and serve him, and serve him faithfully ; but from no lesser principle willingly than this, that the King himself be subject to the King of kings." [2]

It needed not this to bring the Committee of Estates into sharp collision with the Remonstrants. Dunbar had had its effect even upon a body which had authorised the purging in August and September. Its members were now passing slowly but surely over to the position that, whatever might become of the morality of the country, its defence must first be attended to. As yet, however, they contented themselves with condemning the Remonstrance as causing divisions in the face of the enemy. On the 19th they decided upon a conference with the Commission of the Kirk. The Commission of the Kirk, under the influence of Guthrie and Gillespy, gave but a half-hearted answer, and finally, on the 25th, the Committee of

Margin notes:
Nov. Strachan retires.

Ker's position.

A partisan warfare.

Ker does not relieve Borthwick Castle.

Feeling in the Committee of Estates.

Nov. 19. They confer with the ministers.

Nov. 25. The Committee of Estates condemns the Remonstrance.

---

[1] *Letters from Headquarters*, E, 615, 14 ; *Balfour*, iv. 165 ; summons to Borthwick Castle, Nov. 18, *Carlyle*, Letter clii.

[2] Ker to Lothian, Nov. 22, *Ancram and Lothian Correspondence*, ii. 319.

Estates issued in its own name a Declaration highly condemnatory of the Remonstrance. In these discussions no one
spoke more strongly against the Remonstrants than Argyle.[1]

On the 26th Parliament met at Perth. Almost its first act
was to despatch Colonel Montgomery, a son of the Earl of
Eglinton, whose influence was great in the West, to
bring Ker to his senses. Before Montgomery could
reach him Ker had rushed on his destruction. Cromwell, finding that the Western army would not declare
for either side, resolved to abate the nuisance, and marched
against it.

Parliament meets. Montgomery sent to the West.

In the early morning of December 1, whilst it was still dark,
Ker attempted to surprise some troops quartered at Hamilton
under Lambert. He was repulsed without difficulty,
and he himself was wounded and remained a prisoner
in the hands of the enemy. After the fight Strachan
once more appeared on the scene, doing his best to rally the
dispersed troops. Failing in this, he gave himself up to Lambert
and accompanied him in his return to Edinburgh on the 10th.[2]
From that time all Scotland south of the Forth and Clyde was
in Cromwell's power, with the single exception of the Castle of
Edinburgh.[3]

Dec. 1. Ker overthrown at Hamilton.

The Castle did not long hold out. A mine, from which so
much had been expected, was baffled by the hardness of the
rock, when the arrival of heavy guns from England
relieved Cromwell from his difficulties. On the 12th
after summons given and refused, a furious fire was
opened on the defences. On the following day a
negotiation for the surrender was in progress, ex-
pedited probably by news of the alliance between the
King and the enemies of the Kirk brought in by a
handful of men who had contrived to break through
the English guards and make a lodgment in the Castle. From
this time the negotiation took the usual course, and on the

Preparations for attacking the Castle.

Dec. 12. Fire opened.

Dec. 13. A negotiation carried on.

---

[1] *Balfour*, iv. 166–179.   [2] *Merc. Pol.* E, 620, 8.
[3] *Ib.* E, 618, 9.

19th the Governor, Walter Dundas, agreed to surrender the
fortress on the 24th.   When the English soldiers marched in,

Dec. 24.
Surrender of
the Castle.

it was their opinion that the Castle could easily
have held out many weeks, and the suspicion that
the surrender was prompted by other than military
motives was confirmed by the subsequent proceedings of Dundas.   Having first recommended his soldiers to betake themselves to their homes, he gave himself up to Cromwell.
Whether his neglect of a soldier's duty was owing to pusillani-
mity or to his sympathy with the Remonstrants, there are no
means of judging.[1]

For some time Cromwell's headquarters were fixed at Edinburgh.   He had to send out parties to suppress moss-troopers

Cromwell
in Edin-
burgh.

as well as to reduce such fortified houses as still held
out in the South.   A Scottish winter was not favourable to active operations.   On the whole, in spite of
the ill-treatment of deserted churches and houses, and of the
fact that a part of Holyrood Palace was unfortunately destroyed
by fire through the carelessness of the soldiers, the army won
for itself a good reputation in Edinburgh.   The stout English
soldiers contrived to make themselves agreeable to the lasses,
and scarce a day passed without the skirling of the bagpipes in
honour of the marriage of one or other of the victors of
Dunbar.[2]

The evolution in Scottish politics which had commenced
after the great defeat had been quickened by the meeting of

Nov. 26.
Parliament
at Perth.

Parliament.   There was now no humiliation to which
Charles would not stoop, and on the 27th, in his
opening speech, he expressed his confidence in the
continuance of God's favour on the ground that He had moved
him 'to enter into covenant with His people—a favour no
other King can claim.'   Parliament showed as little straight-
forwardness as the King himself.   Professing itself to be the
real defender of the two Covenants, it allowed scarcely a

---

[1] *Carlyle*, Letters cliv.–clxi.   *Merc. Pol.* E, 620, 17 ; E, 621, 4.
[2] *Merc. Pol.* E, 618, 9.

day to pass without readmitting some Royalist or Engager, who for form's sake consented to give his consent to the Covenants. Even Hamilton and Lauderdale found the decree of banishment against them repealed, and Seaforth was soon in the same case. In vain the Commission of the Kirk attempted to put off the evil day on which it would have to follow the tide. On December 6 a letter was read in Parliament from the Moderator stating that the Commission could not meet till the 23rd. Parliament at once sent a sharp reply that unless the Commission met on the 12th, 'Parliament would be forced to act without their desired advice and concurrence : otherways the world might see that they had failed to concur with the Parliament to succour their country in time of her distress and greatest need.' [1]

Dec.
The admission of Royalists and Engagers.

A reproof to the Kirk.

At last the lay mind, careless about principles, but tenacious of its own rights, was raising a voice long silenced in Scotland. That voice could be raised with greater effect, because the clergy itself was divided in opinion. On the one side were the Remonstrants, on the other the Resolutioners, as those were styled who stood by the Resolutions of Parliament against the adherents of the Remonstrance. Many a minister, to whom the two Covenants were as a voice from Heaven itself, felt qualms about the exclusion from military service of any son of Scotland, not because he absolutely rejected the Covenants, but because there were reasons for believing that his acceptance of them was not whole-hearted. When once it appeared that the Commission of the Kirk might be won to consent to the practical point of the readmission of repentant opponents, Parliament was quite ready to meet the ministers more than halfway in all matters of religious formality.[2] On December 13 the Commission notified to Parliament that it had ceased to be obdurate on this matter. On the 14th Parliament effusively acknowledged its own members to be guilty of all the sins charged against

Laity and clergy.

Dec. 14.
Declaration of Parliament.

[1] *Balfour*, iv. 179.   [2] *Baillie*, iii. 125-127.

them.[1]　It was now possible to proceed to order the levy of a fresh army in the North,[2] from which no one who professed

Dec. 30.
Adjourn-
ment. repentance was to be excluded.　On December 30 Parliament, having done its work, was adjourned to February 5.

One more act of formality remained to be accomplished. The King's coronation was fixed to take place at Scone, on the first day of the new year.　To prepare the way for the cere-

Dec. 22.
A nation's
fast. mony, two fasts were held.　On December 22 the nation was called on to humiliate itself.　On

Dec. 26.
The King's
special fast. December 26, the covenanted King was asked to mourn publicly for his own sins, and for the sins of his father and grandfather as well.[3]　Charles made no objection, but he was not likely to forget his abasement. " I think," he is reported to have said when all was over, " I must repent too that ever I was born." [4]　On the same day, Lauderdale—most remarkable of penitents—swore to the Covenants and was received back into the bosom of the Kirk.[5]

On January 1 the church at Scone was filled with a resplendent throng.　When the young King had been led in

1651.
Jan. 1.
The corona-
tion. by such of the nobility as were permitted to take part in the ceremony, he took his place in a chair from which he listened to a lengthy sermon by Robert Douglas with all the appearance of interest.　When the

Charles
swears to
the Cove-
nants. sermon was ended, Charles swore to the two Covenants and subscribed them both, promising not merely to approve of them in Scotland, but to give his ' Royal assent to acts and ordinances of Parliament passed or to be passed, enjoining the same in his other dominions.' The Ministers present reported that he carried himself ' very seriously and devoutly, so that none doubted of his ingenuity and sincerity.'　Then followed the coronation itself.

---

[1] *Acts of the Parl. of Sc.* vi. part ii. 619.
[2] *Ib.* vi. part ii. 624 ; Nicoll's *Diary*, 38.
[3] Coronation of Charles II., *Somers Tracts*, vi. 117.
[4] Letter from Edinburgh, Dec. 30, in *Merc. Pol.* E, 621, 10.
[5] Lamont's *Diary*, 25.

There was to be no anointing, that rite being held to savour of superstition, but in all other respects the ancient ceremonial He is crowned. was observed. The Marquis of Argyle placed the crown on the King's head, and the Earl of Crawford and Lindsay put the sceptre in his hand. He was then conducted to the throne, Douglas ejaculating pious exhortations at each stage of the proceedings. When the nobles had one by one touched the crown and sworn fidelity, Charles addressed himself to some of the ministers present, protesting his sincerity, and begging of them the favour ' that if in any time coming they did hear or see him breaking that Covenant they would tell him of it, and put him in mind of his oath.' [1] The young man was at all events a consummate actor. It is not likely that he was in any way conscious of degradation. If he felt in any way troubled, he was at least allowed to have recourse to the distractions of golf. [2]

The authorities of the Kirk were now ready to qualify for military service all who submitted themselves to the form of Jan. 12. Middleton does penance. penitence. On January 12 Middleton, who till that hour had stood out against the threats of the clergy, did penance in sackcloth at Dundee, and was released from excommunication. At the same time Strachan was at Perth duly excommunicated and ' delivered over to the devil.' [3]

Strachan excommunicated. It would prove impossible to exorcise the spirit of Strachan. A considerable minority of the clergy continued to uphold the doctrines of the Remonstrance ; and the opinion that it was better to close with Cromwell than to persist in a war in which the enemies of the Covenant would have the upper hand, raised itself from time Wild suggestions. to time. Wild as the notion was, Sir Alexander Hope suggested to Charles that he would do well to

[1] Coronation of Charles II., *Somers Tracts*, vi. 117 ; *Life of Blair*, 256.

[2] A memorandum of Lothian's (Jan. 9) direct that some of the King's guards shall attend him ' at the church, and also when he goeth to the fields to walk or goff.' *Ancram and Lothian Correspondence*, ii. 332.   [3] *Balfour*, iv. 240.

compound with Cromwell for the retention of Scotland
north of the Forth, by the abandonment of the remainder of
his dominions.   Not long afterwards, much to Charles's surprise,
this suggestion was repeated by the Earl of Roxburgh, a nobleman who had recently succeeded to the title, and from whom
he expected better things.[1]

   It was impossible but that, with a King set upon rallying
all parties round his standard, Argyle should find his own
position shaken.   Now that the most strenuous Covenanters
had cast him off, there was nothing for the old chief of the
Covenanting party to do but to accommodate himself to his
young master's wishes ; and, according to one account, he had,

*Argyle's
language
at the
coronation.*
on the day of the coronation, gone so far as to express to Charles his approval of an Act of Oblivion
which, in his opinion, the King might obtain whenever
he wished.[2]   Yet it was one thing to give an enforced consent

*Jan. 17.
He leaves
the Court.*
to the inevitable return of his rivals to a share of
power, and another thing to witness their triumph.
On January 17, knowing that Hamilton was to arrive
at Court on the following day, Argyle betook himself to the
Highlands.[3]

   All that Argyle could now hope for was that the combination advocated by the King should receive a Presbyterian
colour ; and, as far as words went, Charles was amenable to
his wishes.   As Charles still counted on a rising of the English
Presbyterians in his favour, he was shrewd enough not to
damage his cause by openly repudiating the promises he had

[1] *Balfour,* iv. 238, 249.

[2] " The Marquis then made answer unto him "—*i.e.* the King—" that
his Majesty did well to observe the expedientness thereof, and that he
might have it passed whenever he pleased." *The Weekly Intelligencer,*
E, 626, 12.   " Argyle, however he act outwardly, and did not long ago in
Parliament protest that, if Colkitto were yet alive, he should rejoice in his
actings in opposition to us, yet he is not without his fears," [*forces* in the
text] " and to those he counts his friends he will often say that, in conclusion, he verily believes they will shuffle him out." Letter from Edinburgh, Jan. 9, *Merc. Pol.* E, 622, 8.   Cromwell had spies at Perth.

[3] Letter from Edinburgh, Jan. 21, *Merc. Pol.* E, 622, 12.

made at his coronation. When on January 21, after Argyle's departure, he despatched Colonel Titus to beg Henrietta Maria to use her influence in his favour on the Continent,[1] he asked her to send him Jermyn and Holles to act as his Secretaries of State, apparently as an evidence of his resolution to support Presbyterianism in England.[2] On January 23, Charles privately instructed Titus to express a hope that his mother would approve of his marriage with Argyle's daughter. Argyle, Titus was to say, 'is a person of great interest, of a very ancient and noble family that hath been always loyal to the Crown and sometimes allied to it, and himself in all transactions between me and my subjects of this kingdom hath particularly merited of me.' This marriage, the messenger was to add, would 'be a great satisfaction and security to all the Church and the Presbyterian party, and the best means to unite all parties and remove all differences occasioned by the late troubles.' Finally, 'the strength of Scotland being united, it will be the greatest encouragement of all of loyalty in England.'[3]

Jan. 21.
Mission of Colonel Titus.

Jan. 23.
His secret instructions.

It is possible that Charles merely counted on securing the continuance of Argyle's support during the two or three months of Titus's absence. His own energy was thrown into the task of gathering a numerous and devoted army. During the early part of February[4] he was riding along the banks of the Forth and attending to the works thrown up for defence. On the 21st he set out for Aberdeen, where Cant and some other ministers were throwing doubts on the propriety of enlisting unsanctified persons in the north under Middleton's command. Argyle,

Feb.
Charles's activity.

Feb. 21.
He starts for Aberdeen,

---

[1] Instructions to Titus, Jan. 21, Hillier's *Narrative of the Attempted Escapes of Charles I.*, 328.

[2] Nicholas to Norwich, March $\frac{11}{21}$, *Nicholas Papers*, i. 227.

[3] Private Instructions to Titus, Jan. 23, Hillier's *Narrative of the Attempted Escapes of Charles I.*, 328.

[4] The Earl of Brentford, who had once been the Commander-in-Chief of the army of Charles I. during the greater part of the first Civil War, died almost unnoticed on the 2nd of this month.

who had now returned to Court, urged the King on, though
Hamilton for some unexplained reason would have had him
Feb. 25.
where he
persuades
the ministers
to drop their
opposition. draw back. On the 25th Charles arrived at Aberdeen,
where his winning address overcame the reluctance
of the severest ministers, and Middleton was allowed
to proceed with his levies unopposed by the Kirk.[1]

For all but the most resolute of the clergy it was hard to
resist a young king who urged Scotsmen to think of their
country rather than of their ecclesiastical parties. " I see no
Waugh's
sermon. reason in Scripture," urged one of the ministers in
the pulpit, "forbidding any man to repent, and if
they once repent they are no longer malignants." There would
be no lack of penitents on these terms. Hamilton indeed was
allowed to qualify himself for a return to the fold by pro-
nouncing the Engagement to have been unlawful, without the
obligation of clothing himself in sackcloth or sitting on the
stool of repentance ; but though this favour was accorded to no
one else, few indeed were likely to be excluded by the necessity
of observing a humiliating ceremony.[2]

It was less easy to bring the remonstrant clergy to submission. Under the influence of James Guthrie the Presbytery of
Feb. 20.
Guthrie
and Ben-
net con-
fined to
Perth. Stirling had declared against the northern levies, and,
in spite of a protestation that the liberties of the
Kirk were thereby endangered, Guthrie and his
colleague, Bennet, were confined to Perth by order of
the Committee of Estates.[3]

When Parliament met again on March 13, it was well
known that Charles would ask that countenance might be shown
March 13.
Meeting of
Parlia-
ment. to the northern levies, even if he did not press for an
absolute repeal of the Act of Classes. In the former
demand, at least, he had Argyle still on his side,[4]

---

[1] *Balfour*, iv. 246 ; Letter from Edinburgh, Feb. 18, *Merc. Pol.* E, 625, 6.

[2] Letter from Edinburgh, Feb. 18, *Merc. Pol.* E, 625, 6 ; *The Weekly Intelligencer*, E, 626, 6.

[3] *Balfour*, iv. 247 ; *Acts of the Parl. of Sc.* vi. part ii. 641.

[4] *Baillie*, iii. 133.

though Loudoun, so long the subservient follower of Argyle, shrank from admitting into the army the wild clans of the north in whom Montrose had found his chief support. Accordingly the first act of the Parliament was to thrust Loudoun out of the President's chair, which he had occupied ever since the rout of the Hamiltons in 1648, and to substitute for him Lord Balfour of Burleigh, a supporter of the prevailing party of conciliation.[1]

It refuses to re-elect Loudoun president.

Even the Commissioners of the Kirk were now under the same influence. On the 22nd, in answer to a question put to them by Parliament, they gave their opinion that, with the exception of a few prime offenders, all who gave satisfaction to the Kirk might sit on the Committee of Estates.[2] The main question, however, was not whether the repentant sinners should sit on the committee, but whether they should hold commands in the army. When, on March 26, it was proposed that a new committee should be erected for the management of the army, on which Hamilton and his partisans should be fully represented, even Argyle voted against the scheme, though Charles had recommended it to the House with his own lips. Lothian, at least, did not mince his words. He reproved Charles to his face for his inconstancy ' in deserting his best friends, who had brought him into the country.' Argyle's party was, however, no longer predominant. Before Parliament broke up on the 31st, it had not only sanctioned the appointment of the new committee, and had requested the King to take upon himself the conduct of the army, but had requested the commissioners of the Kirk to take into consideration the removal of the obstacle which hindered the taking in of all persons excluded by the Act of Classes, 'that there may be a general unity in the kingdom.'[3]

March 22. The Commission of the Kirk in favour of the re-admission of penitents.

March 26. A committee for the army.

March 31. End of the session.

Parliament was to have met again on April 17, but, owing

[1] *Acts of the Parl. of Sc.* vi. part ii. 640; *Balfour,* iv. 254, 262.

[2] *Balfour,* iv. 270.

[3] *Ib.* iv. 274–281; *Acts of the Parl. of Sc.* vi. part ii. 662.

to the active intervention of the Campbells, its assembly was postponed till May 23. By that time Argyle knew that his day of power was irrevocably at an end. Titus had returned from France,[1] the bearer of a distinct warning from Henrietta Maria against her son's marriage with Ann Campbell.[2] If the Act of Classes were indeed repealed, Argyle would therefore be confronted in court and camp by his bitterest enemies without the shelter of a Royal alliance. The blow was not long in falling. On June 2 the Act of Classes was repealed,[3] and Charles was left at liberty to avail himself of the services, not only of the Engagers, but of those resolute opposers of the discipline of the Kirk who had once gathered round Montrose.

Ostensibly, indeed, Argyle was what he had been before. There was no dismissal from Court, no declaration of his incapacity for office. Yet, for all that, his fall was irrevocable. Having built his power on a party hostile to monarchy, he had assumed an attitude of friendliness towards the English republicans which it was impossible for him to maintain in presence of the horror caused by the execution of Charles I. Yielding to his own followers when he ceased to be able to direct them, he had taken part in the invitation to the young King to visit Scotland as the slave of the fanatical clergy. It was not a promising experiment, and any little chance of success that it might have had was brought to a sharp end at Dunbar. Men like Guthrie and Gillespy in the Church, and like Ker and Strachan in the army, could follow their principles whithersoever they might lead. Argyle, clear-sighted as he was, had no idea of becoming a martyr to any principle whatever. He clung to power, hoping to entangle his

Sidenotes: May. Return of Titus. June 2. Repeal of the Act of Classes. Argyle's fall.

---

[1] Titus returned by way of the Hague, and the last letter which is known to mention him as being there is dated on $\frac{\text{April 23}}{\text{May 3}}$, *Nicholas Papers,* i. 240.

[2] Instructions of Henrietta Maria, April $\frac{5}{15}$, Hillier's *Narrative of the Attempted Escapes of Charles I.,* 332.

[3] *Acts of the Parl. of Sc.* **vi.** part ii. 676 ; Argyle to Lothian, June 16, *Ancram and Lothian Correspondence,* ii. 359.

Sovereign in a family alliance, and offering even to welcome his enemies to some share of influence as long as they did not burst in like a flood to occupy all. It was to no purpose, and the statesman who had given over Scotland to the rule of the middle classes, and had taught her that her safety lay in associating herself with England whilst preserving her own national independence, fell unaided and unregretted because a base intrigue for the maintenance of his own influence had taken the place of manful championship of his nation's cause.

The hand that dealt the blow was even more ignoble than Argyle's. Charles had in a few months gained a position in Scotland to which his father could never have attained. With no scruples to hold him back, he had lied his way into the commanding position which was now his. By temperament as well as by intelligence averse to any cause which might rouse avoidable hostility, he was prompt to seize each opportunity as it offered, and to bear with steady but not violent pressure on the line of least resistance. It was Cromwell, indeed, who had discomfited the fanatics at Dunbar, but it was Charles who availed himself of the resulting growth of national feeling to disembarrass himself of all rivals. What was of still greater moment was that in the hour of his triumph no sharp sayings or sharper deeds are recorded against him. Charles I. would have done his best to send Argyle to the dungeon or the scaffold. Charles II. contented himself with continuing him in his service whilst depriving him of power. Whether Charles would succeed in subjugating not Scotland alone, but England also, was a question on which Cromwell and his victorious army would have a word to say.

Charles's success.

END OF THE FIRST VOLUME

Spottiswoode & Co. Ltd., Printers, New-street Square, London